Post-Reformation Reformed Dogmatics

Volume 1
Prolegomena to Theology

Richard A. Muller

BAKER BOOK HOUSE
Grand Rapids, Michigan 49516

To

Karl

and

Elizabeth

Contents

Preface

The plan for this study of post-Reformation Reformed dogmatics arose a decade ago as I brought my doctoral studies to a close—with the distinct impression that my approach to Reformed orthodoxy would be incomplete if not supplemented by another study. What I had written about Christology and predestination and about the way in which these two doctrines relate in a Reformed orthodoxy that was both christocentric and predestinarian, but neither excessively metaphysical nor philosophically rationalistic, pointed directly toward a further study of the fundamental teaching on Reformed orthodox dogmatics. My primary research in this subject—an inquiry into the development of the contents of the orthodox doctrines of theology, Scripture and God—was done in 1978/79 under a post-doctoral research grant from the Mellon Foundation.

The monograph waited and, in fact, was placed on a "back burner" while I revised the dissertation for publication as *Christ and the Decree* and wrote a *Dictionary of Latin and Greek Theological Terms, Drawn Principally from Protestant Scholastic Theology*. When I returned to the project, my bibliography had expanded and my thoughts on the subject had elaborated considerably. What appears here is the first volume of a projected three-volume work. Prolegomena to theology are discussed in the present book; studies of the doctrines of Scripture and God should follow shortly. In all three volumes, the intention is to provide both a statement of the doctrine taught by the Reformed orthodox and an analysis of Protestant orthodoxy in the context of contemporary scholarly and theological discussion.

Several apparent deficits in the present volume will be remedied in the subsequent portions of the study: readers will note the absence of a concluding chapter, a bibliography and an index. All will appear at the end of volume 3. The absence of a concluding chapter is offset somewhat by the presence of introductory chapters, the first of which should serve as a general introduction to all three volumes.

A word of thanks is due, finally, to several persons and institutions. John Patrick Donnelly of Marquette University and Douglas F. Kelly of Reformed Theological Seminary read the manuscript with great care and made many helpful suggestions. To John Farthing of Hendricks College and Brian Armstrong of Georgia State University, I offer thanks for hours of enlightening discussion and for several important references to Protestant orthodox authors and their writings. The libraries of Duke University and Fuller Theological Seminary and the Huntington Library have been my major resources. Donn Michael Farris of Duke Divinity

School library, John Dickason of Fuller and Peter de Klerk of Calvin College and Seminary deserve special thanks for their help in obtaining much-needed resources.   Special thanks is also due to Sandy Underwood Bennett and Jan Gathright of the word processing office at Fuller for the production of the basic manuscript and camera-ready copy.

I offer finally the thanks of a husband and father who knows that the writing of books depends in no small measure upon the love and support of his family.   I dedicate this book to my children, Elizabeth and Karl, who may never read a page of it, but whose presence in my life gives me reason to live and work and, as part of that work, to write. And, after all, today is Karl's birthday.

Epiphany, 1987   Richard A. Muller

Part 1

Introduction

1

The Study
of Protestant Scholasticism

1.1 Orthodoxy and Scholasticism in Protestant Thought

The theology of orthodox or scholastic Protestantism has never been accorded the degree of interest bestowed upon the theology of the great Reformers and has seldom been given the attention it deserves both theologically and historically. Codifiers and perpetuators like the theologians of the late sixteenth and seventeeth centuries simply do not receive the adulation given to the inaugurators of the movement. Nor do codifiers need to be defended as zealously as inaugurators—if only because the codifiers themselves have provided the first line of that defense. If, however, these codifiers and perpetuators have been neglected in favor of the Reformers themselves, the neglect is clearly unjustified: what the Reformation began in less than half a century, orthodox Protestantism defended, clarified and codified over the course of a century and a half. The Reformation is incomplete without its confessional and doctrinal codification. What is more, Protestantism could not have survived if it had not developed, in the era of orthodoxy, a normative and defensible body of doctrine consisting of a confessional foundation and systematic elaboration.

The contribution of the orthodox or scholastic theologians to the history of Protestantism, then, was the creation of an institutional theology, confessionally in continuity with the Reformation and doctrinally, in the sense of the larger system of doctrine, in continuity with the great tradition of the church. The Reformers had developed, on the basis of their exegesis of Scripture, a series of doctrinal issues that were embodied, as the distinctive concerns of Protestantism, in the early confessions of the Reformation. In developing these insights, however, the Reformers identified themselves and their theology with the cause of catholic or universal Christian truth. The Protestant orthodox held fast to these Reformation insights and to the confessional norms of Protestantism and, at the same time, moved toward the establishment of an entire body of "right teaching" in continuity both with the Reformation and with the truths embodied in the whole tradition of Christian doctrine. They recognized that the claim of Protestantism to represent the church could be maintained only if the witness of the Reformation proved to be the key not only to the reform of a series of ecclesiastical abuses but also to the reformulation of the body of Christian doctrine. The selectivity of the Reformation in its polemic had to be transcended in the direction of a reformed catholicity.

This post-Reformation development of Protestantism can be divided, for the sake of convenience, into three periods: early, high, and late orthodoxy. Early orthodoxy extends roughly from 1565 to 1630 or 1640 and is the era of the confessional solidification of Protestantism. As of 1565, the great second-generation codifiers of the Reformed faith (John Calvin, Wolfgang Musculus, Peter Martyr Vermigli, and Andreas Hyperius) were all dead—the single eminent exception being Heinrich Bullinger, who lived until 1575. Reformed theology passed into the hands of Zacharias Ursinus, Caspar Olevianus, Jerome Zanchi, Theodore Beza, Francis Junius, and Amandus Polanus. The theologians who sat at Dort and perpetuated its carefully outlined confessionalism in the early seventeenth century—Antonius Walaeus, Johann Poliander, Sibrandus Lubbertus, Franciscus Gomarus—together with writers like William Ames and J. H. Alsted also belong to the early orthodox period.

High orthodoxy spans the greater part of the seventeenth century. It represents a still broader theological synthesis than early orthodoxy: it rests upon a confessional synthesis of the faith, has a somewhat sharper and more codified polemic against its doctrinal adversaries, and possesses a broader and more explicit grasp of the tradition, particularly of the contribution of the Middle Ages. In this period are found such authors as Franz Burmann, Francis Turretin, Peter van Mastricht, Hermann Witsius, Johannes Marckius, Edward Leigh, John Owen, and Benedict Pictet. After 1700, the theology represented by these writers ceased to be the dominant intellectual pattern in the church and in the theological faculties of the great Protestant universities. Theology after 1700 is less secure in its philosophical foundations, less certain of its grasp of the biblical standard, and less willing to draw out its polemic against other "orthodox" forms of Christianity.   Nonetheless, even in this altered climate, a more or less traditional Reformed theology continued to be produced by such late orthodox writers as Johann Friedrich Stapfer, Herman Venema and Bernhard de Moor.

When this orthodox or scholastic Protestantism is examined in some depth and viewed as a form of Protestant theology in its own right rather than as merely a duplication or reflection of the theology of the Reformation, it is clearly a theology both like and unlike that of the Reformation, standing in continuity with the great theological insights of the Reformers but developing in a systematic and scholastic fashion different from the patterns of the Reformation and frequently reliant on the forms and methods of the thirteenth, fourteenth and fifteenth centuries.   This double continuity ought not to be either surprising or disconcerting. Instead, it ought to be understood as one example among many of the way in which the church both moves forward in history, adapting to new situations and insights, and at the same time retains its original identity as the community of faith.   It ought to be understood as one example of the way in which the Christian intellectual tradition maintains useful forms, methods and doctrinal ideas while at the same time incorporating the advances of exegetical and theological investigation.

The contemporary relevance of Protestant orthodox theology arises from the fact that it remains the basis for normative Protestant theology in the present.   With little formal and virtually no substantial alteration, orthodox or scholastic Reformed theology appears in the works of Charles Hodge, Archibald Alexander Hodge and Louis Berkhof.   Even when major changes in perspective are evident—as in the theology of Emil Brunner, Karl Barth and Otto Weber—the impact of Protestant orthodoxy remains clear both in terms of the overarching structure of theological system and in terms of its basic definitions.   Charles Hodge's *Systematic Theology* draws heavily on Francis Turretin's *Institutio theologiae elenticae* and represents, particularly in its prolegomena, an attempt to recast the systematic insights of orthodoxy in a nineteenth-century mold. Of the other writers, Karl Barth most clearly shows his indebtedness to the orthodox prolegomena—not always in terms of direct appropriation of doctrine but rather in terms of sensitivity both to the importance of prolegomena and to the issues traditionally raised at this preliminary point in dogmatics.

Similar statements can be made with reference to the two *principia* or foundations of theology, the doctrines of God and Scripture, and indeed, with reference to the whole of the Protestant orthodox system.

Just as the orthodox prolegomena represent the Protestant appropriation of basic theological presuppositions and, as such, still affect our view of theology today, so also the orthodox doctrine of God and Scripture represents the fundamental statement of these underlying *principia* for Protestantism. We continue to be influenced by the orthodox language of an immutable, omnipotent, omniscient but nonetheless historically active God—and we continue to wrestle, particularly in conservative or evangelical circles, with the implications of the traditional doctrine of Scripture, given its place of final doctrinal authority by the Reformers, but codified and stated for us by the Protestant orthodox. The impact of scholastic Protestantism remains. This theology and its relationship to earlier ages—specifically, the Middle Ages and the Reformation—must be understood if contemporary Protestantism is to come to terms with its own relationship both to the Reformation and to the Christian tradition as a whole.

The development of Protestant thought in the two centuries following the Reformation is a highly complex phenomenon that defies facile classification. The two terms, orthodoxy and scholasticism, however, do provide a convenient point of departure for classification and description. "Orthodoxy," of course, simply means "right teaching." In one sense, this right teaching was the goal of the Reformation from its moment of inception. Luther, Zwingli, Bucer, and the other early Reformers saw a host of abuses and nonscriptural doctrinal accretions in the practices and teachings of the church. Their goal in attacking these abuses and accretions was to reform both Christian life and teaching. The earliest confessions of the Protestant churches are quite specific in this goal. They do not present entire bodies of doctrine but only those particular points of doctrine—such as grace, faith, justification, and the sacraments—where a return to right teaching was needed.

The division of Christendom and the establishment of Lutheran and Reformed churches independent from Rome led, in the fourth and fifth decades of the sixteenth century, to the rise of another form of Protestant confession and to a somewhat different pressure toward orthodoxy. Whereas the earliest confessions—like the Augsburg or Tetrapolitan—state only disputed points, the later documents—the First and Second Helvetic, the Gallican and Belgic Confessions—provide definitions of all doctrines belonging to the faith of the confessing church. Right statement of a whole body of doctrine, of all the basic articles of faith, is characteristic of institutionally established Protestantism. In other words, orthodoxy and institutionalization are but two aspects of one development—indeed, they are corollaries of one another.

The intention of the theologians of the late sixteenth and seventeenth centuries, as witnessed both by their detailed positive construction of theological system and by their frequently bitter polemic against doctrinal adversaries, was to produce, in the context and frequently on the model of the great Protestant confessions, an entire body of true doctrine. This task was necessary to ensure the survival of Protestantism. The first and second generations of Reformers, the teachers of the first half of the sixteenth century, had been trained in Christian doctrine on the medieval model and had, in their work as Reformers, rendered that model inadequate for the teaching of the next several generations of Protestants. The Reformers, however, did not provide those generations with a fully-developed theological system. Even Calvin's *Institutes* was no more than a basic instruction in the doctrines of Scripture and not a full system of theology written with the precision and detail of the systems of Calvin's own Roman Catholic opponents.[1] The Protestant theologians of the second half of the sixteenth century--writers like Ursinus, Zanchi and Polanus--took up the task of writing a complete and detailed system of theology both for the sake of positive teaching and for the sake of polemical defense.

This development of Protestant orthodoxy, like the doctrinal movement of the Reformation itself, did not occur in isolation from theological system or from the Western philosophical tradition. Although the Reformers and their orthodox or scholastic successors agreed that Scripture ought to be the sole absolute norm of doctrine, they never intended that the whole body of Christian doctrine be reconstructed without reference to the doctrinal developments and systematic constructions of the past--and even if that had been their intention, it would have hardly been possible. The Reformers, after all, assumed the truth of the larger body of received doctrine and attacked only what they perceived to be errors. They did not intend to reconstruct the doctrine of the Trinity or of the Person of Christ or of the creation of the world and the providence of God. The development of Protestant doctrine, therefore, in the great confessions of the mid-sixteenth century and in the orthodox or scholastic systems of the late sixteenth and seventeeth centuries was not a development from kerygma to dogma but rather a development consisting in the adjustment of a received body of doctrine and its systematic relations to the needs of Protestantism, in terms dictated by the teachings of the Reformers on Scripture, grace, justification, and the sacraments.

The term *scholasticism* well describes the technical and academic side of this process of the institutionalization of Protestant doctrine.

The theology of the great systems written in the late sixteenth and seventeenth centuries, like the theology of the thirteenth-century teachers, is preeminently a school-theology. It is a theology designed to develop system on a highly technical level and in an extremely precise manner by means of the careful identification of topics, division of these topics into their basic parts, definition of the parts, and doctrinal or logical argumentation concerning the divisions and definitions. In addition, this school-method is characterized by a thorough use and technical mastery of the tools of linguistic, philosophical, logical, and traditional thought.[2] The Protestant orthodox themselves use the term "scholastic theology" as a specific designation for detailed, disputative system, as distinct from biblical or exegetical theology, catechetical theology and discursive, ecclesial theology. The term "scholastic" is, therefore, applicable particularly to the large-scale, systematic development of seventeenth-century Protestant theology. This approach to Protestant scholasticism, based directly on the definitions and the methods evidenced in the seventeenth-century systems, explicitly opposes the view of several recent scholars according to which "scholasticism" can be identified specifically with a use of Aristotelian philosophy, a pronounced metaphysical interest, and the use of predestination as an organizing principle in theological system.[3]

In this broad sense, the term "scholasticism" can be applied to a theology that is not a duplication of medieval scholastic teaching and method, that is distinctly Protestant, and that is not nearly as concerned to draw philosophy into dialogue with theology as the great synthetic works of the thirteenth century. Scholasticism, then, indicates the technical and logical approach to theology as a discipline characteristic of theological system from the late twelfth through the seventeenth century. Since scholasticism is primarily a method or approach to academic disciplines it is not necessarily allied to any particular philosophical perspective nor does it represent a systematic attachment to or concentration upon any particular doctrine or concept as a key to theological system. This latter point has always been clear with respect to medieval scholasticism, but it needs to be made just as decisively with regard to Protestant scholasticism.

The theology of Protestant orthodoxy, developed in the late sixteenth and seventeenth centuries as a final, dogmatic codification of the Reformation, occupies a position of considerable significance in the history of Protestant thought. Not only is this scholastic or orthodox theology the historical link that binds us to the Reformation, it is also the form of theological system in and through which modern Protestantism has received most of its doctrinal principles and definitions. Without detracting at all from the achievement of the great Reformers and the earliest codifiers of the doctrines of the Reformation—men like Melanchthon, Calvin and Bullinger—we need to recognize that not they but rather subsequent generations of "orthodox" or "scholastic" Protestants are responsible for the final form of such doctrinal issues as the definition of theology and the enunciation of its fundamental principles, the fully-developed Protestant forms of the doctrine of the Trinity, the crucial christological concept of the two states of Christ, penal substitutionary atonement, and the theme of the covenant of works and the covenant of grace.

If the theology of the Reformation was not the source of the final formulation of these major doctrinal issues, neither was it the source of most of the precise definitions and careful distinctions necessary to the creation of a complete theological system. Where the Reformers painted with a broad brush, their orthodox and scholastic successors strove to fill in the details of the picture. Whereas the Reformers were intent upon distancing themselves and their theology from problematic elements in medieval thought and, at the same time, remaining catholic in the broadest sense of that term, the Protestant orthodox were intent upon establishing systematically the normative, catholic character of institutionalized Protestantism, at times through the explicit use of those elements in patristic and medieval theology not at odds with the teachings of the Reformation.

In this introductory essay and in the study of *prolegomena* and *principia* that follows, I propose to develop part of the groundwork for the reassessment and further study of Protestant scholasticism. This is essentially a topical, dogmatic study which presents only the most basic biographical material and which makes no pretense at providing a history of the rise and development of Protestant orthodoxy. All too often, a biographical and historical approach duplicates arguments and omits many doctrinal topics when it attempts to merge a chronological and historical narrative with systematic or doctrinal exposition. Ritschl's *Dogmengeschichte des Protestantismus* deals, for the most part, only with doctrinal controversies or with the doctrines of predestination and justification.[4] Weber's *Reformation, Orthodoxie und Rationalismus* follows a similar pattern.[5] In none of the older histories, moreover, do we find either a consistently presented biographical, institutional and historical narrative or a thorough overview of theological systems.[6]

The scope of the present work also demands some explanation. Discussion is limited to the topics of *prolegomena* and *principia*, the former consisting in the definition of theology as a discipline and the latter consisting in the doctrines of Scripture and God. There are two reasons for this focus: first, the shape of Protestant scholastic system, and second, the need for closer, scholarly consideration of these particular *loci* in the Reformed orthodox systems. In the first place, then, the topics of theology, Scripture and God stand together at the beginning of most of the Protestant scholastic systems and together provide the basis for understanding the subsequent treatment of all other doctrines. The *prolegomena* on "theology" present a discussion of fundamental issues of method, its presuppositions and basic intentions, and provide a clear identification of the *principia* of theology, the cognitive and essential grounds of the discipline, namely, Scripture and God. An examination of these three *loci* in their proper sequence provides the best point of entry into the theology of the late sixteenth and seventeenth centuries.

In the second place, there is a genuine need to review the theology of Protestant orthodoxy and to examine its presuppositions and principles in view of the frequently inaccurate presentation of scholastic Protestantism in histories of Christian thought and even in scholarly monographs dealing with the late sixteenth and seventeenth centuries. This inaccuracy reflects several levels of misunderstanding. Much of the literature assumes a discontinuity between the thought of the Reformers and their orthodox successors without recognizing that a change in form and method does not necessarily indicate an alteration of substance. Scholastic Protestant theology has been described as rationalistic, intellectually arid and theologically rigid—without due attention to its own statements concerning the use of reason and the import of dogmatic system for faith. Such descriptions ignore the process of development— itself quite original and creative—that brought about the orthodox or scholastic Protestantism of the seventeenth century.

Stated methodologically, these problems in scholarship point toward the broader issue of historical continuity and discontinuity that must be addressed on a whole series of issues and subissues. First, there is the standard issue of continuity or discontinuity with the Reformation. Traditionally this issue has been stated either in terms of single doctrines (principally predestination and Scripture) or in terms of the relationship between the phenomenon of orthodoxy and the theology of individual writers in the Reformation era. Whereas the former pattern promises to provide a useful index to the development of orthodoxy, the latter is quite defective insofar as it limits the scope of investigation to the influence (or lack thereof) of a specific thinker, when the antecedents of orthodoxy in the Reformation are in fact quite complex and involve the transmission of doctrinal themes from a variety of first- and second-generation sources to a whole series of rather diverse successors in the third-and fourth-generation Protestantism.

Second, there is the equally important issue of development--in continuity and discontinuity with the past--in the context of the larger tradition of Western Christianity. It is clear that Protestant orthodoxy drew on patristic and medieval sources for theological models as well as on the theology of the Reformers. Here we need to ask whether continuities with patristic or medieval models indicate discontinuities with the Reformation or not.   This question, moreover, must be asked both theologically and methodologically, with attention to methodological changes that retain and even reinforce in new contexts the substance of a theological issue formerly treated according to a different method. Specifically, can the theology of the Reformation be retained in and through the use of scholastic forms and distinctions--and to what extent are the Protestant orthodox sensitive to the need to reinterpret distinctions and alter forms for the sake of preserving continuity of doctrine, albeit in an altered form?

Third, the question of development must be asked in its own right, doctrinally and philosophically.   Continuity must not be conceived simplistically as static reproduction and discontinuity must not be explained, equally simplistically, as change. The changes and developments that took place within Protestantism in the two centuries after the Reformation need to be viewed as belonging to a living tradition which needed to adapt and reformulate its teachings as the historical context demanded.   Quite simply, the fact that theological systems in 1659 did not look like Calvin's *Institutes* of 1559, or even maintain all of the definitions provided by Calvin, does not in itself indicate discontinuity.   The issue is to examine the course of development, to study the reasons for change, and then to make judgments concerning continuity and discontinuity in the light of something more than a facile contrast or juxtaposition.

A fundamental misunderstanding of this set of historical relationships, particularly of the relationship between the theology of the Reformers and the theology of post-Reformation orthodoxy, lies at the root of most of the contemporary complaints against both Protestant orthodoxy and its nineteenth- and early twentieth-century descendants. To very little purpose, several recent studies have set "Calvin against the Calvinists"--as if Calvin were the only source of post-Reformation Reformed theology and as if the theology of the mid-seventeenth century ought for some reason to be measured against and judged by the theology of the mid-sixteenth century. Because the orthodox systems do not mirror Calvin's 1559 *Institutes*, they are labeled "distortions" of the Reformation. The genuine historical and theological issue, of course, is one of development and change within a broad tradition, of continuity and discontinuity with the thought, not only of Calvin, but also of Zwingli, Bucer, Bullinger, Musculus, and Vermigli. The latter point needs to be emphasized inasmuch as these studies tend to note the presence of varied perspectives in early Reformed theology and then, despite the historical evidence, insist on the use of Calvin's theology as the norm for evaluating all that follows.[7]

In order for the Reformed scholastics to receive an adequate interpretation, therefore, we must not only allow for development and change within the tradition, but we also need to trace that development and change in terms of a movement of thought not simply from Calvin to the orthodox but from the theology of an entire generation of Reformers, including not only Calvin but also Bullinger, Musculus, Vermigli, and their contemporaries. The viewpoint of the twentieth century, which has selected Calvin as the chief early codifier, must be set aside, particularly in those instances when the formative influence toward the development of a specific doctrinal position came not from Calvin but from one of his contemporaries. Orthodoxy must be understood not as a result of or as a defection from the work of a single thinker but as a doctrinal development resting on a fairly diverse theological heritage. In addition, we must never forget that the Reformation itself stands within the broad tradition of Western theology and in continuity as well as discontinuity with the patristic and medieval heritage.

The present study is an attempt to provide a detailed exposition of the presuppositions and principles of Reformed othodox theology as stated in the prolegomena to the orthodox systems and in the *loci* on Scripture and God. Throughout the study, attention has been paid to the crucial issues of development and change, continuity and discontinuity—not only with the theology of the Reformers but also with that of the medieval scholastic theology drawn upon by the Protestant scholastics in their search for paradigms and definitions. In addition, attention will be given to the way in which the presuppositions, enunciated by the orthodox in their prolegomena, carry through into the initial *loci* of the system, the doctrines of Scripture and God, and through those initial, principial *loci*, determine the character of the system as a whole.

1.2 The Reformation and Theological System

No small part of the task of describing properly the work of Protestant orthodoxy belongs to the discussion of its relationship to the Reformation. In its simplest form, this relationship is one of broad doctrinal continuity together with methodological discontinuity. Of course, the relationship is considerably more complex than this basic statement: methodological changes bring about changes in doctrinal state-ment if only because careful systematization of an idea tends to remove elements of tension and paradox resident in the initial, unsystematic formulation. The difficulty of making this movement toward methodolog-ically controlled and technically sophisticated system without engineer-ing a basic change in the message can be seen most readily in the contrast between Luther's theology and the teaching of later orthodoxy—the former occasional, paradoxical, primarily exegetical or homiletical, and the latter deliberately systematic and argumentative, resting on exegesis but only infrequently stating a theological point in the form of an exegetical exposition. The unsystematic theology of the Reformer belongs to an entirely different genre than the highly systematized theology of his successors.

Not nearly so great a contrast appears, however, if we examine the writings of other Reformers, including contemporaries of Luther like Bucer and Zwingli, or if we examine the Reformation in its historical development toward orthodoxy. Bucer's style as a commentator on the text of Scripture was to move, in the commentary itself, from exegesis of a passage, to the delineation of a doctrinal topic or *locus*, and then to a detailed dogmatic exposition of the *locus*. This model of establishing dogmatic *loci* was subsequently used by Wolfgang Musculus as a means of moving from commentary to theological system, the latter consisting in a collection of such *loci*. Early in the Reformation, Zwingli attempted to develop doctrinal statement both in his extensive exposition of the *Articuli sive conclusiones LXVII* (1523) and in the *De vera et falsa religione commentarius* (1524). The Reformation, thus, is not only a proclamation over against medieval system but also a movement toward the systematization and codification of that proclamation.

Gerhard Ebeling's work, *The Study of Theology*, provides a convenient basis for a critique of scholarly perceptions of the problems of constructing systems of doctrine on either side of the Reformation. Ebeling begins by describing the problem of late medieval scholasticism as a "hypertrophy of doctrine, a multiplication of theological problems" and ultimately as a "self-deception" leading to an absolutization of dogmatic categories as timeless truth.[8]   While there is an element of truth here, the criticism surely cannot be applied uniformly to late medieval theology.   What is more, even a theology aware of its limitations intends to point toward timeless truth.   The Reformation, for Ebeling, not only led to a biblical and exegetical norm for theology but also to an impulse toward a new kind of dogmatics: thus, the efforts of Melanchthon and Calvin were "fundamentally legitimate."[9]

There is a theological judgment present in Ebeling's argument even before his statements regarding Protestant orthodoxy.   Much as Harnack saw Luther as the end of the history of dogma and as a return to the gospel, Ebeling would see Luther as the point at which the historical development of system is broken and after which all further statement of doctrine must be made in terms of a discontinuity with the past.   Luther occupies an Archimedian position outside of the world of dogmatics. Melanchthon and Calvin are legitimized by their relation to this Archimedian position: their theologies appear more as world-moving levers than as attempts at dogmatics in a traditional sense.   This analysis is more accurate as a description of the first editions of Melanchthon's *Loci communes* and Calvin's *Institutio christianae religionis* than it is of the final editions.   It is also more accurate as a description of the fundamental attitude of the first editions of these works—as proclamations of the truth of the gospel—than it is of the well-defined dogmatic context out of which these works, even at their earliest points of development, function.

When Ebeling approaches the problem of a fully-developed Protestant orthodoxy, his theological appreciation of the existential character of Luther's theology comes to the fore.   Although he recognizes the need for historians to understand the context that produced Protestant orthodoxy, he nonetheless refers to it as embodying "false developments" in theology such as the Reformation had attempted to combat.[10]   The Protestant scholastics incorrectly assumed that the Reformation called for "detailed dogmatic corrections" in traditional system and for a reappraisal of the relation between theology and both the tradition of the church and the categories of philosophy.   The orthodox failed to see that the central issue of the Reformation was, instead, the inability of any system to do justice to "the event of word and faith": the orthodox system ignored the character of the event, "cast [it] into a sequence," and "domesticated it."[11]

We must not forget that the Reformers were trained in the late medieval scholastic system.   Theirs was not a simple representation of doctrine accomplished by a leap into the gospel; what they saw as gospel

was seen through the glass of centuries. If their primary interest was
the return to a scriptural faith, their secondary impulse was toward a
reconstruction of established doctrine on the basis of Scripture. The
only real exception to this generalization is Luther, who expressed
little or no interest in system of any kind—but even he, perhaps
preeminently so, was trained in the system. Indeed, Ebeling's point
concerning the existential impact of the Word as event applies, in its
strict implications, only to the theology of Luther: the necessary
process of "domestication" was well under way already in 1521 with the
publication of Melanchthon's *Loci communes*. The historical issue,
moreover, in spite of Ebeling's desire to state the contrary, is the
impact of the Reformation on the scholastic approach to theology that
existed both before and after the Reformation—and, therefore, the impact
of the Reformation on theology not in the sense of the creation of an
absolutely new beginning but rather in the sense of the demand for an
alteration of extant theological structures.

At the heart of Ebeling's criticism and, indeed, at the heart of
much of the critique of Protestant orthodoxy, lies a theological preference for preaching that embodies "the event of word and faith" and that
places upon its hearers an existential demand for commitment over a
doctrinal or dogmatic teaching that presents the elements of the faith in
a coherent sequence. Such a critique can only have the effect of driving
a destructive wedge between the *fides qua creditur* and the *fides quae
creditur*, the subjective faith by which we believe and the objective
faith that is believed. Such a critique also ignores profound distinctions of literary genre—as if the preaching of the Word somehow excludes
from the life of the church the work of codifying doctrine and constructing system. Ideally, the *fides qua* and *fides quae* stand in an
intimate relation, the former accepting the teaching of the latter.
Ideally, the sermon will reflect at the level of piety and personal need
the objective teaching of confession and system, while confession and
system will not become insensitive to piety. If we find this balance of
subjective need and objective statement indicated in the *prolegomena* and
principia of orthodox system, we will have shown that the critique does
not genuinely address the theological issues raised by Protestant
orthodoxy.

J. S. Whale, in contrasting the preaching of Luther with the
"system" of Calvin, refers to ". . . the scholastic system, the beginnings of which we see in Melanchthon's *Loci*, *The Augsburg Confession* in
Germany, the *Helvetic Confession* in Switzerland, the *Thirty-nine Articles*
in England, and the *Formula of Concord*. . . ."[12] In a sense, Luther was

the only Reformer who truly challenged system with nonsystematic and even antisystematic preaching. From the very beginning the Reformation was an attempt to reformulate the system under the terms and in the aftermath of his preaching. The issue of literary genre is, moreover, quite important to the discussion of the movement toward systematic reformulation. A theological system like Polanus' *Syntagma theologiae christianae* (1609) is quite different in form and method from a sermon of Luther or of Calvin—but the difference arises not only from the fact of Polanus' scholastic method but also from the fact that the *Syntagma* is a system and not a sermon. Protestants did not cease to preach or to write catechisms; they simply added a new genre to their theological writings, the theological system. That system, in turn, was subject to a technical development quite distinct from the development of sermons, catechisms and the like.

This positive development of the theology of the Reformation into a dogmatic system—or the radical adaptation of the dogmatic system to conform to the exegetical, anthropological, and soteriological insights of the Reformers—is the natural and perhaps necessary result of the Reformers' need to train followers and successors in the faith. This motive toward the development of dogmatics—the recognition of the practical necessity of having a systematic point of view—appears not only in the *Loci communes* of Melanchthon and the *Institutes* of Calvin but also in the *Loci communes* (1560) of Wolfgang Musculus, the *Compendium christianae religionis* (1556) of Heinrich Bullinger, the *Methodi theologiae* (1568) of Andreas Hyperius, the *Examen theologicum* (1557) of Benedict Aretius, and the Reformed confessions up to and including the *Confessio Helvetica posterior* (1562/66).

The fact of this gradual historical development toward orthodox system does not, of course, absolve the historian from examining differences between the theology of the Reformers and the theology of the orthodox; it only makes the task of examination more difficult and the problems and issues encountered more subtle. We cannot, as noted above, make facile comparisons between the perspective of Calvin and that of Protestant orthodoxy in general. Instead theological patterns and definitions presented in a variety of early and second-generation Reformation writings need to be compared with a number of orthodox systems, recognizing the variety and variance both among the Reformers and among the orthodox. Some doctrines emphasized by the Protestant orthodox—like covenant—are not at all prominent in the thought of Calvin but are presented in some detail in the works of authors like Bullinger and Musculus. The development is complex at every stage—whether with Calvin and his contemporaries; with the next generation following Calvin, in the thought of writers like Ursinus, Olevianus, Beza, and Zanchi; with the early orthodox codifiers, Junius, Polanus, Perkins, Scharpius, Kecker- mann, and others; or with the subsequent generations of Protestant scholastic teachers.   At each stage, the patristic and medieval back- ground is an important factor in the development of ideas.   In addition, the mutual interaction of the thoughts of contemporaries is equally as important as the impact of specific earlier Protestant theologies on any particular thinker or system.

The fact is that a simple kerygma to dogma model or existential event to domestication-of-the-event pattern of doctrinal development cannot be applied to the historical development of Protestant orthodoxy. The kerygma arose and the existential event of the proclamation occurred within the framework of an extant system and a richly elaborated intel- lectual tradition.   The earliest Reformers were all trained in this extant theology—some, like Luther and Bucer, in considerable depth.   The Thomist, Scotist and Nominalist models carry over into the Reformation in the thought of Vermigli, Zanchi, Calvin, and Musculus.   When the tradi- tion reappears in full force and the medieval theological models are again used explicitly by the early Protestant orthodox, it is not because the early orthodox have deviated widely from the theology of the Reformers.   Rather, the systematic models within which the Reformers worked and against which they reacted, are examined again, now by the early orthodox, for the sake of setting forth a critically altered theological system in which the insights of the Reformers have been used as the basis for determining and developing not only individual doctrines but entire patterns of exposition and doctrinal interrelationship.

The development of Protestant system, therefore, resulted in a theology that was neither the theology of the Reformers nor the theology of the medieval scholastics.   Just as the continuity of Christian Aristotelianism is characteristic of the historical path of Western philosophy from the thirteenth through the seventeenth centuries,[13] so the continuity of a dialectical and argumentative scholastic method is a feature of both Catholic and Protestant theological system during the same period.   The impact of the Reformation on this development must not be minimized by a view of Protestant scholasticism as a departure from or distortion of the theology of the Reformation, as if continuity with the Reformation can be identified only in cases of simple duplication of its theology.   Instead, the impact of the Reformation must be considered in terms of the massive reworking of system as undertaken gradually by post-Reformation Protestants.

1.3 The Rise of Orthodoxy and the Structures
of Protestant Scholastic Theology

In order to understand this reworking of theological system that became the primary task of Protestant theology from the mid-sixteenth to the end of the seventeenth century (a period, we note, some three times longer than the Reformation) we must examine the characteristics of scholastic orthodoxy through the several phases of its development.   A full history of orthodoxy cannot be presented here, but the synthetic and doctrinal character of the present study does demand a historical prologue, if only for the sake of noting explicitly the broad stylistic changes that took place in Protestant theology and that must stand in the background of the discussion of each doctrinal point.

The first period of Reformed theology runs roughly from Zwingli's *Articuli sive conclusiones* (1523) and the *Theses Bernenses* in 1528 to the promulgation of the *Heidelberg Catechism* (1562-63) and the death of Calvin in 1564. The *Theses Bernenses*, which grew out of theses presented at several earlier disputations, represents the first distinctively Reformed confessional writing. In contrast to the Lutheran confessional writings, the theses begin with a description of Scripture as the Word of God and therefore as the ground of theology and the church. Following 1523 we see the rise of the major early Reformed writers (Zwingli, Bullinger, Calvin, Musculus, Vermigli) and the publication of their crucial theological works.   It is a period of great variety in theological formulation despite general doctrinal consensus and it defies harmonization of its various theologies into a single analysis of doctrine. By the death of Calvin, all of these founders of the Reformed tradition had produced their major writings and had prepared their churches for the next generation, represented by the *Heidelberg Catechism* and the system of doctrine founded on it. The basic doctrinal positions were stated, but orthodoxy would elaborate, refine, draw out conclusions and, in addition, make more explicit the rootage of Protestantism in the Christian tradition.   In other words, most of the presuppositions and premises of Protestant theology were enunciated during this period, but system as such was not fully developed nor had theology yet received a full Protestant treatment as an academic discipline.

The next period, which represents the beginnings and the initial codification of Reformed orthodoxy, and which we shall label for convenience "early orthodoxy," runs from the *Heidelberg Catechism* to the time when the theologians who sat at the Synod of Dort (1618/19) ceased to dominate Reformed theology (somewhere between 1630 and 1640).[14]   The *Heidelberg Catechism* had two major effects on Reformed theology. First, it set the tone of Dutch and German Reformed piety and doctrine for many decades to come and, second, it provided the basis in Heidelberg for a scholastic approach to theology as taught by one of the authors of the catechism, Zacharias Ursinus. Ursinus revived the *quaestio* as a device for teaching theology, utilizing the catechism itself as the basic form for theological discourse. Ursinus' successor to the chair of theology, Jerome Zanchi, was trained in Thomism and late medieval scholastic thought; the nascent Protestant scholasticism of Ursinus was developed and refined under his tutelage.

As we move from the initial period of Reformed theology into the early orthodox period, a major change in style can be noted. Some of this change relates directly to the increasingly formal, institution-alized character of theology in general. Protestant theology is no longer, in the latter period, reforming a church—it is establishing and protecting the church. Theology itself is more and more a creature of the schools. In the early period theology has strong homiletical and catechetical motives; in the latter period these characteristics are no longer as obvious in the system. At this point we must be wary of making artificial contrasts, for the homiletical and catechetical instruction of the orthodox maintains much of the earlier warmth and dynamism. Preaching and teaching of piety have been separated from instruction in doctrine by the increasing need to deal with the language of technical school-theology. We must bear this in mind in our comparison, since a system like Bullinger's *Compendium* or Calvin's *Institutio* is not perfectly analogous in intention and use to a system like Polanus' *Syntagma* or Scharpius' *Cursus theologicus*. The justice of these remarks is apparent in the works of such thinkers as Zanchi and Walaeus who produced both introductory doctrinal instructions and systems of theology.

The issue of style conjoins, then, with the issue of literary genre. The earliest systematic efforts of the Reformation, whether Zwingli's *Commentarius*, Bullinger's *Compendium*, Calvin's *Institutes*, or any of the various *Loci communes* written before 1564, are intended to be instructions in the basic teachings of Scripture, preparations for biblical study. In the case of Bullinger's *Compendium* and Calvin's *Institutes*, the parallel between this basic instruction and the forms of catechetical instruction is obvious. The style, moreover, is discursive—as one would expect at this level of preparatory and at times hortatory instruction. The passage of Reformed theology into the era of early orthodoxy can be charted in terms of the movement from basic, discursive instruction to a more sophisticated, dialectical model.

Part of the reason for this development lies in the polemic in which the Reformers and their successors were continuously engaged.[15]   The growth and development, for example, of Calvin's *Institutes* represents not only the positive creation of a more inclusive doctrinal statement but also the polemical engagement with an ever increasing series of adversaries.   It is painfully apparent in the later editions of the *Institutes* that the discursive model was strained and its clarity of doctrinal exposition threatened by the addition of polemics that interrupt the flow of thought and frequently move in directions not dictated by the positive statements of doctrine.   The early orthodox development of larger, more detailed, dialectical or scholastic argumentation must be viewed, in large part, as an accommodation to the needs of debate.   Thus Ursinus will argue in the form of the *quaestio*, with objections and replies, while writers like Scharpius and Trelcatius will add entire polemical sections to each doctrinal *locus*.   In the later phases of orthodoxy, Wendelin and Turretin will write elenctical or disputative systems and Mastricht will include a polemical section alongside the exegetical, dogmatic and practical divisions of his *loci*.

Early orthodoxy is also the period of Ramism.   If the Heidelberg theology, particularly in the works of Zanchi, tended toward the treatment of *loci* on a massive expository scale, the theology and dialectic of Petrus Ramus (1515–1572) had an opposite effect.   In his attack on the Aristotelianism of his day, Ramus produced a method of logical discourse by means of partition or dichotomy which gave to Reformed theology an extreme clarity and conciseness of approach.   This clarity and conciseness appears in the writings of Perkins, Polanus, Ames, Scharpius and, to a lesser extent, Walaeus and Maccovius.   If not universally accepted— indeed, opposed bitterly by Beza and Olevianus—Ramism is characteristic of the striving of early orthodoxy toward a careful and viable enunciation of theological method.

The early orthodox, whether Ramist or anti-Ramist, shared the desire to create a theological system suited to the successful establishment of Protestantism as a church in its own right, catholic in its teaching, capable of being sustained intellectually against its adversaries, and sufficiently technical and methodologically consistent to stand among the other disciplines in the university.[16]   This concern for method and structure marks a point of genuine distinction between the theological approach of the Reformers and that of the early orthodox.   Method, although a concern of Reformation writers like Melanchthon and Hyperius,[17] was not a dominant theme.   The gradual expansion of Calvin's *Institutes* manifests virtually no concern for approach, method or overarching unity until the final edition of 1559, when Calvin reorganized the whole of the *Institutes* on the pattern of the creed. Even in this final edition, the issue addressed by Calvin was the arrangement of all his chapters—including noncredal topics—under the credal form and not the development of a consistent approach, either synthetic or analytic, to the organization of doctrine. The early orthodox era, drawing on Hyperius and given direction by Ursinus, Zanchi and the Ramists, strove toward cohesive method and arrangement of doctrine as well as toward precise definition. Typical of the era is a concern to distinguish between a theoretical, somewhat deductive and teleological approach to system, usually called "synthetic," and a more practical, somewhat inductive approach usually called "analytic." The synthetic model, which became the dominant pattern for system, begins with prolegomena and the doctrine of Scripture and moves from the doctrine of God, via the historical path of sin and redemption, to the last things. Analytic patterns can, for example, begin with the problem of sin and move, via the work of redemption, to faith and the articles of the faith.

Intimately bound up with the early orthodox concern for method is the role of early orthodoxy in the positive development of Protestant theology in the form of system. Several of the earlier historians of Protestant orthodoxy, particularly those enmeshed in the theological problems of the nineteenth century, have spoken of this positive systematic development as the working out of an inner logic of Protestant doctrine. Most notable here are the writings of Alexander Schweizer, Wilhelm Gass and Ernst Troeltsch.[18] The two former writers argue for a metaphysical and predestinarian systematization, while Troeltsch, more on the Lutheran side of orthodoxy, tended to emphasize the inner logic of system. While we will take issue, below, with the notion of a predestinarian metaphysic in the Reformed systems,[19] we need to recognize here the fact of the positive, synthesizing drive evident alongside of the polemics in the early orthodox systems.

Rather than view this drive as arising from the inner logic of certain central dogmas, we ought to view it, more simply, as the result of the forces of institutionalization witnessed both in the Protestant confessions and in the larger theological context of the catholic or universal churchly tradition of which the Reformers and their successors strove to be a part. Thus the Protestant orthodox systems increasingly adopt a confessional structure and include all the doctrinal points noted in earlier theological system, specifically in the sentence commentaries and theological summas of the later Middle Ages. This positive development, moreover, provided a more suitable systematic vehicle in and through which to surmount objections leveled by Roman Catholic polemicists.

This movement toward a lucid schema of doctrine was accompanied by a response to a still more sophisticated Roman polemic—principally in the writings of Robert Bellarmine.[20]   As a result we see a tendency to produce complete formulations of doctrine on points left vague or unfinished by theologians of the Reformation.   In addition, the sophistication of the polemic led these early orthodox to adapt for their own use many of the distinctions used by the medieval scholastics.   Now, more than in earlier times, Protestantism began to develop a self-conscious "church dogmatics" formulated in continuity with the tradition of Christian systematic theology and aware of the need for philosophical as well as theological consistency.   This drive toward system may be regarded as one of the causes of the debate with Arminius and the confessional determination of that debate at Dort.   There was no room left within the system for variance such as that of the Remonstrants which now stood out so clearly against the background of a more closely defined system identified as the particular theology of the Reformed churches.

On the second point, it must be admitted that, despite the level of rancor and invective reached in the doctrinal debates of the seventeenth century, the Protestant scholastics seldom misunderstood or misrepresented the doctrinal statements of their opponents.   We may find excessive the claim made by the Lutherans and the Reformed against each other that their respective Christologies, if followed to their logical conclusions, would mean the destruction of the doctrine of the Person of Christ and the eventual loss of faith in the incarnation.   Nonetheless, the actual statement of Reformed doctrine by Lutherans and of Lutheran doctrine by the Reformed for the sake of confutation were generally accurate, as were the Reformed and Lutheran representations of the views of their mutual adversaries, like the Roman Catholics and the Socinians. The primary purpose of polemics was the assault on and demolition of error.   That purpose was best served by the accurate statement of an opponent's position.

In addition to these doctrinal and institutional pressures, both positive and polemical, early orthodoxy was faced by the intellectual and academic pressure of establishing a new dialogue, suitable to the Protestant context, between theology and philosophy.   As Lewalter has argued, the nominally metaphysical issues necessarily addressed by fully developed theological system could only be dealt with adequately by the adoption (or adaptation) of a philosophical metaphysic congenial to that system.   The Protestant orthodox looked both to the precedents provided for a synthesis of philosophy and theology, reason and revelation, by the scholastics of the thirteenth, fourteenth and fifteenth centuries and, as emphasized by Lewalter, to the revived Aristotelianism of Zabarella and Suarez.

The theology of the Reformation manifests a certain degree of continuity with the critical theology of the later Middle Ages, specifically with the Scotist and Nominalist emphasis on the diastasis of revelation and reason and on the need for reliance on authority in the construction of a body of Christian doctrine.   Even so, the theology of Protestant orthodoxy, when it seeks medieval models, manifests an affinity with the more critical perspective of the fourteenth and fifteenth centuries rather than the more optimistic approach of the thirteenth-century Dominicans and their views on the relationship of revelation and reason.   Where the Thomistic line of thought continues into the Reformation—for example, in the writings of Vermigli, Zanchi and, to a certain extent, Keckermann—it is modified by a more negative assessment of the powers of reason and by a sense of diastasis between the ways of God and the ways of man that virtually cancels a Thomistic use of the analogia entis in theology.[21]

The Protestant interest in the philosophy of Zabarella and Suarez, evidenced in the works of Keckermann and Alsted, arose out of the desire to find a suitable metaphysic for the Protestant academy.   The theological impact of this new philosophical alliance can be described, on the one hand, as a reinforcing of the modified Thomism already present in Reformed thought through the work of Vermigli and Zanchi and, on the other, as the creation of new systematic and linguistic possibilities for Protestant thought.   Now Protestant theology could draw, with philosophical rigor, on the language of potency and act, of essence and existence, and of intellectual habits or dispositions.   In other words the language and therefore the systematic conceptuality of being, both finite and infinite, and of human psychology was once again available in a cohesive and coherent form.[22]   The effect on theological system was twofold: first, the systematic broadening, that we have already noted as a positive development of the implications of the Reformation for theological system as a whole, was facilitated, and, second, theology was placed in dialogue with collateral disciplines far more than it had been during the era of the Reformation.   The grounds for this dialogue now had to be described in theological prolegomena even as its effect became evident in other loci, specifically, the doctrines of God and providence.

We can affirm four forces contributing to the rise and development of Protestant orthodoxy, (polemics, pedagogical needs, the working out of systematic issues, and the striving for philosophical breadth and coherence) and rule out a fifth (concentration on a metaphysical principle or central dogma). We concur with Scharlemann's comment concerning Lutheran orthodoxy, that the development was not a "relapse" into "earlier concept-splitting 'school philosophy'" but rather a development manifesting a "theological continuity" between the sixteenth and seventeenth centuries.[23]   However, it seems that response to polemic was more important for the development of individual *loci* than Scharlemann would allow and that continuity must be defined in terms of the broadening of the Protestant theological perspective to include more of the tradition of the church than had been utilized by the Reformers. In addition, it is also crucial to recognize, underlying all of these individual forces or pressures toward scholastic orthodoxy, the pressure of institutionalization. Inasmuch as the Reformation itself intended to correct doctrinal errors and abuses, its success as a movement virtually demanded that Protestant theologians create an orthodoxy, an institutionally viable, genuinely catholic body of right teaching resting upon, elaborating and defending the church's confessions.

It is also during the early orthodox period that Reformed theology assumed truly international dimensions. The systems of Calvin, Vermigli, Musculus, and Bullinger had extensive circulation not only in Switzerland but also in German Reformed territories, the Netherlands and England. Writers of the third and fourth generations of the Reformed churches—Ursinus, Olevianus, Szegedinus, Zanchi, Polanus, Perkins, Ames—were well known and widely read throughout Europe. Indeed, by the time of the Synod of Dort, the international character and broad, international consensus in Reformed doctrine was such that delegates were gathered from the Dutch states, the German Reformed cities, Switzerland, and England.

The English—Perkins, Ames, Downame, Ussher, Charnock, and Leigh, not to mention commentators and theologians who did not produce systems— fall generally within the bounds of mainline Reformed theology and have only been neglected in studies of Protestant orthodoxy because of the insular approach not only of English but also of continental historians. In the sixteenth and seventeenth centuries England was receptive to continental thought, as citations of European thinkers in English works testify. If the English were not as ready to develop a fully scholastic systematic theology as their Dutch, German and Swiss brethren, they were sensitive to this fact and made up for their hesitancy by an omnivorous reading of continental works. On the other hand, major English thinkers like Perkins, Ames, Whittaker, Gataker, and Owen were much appreciated on the continent--as is manifest by the European editions and citations of their works. A full picture of Reformed orthodoxy cannot afford to omit the English contribution to Protestant scholasticism.

Although this period (from roughly 1564 to 1635) is also the era during which the new science was being set forth by Kepler, Galileo and Bacon and the new rationalism was being expounded by Descartes and Lord Herbert of Cherbury, the rise of modern science and modern rationalism did not directly affect Protestant theology until the close of the seventeenth century. For the most part Protestant theologians doubted the new cosmology and rejected rationalist philosophy. The former had to wait until Isaac Newton's physical and mathematical discoveries to make any sense at all and the latter, particularly in the deductive model presented by Descartes, has never proved congenial to traditional theology.[24]

Just as the Ptolemaic universe remained the basis of the Western worldview until the end of the seventeenth century and continued to affect literary and philosophical forms of expression well into the eighteenth,[25] so did Christianized Aristotelianism remain the dominant philosophical perspective throughout the era of orthodoxy. Here too, as in the area of theological system, important developments took place in the context of the Protestant universities in the late sixteenth century. Where Melanchthon, Vermigli and others of their generation had tended to content themselves with the teaching of rhetoric, logic, ethics, and physics without giving particular attention to the potential impact of these disciplines on theology, in the second half of the century the philosophical disciplines began to have a marked effect on Protestant theology. Aristotelian physics served the doctrine of creation in the works of Daneau and Hyperius, Agricolan and Ramist logic began to clarify the structure of theological systems, and metaphysics re-entered the Protestant classroom in the writings of Schegk, Martinius, Keckermann, Alsted and Timpler.[26]

This development of Christian Aristotelianism in the Protestant universities not only parallels the development of Protestant scholasticism but bears witness to a similar phenomenon. The gradual production of philosophical textbooks by Protestants does not indicate a period during which the philosophical tradition was set aside followed by a sudden return to philosophy. Instead it indicates a transition from medieval textbooks, like the *Summulae logicales* of Peter of Spain and the *De dialectia inventione* of Rudolf Agricola, to textbooks written by Protestants for Protestants, like Seton's *Dialectica* (1545), Ramus' *Dialectica*

(1543) and the spate of works based upon it, or Burgersdijk's *Logica*
(1637). In other words, the absence of Protestant works from the era of
the early Reformation does not indicate an absence of logic or philosophy
as much as it indicates a use of established textbooks prior to the
development of new ones under the pressure not only of Protestant theology but also of humanism and of changes and developments in the philosophical disciplines themselves. Schmitt summarizes the situation neatly:

> . . . Latin Aristotelianism stretching from the twelfth to the
> seventeenth century had a degree of unity and organic develop-
> ment that cannot be easily dismissed. . . . the differences
> distinguishing the Catholic, Lutheran, or Calvinist varieties,
> are far outweighed by a unifying concern for the same philo-
> sophical and scientific problems and an invocation of the same
> sources of inspiration by which to solve them.[27]

The period following 1640 and extending to the end of the seventeenth century can be called the period of high orthodoxy, defined most
clearly by further changes in the style of dogmatics. The architectonic
clarity of early orthodoxy is replaced to a certain extent or at least
put to the service of a more broadly developed and even discursive
system. Much of the change relates to the incorporation of expanded
polemical argumentation into the system and of elaboration of ideas
already present in system as basic definitions into more extended *loci*.
In addition, the creative phase of orthodoxy, during which the Protestant
scholastic system was built out of materials drawn from the Reformers,
the tradition and Scripture, was over by 1640. High orthodoxy did not
create system; it modified, developed and elaborated extant system.

The early orthodox systems and compendia, with their lucid and
neatly argued structures, provided as it were the skeleton of the high
orthodox dogmatics. One can almost imagine the high orthodox system as
an extended meditation on all tangential subjects and controversial
topics adumbrated by the individual propositions and partitions of the
early orthodox system. This appears quite clearly in Rissen's *Summa
theologiae* wherein doctrine is stated in neatly numbered propositions
between which the related controversies are argued and resolved. Nevertheless, the early orthodox structure, however well-conceived, did not
resolve all the problems of form and order—not even in the prolegomena.
Together with the elaboration of extant *loci*, the high orthodox further
elaborate system as a whole by the addition of new *loci* and, in particular, new subdivisions of *loci*. For example, the doctrine of the *pactum
salutis* appears in the discussion of covenant and the question of fundamental articles in theology is added to the prolegomena.

Whereas the major polemics of early orthodoxy were directed against
Rome—in particular against Bellarmine—and, on a limited set of

doctrinal issues, against Lutheranism and the traditional heterodoxies of Christianity, the polemic of high orthodoxy encountered a wider variety of antagonists, some of them more closely related to the heart of Reformed theology (the Remonstrants, Conrad Vorstius, and the Socinians). The *loci de theologia* and *de Deo*, during the early orthodox period, developed for the most part as positive doctrine drawing nonpolemically upon the resources of medieval scholasticism with emphasis on modified Thomist, Augustinian and Scotist formulations. The *loci de scriptura sacra* and *de trinitate*, however, developed in controversy—the former against Rome and the latter against scattered antitrinitarian heresies. In the high orthodox period, beginning in the 1640s with thinkers like Cloppenburg, Hoornbeeck, and Wendelin, the polemical or controversial element begins to pervade all the *loci*—particularly in view of the rise of Socinian theology and its attack not only on the Trinity but on the traditional view of God, and in view of the Remonstrant systems (first Episcopius, then Curcellaeus, Grotius, and Limborch) and their nearly total alternative view of theology which touched not only the system proper but the entire prolegomena including the *locus de theologia* and the problem of religion in general.

The Remonstrant theology in particular posed a major threat since it was, in its beginning, an offshoot of the Reformed system and, in its development, a highly rationalistic structure allied with both Cartesian and Lockean thought. Polemic became particularly bitter over the Remonstrant–Cartesian association since Cartesian philosophy, as the reigning new movement of the age, had also made inroads into Reformed theology among the federal theologians. Here, the near contact between the Reformed and their Remonstrant opponents was most obvious. The Remonstrant system had retained some strong resemblances to the Reformed system, and especially in the area of the federal doctrines had developed a dispensational structure close to that argued by Cocceius and his followers.[28] The Cocceian theology, however, once the initial polemic had subsided somewhat and the various hermeneutical problems inherent in Cocceius' rather idiosyncratic notion of a gradually abrogated covenant of works had been overcome by theologians like Burmann and Witsius, provided the covenantal model which became a central architectonic feature of the orthodox Reformed system. Such unquestionably orthodox thinkers as Turretin, Heidegger and Mastricht employ the covenant as a focal point of system between the *loci* on creation and fall and the locus of redemption in Christ.[29]

High orthodoxy, then, is the era of the full and final development of Protestant system prior to the great changes in philosophical and scientific perspective that would, in the eighteenth and nineteenth centuries, utterly recast theological system into new forms.   There is perhaps some justification in dividing seventeenth-century orthodoxy into a phase of polemical codification during which theologians like Hoornbeeck, Cloppenburg, and Voetius developed primarily polemical systems in response to all known adversaries past and present, and a synthetic phase following 1660 when the tendency was toward the creation of a theological synthesis in which the results of Protestant exegesis, the dogmatic forms of Protestant doctrine, the polemical establishment of those doctrines, and an exposition of the practical implication of doctrine could be gathered into a systematic whole, as witnessed by Mastricht at the end of the century.   Nevertheless, the entire period from 1635 or 1640 to the end of the century bears witness to a confessional homogeneity and to a fairly consistent development of the language of scholastic Protestantism as set forth by the great formulators of system in and following the era of confessional synthesis.   By 1640 the theologians of the era of Dort were being replaced by pupils and successors and the final codification both of polemics and of positive dogmatic theology had begun in the Reformed Church. This work of the final codification of orthodoxy was complete by 1700 in the works of Turretin, Marckius and Heidegger.

Following 1700 (and beyond the emphasis of the present study) there are two basic historical divisions of late orthodoxy, both fraught with dramatic changes in attitude and orientation.   Between 1700 and 1739 theologians became wary of the more dogmatic orientation of exegesis in the preceding period and also of the use of philosophical systems in theology.   This brief interlude might be called the "pietistic-eclectic phase" of orthodoxy.   Its theologians include J. A. Turretin, Samuel Werenfels, J. J. Rambach, J. F. Osterwald, and F. A. Lampe.   In 1740, Christian Wolff was returned to the chair of philosophy in Halle over the objections of his pietist detractors, inaugurating a new era in the development of Protestant theology.   Although Wolff had a more massive following among the Lutherans, he did count among his Reformed followers Endemann, Stapfer, Wyttenbach, and Beck.   In the writings of these theologians we see a more positive use of natural theology and reason and the definitive marriage of theology to rational, supranaturalistic philosophy.   In addition, through the hermeneutical work of J. A. Turretin and J. J. Rambach, the critical-textual methods of Cappel and the school of Samur came more and more into use, disrupting the older hermeneutic of the *analogia fidei*.[30]

With the pietist or transitional phase of Protestant theology and the subsequent rise of a rationalistic dogmatics, the phenomenon of

Protestant orthodoxy comes to an end. Whereas Wolffian dogmatics may still be considered "scholastic" in form, the content of traditional dogmatics has been consistently removed from theological system: neither the scriptural principle nor the subordination of reason to revelation govern theological statement in these systems. The few genuinely orthodox systems written in the eighteenth century, like those written in the nineteenth and twentieth centuries, hardly represent a living theological movement: they tend to reproduce doctrine in the hope of maintaining the correct statement of earlier generations against the shifting patterns of philsophical opinion and linguistic expression. Here, finally, as never before in the history of orthodoxy, do we have epigoni who replicate the systems of their predecessors.

The decline of Protestant orthodoxy, then, coincides with the decline of the interrelated intellectual phenomena of scholastic method and Christian Aristotelianism. Rationalist philosophy was ultimately incapable of becoming a suitable *ancilla* and, instead, demanded that it and not theology be considered queen of the sciences. Without a philosophical structure to complement its doctrines and to cohere with its scholastic method, Protestant orthodoxy came to an end. (A similar decline of scholastic theological system occurred in the Roman Catholic Church in the eighteenth century.[31])

The continuity of Christian Aristotelianism and scholastic method from the medieval into the early modern period together with the relationship of these two phenomena to Protestant orthodoxy pinpoint one further issue to be considered in the study of orthodox or scholastic Protestantism. It is not only an error to attempt to characterize Protestant orthodoxy by means of a comparison with one or another of the Reformers (as in the case of the "Calvin against the Calvinists" thesis). It is also an error to discuss Protestant orthodoxy without being continually aware of the broad movement of ideas from the late Middle Ages, through the Reformation, into post-Reformation Protestantism. Whereas the Reformation is surely the formative event for Protestantism, it is also true that the Reformation, which took place during the first half of the sixteenth century, is the briefer phenomenon, enclosed as it were by the five-hundred-year history of scholasticism and Christian Aristotelianism. In approaching the continuities and discontinuities of Protestant scholasticism with the Middle Ages and the Reformation, the chief task is to assess the Protestant adjustment of traditional scholastic categories in the light of the Reformation and the patterns according to which it mediated that tradition, both positively and negatively, to future generations of Protestants. This approach is not only more adequate to the understanding of Protestant orthodoxy, but is also the framework for a clearer understanding of the meaning of the Reformation itself.

1.4 A Survey of Authors and Sources

The study of Protestant orthodoxy has been greatly hampered by a general lack of knowledge of the authors and writings of the post-Reformation era of Protestantism. The following list is not exhaustive. It only serves to identify, in brief compass and by period, the authors and first editions of documents important to the development of post-Reformation Reformed theology. Medieval scholastics have not been included in the list but several orthodox Lutheran writers and sources have been noted. For modern editions and collected works used in this essay, the reader should consult the footnotes of the present volume. This information will also appear in the bibliography at the end of volume 3.

The Era of the Reformation (ca. 1517–1565)

Heinrich Bullinger (1504–1575); studied in Cologne and became involved in the Reformation through encounter with the writings of Luther and Melanchthon. He succeeded Zwingli as pastor of the Grossmünster of Zurich in 1531, a post he held until the end of his life. Major doctrinal works: *Sermonum decades quinque* (1549–1551); *Compendium christianae religionis* (1556); *Confessio et expositio simplex orthodoxae fidei* (1566). The latter work is commonly known as the *Second Helvetic Confession*.

John Calvin (1509–1564); studied law and classical languages at Orleans, Bourges and Paris. From 1536 to 1538 and from 1541 to 1564 Calvin led the Reformation in Geneva. His major dogmatic work is the *Institutio christianae religionis* which went through four major editions (1536, 1539/41, 1554, and 1559). The last of these editions represents its final and, to Calvin's mind, definitive form.

Andreas Gerardus Hyperius (1511–1564); studied at Tournai and Paris; visited England (1537–1541) and in 1542 was appointed professor of theology at Marburg, a post he held to the end of his life. His theology mediates between Lutheran and Reformed and is important to the development of both traditions. Major works: *De theologo, seu de ratione studii theologici, libri IIII* (1556); *Elementa christianae religionis* (1563);

Methodi theologiae, sive praecipuorum christianae religionis locorum communium, libri tres (1568).

Philip Melanchthon (1497–1560); studied at Heidelberg and Tübingen; was called to Wittenberg in 1518 as professor of Greek; his subsequent teaching of rhetoric and ethics in a classical mode and its influence on German education have given him the title *Praeceptor Germaniae*. His theological views caused considerable debate in early Lutheranism, but his systematizing influence cannot be questioned. The relevant systematic works are: *Loci communes rerum theologicarum* (1521; revised and augmented, 1535, 1543/44, 1559); *Brevis discendae theologiae ratio* (ca. 1530).

Wolfgang Musculus (1497–1563); studied in the Benedictine monastery near Lixheim; advocated reform after reading early tracts by Luther and fled the monastery in 1518. From 1529 to 1531 he studied at Strasbourg and was a preacher in Augsburg from 1531 to 1548. Forced out of Germany by the Augsburg Interim (1548) he went to Switzerland and was appointed professor of theology in Bern (1549), a post he held until his death. Major dogmatic work: *Loci communes sacrae theologiae* (1560).

Peter Martyr Vermigli (1500–1562); studied at Padua and Bologna; while prior of St. Pietro ad Aram near Naples he encountered the reform ideas of Juan de Valdés. In 1542 he more openly espoused reform and left Italy for Basel and Strasbourg. In December of 1542 he succeeded Capito as professor of theology in Strasbourg. From 1547 to 1553, Vermigli taught at Oxford. On the accession of Mary he returned to Strasbourg (1553–1556) but ended his career in Zurich (1556–1562). His great dogmatic testament, the *Loci communes*, was gathered out of his writings and published posthumously by Robert Masson in 1576.

Pierre Viret (1511–1571); studied in Paris but renounced his training and joined William Farel in the Swiss reform (1531). He taught at Bern (1537) and served as a preacher in Geneva, Lausanne and Lyons. His systematic works include: *Exposition familière sur le Symbole des Apostres* (1560); *Exposition de la doctrine de la foy chrestienne* 1564; and *Instruction chrestienne en la doctrine de la loy et de l'Evangile* (1525).

Ulrich Zwingli (1484–1531); studied at Vienna and Basel (1500–1506); he served as pastor at Glarus and Einsiedeln before becoming the chief preacher and pastor at the Grossmünster in Zurich in 1518. Between 1522 and 1524 he instituted the reforms and conducted the disputations that solidified the Zurich Reformation. Zwingli's most important systematic essay is the *De vera et falsa religione commentarius* (1525).

Early Orthodoxy (ca. 1565–1640)

Johann Heinrich Alsted (1588–1638); studied at Herborn.   In 1610 he was appointed professor of philosophy at Herborn and in 1619 professor of theology.   He represented the Reformed church of Nassau at the Synod of Dort in 1618/19.   He left Herborn in 1629 for the University of Weissenburg.   Alsted was a codifier and compiler of knowledge whose major works include: *Cursus philosophici encyclopaedia* (1620) and the *Methodus sacrosanctae theologiae octo libris tradita* (1614).

William Ames (1576–1633); studied at Christ's College, Cambridge. He went to Leyden in 1611; in 1618/19 he sat at the Synod of Dort as an assistant to its president, Johannes Bogerman.   He became professor of theology at Franecker in 1622 and rector of the university in 1626.   His major dogmatic work is the *Medulla ss. theologiae* (1623).

Benedictus Aretius (1505–1574); studied at Strasbourg and Marburg; served as professor of logic at Marburg and, beginning in 1564, as Wolfgang Musculus' successor as professor of theology in Bern.   His major dogmatic works are *Examen theologicum* (1557) and *SS. theolgiae problemata, seu loci communes* (1573).

Theodore Beza (1519–1605); studied at Paris, Orléans, and Bourges. In 1548, Beza visited Geneva, Tübingen and Lausanne, solidifying his connection with Calvin and receiving an appointment as professor of Greek at Lausanne.   In 1558 Beza went to Geneva where he became an increasingly important spokesman for the Reformed faith and, ultimately, Calvin's successor (1564).   His most significant doctrinal works are: *Confession de la foy chrestienne* (1558); *Quaestionum et responsionum Christianarum libellus* (1570; second part, 1576).   The *Summa totius christianismi* (1555) with its famous *Tabula praedestinationis* should also be mentioned.

Gulielmus Bucanus (d. 1603); served as professor of theology at Lausanne from 1591 to 1603.   He was called to teach at the new academy at Samur in 1603 but died before he could accept the post.   His major dogmatic work is the *Institutiones theologicae seu locorum communium christianae religonis* (1602).

Antoine de la Roche Chandieu (1534–1591) or Sadeel; studied at Toulouse and Geneva and served as pastor of the Reformed congregation in Paris (1556–62).   He played a major role in the national synods of the French Reformed Church in the sixteenth century.   After the St. Bartholomew's Day massacre he fled to Switzerland and lived in Geneva, Lausanne and Aubonne.   His major theological treatises include: *De verbo Dei scripto* (1580) and *De veritate naturae humanae Christi* (1585).

Lambert Daneau (1530–1595); studied law at Orléans, went to Paris (1547–52) and then returned to Orléans where he received his doctorate in law in 1559. His sympathies with the Reformation led him to Geneva in 1560. He held a pastorate from 1561 to 1574, and was appointed as professor in the Academy at Geneva in 1574. In 1581 he was called to the University of Leiden and to a pastorate in that city. He held the post for only a year. He served several churches in Ghent, Orthez and Lescar until called to Castres in 1593, where he remained until his death. His chief dogmatic work is the *Christianae isagoges ad locos communes* in five parts (1583–88); he also wrote a *Compendium sacrae theologiae* (1595).

Franciscus Gomarus (1563–1641); studied at Strasbourg, Neustadt, Oxford, Cambridge, and Heidelberg. In 1594 Gomarus was appointed professor of theology at Leiden. When his theological adversary, Arminius, died in 1609 and was succeeded on the theological faculty of Leiden by Conrad Vorstius, Gomarus resigned his position in protest over the appointment. In 1614, he went to Samur as professor of theology and in 1618 to Groningen. He retained his post at Groningen until his death in 1641. He was a delegate to the Synod of Dort. Gomarus' theological system is the *Disputationes theologicae* (1644).

Franciscus Junius (1545–1602); studied in Geneva. He was professor of theology at Neustadt (1576–1584), Heidelberg (1584–1592) and Leiden (1592–1602). Junius' major theological works are the treatise *De vera theologia* (1594) and the theological compendium, *Theses theologicae*, from his years at Leiden.

Bartholomaeus Keckermann (1571–1609); studied at Wittenberg, Leipzig and Heidelberg. His years at Heidelberg (1592–1601) were divided between study and teaching. Keckermann taught Hebrew and theology. From 1601 until his death in 1609, Keckermann was rector of the gymnasium and professor of philosophy in his native Danzig. His major theological work is the *Systema sacrosanctae theologiae, tribus libris adornatum* (1602).

Sibrandus Lubbertus (ca. 1556–1625); studied in Bremen, Wittenberg, Marburg, and Geneva. In Geneva, he studied under Beza. After 1577 he studied in Basel and Neustadt and in 1585 began to teach theology in Franecker. He was awarded a doctorate in theology by the University of Heidelberg in 1587. He was a delegate to the Synod of Dort. He authored the *De principiis christianorum dogmatum libri VII* (1591).

Johannes Maccovius (1578–1644); studied at Franecker and became professor of theology at that institution in 1615. He is remembered for his extreme and polemical advocacy of supralapsarianism against Lubbertus and for the censure he received for his speculative and philosophical approach to theology by the Synod of Dort. His chief works are *Collegia theologica* (1623) and *Loci communes theologici* (1650).

Pierre du Moulin (1568–1658) or, frequently, Petrus Molinaeus; studied at Sedan, Paris, Cambridge, and Leiden. In 1592 he was appointed professor of philosophy at Leiden, a post he vacated in 1599 to become a preacher at Paris and Charenton. In 1615 he went to Cambridge and received his doctorate in theology. He returned to Sedan in 1625, where he remained until his death. His *De cognitione dei tractatus* appeared in 1624.

William Perkins (1558–1602); studied at Christ's College, Cambridge (1577–1582). Following 1582 he served as a fellow of the college. Perkins was an influential teacher. His works include *Armilla aurea* (1590), translated into English as *A Golden Chaine* (1591); *The Foundation of the Christian Religion gathered into sixe Principles* (1590); and *An Exposition of the Symbole or Creed of the Apostles* (1595).

Amandus Polanus von Polansdorf (1561–1610); studied at Tübingen, Basel and Geneva. He was appointed professor of Old Testament at Basel in 1596 and served as dean of the theological faculty from 1598 to 1609. His dogmatic works are *Partitiones theologicae, pars I* (1590), *pars II* (1596); and *Syntagma theologiae christianae* (1609).

Johann Poliander (1568–1646); studied at Bremen, Heidelberg and Geneva. In 1591 he became pastor of the Walloon congregation at Dordrecht and in 1611 succeeded Gomarus as professor of theology at Leiden. He sat at the Synod of Dort. He is also remembered as coauthor with Rivetus, Walaeus, and Thysius of the *Synopsis purioris theologiae* (1626).

Peter Ramus (ca. 1515–1572); studied at Paris; taught briefly at Heidelberg (1570) and returned to Paris only to perish in the St. Bartholomew's day massacre in 1572. Ramus is most famous for his anti-Aristotelian logic, the *Dialecticae institutiones* (1543) and the *Dialecticae partitiones* (1543). He also wrote a brief work on theology, the *Commentarii de religione christiana* (1576).

Johannes Scharpius (ca. 1572–1648) or John Sharp; studied at St. Andrews, receiving his M.A. in 1592. In 1601 he became minister of Kilmany in Fife, where he served until 1605. In that year he so opposed the religious repression of James VI that he was banished for life. In 1608 he was appointed professor of theology at Die in the Dauphiné. He was ordered out of France in 1630 and returned to Edinburgh where he became professor of theology. His major work is the *Cursus theologicus* (1618).

Stephanus Szegedinus (1515–1572); otherwise Stephen Kis, was born at Szeged in Hungary, whence his last name. He studied at Vienna, Crakow and Wittenberg (1543–54). He served as a teacher in Hungary until driven from his post in 1552 by the Roman Catholics. In that year he fled to the part of Hungary under Ottoman rule where, except for a year-long imprisonment (1563), he continued his work as a teacher and church superintendent. His major systematic work is the posthumous *Theologiae sincerae loci communes de Deo et homine cum confessione de Trinitate* (1585).

Lucas Trelcatius, the younger (1573–1607); studied at Leiden and became professor of theology there in 1603. He participated in the debate with Arminius over predestination and Christology. His major work is the *Scholastica et methodica locorum communium s. theologiae institutio* (1604).

Zacharius Ursinus (1534–1583); studied with Melanchthon at Wittenberg from 1550 to 1557; after being attacked as a "sacramentarian" or crypto-Calvinist, he went to Zurich (1560) and was appointed director of the *Collegium Sapientiae* in 1561. Together with Caspar Olevianus he authored the *Heidelberg Catechism*. He was professor of theology in Heidelberg from 1562 to 1568. His great theological work is surely the lectures on the *Heidelberg Catechism*, the *Doctrinae christianae compendium* (1584), published in revised form by his pupil Paraeus as *Explicationum catecheticarum* (1594). Ursinus also wrote a fragment of a major system, the *Loci theologicae* (1612).

James Ussher (1581–1656), studied at Trinity College, Dublin, gaining his B.A. in 1597. He was made a fellow in 1599 and was granted the M.A. in 1601. In 1605 he was appointed chancellor of St. Patrick's cathedral in Dublin and awarded the B.D. He was appointed professor of theology at Trinity College in 1607 and awarded his D.D. in 1614. In 1615 he wrote the strongly Reformed *Irish Articles of Religion*. He was elevated to the archepiscopate of Armagh in 1625. In 1640, he left Ireland for England where he resided for the remainder of his life. He was noted as a scholar and theologian, being offered the chair of theology at Leiden in 1641 and being twice offered a seat in the Westminster Assembly. His major theological works are *Gotteschalci et praedestinatione controversia historica* (1631), the *Annales Veteris Testamenti* (1650–54) and his *The Principles of Christian Religion* (1644) also published as *A Body of Divinitie* (1645). This latter work is a three-part theology that begins with a short catechism, follows it with a more elaborate "Method," and concludes with a full system entitled "The Sum and Substance of Christian Religion."

Matthieu Virel (fl. 1561–1595); virtually nothing is known of Virel's life other than that he preached reform in Namur (1561), and served the French congregation in Basel after 1588. He may have lived for a time in England. His major work is the popular *Dialogue de religion chrestienne* (1582) which went through fourteen English editions from 1594 to 1635 as *A Learned and Excellent Treatise Containing all the Principall Grounds of Christian Religion* (1594).

Antonius Walaeus (1573–1639); studied at Leiden (1596–99), lectured in Geneva (ca. 1600), held several pastorates in the Netherlands, and was appointed professor of theology at Middelburg in 1609. He attended the Synod of Dort and, after the close of the Synod, became professor of theology at Leiden (1619). He collaborated with Poliander, Thysius and Rivetus in writing the *Synopsis purioris theologiae* (1625). His own dogmatic essays, the *Enchiridion religionis reformatae* and the *Loci communes theologici*, appear in his collected *Opera* (1643).

Marcus Friedrich Wendelin (1584–1652); studied at Heidelberg; taught privately in Geneva and served as rector of the gymnasium in Zerbst from 1612 until his death. He marks the transition from early to high orthodoxy. He wrote *Christianae theologiae libri ii* (1634) and the *Christianae theologiae systema maius* (1656).

Johannes Wollebius (1586–1629); studied at Basel; in 1607 he succeeded Johann Jacob Grynaeus as preacher in the cathedral and was appointed professor of Old Testament. His major work is the *Compendium theologiae christianae* (1626), modeled on the thought of Polanus.

Jerome Zanchi (1516–1590); studied at Padua; was a member of the Augustinian order, associated with Peter Martyr Vermigli at Lucca. His evangelical preaching forced him to flee Italy. He was appointed professor of Old Testament at Strasbourg, a post he held until 1563. In 1568 he went to Heidelberg as Ursinus' successor in theology. He left Heidelberg for Neustadt in 1576 on the accession of the Lutheran elector, Ludwig VI, and remained there as professor of theology until his death. His works include the beginning of a vast *Summa* of the Reformed faith: *Praefatiuncula in locos communes*; *De tribus Elohim*; *De natura Dei*; *De operibus Dei*; and *De primi hominis lapsu, de peccato et de lege Dei* (all in *Opera*, 1617). Zanchi also wrote an extended confession of faith, *De religione christiana fides* (1585).

High Orthodoxy (ca. 1640–1700)

Johann Wilhelm Baier (1647–1695); a Lutheran theologian who studied at Altdorf (1664–1669) and Jena (1669–1674). In 1675 he was appointed professor of church history and in 1694 became professor of theology and rector of the University of Halle, a post that he vacated because of conflict with the Pietists after only a year of service. He died shortly thereafter. He is famous for his *Compendium theologiae positivae* (1686; enlarged, 1691), a genuinely representative essay in orthodox Lutheranism.

Franz Burmann (1632–1679); pastor at Hanau (1651); rector of the university at Leiden (1661) and professor of theology at Utrecht (1662). Burmann also taught church history at Utrecht following 1671. His major work is the *Synopsis theologiae, & speciatim oeconomiae foederum Dei* (1671–72).

Stephen Charnock (1628–1680); studied at Emanuel College, Cambridge and afterwards served as a minister in Southwark. In 1649 he became a fellow at New College, Oxford and received his M.A. there in 1652. He served as Henry Cromwell's chaplain in Ireland and from 1675 until his death was joint pastor with Thomas Watson of a Presbyterian congregation in London. His most famous work is his *Discourses upon the Existence and Attributes of God* (1681). He also wrote A *Discourse on the Knowledge of God* (1684); A *Discourse on the Knowledge of God in Christ* (1684); and A *Discourse of Divine Providence, General and Particular* (1684).

Johannes Cocceius (1603–1669); studied at Bremen, Hamburg and Franecker. In 1630 he was appointed professor of biblical philology at Bremen and in 1636 professor of Hebrew at Franecker. In 1650 he succeeded Friedrich Spanheim the elder as professor of theology at Leiden. His *Summa doctrina de foedere et testamento Dei* (1648) and *Summa theologiae ex sacris scripturis repetita* (1662) are his major doctrinal essays.

Abraham Heidanus (1597–1678); studied in Amsterdam and Leiden. He served as a pastor in Leiden (1627–1648) and in 1648 was appointed professor of theology at Leiden. His major theological work is the *Corpus theologiae christianae in quindecim locos* (1686).

Johann Heinrich Heidegger (1633–1698); studied at Zurich, Marburg and Heidelberg. From 1659 to 1665 he taught dogmatics and church history at Steinfurt. In 1665 he accepted the post of professor of ethics at Zurich and succeeded J. H. Hottinger as professor of theology in 1667. His major dogmatic writings are the *Medulla theologiae christianae* (1696) and the vast *Corpus theologiae* (1700).

Johannes Hoornbeeck (1617–1666); studied at Leiden and Utrecht. In 1644 he was appointed professor of theology at Utrecht. He moved to Leiden in 1654 where he polemicized against Cocceius and Heidanus. He wrote a massive polemical theology, *Summa controversiarum religionis, cum infidelibus, haereticis, schismaticis* (1653) and a theological system, *Institutiones theologicos ex optimis auctoribus concinnatae* (1653).

Edward Leigh (1602–1671); studied at Magdalen College, Oxford where he received the B.A. in 1620 and the M.A. in 1623. His dogmatic works are A *Treatise of Divinity* (1646), later incorporated into his A *System or Body of Divinity* (1654), and A *Treatise of Religion and Learning* (1656).

Johannes Marckius (1656–1713); studied at Franecker and Leiden. He received his doctorate from Franecker in 1675 and was appointed professor of theology there in the following year. In 1682 he went to Groningen as professor of theology and preacher to the university; he went to Leiden in 1689 where he remained for the rest of his life as professor of theology and, following the death of Spanheim in 1702, professor of church history. Most of his writings are commentaries on Scripture, but he also produced the influential *Compendium theologiae christianae didactico-elencticum* (1686).

Samuel Maresius (1599–1673), often Desmarets; studied in Paris, at Saumur under Gomarus, and in Geneva. He preached at Laon (1620–1624) and was appointed professor at Sedan in 1625. From 1632 to 1636 he was a pastor at Mastricht and then, successively, professor of theology at Bois-le-Duc (1636–1643) and Groningen (1643–1673). His most influential doctrinal work is the *Collegium theologicum sive systema breve universae theologiae* (1645).

Petrus van Mastricht (1630–1706); studied at Duisburg and Utrecht. He served as a pastor in Cleves and Gluckstadt before being called in 1662 to be professor of oriental languages and practical theology at Frankfurt-on-the-Oder. In 1669 he was appointed professor of theology at Duisburg and in 1677 succeeded Voetius as professor of theology at Utrecht. *Theoretico-practica theologia* (1714) is his major theological work.

John Owen (1616–1683); studied at Oxford where he received his B.A. in 1632 and the M.A. in 1635. He served in several parishes before he was appointed dean of Christ Church, Oxford by the House of Commons (1651). He became vice-chancellor of the university in 1652. He lost these posts in 1660 with the restoration of the monarchy. His theological works include: *Theologoumena pantodapa* (1661); *The Reason of Faith* (1677); and *The Causes, Ways, and Means of Understanding the Mind of God as Revealed in his Word* (1678).

Benedict Pictet (1655–1724); studied in Geneva. After serving as a pastor in that city, he was appointed professor of theology at the University of Geneva (1686). His major dogmatic work is the *Theologia christiana* (1696).

Leonhard Riissen (ca. 1636–1700) or Ryssen; studied at Utrecht and received his doctorate in theology from that university in 1655. He served as a pastor and never occupied an academic post. He wrote a *Synopsis theologiae elencticae* (1671) but his best-known work is his *Summa theologiae*, based on Turretin and also entitled *Compendium theologiae didactico-elencticae* (1695).

Francis Turretin (1623–1687); studied at Geneva, Leiden, Utrecht, Paris, Samur, Montauban, and Nimes. He was called to be pastor of the Italian congregation in Geneva in 1648 and was appointed professor of theology in the university in 1653. His major theological work is the *Institutio theologiae elencticae* (1679–1685); his *Opera* also contains a disputation *De sacra scripturae authoritate*.

Gisbert Voetius (1589–1676), studied at the University of Leiden (1604–11) under Gomarus. Between 1611 and 1634, he served several congregations and in 1618 was one of the delegates from South Holland to the Synod of Dort. In 1634 he was called as professor of theology to the newly established University of Utrecht. Voetius was both a bitter polemicist against the Cocceians and Cartesians and a major influence on the development of Reformed piety and practical theology. His major, and highly scholastic, theological treatises are found in the *Selectae disputationes theologicae*, 5 vols. (1648–1669).

Thomas Watson (d. ca. 1689); studied at Emanuel College, Cambridge and served from 1646 to 1662 as pastor of St. Stephen's, Walbrook. After 1672 and the Declaration of Indulgence he again served as a pastor at Crosby Hall, London. His major work is the posthumous *A Body of Practical Divinity . . . One Hundred and Seventy Six Sermons on the Lesser Catechism* (1692).

Hermann Witsius (1636–1708); studied at Utrecht and Groningen. From 1656 to 1675 he served as pastor at Westwoud, Wormer, Goes and Leeuwarden. In 1675 he was appointed professor of theology at Franecker. He was called to a professorship at Utrecht in 1680. He ended his career as professor of theology at Leiden (1698–1707), being forced to retire because of ill health one year before his death. His major dogmatic works are *De oeconomia foederum Dei cum hominibus libri quattuor* (1677) and *Exercitationes sacrae in symbolum, quod Apostolorum dicitur* (1681).

Late Orthodoxy (ca. 1700–1790)

Sigmund Jacob Baumgarten (1706–1757); Lutheran; studied at Halle. He was appointed to the faculty at Halle in 1730 and promoted to the rank of professor of theology in 1743. He is remembered as one of the first theologians to adopt the philosophical principles of Wolffianism. His major dogmatic works are the *Evangelische Glaubenslehre* (1759–60) and the *Theses dogmaticae* (1736).

Johann Christoph Beck (1711–1778); studied at Basel and received the M.A. in 1729. He was appointed professor of history at Basel in 1737. In 1744 he was awarded the degree of doctor of theology and appointed professor of theology as well. From 1759 until the end of his life he served as professor of Old Testament. His major dogmatic work is the *Fundamenta theologiae naturalis et revelatae* (1757).

Johann Christoph Doederlein (1745–1792); Lutheran; studied at Altdorf and was appointed professor there in 1772. In 1782 he went to Jena as professor of theology. His *Institutiones theologi christiani* (1780), where he blends the results of critical textual study with a nominally orthodox dogmatics, is his major work.

Samuel Endemann (1727–1789); studied at Marburg under Wyttenbach. He served as a pastor in Jesberg from 1750 to 1753 and as a pastor, school inspector and district church superintendent in Hanau from 1753 to 1782, when he was called to be professor of theology and church superintendent at Marburg, a post that he held until his death in 1789. His major theological works are: *Institutiones theologiae dogmaticae*, 2 vols. (1777–78); *Compendium theologiae dogmaticae* (1780); and *Theologia moralis*, 2 vols. (1780).

Georg Christian Knapp (1753–1825); Lutheran; studied at Halle and Goetingen. In 1777 he was appointed to the theological faculty at Halle and in 1782 raised to the rank of professor of theology. His theological lectures were published posthumously: *Vorlesungen über die Christliche Glaubenslehre* (1827); translated as *Lectures on Christian Theology* (1831).

Bernhard de Moor (1710–ca. 1765); studied at Leiden (1726–1731). From 1732 to 1735 he was a pastor at Ingen and Brock. In 1736 he returned to Leiden to study and was subsequently awarded the doctorate in theology. After serving as pastor at Ostsaandam and Enthuisen (1738–1744), he was called first to Franecker (1744) and then to Leiden as professor of theology. His major dogmatic essay is the six-volume *Commentarius perpetuus in Joh. Marckii compendium theologiae christianae didactico–elencticum* (1761–1771).

Johann Reinbeck (1682–1741); Lutheran; studied at Halle from 1700 to 1702. In 1702 he was appointed as an adjunct instructor in the faculty of theology. From 1709 until his death he served as pastor, superintendent of churches and inspector in the Prussian church. He was awarded the degree of doctor of theology at Königsberg in 1739. His major theological work is the massive and fragmentary *Betrachtungen über die in der Augspurgischen Confession*, 4 parts (1731–1741).

Thomas Ridgley (ca. 1667–1734); studied for the ministry in Wiltshire at Trowbridge with John Davidson. In 1695 he was called as assistant to Thomas Gouge in the independent church at Three Cranes, Thames Street, London. When Gouge died in 1700, Ridgley succeeded him as pastor of the congregation, a post he held until his death. In 1712, Ridgley was appointed tutor in divinity at the Fund Academy, Tenter Alley, Moorfields. He was viewed as a defender of orthodoxy against Arianism and Arminianism. He was granted the D.D. by the University of Aberdeen for his *A Body of Divinity* (1731).

Johann Friedrich Stapfer (1708–1775); studied at Bern and Marburg. He served as a private tutor at Diessbach from 1740 to 1750 and subsequently as a pastor in the same city from 1740 to 1775. He declined numerous offers of university positions. Stapfer's major dogmatic works are the *Institutiones theologiae polemicae*, 5 vols. (1743–47) and the *Grundlegung zur wahren Religion*, 12 vols. (1746–53).

Hermann Venema (1697–1787); studied at Groningen (1711–1714) and Franecker (1714–1718). In 1723 he succeeded the younger Vitringa as professor of theology at Franecker, a post he held until his retirement in 1774. His dogmatic work was published posthumously in English translation: *Institutes of Theology* (1850).

Salomon van Til (1643–1713); studied at Utrecht and Leiden. From 1666 to 1684 he served as pastor in Huisduinen, De Rijp, Medemblik, and Dort. He was called in 1684 to teach biblical languages at Dort and in 1685 to teach theology. In 1702 he was appointed professor of theology at Leiden. His chief dogmatic work is the *Theologiae utriusque compendium cum naturalis tum revelatae* (1704).

Jean Francois Turretin (1671–1737); studied in Geneva and Leyden. He became a pastor in Geneva in 1693 and was appointed professor of church history in the university in 1697. He is important for the latitudinarian or "broad church" views that led him to oppose the *Formula Consensus Helvetica* and work toward its abolition in 1725. His major theological essays include the *Brevis & pacifica de articulis fundamentalibus disquisitio, qua ad protestantium concordiam mutuamque tolerantiam via sternitur* (1719) and the treatises on natural and revealed theology in the *Cogitationes et dissertationes theologicae* (1737).

Campegius Vitringa (1659–1722); studied at Franecker (1675–78) and Leiden (1678–79). He was appointed professor of oriental languages at Franecker in 1681. In 1683 he succeeded Marckius as professor of theology and in 1693 assumed the chair of church history. He retained this position until his death in 1722. His system of theology is the *Doctrina christianae religionis, per aphorismos summatim descripta* (1690) augmented to the size of a full system with his *Hypotyposis theologiae elencticae* (1702) which follows the outline of the aphorisms.

Daniel Wyttenbach (1706–1779); studied at Marburg, in the Netherlands and in Paris. From 1740 to 1746 he served as an assistant in the Heiliggeistkirche in Bern. He was appointed professor of polemical theology at Bern in 1746. In 1756 he went to Marburg where he served as professor of theology and the inspector or superintendent of schools and churches. His major dogmatic work is the *Tentamen theologiae dogmaticae*, 3 vols. (1747–1749).

2

The Development
of Theological Prolegomena

All theology rests upon presuppositions and principles. The explicit
enunciation of those presuppositions and principles, however, is one of
the last tasks undertaken in the historical development of theological
system.   This generalization applies both to the experience of the
medieval scholastics and to that of the Protestant orthodox.   Medieval
theology received from the church fathers a great body of highly detailed
doctrine.   This body of doctrine was further clarified and systematized
by the controversies of the Carolingian era and of the eleventh and
twelfth centuries—to the point that, toward the close of the twelfth
century, the theological teachers of the cathedral schools and monaster-
ies were able to draw doctrine together into collections of theological
statements and definitions, the *sententiae*.   Only with this latter codification of theology as an academic discipline do prolegomena as such
became possible or desirable.   A similar situation obtains in the much
more rapid development of a Protestant system of theology. Protestant
system begins to develop within a few years of the posting of the *Ninety-
five Theses* in 1517; genuine theological prolegomena appear after 1590.

Despite their late appearance and academic origin, however,
theological prolegomena address issues that are always present and must
always have their effect on doctrinal statement.   The production of any
theological formula brings with it fundamental questions of the relationship of language to divine truth, of the capability of any human
statement to bear the weight of revelation, and of the relationship of

statements concerning God to grammatically identical statements concerning the world of sense and experience. In other words, the inherent
paradox of the use of finite forms to discuss an infinite truth, of the
presentation of concepts relating to an incomprehensible Being and the
unfathomable mystery of his relation to the world and its creatures,
hovers in the background of all theological statement. Prolegomena
merely make these issues explicit. What is theology? What is the relationship of theology to God's own truth? Where does theology stand among
the ways of human knowing? How can a knowledge or wisdom concerning
divine things draw on the resources of human reason and human language?
What are the necessary and irreducible foundations of theological
statement?

Otto Weber asks the crucial question concerning prolegomena in his
Grundlagen der Dogmatik—namely, whether and under what circumstances the
prolegomena are *vordogmatisch*, or predogmatic.[1] When dogmatics rests on
prior, nontheological, ontological, or anthropological presuppositions,
and these presuppositions are set forth in the prolegomena, then indeed
the prolegomena are *vordogmatisch*—but is this then a Christian
dogmatics? Weber concludes that Christian dogmatics can have no true
prolegomena, but only an introduction which shares in the presuppositions
of the system of dogmatics as a whole. Although this specific point is
not made in the orthodox prolegomena, it is clearly reflected both in the
explicit concerns of the prolegomena and in the dependence of the
prolegomena upon the system itself for many of their basic arguments.

The prolegomena, therefore, provide a crucial index to the character
and intention of a theological system. Thus, any attempt to present an
accurate picture of Protestant orthodox theology must include and,
preferably, begin with an analysis of the orthodox prolegomena. Moreover, only by investigating these presuppositional statements can the
questions typically asked about the character and intention of Protestant
orthodox theology be properly and correctly answered. For example, what
is the relationship of orthodoxy to the Reformation? Is it a simple
continuation and development of the thought of the Reformers or is it in
some ways a distortion of or departure from the Reformation? Is orthodoxy a form of rationalism or a movement toward rationalism? Is Reformed
orthodoxy a predestinarian system? We have already provided, in chapter
1, a tentative answer to the first question: orthodoxy stands in
continuity both with the Reformation and with the church's tradition but
also evidences elements of discontinuity. This tentative answer provides
us with an approach, a method, for answering the other two questions in

and through an examination of the prolegomena and *principia* of the orthodox systems.

2.1 Medieval Prolegomena

The development of Protestant theological system was a complex process in which elements of extant theological system, inherited from the later Middle Ages, were used, modified, and brought into intimate contact with the insights of the Reformers. This process is nowhere more prominent than in the development of theological prolegomena, for here the Reformers provided a whole series of insights into presuppositional issues in theology, such as the relation of reason and philosophy to theological system and the relation of the soteriological content of the system proper to the enunciation of basic principles and presuppositions. However, the Reformer provided no structural models at all. The only extant theological prolegomena were the prolegomena to medieval systems. It was to these prolegomena, particularly to those written in the fourteenth and fifteenth centuries, that the Protestant orthodox looked for models.

The theologians who taught and wrote in the mid-twelfth century-- among them Hugh of St. Victor (d. 1141), Gilbert de la Porrée (d. 1154), Peter Lombard (d. 1160), and Alain of Lille (d. 1202)--agreed that theology needed to be organized and developed according to a consistent method if it was to be taught properly in the schools. Hugh of St. Victor wrote not only a brief book of *Sentences* but also an important essay on education, the *Didascalion*, as well as a lengthy theological system with a prolegomenon, the *De sacramentis christianae fidei*. Although not a formal prolegomenon to theological system, the *Didascalion* provides what might be called an attitudinal introduction to theological study and, in addition, a survey of the discipline of theology just prior to the great drive toward system characteristic of the thirteenth century. Hugh's purpose was to survey all of the sciences--theoretical, practical, mechanical, and logical. He views theology as the highest *scientia* of the theoretical category, similar to philosophy but superior to it. The study of theology, according to Hugh, is an exercise in prayerful spirituality that finds its substance in Scripture and the writings of the fathers. Hugh concludes, in his seventh book, with a discussion of the outline of the body of doctrine that can be drawn from these sources.[2]

Whereas Hugh's *Sententia* begins, not with a prologue on the discipline of theology but rather with a discussion of the three Christian virtues (faith, hope, and love),[3] his *De sacramentis christianae fidei* (*On the Mysteries of the Christian Faith*) does have a formal prologue on Scripture as the foundation and the material of theology, on the study of Scripture, on the relation of all the "arts" to "divine wisdom," and, finally, on the canon of Scripture.[4] This prologue raises several issues that would become of paramount importance to the discipline of theology in the era of scholasticism. In the first place, Hugh makes it clear that Scripture and its correct interpretation are the foundation of theology inasmuch as all of the arts in the trivium (grammar, logic and dialectic) and the quadrivium (arithmetic, music, geometry, astronomy/ physics) are subordinate to theology: ". . . all natural arts serve divine knowledge (*scientia*); and inferior wisdom (*scientia*) rightly arranged is of use to superior."[5] In the second place, Hugh speaks of the knowledge of God gained from Scripture as both *scientia* and *sapientia*, thus emphasizing the terms that the next several generations would use and debate as characterizations of the *genus* of theology. Finally, Hugh prepares the way for debate on the object or material of theology by defining it as the work of founding or creating (*opus conditionis*) and the work of restoring or redeeming (*opus restaurationis*). The *opus conditionis* is the creation of the world and "all of its elements"; the *opus restaurationis* consists in "the incarnation of the Word together with all its mysteries, or, that which has occurred from the beginning of the age . . . to the end of the world."[6] The point is crucial inasmuch as it defines the object of the discipline as practical and redemptive rather than speculative and metaphysical.

Gilbert and Alain are more important than Lombard and Hugh to the development of formal theological prolegomena. Whereas Lombard only briefly encountered the issue of knowledge (*notitia*) before engaging in his discussion of the Trinity, Gilbert and Alain presented, for the first time in the history of theology, a set of rules concerning theological method. Gilbert pressed the point, profoundly important for the development of theological prolegomena, that in theology as much as in the other classical disciplines the rules of argument ought to be suitable to the object of discussion. Alain accepted this basic concept and even more pointedly than Gilbert placed theology in the category of academic disciplines by denominating it a *scientia*. Here, too, we see raised one of the crucial issues to be addressed by all subsequent prolegomena to theology.[7]

Lombard's *Sententiae* is important primarily as the great theological textbook of the Middle Ages. The *Sententiae* provides a cogent arrangement of theological materials into problems. Lombard sets forth an issue, provides the patristic and biblical resources relevant to it, and then sets forth a response--the basic form of scholastic argument. When the *Sententiae* became the standard text in the early thirteenth century, these chapter-length discussions were gathered, probably at the University of Paris by Alexander of Hales, into "distinctions" or major topics. Lombard's overarching pattern of four books--God (I); creation, sin, free will (II); incarnation, Christ's person and work, Christian graces and virtues (III); the sacraments and the last things (IV)--became the basic form for theological system. Nonetheless, Lombard was not as influential in the development of prolegomena as Hugh, Gilbert and Alain. He identifies the subject matter of theology according to the Augustinian model of things and the signs that point toward them. He further identifies the things as *res divinae* and then divides these "divine things" into the Augustinian categories of enjoyment (*frui*) and use (*uti*), the former indicating God as Trinity and the latter the entire created order.[8] This model implies the later definition of the object of theology as God and all of God's works, and also the later identification of theology as a mixed science, both contemplative and practical.

The use of the term *scientia* with reference to theology took on a new meaning in the early thirteenth century with the rise of interest in the larger Aristotelian corpus. Whereas the Aristole known to the early Middle Ages was the logical Aristotle of the *Organon*, the new Aristotle presented to the thirteenth century was the Aristotle of the *Metaphysics* and *Ethics*. The latter document is of particular importance since it is the place where Aristotle delivered his arguments for the classification of the forms of knowing: understanding (*intelligentia*), knowledge or science (*scientia*), wisdom (*sapientia*), prudence or discretion (*prudentia*), and art or technique (*ars*).[9] William of Auxerre (d. 1231) argued, following Aristotle, that all sciences properly so-called rest upon their own *principia* or first principles. Theology, therefore, must have its own self-evident principles (*principia per se nota*) which, in turn, provided the basis of argument for the sake of clarifying or proving the faith.[10]

As the great age of scholasticism dawned in the second quarter of the thirteenth century, the various commentators on the *Sentences* of Lombard--Alexander of Hales, Bonaventure, Robert Kilwardby, Albert the Great, and Thomas Aquinas--recognized the need to place methodological discussions, constructed along the lines indicated by Gilbert de la

Porrée, Alain of Lille and William of Auxerre, at the beginning of their commentaries, as prolegomena set prior to the first set of distinctions made by Lombard. These early thirteenth-century prolegomena are not, as a rule, highly elaborate, but they do identify theology as a word concerning God resting on a revelation given in this life to the Christian pilgrim, the *viator*. They also pose, in the causal language of the scholastic era, questions concerning the sources, object and purpose of theology. Kilwardby in particular viewed the questions of material and formal, efficient and final causality of theology as crucial to the definition of theological science.[11] In addition, these prolegomena and all those that followed in the medieval period raise the question of the nature of theological knowledge in terms of the character of theology as theoretical, practical or affective, and in terms of the nature of theological knowing as science (*scientia*) or wisdom (*sapientia*). This contrast of *sapientia* with *scientia*, moreover, carries with it, implicitly, a contrast between the older patristic and specifically Augustinian heritage of the Middle Ages and the new Aristotelianism of the thirteeth century. Augustine had preferred the term *sapientia* for theology not only because of its biblical and traditional usage but also because he viewed *sapientia*, wisdom, as an understanding of goals, specifically, of God as the highest good, and *scientia*, knowledge, as an understanding of the temporal order. In the Aristotelian model, however, *sapientia* belonged to a general paradigm of temporal knowing and, strictly defined as an understanding of *principia* and ends, was less applicable to theology as an academic discipline than was the Aristotelian definition of *scientia*—a knowledge of principles and the conclusions drawn from them. Indeed, for Aristotle, *sapientia* properly understood was the highest kind of *scientia*, in view of its grasp of ultimates.[12] All of these issues would reappear in the Protestant scholastic systems.

Over against the Thomistic perception of theology as science, the great Franciscans, Alexander of Hales and Bonaventure, insisted on the affective, experimental and moral character of theology and argued that this character of the discipline prevented it from being considered as a *scientia* in the Aristotelian sense of a rational or demonstrative discipline. Thus Alexander could write that there is "one mode of certainty in *scientia* taught according to the human spirit and another in *scientia* taught according to the divine Spirit" and that this latter mode, a "certainty concerned with disposition" (*affectus*), is more certain than the "certainty of speculation" or the "certainty of experience" belonging to other sciences.[13] Bonaventure, even more than Alexander, stresses

inward illumination as the source of theological knowledge rather than a
scientia resting upon the perception of externals.[14]

Bonaventure had already distinguished between the theology of the
sacra pagina, that is, Scripture, and the theology of his commentary on
the Sentences.   The former follows a "revelatory, preceptive mode"
whereas the latter adopts a "ratiocinative or inquisitive mode."   Nonetheless, as Chenu pointed out, Bonaventure's adoption of a logical rather
than an exegetical or expository model did not result in the formal
definition of theology as a discipline, a science among the other
sciences and standing in clear relation to them.[15]   That step was taken
by Thomas Aquinas who joined the concept of theology as a raticcinative
discipline characterized by definition and division of the subject for
purposes of debate to the Aristotelian concepts of scientia and scientia
subalterna, subalternate science.[16]

This "scientific" character of theology in relation to the problems
of the knowledge of its principia, of the identification of its proper
subject (or object), and of the construction of proper theological arguments and demonstrations become the central concern of Aquinas' preliminary remarks in the Summa theologiae.[17]   Aquinas deals with the problem
that revealed principia are not self-evident but are derived from a
higher science, namely, from the divine self-knowledge.   Theology is,
thus, a subalternate science which, after the manner of all scientiae,
utilizes its principia as the means by which less evident teachings are
explicated and understood.   The place of reason is clearly instrumental
and ancillary, although Aquinas does permit reason to work with revealed
truths in order to deduce truths not explicitly given in revelation:
reason deduces and supports truths for sacred theology but does not
provide them in and of itself.   In this context, Scripture and the great
creeds are easily understood as the sources of the principia of theological science and theological science itself can turn to the elaborate
development of doctrine as a faithful but also eminently rational derivation of conclusions from its revealed principia.   Although the development of doctrinal formulae had been going on for centuries, surely since
the age of the second-century Apologists, we now have, for the first time
in the history of doctrine, a formally defined model for the construction
of a body of doctrine beyond the simple discursive presentation of the
results of exegesis.

The great codifier of thirteenth-century theorization on the presuppositions of theological system just prior to the intense critique
launched by Scotus and the nominalists was Henry of Ghent (d. 1293).
Henry's Summae quaestionum ordinariarum theologi deals at length with the

question of theology as *scientia* in relation to other sciences (art. VI–VII), the causality of theology (the author and the authority of Scripture; art. VIII, IX, XIX), the *materia* or substance of this divinely given knowledge, the theoretical and practical character of theology, and the problem of theological method and its exercise by human teachers (art. XI–XVIII). The latter discussion is particularly significant because it is not usually encountered in theological prolegomena, especially not at such length. Henry's discussion of the role and attitude of the theological teacher, like Hugh of St. Victor's marriage of theological study and spirituality, represents the scholastic continuation of the Augustinian model for biblical study and interpretation found in the great treatise *On Christian Doctrine*. In the Augustinian perspective, the interpretation of Scripture is directly related to the spiritual pilgrimage of the believer from a legal fear of God to the final earthly preparation of the human spirit for the beatific vision.[18] For Henry, as for the other scholastics of his time, the causality of theology mirrors and explains this pilgrimage.[19]

Leff refers to Henry as "undoubtedly" the greatest of those thirteenth- and fourteenth-century theologians not affiliated with either the Franciscan or Dominican orders. In a sense, Henry must be regarded as the bridge from the thirteenth-century attempts at synthesis to the more critical perspective of Scotus—just as Scotus can be viewed as the point of transition to nominalism. Henry's importance lies in his sense of "the limitations of classical Augustinianism" and "the dangers of Aristotelianism."[20] The critical balance that he achieved provides an important model for later theology, including that of the Protestant scholastics.

Henry's prolegomena are closely mirrored in the preliminary questions of Gerard of Boulogne's *Summa*. Here, too, the causality of theology is discussed as well as the disposition of theological students and teachers. In addition, as with Henry's *Summa*, the question of causality arises directly out of the divine authorship of Scripture and the necessary rootage of theology therein.[21] Like the argument of several *Sentence* commentators and of Henry of Ghent's *Summa*, Gerard's meditation on causality must be regarded as a heuristic device rather than as some sort of necessitarian language. The focusing of these prolegomena on Scripture, moreover, renders them as important for the later development of a Protestant doctrine of Scripture as they are important for the development of Protestant scholastic prolegomena.

A new and critical phase, crucial for the development of theological prolegomena, begins with the lectures of Duns Scotus (d. 1308) at Oxford and Paris. In one sense, Scotus manifests a continuity of perspective with the great Franciscans of the thirteenth century, Alexander of Hales and Bonaventure. He echoes their hesitancy to accept the alliance between Christian theology and Aristotelian philosophy. Nonetheless, Scotus is responsible for the incorporation of much Aristotelian teaching into Franciscan theology. In another sense, however, Scotus presents a highly original model and, with it, a critique of virtually all previous scholastic theology. He differs from Alexander and Bonaventure in his assumption of two ways of knowing, faith and reason, and from Aquinas in his assumption of a radical diastasis between the two. Scotus radically limits both natural and supernatural knowledge, moreover, on the assumption of the incapacity of the finite for the infinite.

This perspective led Scotus to deny that theology can be a *scientia* proper. The principles of theology, gained by revelation, cannot approach the principles of the *scientia Dei* or claim to identify God as he is in himself. As Congar aptly observes, Scotus' theology is characterized by "the constant intervention of disjunctions between the order *in se* and the order of fact,"[22] in this case between the infinite and perfect *theologia in se* and the finite *theologia nostra*, our theology, Scotus' equivalent of *theologia in via*. Since there is no proportion between divine theology in itself and our theology, God alone is truly a theologian. (Significantly, this identification of God as the true theologian or as the only true *doctor* of the wisdom in Scripture, which rested on the language of Augustine's *On Christian Doctrine*, had been used by earlier scholastics, like Henry of Ghent, to indicate the divine source of all true theology—but not to press so radically the disjunction between the divine self-knowledge and revealed knowledge of God.[23])

Similar views are expressed by Scotus' contemporary, Durandus de Saint Pourçain (d. 1334), who also refused to view theology as a science in the strict sense of the term. Rather, theology is merely a mental disposition (*habitus*) according to which the articles of Christian faith are drawn from the *principia* found in Scripture. Durandus addresses this problem, moreover, by dealing with theology in terms of its four causes and then comparing this causality with the causality of other "sciences."[24] Peter Aureole (d. 1322) follows a line of argument much like that of Durandus but concludes that theology is a *scientia subalterna* or, more precisely, a *scientia consequentiarum*, a knowledge of consequences, resting upon the articles of faith and upon Scripture as *principia*. Aureole does not assume that such principles are self-evident but rather that they have a certainty, in view of their divine origin, sufficient for the denomination of theology as *scientia subalterna*.[25]

One of the other results of the line of argument on the causes and ends of theology that begins in Kilwardby and moves through Henry of Ghent to Duns Scotus was an increasing interest in the question of whether theology was a speculative or a practical discipline.   Whereas the Dominican theology, influenced by Aquinas, had emphasized the theoretical or speculative side of the *scientia*, inasmuch as theology can be known in and for itself, the Fransciscan theology, with its mistrust of the language of *scientia*, tended to stress the practical aspect of theology and, in the work of Scotus, to argue that theology, considered as a discipline oriented toward the ultimate goal of mankind in God, is essentially a *praxis*.   This argument, taken up by Ockham, would have considerable influence on Protestant theology.

It is also characteristic of later medieval prolegomena, written in the wake of Scotus' critique, that the disjunction between divine self-knowledge and human knowledge of God appears in the language of *theologia nostra*, now used by virtually all of the commentators, and in the frequently pointed debate over the proper subject or object of this *theologia nostra*.   In view of the limitation of knowing in the human subject, the object of that knowing must also be limited or restricted—not, of course, in itself but insofar as it is known.   We encounter this concern in the prolegomena of such thinkers as Peter Aureole, Durandus, Richard of Middleton, Gregory of Rimini, Marsilius of Inghien, and Gabriel Biel.   Parallel to this development, we also see in these later medieval prolegomena little concern to conjoin theology with philosophy—indeed, a fundamental break has occurred between theology and philosophy such that the service of philosophy to theology has been virtually confined to logic and dialectic.

Finally, we need to recognize that many of the pressures toward change leading to the development of nonmedieval patterns—such as the organization of dogmatics by *locus*—in Protestant theological system were pressures universally felt and also of importance to the development of Roman Catholic theology in the sixteenth and seventeenth centuries.[26]   On the one hand, the dominance of Lombard's *Sentences* as the basic form of theological system came to an end as the Dominicans, following the model of Cajetan, began to comment on Thomas Aquinas' *Summa* instead.   More importantly, Catholic scholasticism also began to develop entirely new forms in the sixteenth century.   Following the example of Melchior Cano, his followers at the University of Salamanca set aside the medieval form of the *quaestio* as well as the model of the *Sentences* and, much like their Protestant foes, developed a system of theologial *loci*, resting at least in part on the new logic of Rudolf Agricola.[27]   The theologians who maintained the tradition of commenting on the *Sentences*, moreover, were hardly immune to these developments. The new methodology, with its concentration on *loci* in Scripture and tradition as material sources of theology, had its impact.

2.2 The Reformation and Its Theological Presuppositions

The theology of the Reformation, in its doctrinal statements and in its presuppositions, stands as both the rejection of the late medieval theological world and as a direct outgrowth of that world, dependent in large measure upon the medieval science of theology for insight into the nature of the theological task. Although too much can be made of the continuity of medieval Augustinianism with the theology of the Reformation, it is clear that not only the theory of salvation by grace but also the view of divine transcendence and omnipotence associated with it carries over from the late medieval period into the sixteenth century.[28] In addition, there was an important tradition in medieval theology which identified Scripture as the soteriologically sufficient source of Christian doctrine and, within that tradition, an anti-ecclesial argument that pitted the authority of Scripture against the authority of the church or, in its less polemical forms, argued the priority of the scriptural over the traditionary norm of doctrine.[29] Beyond these basic doctrinal and principial continuities, the Reformation protest against the highly speculative arguments engendered by nominalism and its corresponding demand for a biblical theology responsive to the needs of piety and worship also had ample precedent in the late Middle Ages. What is more, the Scotist and nominalist critiques of earlier scholastic theology, considered apart from the excesses that brought about the Reformation, created an emphasis on revelation and a separation of theology from metaphysics that carried over into the theology of the Reformers.

The Reformation, in spite of its substantial contribution to the history of doctrine and the shock it delivered to theology and the church in the sixteenth century, was not an attack upon the whole of medieval theology or upon Christian tradition. The Reformation assaulted a limited spectrum of doctrinal and practical abuses with the intention of reaffirming the values of the historical church catholic. Thus, the mainstream Reformers reconstructed the doctrines of justification and the sacraments and then modified their ideas of the *ordo salutis* and of the church accordingly; but they did not alter the doctrines of God, creation, providence, and Christ, and they maintained the Augustinian

tradition concerning predestination, human nature and sin. The reform of
individual doctrines, like justification and the sacraments, occurred
within the bounds of a traditional, orthodox and catholic system which,
on the grand scale, remained substantively unaltered.

Characteristic of this first stage of the Reformation is the absence
of a formal doctrine of Scripture and of discussion concerning its
relation to the church and theology. The Protestants stated a scriptural
principle but not a doctrine of Scripture. Nevertheless, from the outset, that principle both reflected the medieval background and contained
the foundation of later formulations belonging both to the theological
prolegomena and to the doctrine of Scripture. Although the orthodox
doctrine would be shaped by polemical as well as positive considerations,
its basic form can be traced directly to the wellsprings of reform, even
to that day in April of 1521 when Martin Luther stood before the Diet of
Worms, refusing to recant:

> Unless I am convicted by Scripture and plain reason—I do not
> accept the authority of popes and councils, for they have
> contradicted each other—my conscience is captive to the Word
> of God. I cannot and I will not recant anything, for to go
> against conscience is neither right nor safe. God help me.
> Amen.[30]

In an eloquent and concise form Luther stated all the elements of the
later Protestant doctrine of Scripture: the Bible is the ground of
doctrine, to be interpreted by reason in order that logical conclusions
might provide a basis for doctrines not explicitly stated therein. In
addition, Luther insisted on the fallibility of all human authority and
the consequent demand that all interpreters be bound to the living word
as it speaks directly to the believer.[31]

These presuppositions of Luther's doctrinal revolt have direct
relevance to the development of Protestant dogmatics, specifically, of
theological prolegomena. As Paul Althaus argued, Luther stated his
theology in a highly individual manner, but nonetheless strove to
"explicate rightly the truth contained in the Holy Scriptures and the
dogma of the orthodox church" rather than to state a unique or original
position.[32] Luther never intended to set aside tradition, but assumed,
following late medieval writers like Wessel Gansfort, the secondary or
derived authority of that tradition.[33] This perspective, together with
the assumption of the role of recta ratio (right reason), remained at the
foundation of Protestant dogmatics.

Some, though not all, of Luther's doctrinal revolt can be associated
with the reigning theologies of his day. When he read the more nominalistic thinkers, like Gabriel Biel or his teacher at Erfurt, Jodokus

Trutfetter, he was confronted by an almost unprecedented emphasis on the authority of the church created by the failure of human reason to ascertain the truth of God.[34]   If, however, he turned to the Thomists, like von Gorichem or Capreolus, he was faced with a seemingly excessive trust in the rational, scientific character of theology—particularly by way of contrast with nominalist theology.   The Thomists' systematic fault was more one of omission than commission: they tended to set aside preliminary epistemological considerations, to assume, against the nominalist objections, a continuity of reason and revelation, and to apply, with considerably more rigor than had Thomas Aquinas, the Aristotelian conception of a science to their theological investigations.[35]   Luther, in reaction against both extremes of thought, took from the Scotist and nominalist systems a sense of the rift between theology in itself and theology in fact—the epistemological restriction of the *theologia viatorum*—but radically altered it. Under the pressure of his Augustinian anthropology with its powerful sense of human sinfulness and guided by his sense of the soteriological necessity of the revealed Word, Luther produced the epochal contrast between *theologia gloriae* and *theologia crucis*.[36]

Prior to and at the root of Luther's distinction between *theologia gloriae* and *theologia crucis* in the Heidelberg Disputation is the dissatisfaction over scholastic enunciation of theological principles that he had voiced some eight or nine years earlier in his lectures on the *Sentences*.   Luther seems to have been deeply struck by the prephilosophical or pre-Aristotelian character of Lombard's thought in contrast to the thought of the commentators.   Vignaux notes in particular Luther's fairly extensive and antagonistic notes on the consideration of the divine essence as a philosophical and metaphysical problem apart from the doctrine of the Trinity.[37] According to Luther, Lombard had begun with the Trinity and used it as the basis of his discussion of God whereas after Aquinas theologians had distorted doctrine and engaged in what Althaus calls "men's autonomous search for God."[38]   The distinction between *theologia gloriae* and *theologia crucis*, thus, not only partakes of a distinction between *theologia in se* and *theologia in subiecto* but also adds, together with its soteriological thrust, a re-evaluation of the language of the object of theology.   We cannot discuss God as such, but God according to the form of his revelation.[39]   This point had been made by the medieval doctors, but without the intensity and impact of Luther's insistence on a *theologia crucis*.

As noted above in the discussion of the relationship of the Reformation to theological system, Luther's antisystematic or at least nonsystematic approach to theology sets him apart not only from the orthodox or scholastic Protestantism of the late sixteenth and seventeenth centuries, but also from the efforts of many of his contemporaries, both Lutheran and Reformed, to gather together the elements of a Protestant body of doctrine, most typically in the form of *loci communes*. Thus even the first edition of Melanchthon's *Loci* (1521) includes a preface on the nature of theology. As one would expect, given the date of the treatise, its preface is highly antagonistic toward philosophy and even toward the more speculative elements of traditional dogmatic system. As Melanchthon's *Loci* developed through successive editions, traditional dogmas reappear and the highly polemical elements of its prologue are removed, giving way to more positive statements concerning the presuppositions and contents of theological system.

Although Melanchthon did not develop a formal prolegomenon to theology, elements of a presuppositional structure for theology appear both in his various prefaces to the *Loci communes* and in the *locus* on God in later editions. Here Melanchthon notes the necessity of adopting the proper order or arrangement of topics: the author must identify the principal topics (*praecipui loci*) and, as well, the issues which are unnecessary or detrimental to the edifice as a whole. With this in mind, the beginning, middle and end of the whole must be identified. The precedence of causes over effects must be noted. Theology begins by considering God and then creation, next the fall and then redemption. The *scripturae series* of the biblical events must be noted—the movement of revelation from sin to redemption, law to promise.[40] Similarly, the ancient creeds provide architectonic models for theological system.[41] These views on the *methodus theologiae* or "way through theology," drawn primarily from the 1533 *Loci communes*, are among the earliest Protestant comments on the organization of theology and have profound impact on the rise of orthodoxy and its organization of dogmatics.[42]

Melanchthon also wrote a *Brevis discendae theologiae ratio* (ca. 1530) in which he discusses a plan for proper biblical study: the student begins with Romans, proceeds through the Epistles to the Gospels, (concluding with the Gospel of John), and then works through the Old Testament (from Genesis to Deuteronomy followed by the Psalter and the prophets).[43] This brief essay is hardly a full theological prolegomenon but, as in the various prefaces to the *Loci communes*, Melanchthon manifests a strong interest in the elicitation of theological topics from the text of Scripture. The Epistle to the Romans provides a *methodus* or way through the whole Scripture by setting forth the "principal topics of Christian doctrine": justification, the use of the Law, the distinction of Law and gospel. From the Gospel of John we learn about the Trinity, creation, the two natures of Christ, original sin, free will, the righteousness of faith, the church, and the office of the keys.[44] Melanchthon followed this approach in his *Loci communes*.

In the *locus de Deo* Melanchthon included a series of comments on natural revelation and the use of human reason. Whereas his earliest comments on reason and philosophy were negative to the point of being bitter, Melanchthon ultimately tempered his views and identified the function of reason with that of Law and the function of revelation with that of the gospel.[45] True knowledge of God, argues Melanchthon, has been preserved since the fall in the revelation of the promise—while at the same time human sinfulness has created distortions of divine truth. At best nature provides knowledge of the existence and attributes of God and a sense of the moral commands of God, but this knowledge is legal and not saving.[46] Melanchthon poses, as a rhetorical question, the problem of rational knowledge of God: is it like our knowledge of mathematics? The answer, by implication, is that theological certainty rests on revelation; rational certainty in theology cannot be attained immediately but rather by the reason's acceptance of revealed truth.[47] This distinction between mathematical and theological certainty was crucial for orthodox dogmatics.[48]

The influence of Melanchthon, via his own *Loci communes* and via the works of Ursinus, Hyperius and Szegedinus, must be noted without being overestimated. The *scripturae series* and the demand for a *methodus*, together with the establishment of a set of theological *loci*, are all crucial for the creation of orthodox theology, although the use of *loci* was certainly not Melanchthon's invention. Melanchthon's Aristotelianism and his emphasis on reason are also of considerable importance to Reformed theology but, again, he did not create these emphases but rather supplemented the similar emphases brought to Reformed theology by Thomists like Vermigli and Zanchi.

On the Reformed side, there is not only a movement toward system—as in Zwingli's *De vera et falsa religione commentarius* (1524), the *Confessio fidei Basileensis prior* (ca. 1532) of Oecolampadius and Myconius, and the *Confessio Helvetica prior* (1536)—but also a growing interest in setting forth theological presuppositions at the beginning of the body of doctrine. Thus, beginning with the *Confessio Helvetica prior*, Reformed confessions virtually without exception present a doctrine of Scripture as the first point to be addressed. As early as Zwingli's *De vera et falsa religione*, one of the basic issues of future prolegomena is presented at some length—that is, the issue of religion.

Bound up with the problem of religion, moreover, is the problem of the effect of sin on knowledge of God and the blurring or distortion of the natural knowledge of God still possible because of the *semen religionis* or "seed of religion" in the mind.[49]

Similarly, we see in Bucer's *Summarischer Vergiff* (1548), as in his earlier summary of Christian teaching (1523), a strong sense of the problem of knowledge of God caused by the fall.   In the later document, Bucer spells out at some length both the problem and the solution: because of the fall, mankind has sunk into an idolatrous ignorance of God, divine truths, and the will of God.   This sinful ignorance is such that man has neither a valid knowledge of God nor a valid knowledge of himself.   True knowledge of God, then, arises not out of fallen human nature but only out of the biblical revelation, and it involves not merely knowing the truth concerning God and Christ as a datum, but also accepting that truth in repentance and faith.[50]   Bullinger's brief *Ratio studii theologici* also emphasizes the union of theological study with piety by recommending not only the careful study of Scripture but also the careful preparation of body and mind, even counseling attention to proper diet.[51]

This development toward enunciation of presuppositions and principles is also evident in the successive editions of Calvin's *Institutes*.[52] The first edition of 1536 was simply an extended introductory discourse on the basic subjects of catechesis—the Law, the Creed, the Lord's Prayer, and the sacraments—to which Calvin appended a chapter on Christian freedom and the relation of church and state.   In 1539 Calvin changed the *Institutes* from a catechetical manual to a summary of basic Christian doctrine, covering such subjects as predestination and providence, and repentance and justification in separate chapters; he also added an introductory discussion on the knowledge of God.   The next expansion of the *Institutes* (1543) juxtaposed the knowledge of God with the knowledge of man and thereby recast the whole system in the light of the problem of human knowing in its finitude and sinfulness after the fall.   The final edition of Calvin's *Institutes*, published in 1559, not only expands these chapters but adds the theme of a twofold knowledge of God, the *duplex cognitio Dei*—knowledge of God as Creator and as Redeemer —that provides not only a further presuppositional focusing of Calvin's theology but also a structuring device identifying Scripture as the ground of all true knowledge of God and then setting forth the order of the first two books of the *Institutes*: "Knowledge of God the Creator" and "Knowledge of God the Redeemer."[53]

Perhaps even more than Calvin's *Institutes*, the Vermigli–Massonius *Loci communes*[54] and Musculus' *Loci communes* provide models for the methodological and doctrinal development of Reformed orthodoxy. Unlike the *Institutes*, both of these systems follow the *locus* method that would be adopted by the orthodox in preference to the discursive model presented by Calvin. In addition, both Vermigli and Musculus, in their individual *loci*, manifest a closer relationship than does Calvin to the traditional contents of theological discussion. Calvin, as frequently noted by those who would drive a wedge between early Reformed theology and Reformed orthodoxy, does not provide a detailed discussion of the divine attributes, but such discussion was available as a model for orthodoxy in the *Loci communes* of Vermigli (I.xii) and Musculus (cap. 47–60). In Musculus' *Loci* the discussion is of considerable length, equalling the extent of elaboration in virtually any seventeenth-century Reformed system.

The tendency of Vermigli and Musculus—who were more carefully and thoroughly trained in the intricacies of late medieval theology than Calvin—to state traditional theological topics at greater length and in greater detail than Calvin is matched by their interest in the presuppositions of theological discourse. Thus, the introductory chapters of Vermigli's *Loci* contain discussions of the various forms of revelation (I.ii) and of natural knowledge of God (I.iii–v) prior to the *locus* on Scripture and its interpretation (I.vi). In addition, a discussion of the relationship of philosophy to theology (II.iii) indicates a more positive relationship between faith and reason, theology and philosophy than that argued by Calvin.[55] Vermigli, trained at Padua as a Thomist, manifests a willingness to deal with the complex questions of the relationship of faith—which is a rational disposition of the soul—to rational argumentation, within the context of his thoroughly Augustinian anthropology.[56] In other words, Vermigli maintains the *sola gratia* of the Reformation but also develops a more sophisticated view of the theological and philosophical functions of reason than Calvin ever attempted.[57]

Since Musculus' lengthy discussion of the knowledge of God occurs later in his system (cap. lxi), his theological prolegomenon is quite brief. Before the exposition of his first locus, *de Deo*, Musculus addresses the question "whether there is a God." He offers no formal proofs but rather indicates that the existence of God either is or ought to be self-evident. This perspective, in turn, raises the question of the knowledge of God. The topic is treated only briefly, however, as

Musculus reserves his broad exposition of the problem of knowledge for the later *locus*.

Consequently, Musculus devotes several sections of his *Loci communes* to the discussion of the problem of knowledge of God, with no less insistence than Calvin and Vermigli on the problem of man's sinfulness, but with more interest in the several elements of the knowledge of God and in their arrangement and relation to the progress of human salvation. Musculus here manifests reliance on the traditional view of faith as consisting in *notitia*, *assensus*, and *fiducia*. He also clearly indicates the central place of Christ in saving knowledge and its personal appropriation.[58] Significantly, Musculus devotes a fairly lengthy discussion to the content of our natural knowledge of God and its function in the setting aside of impiety and coming to the truth of God—with the implication that philosophical knowledge of God contains important, albeit unsaving, truths potentially useful to theology. In any case, Musculus provides further insight into the early Reformed contribution to theological prolegomena. Like Calvin and Vermigli he manifests an epistemological concern and, more like Vermigli than Calvin, he notes a certain philosophical and theological complexity to the problem of natural knowledge of God.

A formal, methodological prolegomenon appears in Andreas Hyperius' posthumous *Methodi theologiae* (1568). Here the Melanchthonian concern for method and order bore fruit in an extended discussion of the *locus* method of theology.[59] Together with Vermigli and Musculus, Hyperius represents the technically trained theological mind of second-generation Reformed theology. Hyperius' theology, far more than Calvin's, reaches into the historical tradition of the church for its paradigms—and sees the usefulness of systematic essays like Augustine's *Enchiridion*, John of Damascus' *On the Orthodox Faith*, and Lombard's *Sentences*. Indeed, Hyperius cites these works specifically as models for theological system.[60] His method, like that of Vermigli and Musculus and more so than that of Calvin and Bullinger, points toward the development of Protestant orthodoxy.

Hyperius also wrote an extended essay on the study of theology, the *De theologo seu de ratione studii theologici libri iiii*.[61] As Preus comments, this essay is by far the most elaborate prolegomenon produced by a Protestant in the first half-century of the Reformation.[62] Hyperius begins, echoing the medieval tradition and Augustine, with a counsel to piety: prayer and the guidance of the Spirit are requisite to theology while growth in Christian love is the proper result of theological study.

Hyperius counsels the study of philosophy, logic and language, but offers a caveat concerning the excesses of Aristotelian metaphysics.   In book II, Hyperius outlines a method for the interpretation of Scripture and in the final two books, he deals at length with the pattern of *loci communes* that he followed in his *Methodus*.[63]

The importance of Hyperius' arguments is enormous.   He is the only member of his generation of Reformed theologians to state clearly a rationale for systematic organization of doctrine and to begin writing with the idea of completed system fully in view.   Calvin began with a catechetical model and modified it; Hyperius constructed system with a view to its traditional shape.   His model is both synthetic or causally controlled and modeled on a movement from genus to species—that is, from first principles to their modification into particulars by means of *differentia*.   Both the logic of movement from first cause to final goal with its language of synthetic or constitutive arrangement, and the structuring of system in relation to first principles have an enormous impact on orthodox system and its prolegomena.[64]

Pierre Viret, a thinker whose name is closely associated with the Reformation in Lausanne and whose doctrine stands in firm continuity with that of Calvin, wrote in a more popular style than that of Calvin and produced theological works primarily in the vernacular rather than in the more scholarly Latin.   He must be regarded as a theologian of less importance than Calvin to the systematic development of the Reformed faith but of great importance to its popular diffusion both in the French-speaking cantons of Switzerland and in France itself.   Viret frequently wrote his works in the form of dialogues.

Viret produced several more or less systematic works, the largest in scope being his *Instruction chrestienne en la doctrine de la loy et l'Evangile, et en la vraye philosophie et théologie tant naturelle que supernaturelle des chrestiens, et en la contemplation du temple et des images et oeuvres de la providence de Dieu en tout l'univers, et en l'histoire de la création et cheute et reparation du genre humain. Le tout divisé en trois volumes* . . . (Geneva, 1564).   According to Viret's biographer, Barnaud, only the first two volumes appeared, while the third (which was to deal with providence and predestination) was left unpublished.[65]   The first part of this work is a catechetical summary of the faith, a beginning instruction,[66] while the second—although it retains the form of a dialogue—enters into considerably greater detail.[67]

Viret's emphasis on a Christian philosophy as well as theology and upon natural and supernatural knowledge of God stands in greater continuity with traditional views on theology and its ancillae than does Calvin's thought—as does his emphasis on knowledge of God drawn from creation as well as from the biblical history of salvation. We must note too, however, the important phrase, *"l'histoire de la création, cheute et reparation de la genre humaine,"* which points to the emphasis of Reformed theology, following Hyperius, Calvin and Melanchthon, on the historic series of Christian doctrine. Although Viret stands considerably below the rank of Calvin, Hyperius, Musculus or Vermigli, his work also indicates the strong early Reformed emphasis on preliminary questions of knowledge that would eventuate in the orthodox prolegomena.

Several points must be made clear if we are to understand the relation of theology in the period of formulation to the theology encountered during the formation and development of orthodoxy. In the first place, the elements of prolegomena found in these early attempts at a Reformed system do not always occur at the beginning of the doctrinal treatises: the order of theology is not yet fully established. Nevertheless, there are enough treatises and confessional documents adumbrating the later synthetic order of system to make this gathering of "elements of prolegomena" from the early Reformed systems and compends a legitimate undertaking. More importantly, the gathering of these presuppositional reflections from the early Reformed systems provides a useful gauge to the development of the orthodox or scholastic systems and to their continuity with the teaching of the Reformation.

These early Reformed statements concerning theological presuppositions focus, virtually without exception, on the problem of the knowledge of God given the fact not only of human finitude but also of human sin. In other words, the critique leveled by the Reformation at medieval theological presuppositions added a soteriological dimension to the epistemological problem. Whereas the medieval doctors had assumed that the fall affected primarily the will and its affections and not the reason, the Reformers assumed also the fallenness of the rational faculty: natural theology, according to the Reformers, was not merely limited to nonsaving knowledge of God—it was also bound in idolatry.[68] This view of the problem of knowledge is the single most important contribution of the early Reformed writers to the theological prolegomena of orthodox Protestantism. Indeed, it is the doctrinal issue that most forcibly presses the Protestant scholastics toward the modification of the medieval models for theological prolegomena.

2.3 Theological Prolegomena in Reformed Orthodoxy

The Reformers and their immediate successors contributed several of the elements of Protestant theological prolegomena but produced no fully developed statement of the presuppositions and principles of theology. More importantly, they did not define either the theological enterprise itself or the task of theological system. The reason for this omission is simple: the first two generations of Protestant thinkers were fully occupied in establishing exegetically and discursively the basic theological positions of Protestantism. They did not engage in the task of adapting the theological propositions of Protestantism to the needs of university-level training in theology as system. In view of their polemical relationship to late medieval theology, they were bound not to teach the system as they themselves had learned it. In the next two generations, however, that is, in the works of the theologians of the latter third of the sixteenth century, the movement toward institutional-ization and toward the disciplined academic teaching of theology is evident. With this movement, moreover, came the need to define theology as a discipline with its own presuppositions and principles.

The theological prolegomena of the seventeenth century are, argu-ably, the most exhaustive and most finely tooled prolegomena in the history of theology. The intense polemics of the century following the Reformation forced all parties in the theological debate to examine, clarify and defend their presuppositions more carefully than ever before. This generalization is as true of the Roman Catholic systems of the day as it is of the Protestant ones. In the case of the Protestant theolo-gians, however, the construction of prolegomena was a twofold or even threefold endeavor involving the statement of views of the theological task grounded in the experiences of the Reformation, the appropriation and modification of the earlier tradition of prolegomena, and the polemical and apologetic defense of Protestant theological presupposi-tions over against Roman Catholic attack. The resulting prolegomena manifest a mastery of the issues and debates underlying the theological enterprise that has seldom been achieved in the history of theology either before or since. Without exaggeration, the theological prole-gomena of the seventeenth-century Protestant scholastics provide a model for the development of a distinctively Protestant but nonetheless universally Christian or catholic theology—a model that Protestant theology today can ignore only at great risk.

The development of theological prolegomena is, in a sense, the cen-tral issue of post-Reformation theology, grounded in the hermeneutical cast of Luther's own thought and in the theological background of his protest. Here, in the developing prolegomena, the great themes of the Reformation theology and its theological antecedents converge and coalesce. On the one hand, we see the impact of the evangelical reform with its watchword of *sola scriptura* while on the other, lingering first in the background of the Reformers' thought and then becoming explicit in the age of early orthodoxy, we encounter the Scotist and nominalist realization of the inaccessibility and unknowability of God apart from revelation. The theological prolegomena of post-Reformation Protestantism rest upon the scriptural standard, accepting philosophical categories only insofar as they can be used after the collapse of the *analogia entis*. On the Reformed side of Protestantism, the ontological and epistemological premise of the prolegomena would be *finitum non capax infiniti*.

The continuities of theological interest and discontinuities of method that we have already noted in the context of the development of Protestant thought concerning theological presuppositions and principles, from Luther's initial protest to the rise of Reformed system in the writings of Calvin, Musculus, Vermigli, and Viret, remain characteristic of Reformed theology as it developed past the age of Calvin into its third and fourth generations of thinkers. It is in the thought of these writers that the pressures of institutionalization and academic instruction begin to bear fruit in the form of more explicit considerations of presuppositions, methods and principles in theology. As in the earlier period, change is not sudden and the recourse to the tradition, particularly that of the Middle Ages, is somewhat hesitant and only occasionally explicit. Nonetheless, the development of actual theological prolegomena forced these early orthodox to look to the centuries before the Reformation for models.

The prefatory remarks at the beginning of Ursinus' posthumously published *Doctrinae christianae compendium* are of importance to the development of Reformed theological prolegomena and to the rise of a doctrine of Scripture in Reformed orthodoxy. The *compendium* consists of the catechetical lectures of Ursinus with some editorial additions from other works—in the case of the prolegomena, the preface to the catechetical lectures is conflated with the *locus* on Scripture found in Ursinus' fragmentary *Loci communes*. There is no discussion of theology as such but rather a distinction between true religion, founded on Scripture, and false religion, founded on the mental exertions and idolatrous fears of unbelievers. Ursinus also briefly notes three methods characteristic of the study of theology: catechetical instruction (which briefly sets forth a summary of beliefs), the development of *loci communes* or commonplaces (according to which different points of doctrine are handled "together with their divisions, reasons and arguments"), and meditation on the Scriptures (from which catechesis and commonplaces arise and to which the study of the catechism and the *loci* returns the reader).[69] This model is retained by the later Reformed orthodox—as is Ursinus' definition of scholastic method in the handling of the *loci*.

Zanchi's *Praefatiuncula in locos communes* must be counted among the first of the early Reformed orthodox attempts at prolegomena. What is surprising about this work is Zanchi's unwillingness to proceed in any great detail beyond a preliminary statement concerning the meaning and method of theology affixed to a statement of the doctrine of Scripture— this despite Zanchi's training in late medieval theology and his certain acquaintance with the prolegomena to medieval systems. We hear no echo, in Zanchi's *Praefatiuncula*, of the questions presented by Aquinas concerning the scientific character of theology or the relation of theology to *praxis*. "What indeed is Theology," Zanchi declares, "unless it is the doctrine concerning God, drawn out of the Word of God."[70] Thus Scripture is the *fundamentum totius Theologiae* and ought to be the subject of the first *locus* in theology.

There are, Zanchi argues, two principal methods of teaching theology, the synthetic and the analytic. The synthetic or "compositive" method is properly employed in the binding together and teaching of theological *loci*, while the analytic or "resolvative" method is properly applied to the explication of Scripture. Theology, therefore, begins analytically with the text of Scripture, presenting first the scope of an author's argument in a particular place, then presenting issues springing from the passage, and finally formulating questions or propositions that arise from discussion of the issues.[71] This approach is followed closely by Zanchi in his commentary on Ephesians. The next step in theological method is the movement from commentary to system, the synthetic or compositive use of the questions and propositions in the construction of a set of theological *loci*.

From this period we also have the brief *Examen theologicum* (1557) and more extensive *S. S. theologiae problemata* (1573) of Benedict Aretius, Musculus' successor in Bern.[72] Both of these works carry forward the methodological concentration on scripturally based *loci communes*, but neither makes any contribution to the development of formal theological prolegomena. The *Theologia problemata* is significant for its extended opening discussion of natural theology as the fruit of gentile philosophy and its juxtaposition of that theology with the revealed truths of the Christian faith.[73]

The early orthodox interest in method, specifically in the issue of an obviously "scholastic" approach to theology, finds its clearest statement in the preface to Antoine Chandieu's *De verbo Dei scripto* (1580). On the one hand, Chandieu distances himself from the "errors" of the medieval scholastics who, he notes, used logical rather than biblical principles and who obscured truth in sophistic argumentation—but, on the other hand, he recognizes the need to dispute with the Roman opponents of Protestantism in carefully constructed scholastic debate. He therefore proposes an approach "at once theological and scholastic" that holds biblical *principia*, refuses to subordinate them to human wisdom, and adopts a method sufficient to the task of refuting adversaries of the faith.[74]   Chandieu, in short, proposed explicitly a program for Protestant scholasticism.

Although primarily an essay written in defense of the Protestant doctrine of Scripture, Sibrandus Lubbertus' *De principiis Christianorum dogmatum libri vii* (1591) also deserves mention both as an example of the impact of polemic on the construction of Protestant dogmatics and as a contribution to one of the topics of theological prolegomena, the principles or *principia* of theology. Lubbertus wrote in response to Bellarmine's treatises on the Word of God and the teaching authority of the church. The scholastic detail and mastery of sources typical of Bellarmine's work press Lubbertus to deal with writings of the fathers, the scholastics, the church councils, and Aristotle (on the subject of *principia*) in detail atypical of the Reformers. In addition, out of the polemic arises a distinctly Protestant understanding of theological *principia*: the divine materials of theology necessitate divine or divinely guaranteed *principia*. Scripture alone is the principle or foundation of such a discipline. Lubbertus provided Reformed theology, at the beginning of the formulation of its prolegomena, with the identification of Scripture as the *principium* in the dogmatic sense of the term.

The most important contribution to the development of a Protestant theological prolegomenon during the era of early orthodoxy came from Franciscus Junius. Indeed, all of the Reformed and most of the Lutheran prolegomena in the following century bear some trace of the impact of Junius' work. Several of the more important early orthodox Reformed prolegomena, like those of Polanus and Scharpius, were modeled directly upon Junius' arguments, sometimes with a verbatim borrowing of definitions. Junius introduced into Reformed system not only a lengthy definition of theology as a discipline but also the view, typical of later orthodoxy, of our theology (*theologia nostra*) as a form of ectypal theology resting on the divine archetype. Junius also manifests, in the changing patterns of his own thought, the tendency of Protestant orthodoxy to move away from a Thomistic view of theology as *scientia* toward a definition of theology as *sapientia* or wisdom.[75]

In the three decades following the appearance of Junius' *De vera theologia* (1594), a massive development of theological prolegomena occurred within Reformed theology. With Polanus' *Syntagma theologiae christianae* (1609) virtually all of the scholastic questions concerning theology as a discipline have reappeared, now interpreted through a distinctly Protestant glass. What is theology? What are its divisions or parts? Is it a science? What are its causes and ends? Is it theoretical or practical? What are its *principia*? Later orthodoxy would add further questions and, under the impact of polemic, elaborate some others—such as the questions of the relation of theology to philosophy and the existence of fundamental articles in theology—but the basic form of system is established in Polanus' *Syntagma*. In the writings of both Junius and Polanus, though medieval scholastics are seldom cited directly, medieval models are evident in the language used and in the issues addresssed. We note, at this stage of development of Protestant system, a conscious effort to take old forms and infuse them with the message of Protestantism.[76]

Polanus' *Syntagma*, which is profoundly dependent upon Junius' *De vera theologia*, marks a watershed in the development of Protestant orthodoxy. Apart from the vast pieces of Zanchi's fragmentary *Summa*, the *Syntagma* is surely the most elaborate dogmatic system produced by a Reformed theologian up to that time. In it, Reformed theology attains its orthodox form, replete with references to patristic and medieval theology. A parallel development had, of course, occurred in Lutheranism: the year following the appearance of Polanus' *Syntagma* saw the publication of the first portion of Johann Gerhard's *Loci theologici*, the great formative work of Lutheran orthodoxy.

Once the basic definitions of theology had been established by Junius and were brought to bear on full system by Polanus, they passed into the somewhat less elaborate prolegomena of systematizers like Johannes Scharpius, Antonius Walaeus, William Ames, Francis Gomarus, and Johannes Maccovius. In these writers' works, the prolegomena are reduced to basic statement of definitions and principles, while at the same time new emphases are seen to take root—such as the description of theology as theoretical and practical and, in the cases of Ames and Maccovius, the definition of theology as the science of living blessedly forever, a definition of importance to Reformed piety in the seventeenth century. We ought also to mention here the contribution of Bartholomaus Keckermann to the problem of the relationship of philosophy and theology, an issue significant for the high orthodox development of prolegomena. Among the German Reformed, Johann Heinrich Alsted represents the embodiment of all of these concerns, particularly the desire to establish the interrelationship of the disciplines of philosophy and theology.

Alsted's *Methodus sacrosanctae theologiae* (1614) deserves special mention as the most important of the early orthodox systems after Polanus. Unlike most of the theological systems of the day, Alsted's is organized primarily according to the form or kind of theology and only secondarily according to the internal logic of system: the concern for method governs the organization of the work. Thus Alsted begins with the two books of *Praecognita*—one a formal prolegomenon on the nature of theology, the other an instruction on the study of theology—and then proceeds to separate studies of natural theology, catechetical and scholastic theology, ethical casuistry, preaching, and arcane or mystical theology. Alsted's *Praecognita* provide us with the most elaborate of the early orthodox prolegomena although they provide little new material on the nature of theology beyond the earlier contributions of Junius and Polanus. Indeed, they manifest the importance of Junius' *De vera theologia* in yet another part of the Reformed world, mediated through the work of Polanus. Alsted's greater contribution is to the development of method and to the delineation of patterns in the study of theology, although here again his ideas are not original—the emphasis on piety is part of the patristic and medieval heritage and, as given a distinctly Protestant emphasis in the writings of Bullinger and Hyperius.

A somewhat different approach to prolegomena is also found during the early orthodox period in the systematic works of Perkins and Ames and, for somewhat different reasons, in the systems of Trelcatius, Wollebius, Walaeus, and Gomarus. In the work of these theologians, the lengthy discussion of archetypal and ectypal theology as presented by Junius, Polanus and Alsted is omitted. Rather, their definitions of theology focus on "our theology," the *theologia nostra*. In the cases of Perkins and Ames, this emphasis on the present-day theology of believers in the church arises out of a definition of theology as a *praxis* that can lead believers toward eternal fellowship with God. This definition comes into Reformed theology via the work of Peter Ramus, though certainly not without powerful medieval precedent. In the cases of Trelcatius, Wollebius, Walaeus, and Gomarus, we are dealing with brief compends rather

than systems conceived on the scale of Polanus' *Syntagma* or Alsted's
Methodus. The concept of an archetypal ground for ectypal theology
appears to be assumed without debate while the emphasis of exposition
falls upon "our theology" as the primary material of system. (It is
worth noting that Arminius' several *Orations* on theology together with
the initial chapter of his *Private Disputations* echo this rapid development of Protestant theological prolegomena, draw on the categories of the
Reformed systems and manifest, together with the Reformed, a constructive
and architectonic interest in scholastic categories of argument.[77])

As we trace the development of Reformed prolegomena into the mid-
and late seventeenth century, we find the Ramist line of Perkins and Ames
to be highly influential in the Netherlands, as evidenced by the
technique of bifurcation and the typically Ramist definition of theology
in the *Loci communes* of Johannes Maccovius and the *Theoretico-practica
theologia* of Petrus van Mastricht. As noted in the preceding paragraph,
Walaeus' and Gomarus' systems belong to a group of works that tend away
from massive prolegomena. In terms of the chronology of orthodoxy, these
systems carry the pattern of Trelcatius' *Loci* into the middle of the
century. The tradition of more extended or expansive prolegomena can be
viewed as carrying over into the systems of Maresius, Burmann, Heidanus,
and Marckius as well as into the *Synopsis purioris theologiae* and the
massive works of Turretin, Heidegger and Mastricht. Here, too, as
evidenced by Burmann's *De studio theologico*, Voetius' *Exercitia et
bibliotheca studiosi theologiae* and Owen's *Theologoumena*, the development
and elaboration of prolegomena was paralleled by the production of
separate treatises on propaedeutic themes—continuing the model pioneered
by Hyperius into the late seventeenth century. Marckius' influence,
together with the tradition of extensive and exhaustive prolegomena,
carries over into the eighteenth century in the vast dogmatics of
Bernhard de Moor, whose six-volume commentary on Marckius' *Compendium* was
published in 1761-1771. De Moor's work also provides evidence of the
stubborn survival of theological orthodoxy, long after its era of
dominance, into an otherwise rationalist era, without the loss of its
scholastic balance of the issues of faith and reason, philosophy and
theology, and without the loss of its scriptural principle.

Whereas it is characteristic of the early orthodox prolegomena to
reflect intellectual ties to thinkers like Calvin, Musculus and Vermigli
through extended discussion of the problem of natural theology, the high
orthodox prolegomena tend to accept the results of earlier discussion and
to treat the issue in brief definitions.[78] By way of further contrast,
the high orthodox shift the focus of the discussion of the natural powers

of mind to the extended treatment of the relation of philosophy to theology and the function of reason in theology.[79]   This latter change can be accounted for in no small measure by the successful institution-alization of Protestantism and the identification of theology as an academic discipline in dialogue with philosophy.   This institutional-ization had occurred by the beginning of the seventeenth century.   On the negative and polemical side of the matter, the rise of rationalist philosophy forced the orthodox to enquire into the limits of reason while at the same time disputing with a philosophical adversary far more willing than a medieval or sixteenth-century philosopher to assume the normative status of rational proof in all areas of knowledge, including theology.[80]   The impact of rationalism on theological prolegomena is evidenced in Burmann's and Heidanus' interest in language of "clear and distinct perception" and in the presence in the human mind of innate ideas of the existence of God.[81]   It is equally apparent in the extended discussion of reason, including its principial use in natural theology, that appears in the work of the anti-Cocceian, anti-Cartesian Maresius. Maresius, however, does not represent a majority view—particularly not in the anti-Cocceian and anti-Cartesian party, as the strict limitation set by Voetius on the use of reason "in matters concerning faith" amply testifies.[82]

In addition to this interest in the relation of philosophy to theology, the high orthodox prolegomena, produced by writers like Francis Turretin, John Heinrich Heidegger, Franz Burmann, Herman Witsius, and Leonhard Riissen, develop discussions of the fundamental articles in theology, and more elaborate analyses of the object and genus of theology.   The first of these topics arose in debate with the Lutherans, the latter two out of a closer study of the medieval scholastic systems. Similar developments are seen in the German Reformed theology of Marcus Friedrich Wendelin and in the fully scholastic system of the English theologian, Edward Leigh.   Leigh's system is particularly significant as firm evidence of the constant dialogue between English and continental theologians during the seventeenth century.   In addition, most notably in Turretin's *Institutio*, the Protestant scholastics of this period begin to cite medieval systems directly and to dialogue, critically, with medieval models and paradigms for theology.

From both a historical and a theological perspective, the prole-gomena in succeeding generations of Protestant theological systems manifest a fairly continuous development from the presuppositions of the Reformers through the perceptions concerning systematization or organiza-tion of theology noted by the second-generation codifiers—Calvin,

Vermigli, Musculus, Hyperius, and their contemporaries—to the several stages of construction of theological prolegomena we have associated with the early and high orthodox periods. We note, again, that theological prolegomena are never *vordogmatisch*: they are an integral part of dogmatic system that develops in dialogue with basic dogmatic conclusions after the system as a whole has been set forth. Thus, the Protestant scholastic prolegomena look back to medieval models—in the absence of clear statements of presuppositions and definitions by the Reformers—but do so in the context of an already established Protestant theological tradition as embodied in confessional norms.

Despite the relative infrequency of direct citation of the medieval scholastics in the early orthodox systems, the first Reformed prolegomena tend to appropriate and adapt medieval definitions while those of the high orthodox period tend to add topics that reflect specifically Protestant concerns, such as the identification of *principia*, the relationship of nonsaving natural theology to the Christian theological enterprise, and the identification of fundamental doctrines. The same point may be made concerning the essays on the study of theology which, beginning with Alsted, are associated with or included within theological prolegomena. Such essays are not the first order of business in the construction of theological system but rather arise after the establishment of system and the self-conscious identification of Protestant theological system and its concerns over against the presuppositions of earlier theological systems.   Concomitant with the development of these distinctively Protestant prolegomena is the inclusion in the prolegomena of brief histories of theology that serve to identify the contribution of the Reformers and to distinguish the new scholasticism of the Protestants from the scholasticism of the Middle Ages. Such histories occur in the systems of Alsted, Maccovius and Burmann, in each case associated with the development of distinctively Protestant elements in the prolegomena.

This continuity of Reformed orthodoxy with the Reformation in and through the use of modified medieval models for system was possible because of Christian Aristotelianism, its dialectical method, and because of the training of many of the Reformers in the old systems. Just as the Reformation cannot be seen as a total break with the Middle Ages and just as the medieval forerunners of the Reformation bear witness to principles and presuppositions in theology akin to those of the Reformers, so is it an error to argue discontinuity between the Reformation and post-Reformation Protestantism.   Instead, we must think in terms of the larger continuities of theological and philosophical method—the trajectory of scholasticism from the late twelfth to the late seventeenth century—and in terms of the doctrinal continuity, not without development and change, within Protestantism itself. What is more, genuine room must be allowed for development and change, particularly the development and change associated with the creation of orthodoxy, "right teaching" characteristic of an institutionalized church intent on teaching its theology in universities and manifesting its catholicity in terms of the greater tradition of Christian doctrine. By way of clarification of these points and as final preparation for the discussion of theological prolegomena and *principia*, we raise two very specific issues concerning the development of post-Reformation Reformed theology: the idea of "central dogmas" and the problem of rationalism.

2.4 Reformed Orthodoxy and the Idea of "Central Dogmas"

In this and the following section we address the two basic questions raised by scholars and theologians about the character and intention of Reformed orthodoxy: is it a predestinarian system, and is it a form of rationalism? If Reformed orthodoxy is a predestinarian system and if it is a form of rationalism, it certainly stands in discontinuity with the Reformation. This would also mean that the hope of some theologians to leap over the orthodox and to reappropriate the genuine Protestantism of the Reformers, although probably incapable of fruition, would have some theological and historical justification. The usefulness of orthodoxy to the theological present depends, therefore, in no small measure, on our ability to answer both of these questions in the negative.

Before we address either of these questions, it is of paramount importance to recognize that they are separate questions—separate from each other and from the underlying methodological question of historical continuity and discontinuity. Predestinarianism and rationalism are hardly identical. On the one hand, Reformed predestinarianism rests on an exegetical, not on a philosophical basis and has little in common with the development of a monistic or panentheistic rationalism such as can be found in the seventeenth-century rationalist system of Spinoza. On the other hand, rationalism itself, depending on its anthropological presuppositions, could and did, in the seventeenth century, emphasize freedom rather than determinism. Emphasis on freedom is particularly evident in the inductive rationalism of the seventeenth-century English philosophers standing in the line of Bacon and Lord Hebert of Cherbury. In addition, the underlying issue of continuity and discontinuity is considerably larger than either the issue of predestinarianism or rationalism and it remains an issue after these other two have been set aside.

The analysis of prolegomena and *principia* in post-Reformation Reformed dogmatics provides a partial answer to the claim of earlier scholarship that the Reformed, following the death of Calvin, ignored the essentially Christologically, soteriologically and epistemologically controlled doctrinal perspective of the *Institutes* and, in its place, introduced a predestinarian metaphysic as the controlling element of Reformed system, in effect, the "central dogma" and fundamental principle of Christian doctrine. The prolegomena of the scholastic Protestant systems were designed specifically for the purpose of presenting and defining the presuppositions and principles controlling the system of theology as a whole. The absence of a predestinarian principle from these discussions, together with some reference to soteriological, epistemological and Christological issues, would provide one side of an argument reappraising and reassessing the character of scholastic Protestant theology. This argument, of course, is only partial. It must be presented in relation to an analysis of developing Reformed orthodoxy in which the doctrine of predestination is shown to be one doctrinal focus among others and not a central pivot of system or overarching motif controlling other doctrines—despite the absence of any reference to it in the prolegomena.

The attempt to describe Protestant scholasticism as the systematic development of central dogmas—predestination in the case of the Reformed, justification in the case of the Lutherans—was, at best, a theological reinterpretation of the Protestant scholastic systems by constructive theologians of the late eighteenth and nineteenth centuries as they attempted to rebuild theological system in the wake of the Kantian critque of rational metaphysics.[83] Hermann Bauke neatly distinguished between this post-Enlightenment "monistic" systematizing tendency and the earlier discursive and scholastic approaches of Protestant theology.[84] The monistic systematizers of the nineteenth century—Alexander Schweizer, Gottfried Thomasius and Albrecht Ritschl—simply read their own method back into the Protestant tradition. At worst, the central dogma theories are an abuse of history that cannot stand in the light of a careful reading of the sources.

In addition, the arguments of Bizer, Hall and others that the little *Tabula praedestinationis* published by Beza in 1555 (nine years *before* the death of Calvin) was a substantive alteration of the systematic perspective of Genevan theology and the basis of a predestinarian restructuring of Reformed system simply does not bear historical scrutiny.[85] Beza's

Tabula is nothing more than a presentation of the doctrine of predestination in its relation to the *ordo salutis*, based on the standard scholastic distinction between the decree and its execution in time.   It is hardly a prospectus for a system.[86]   Similarly, Perkins' A *Golden Chaine*, which appears to be based on Beza's *Tabula*, is an exposition of the decree and its execution—and not at all a theological system.[87]   Thus, there is not only no evidence that Beza's *Tabula* was a predestinarian systematization of theology, there is also no evidence that any of Beza's contemporaries or successors viewed it as the basis for a predestinarian system.   Both Beza and Perkins assume, moreover, a category of divine permission and the existence, as well, of contingent events and free will in the world.   There is not even a tendency toward metaphysical determinism.[88]

A further confutation of this older scholarship concerns the omission of any consideration of the doctrine of predestination from the Reformed orthodox prolegomena.   How could several generations of theologians, all of them quite pointed and persistent in their declaration of presuppositions, definitions, foundations, and principles, fail to recognize or to consider the systematic underpinning of their theology? Yet such would be the case if predestination or the eternal decree were in fact the central dogma of Reformed scholastic theology, for the doctrine of the decrees is not so much as mentioned in the *locus de theologia* of any of the orthodox systems examined in this essay, not even in the supposedly speculative and reputedly "decretal" systems of Gomarus and Maccovius.   The decree is identified neither as a *principium theologiae* nor as an *articulus fundamentalis*.   Indeed, the discussion of *principia* and of *articuli fundamentales* points toward a series of scripturally-based doctrinal *loci* which together determine the character of theological system rather than to a single central dogma.

The actual enunciation and discussion of *principia* by the Reformed orthodox, moreover, manifest both the reason for their treatment of the doctrine of predestination and the reason for its use as one focus, among others, of the theological system.   Briefly, the Protestant scholastics declare two *principia theologiae*, a principle or foundation of knowing (*principium cognoscendi*) and a principle or foundation of being (*principium essendi*).[89]   The former is Scripture, the self-revelation of God, and the latter is God himself, the self-existent ground of all finite existence.   The first and foremost reason for the inclusion of any doctrine in such a system is the fact of its presence as a place or topic—a *locus* or *topos*—in the biblical revelation.[90]   Predestination receives considerable attention in the Pauline letters and, consequently, receives considerable attention in the Reformed system. Its presence in the system, moreover, rests on the foundation of the Augustinian tradition antecedent to the Reformation.

More to the point, however, is the fact of the relationship of the doctrine of predestination to the doctrine of God. Alexander of Hales and Thomas Aquinas, who have never been accused of creating a predestinarian system, noted the logically necessary relationship of the two doctrines by arguing whether predestination ought to be predicated of God.[91] It is, after all, the eternal God who in eternity, promulgates his decree concerning the shape and destiny of creation. This question of proper predication, incidentally, accounts for the occasional practice of Reformed scholastics of including the decree among the divine attributes.[92] They were not attempting to create or to justify a deterministic system by the placement of a particular doctrine: they were simply reflecting a traditional question of predication.

Since predestination can be predicated of God—in other words, since God can be said to decree or predestine, the decretive or predestining will of God becomes an important category of system. It is not, however, an all-embracing category. On the basis of the logic of predication and the prior enunciation of God as the *principium essendi theologiae*, the doctrine of predestination must be a category subordinate to the *principium* of which it is predicated, the triune God, and subordinate also to the will of God, of which it is the representation. Significantly, the early orthodox press home the point that the decree must be understood in terms of the doctrine of the Trinity as well as in terms of the doctrine of the divine essence, and that predestination, defined strictly as the decree to elect some and to reprobate others, is only one category of the divine willing.[93] Particularly in the infralapsarian systems of Reformed theology, the doctrines of creation and providence stand apart from and, in some sense, prior to election and reprobation. In all Reformed systems, the divinity of Christ assures Christology a greater importance in the soteriological portion of system than the doctrine of predestination. In addition, there is no reason that a given system cannot be both predestinarian and soteriologically christocentric, contrary to the claims of some recent essays. Indeed, without the decree manifesting the solely gracious character of salvation, the system could easily cease to be soteriologically christocentric.[94] Such systematic balance can occur, moreover, only when predestination is significant but not principial.

There is, then, sufficient reason to accept the assumption of the Reformed systems that their declared *principia* are their actual *principia*

and that no doctrines other than the doctrines of Scripture and God have
an absolutely determinative effect upon the structure and contents of
theological system.   This conclusion highlights the methodological
problem inherent in one of the more eminent earlier treatises on the
basic principles of Reformed theology, Althaus' *Die Prinzipien der
deutschen reformierten Dogmatik*.   Althaus tries to elicit from select
doctrinal *loci*, typically the *loci de praedestinatione*, *de Deo* and *de
providentia*, what he believes to be underlying principles and tendencies,
without paying particular attention to what the Protestant scholastics
themselves say about *principia*.[95]

In addition, Althaus usefully analyzes the presence of philosophical
and logical structures within the systems.   However, because of his lack
of attention to presuppositions enunciated in their prolegomena, such as
the object of theology, the relation of theology to reason and philosophy, and the legitimate grounds of theological knowing, Althaus
frequently fails to evaluate accurately the general character of Reformed
dogmatics and the implications of arguments and structures within
individual Reformed systems.

Heppe's presentation of *principia* is also marred by a series of
profound problems.   He reduces the complex prolegomena of the orthodox
systems to a discussion of natural and revealed theology and virtually
excludes their extensive inquiry into the nature and forms of theology,
the object and genus of theology, the use of philosophy in theological
systems, and the problem of "fundamental doctrines."[96]   Heppe also
arranges his dogmatics in such a way as to place the doctrine of predestination prior to creation, in relation to the doctrine of God.   This was
a pattern followed by a large number of seventeenth-century systems, but
not by all of the Protestant scholastics—certainly not by all of those
cited by Heppe.   In other words, in this and other discussions throughout
his dogmatics, Heppe's arrangement of doctrine does not reflect the
arrangement of doctrine in the systems he is citing.   Nor does he attempt
to alleviate the problem by describing the order, arrangement and interrelationship of individual doctrines in these systems.   The following
essay attempts to set forth all the elements of the orthodox prolegomena
and *principia*, with attention to the several historical forms of argument
and to the development of orthodox system.

A selection of citations from the Reformed orthodox prolegomena
somewhat more representative of their contents than Heppe's presentation
is available in Schweizer's *Glaubenslehre*.   Here at least we have discussion of theology as a mixed discipline, both practical and speculative;

of God, the highest good, as the end or goal of theology; and of the relationship of philosophy and theology.[97]   Nevertheless, the survey of topics is incomplete: there is no discussion of the object and genus of theology, fundamental articles, or the distinction between the divine archetype and the derived or ectypal forms of theology.   Furthermore, Schweizer's discussion is organized not according to the logic of the sixteenth- and seventeenth-century systems but according to the require- ments of his own Schleiermacherian theological system.   In Schweizer's hands, even the topics of the prolegomena must bear witness to "das Bewusstsein schlechthiniger Abhängigkeit"--the consciousness of absolute or utter dependence.[98]

It is also worth observing that the fact of the absolute dependence of the entire created, contingent order upon God does not necessarily provide a foundation either for a philosophical determinism or for a theological predestinarianism that understands the divine decree as the principle from which an entire system can be deduced.   Without a doubt, the assumption of the absolute dependence of all things upon God will be bound, doctrinally, to a strong concept of the divine decree in provi- dence and predestination.   But it is equally clear that such an assump- tion, when bound to concepts of providential concurrence, the ordained freedom of secondary causes, and the moral freedom and responsibility of human beings, does not lead in the direction of a thoroughgoing deter- minism and does not lead to the discussion of divine determination as an underlying factor in all topics of theological discussion.   Since, more- over, the actual topics of theological system are understood as arising from revelation and not from reason, the synthetic arrangement of those topics does not and cannot indicate their logical deduction from a single central doctrine.   The contrary opinion, that dependence indicates both determinism and the deductive character of theological system, is the fundamental error in Schweizer's conception of Reformed theology.[99]

None of these older essays, therefore, provide an adequate analysis of the actual *principia* of orthodox Reformed theology.   Not only do all in some way or other assume that predestination is the real *principium theologiae* but they also fail to do justice to the actual contents and implications of the Reformed prolegomena.   In the present essay, both the topics and their organization follow the Reformed prolegomena closely, with the intention of presenting all of the issues addressed by the orthodox and the implications of those issues for the orthodox theolog- ical system.

2.5 Reformed Orthodoxy and Rationalism

The rise of Protestant scholasticism and the beginnings of modern philosophical rationalism belong to the same period in history. This coincidence of inception and early development has led scholars to raise the question of the relationship of orthodoxy and rationalism. The question is of broad significance for the history of Western thought inasmuch as the breakdown of Christendom and of the objective churchly standard of authority did open the way for rationalism (or "freethinking" as it has sometimes been called). In addition, the dominance of rationalism in the eighteenth century was historically possible only because of the decline of late orthodox scholasticism, which had polemically opposed both Cartesian, deductive rationalism and the Baconian inductive rationalism at the heart of early modern science.

A particularly subtle thesis concerning the relationship of the Reformation to rationalism was put forth in the middle of the nineteenth century by Armand Saintes. Against the arguments of a generation of German rationalists, who had found the roots of their insistence on reason as the ultimate criterion for religious truth in the theology of the Reformation, Saintes argued the essentially antirationalistic and supernaturalistic stance of the earliest Reformers. Nonetheless, he felt that the historical development of Protestantism in Germany proved "that Rationalism is the inevitable consequence of the establishment of the Reformation" and that "the pursuit and development of the principles which [the Reformation] laid down" were in fact "the preparation, the birth and the progress of . . . Rationalism."[100]

The Reformation, by setting aside the authority of church and tradition and by setting in their place the authority of Scripture and its own confessions, established an essentially arbitrary support of faith which "could not prevent the explanations and contradictions of the human mind" from running their skeptical course and demolishing the scriptural foundation itself.[101] Scholastic Protestantism, according to Saintes, only furthered the cause of rationalism by developing to the point of absurdity a detailed theological system resting, not on sound exegesis, but on polemical assertions concerning the supposedly infallible words of the text of Scripture.[102] Pietism saw the religiously arid character of Protestant scholasticism and endeavored, too late, to rescue the Reformation from the toils of theological system. Yet even pietism, in its assumption that confessions of the church were not absolutely necessary, exercised "the liberty inherent in Protestantism" to the detriment of the biblical standard. Some churchly confession is needed, after all, to identify the meaning of Scripture.[103]

The dogmatic rationalism of the succeeding era in Germany, with its positive acceptance of Christian doctrine as coherent with the rational truths of philosophy, only served to subvert further the doctrinal standards of Protestantism. The new power accorded to reason in matters of religion could all too easily be turned against Scripture itself by the comparison of the text with the findings of science.[104] Indeed, in the absence of genuine institutional norms, the theologians of the eighteenth century could appear to follow the Reformers' own directive to interpret Scripture literally while instead interpreting the text according to rationalistic criteria used in the interpretation of secular texts.[105] The Reformation, therefore, though itself not a rationalistic movement, by its dissolution of churchly, corporate and objective norms in theology opened the door to the rule of the individual rational subject in the determination of truth.

A virtually identical explanation of the historical transition from the age of the Reformation to the era of rationalism, albeit connected with a highly favorable assessment of rationalism, is found in the works of Lecky and Robertson. Both writers view the Reformation as a movement away from antiquated churchly norms toward individualism and secularism that led in some instances toward a "religious semi-rationalism" and in others toward the rise of a standard of rational doubt before it disintegrated into an irrational bibliolatry.[106] Robertson adds to this basic thesis the argument that the development of post-Reformation Protestantism with its "chaos of dispute and dogmatic tinkering" only served to further the demise of the Reformation as a movement and to bring on the rise of rationalism or "freethought."[107]

A related view of the relationship of Protestantism and rationalism was put forth by Hurst, who endeavored to free the Reformation from Saintes' charge of subjectivism while nevertheless placing the blame for the rise of rationalism at the door of scholastic orthodoxy. It was the scholastics whose "dogmatism, with its endless distinctions" cast Protestantism into the intellectual and religious abyss. Rationalism appeared as a new kind of salvation from "idle display of learning . . . imaginary distinctions . . . [and] labored sermons."[108] Rationalism, then, according to Hurst, did not spring from the Reformation's attack on church and tradition but rather from the problematic of Protestant orthodoxy.

These earlier histories of rationalism agree in their placement of the origins of modern rationalism in the gap left by the decline of churchly and biblical authority after the Reformation and the era of orthodoxy. They also agree in their assessment of the Reformation and of orthodoxy as basically fideistic and antirationalistic. In this second assumption, both Saintes and Hurst stand against the position of more recent scholarly investigators of the problem of the Reformation, orthodoxy and rationalism, namely, Weber and Bizer. Weber, whose studies are foundational for Bizer's, argues that theological rationalism had its beginnings in orthodoxy itself. He views the Hoffmann controversy of the late sixteenth and early seventeenth centuries as a convenient point of departure for the examination of the problem. In that debate the "irrationalism" of the proponents of "existential subjectivism" held forth unsuccessfully against the "rationalists" who argued a unity of truth in philosophy and theology and offered, as an alternative to irrationalism and subjectivism, a "rational apologetics" and a "philosophical objectivism."[109]

According to Weber, the expression of this unity of truth becomes most evident in the doctrine of creation: the theological discussions of the causality of the world and of human life are paralleled constructively by philosophical discussions of physics and ethics.[110] Beginning with Melanchthon, who argued traces of divine creative power in creation, the orthodox gradually ceased to view natural knowledge of God as a threat to revealed knowledge and—especially among the Reformed—a relationship came to be argued between natural and revealed theology according to which natural theology occupied the place of Law over against the gospel of revelation. The subsequent history of orthodoxy, according to Weber, is a chronicle of the gradual intrusion of rational argumentation, by way of logical demonstration based on the scriptural principle itself, into the realm of revelation—and the consequent, gradual drawing of the topics of revealed theology into the bounds of natural reason.[111]

The major problem encountered by orthodoxy, therefore, was the establishment of boundaries for reason. Obviously reason was a necessary part of theological discourse and argument insofar as all discourse and argument, all critical examination of issues, is a rational endeavor. But, as the "irrationalists"—like Flacius and Hoffmann—had seen, the use of rational norms could only lead to the ultimate subjection of theological knowledge drawn from Scripture to the "ideal of rational knowledge."[112] This subjection of theological to rational knowing Weber identifies in the tendency of orthodox theologians to point to an inner necessity in their doctrinal arguments, as indicated by the continual use of *oportet* and *necesse est* in argument. The Reformed, in particular, fall into this rationalistic trap through their use of the doctrine of predestination as the underlying category of logical necessity in all theology.[113] This rationalizing tendency, argues Weber, is the problem of all Protestant orthodox dogmatics—to the end that, in the declaration of doctrine, human rationality ultimately becomes the principle according to which the will of God is explained.[114]

Weber's thesis concerning Protestant orthodoxy and rationalism, and the related idea of Reformed orthodoxy as a predestinarian system, have been used more recently by Ernst Bizer in two essays describing problems in the developmnet of orthodox and scholastic Protestantism. His short monograph, *Frühorthodoxie und Rationalismus*,[115] endeavors to document a rationalizing process within early Protestant orthodoxy during the second half of the sixteenth century, and a substantial essay, "Die reformierte Orthodoxie und der Cartesianisimus,"[116] presents the consequences for Reformed theology in the Netherlands of the extended and bitter debate between the orthodox and the Cartesians in the latter half of the seventeenth century. The first of these essays presents Beza's *Tabula praedestinationis* as the basis for an entire system of theology formed in terms of the logical necessity of the divine decrees. Assuming the predestinarian underpinnings of Reformed theology, Bizer moves on to discuss—with obvious reliance on Weber's thesis—the language of logical necessity in Ursinus' treatment of Christ's satisfaction for sin. The final section of Bizer's essay argues the effects of the predestination-based perception of logical necessity in the use of a rationalistic perspective drawn from Aristotelian physics in Daneau's treatise on the creation.[117]

Apart from the problematic nature of the central dogma thesis, there is a major methodological flaw underlying the entire argument presented in Weber's and Bizer's studies of orthodoxy and rationalism. There is no essential relationship between the dogmatic declaration of necessity under the divine decree and the logical declaration of propriety (*oportet*) or necessity (*necesse est*). On the one hand, Reformed predestinarianism ought not to be confused with metaphysical determinism, inasmuch as the Reformed insist on contingent events and free exercise of the will under the decree—and inasmuch as logical argumentation belongs equally to predestinarian and nonpredestinarian topics. Furthermore, the use of logical argumentation within categories determined by revelation is quite different both procedurally and philosophically from the use of the categories of any particular philosophical worldview as the basis for understanding an issue in Christian theology.[118] There is, therefore, no genuine connection between Ursinus' use of logical argumentation and Daneau's references to Aristotelian physics in his treatise on creation.

As Dillenberger has pointed out in *Protestant Thought and Natural Science*, with specific reference to Daneau, the antagonism between orthodox theology and the new science was the product of an increased reliance by the orthodox upon the Bible as a source of propositional knowledge and upon the seeming divergence between a biblical system of knowledge and the ever growing mass of data produced by the new science.[119] Nor does the orthodox Protestant use of Aristotelian physics represent a change of worldview on their part. Indeed, Daneau's treatise, used by Bizer to argue a tendency toward rationalism, appears in its true context as a theological rejection of the rationalistic perspectives of the new science in favor of the older viewpoint, shared by the Refomers and the orthdox, according to which revelation provided the norm for understanding a Christianized version of the Aristotelian-Ptolemaic description of the universe.

Beyond these specific historical considerations, it is also the case that neither Weber nor Bizer distinguish—as did virtually all of the theologians of the sixteenth and seventeenth centuries—between reason considered subjectively as a spiritual capacity of human beings and reason considered objectively as a form of natural or philosophical knowledge.[120] Similarly, neither Weber nor Bizer distinguishes carefully between the rationalizing tendency that is an integral if sometimes unfortunate part of the creation of theological system and the rationalist philosophy of the seventeenth century that identified human reason as the prior and primary norm of all contructive intellectual endeavor. What the earlier historians—Saintes, Lecky, Robertson, and Hurst—saw, without considering in any depth the impact of a systematizing and rationalizing process on the contents of Protestant theology, was the fundamental opposition both of the Reformers and of their scholastic successors to the principial use of reason and the unmodified appropriation of philosophical system in dogmatic theology.

Some distinction needs to be made, therefore, between the rationalizing tendency in theology brought about in the transition from earlier exegetical and discursive models to fully developed scholastic system and the incorporation of rationalist philosophy into Protestant theological system. The former is characteristic of Protestant scholasticism, while the latter occurred only in the eighteenth century following the demise of Protestant orthodoxy and the Aristotelian-Ptolemaic worldview it presupposed.[121] It is, moreover, an inadequate explanation of this transition from orthodoxy to rationalism to view it as a mere passage from the intellectualism of the seventeenth century to the rationalism of the eighteenth century. Orthodoxy and supernaturalism, after all, carried over into the eighteenth century as a conservative theology, somewhat out of step with the philosophical climate of the day but increasingly aware of and interested in the results of critical scholarship, in the systems of writers like De Moor, Doederlein and Morus;[122] and rationalism has a history of its own in the seventeenth century prior to its theological use by the followers of Wolff in the eighteenth century.

Bizer attempts to advance somewhat beyond this obviously problematic position by defining "rationalism" as a system assuming both the standard of scriptural revelation and the standard of rational proof to the end that faith rests upon demonstrable evidence and rational necessity—rather than following the philosophical definition of rationalism as a system accepting reason as the sole norm and source of truth.[123] There are immediately a series of problems with this perspective. In the first place, it leaves us with two distinct phenomena, differently defined, bearing the same name, and existing at the same time. If not an outright denial of the principle of noncontradiction, such a pattern of definition is nonetheless unproductive. In the second place, this redefinition of rationalism is hardly an advance on Tholuck's notion of an "intellectualism" in theology historically prior but not at all conducive to the philosophical rationalism of the seventeenth-century Cartesian or eighteenth-century Wolffian theologians. Third, and finally, the definition itself, much like Tholuck's, does not do justice to the sophisticated approach to the problem of revelation and reason found in the systems of the late sixteenth- and seventeenth-century orthodox.[124]

The rationalization and intellectualization of theology into system characteristic of the orthodox or scholastic phase of Protestantism never set the standards of scriptural revelation and rational proof on an equal par and certainly never viewed either evidential demonstration or rational necessity as the grounds of faith.[125] Quite the contrary, the Protestant orthodox disavow evidentialism and identify theological certainty as something quite distinct from mathematical and rational or philosophical certainty.[126] They also argue quite pointedly that reason has an instrumental function within the bounds of faith and not a magisterial function. Reason never proves faith, but only elaborates faith toward understanding.[127]

In pressing a firm distinction between the methodological rationalizing process integral to the production of a scholastic theology and the acceptance of rationalist philosophical principles, we must also

stress the genuine and positive relationship between Protestant scholasticism and the Christian Aristotelianism of earlier centuries.[128]   This
relationship, as manifest in the Protestant scholastic use of medieval
paradigms for the discussion of the genus and object of theology and, to
a lesser or at least less explicit extent, for the establishment of a
theological epistemology in which faith and reason both had a place, in
fact provided a barrier to the use of seventeenth-century rationalist
philosophy in Protestant orthodox system.[129]   In other words, Protestant
scholasticism was no more conducive to a truly rationalistic philosophy
than were the Augustinian, Thomist and Scotist theologies of the later
Middle Ages.   In the words of one historian of philosophy,

> Scholasticism itself had been the result of a yearning for
> rational insight, of a desire to understand and to find reasons
> for what it believed. . . . the goal of its search was fixed
> by faith: philosophy served as its handmaiden. . . . They did
> not study the world as we study it, they did not pursue truth
> in the independent manner of the Greeks, but that was because
> they were so firmly convinced of the absolute truth of their
> premises, the doctrines of the faith. These were their facts,
> with these they whetted their intellects, these they sought to
> weld into a system.[130]

Although these sentences were written as a description of medieval
scholasticism, they apply with little modification to the systematizing
efforts of the Protestant scholastics, particularly in terms of the
relation of faith and reason, worldview and independent investigation.

Even though the philosophical perspective of most of the Protestant
orthodox was basically the modified Christian Aristotelianism that had
dominated Western theology since the thirteenth century, the orthodox did
not view their theology as bound to any particular philosophical system.
Any use of philosophical concepts by Protestant scholastics involved the
rejection of views noticeably at variance with Christian doctrine.[131]
Just as their medieval predecessors had disavowed the Aristotelian
notions of the eternity of the world and the destructability of the soul,
so did the Protestant scholastics refuse these particular tenets and any
other rational deductions at odds with revealed doctrine—such as the
curious cosmology of Descartes or the occasionalism of Geulincx.   This
generalization extends even to the Cocceian theologians Heidanus,
Burmann, and Wittich who were most influenced by the Cartesian views of
truth and substance.[132]

Bizer's other essay, "Die reformierte Orthodoxie und der Cartesianismus," registers the antagonism between high orthodoxy and the few
Cartesian theologians who had risen within the Reformed ranks.   This
essay, written before *Frühorthodoxie und Rationalismus*, does not yet
propose the new definition of rationalism found in the later essay and

remains within the bounds of the earlier model provided by Tholuck in which rationalism is identified as the Cartesian perspective on reason as sole standard for truth and orthodoxy is viewed as an "intellectualism" manifesting a certain affinity with the rationalist view of truth.[133] Here Bizer carefully documents the disputes between Reformed orthodox and Cartesians in the late seventeenth century, noting Melchior Leydekker's distinctions between the truths of revelation and the ancillary truths of reason and between the self-evident principles of nature and the conclusions drawn from them by reason. In the latter distinction, the rational conclusions are subject to error and therefore stand below revelation in the order of certainty.[134]   What Bizer does not acknowledge is that, despite some superficial similarities between a ratiocinating theology like Leydekker's and rationalism, Leydekker's view falls into the medieval pattern for the relation of faith and reason adopted by Reformed orthodoxy, whereas the rationalist assumption of the priority or at least the equivalency of reason with faith cannot be accommodated either to the Reformed or the medieval perspective.

In short, the phenomenon of Protestant scholastic theology occupies a position somewhere between the extremes of the intellectual spectrum indicated by the opposing views of earlier scholarship: it is neither an irrational fideism nor an incipient rationalism. Rather, it represents a continuation, now in Protestant theological garb, of the traditional quest of scholastic theology and Christian Aristotelianism, to state in terms both theologically acceptable and philosophically adequate the relationship between revelation and reason as forms of divinely given truth. The Protestant attempt to argue the ancillary status of reason ought no more to be called rationalism than the medieval attempt, nor ought it to be dismissed as a form of fideism out of touch with the exigencies of philosophical argument.

Once the opposition between the rationalist view of reason as the norm of truth and the Protestant orthodox view of reason as subordinate to revelation is highlighted as the basis of dispute between the Dutch Reformed and the Cartesians, the element of validity in the older view of the origins of rationalism found in the histories of Saintes, Lecky, Robertson, and Hurst becomes apparent. The highly intellectualized and rationalized structure of Protestant orthodoxy, sound and convincing in the context of an Aristotelian-Ptolemaic worldview, made little sense in the face of the alliance of rationalism with modern science. Saintes, Lecky, Robertson, and Hurst do orthodoxy a historical injustice by assuming absolutely the irrelevance and uselessness of its arguments: Protestant scholasticism only became intellectually problematic with the passing of the worldview to which it was bound as much by historical necessity as by choice.   When that worldview failed, the orthodox theological system also seemed to fail and rationalism, allied to the new science, appeared as a viable alternative particularly in the writings of those rationalist philosophers who were not hostile toward theology.

Indeed, to find the point of contact between Reformed orthodoxy and rationalism, we need to search behind the rationalizing of system within the boundaries of faith and behind the creation of rationalist philosophical system, for a common basis in the intellectual development of the West in the sixteenth and seventeenth centuries.   There is in fact such a common basis of formative significance for both orthodoxy and rationalism: the profound concern of the age for right method.   Orthodoxy itself arose in the context of thinkers like Hyperius, Ramus, Trelcatius and Alsted pressing the issue of proper *methodus* or the proper "way through" the topics or *loci* of theology.[135]   On the side of rational philosophy not only the deductive Descartes in the *Discourse on Method* but also the inductive Bacon in his *Novum organon* bear witness to the new emphasis on right approach to thought.   It is incorrect to separate orthodoxy and rationalism after the fashion of Saintes, Hurst, Lecky, and Robertson, since the interest in method provided impetus to both--but it is equally incorrect to view orthodoxy as a form of rationalism, as do Weber and Bizer, inasmuch as its view of method did not allow reason the status of *principium cognoscendi*.

In addition, it must be noted that high orthodoxy, particularly in the last two decades of the seventeenth century, experienced the strain upon system caused by the demise of the Aristotelian-Ptolemaic worldview, and, in a few cases, tolerated Cartesians when their philosophy seemed not to undercut theological orthodoxy.   This is clearly the case with Daniel Chouet and the Genevan theologians, Tronchin and Turretin.[136]   The transition from the era of orthodoxy to the era of rationalism, then, was not a sudden event but rather appears as the gradual decline of orthodox system brought on not only by the loss of its underlying worldview but also by its own realization that a new philosophical perspective was needed.[137]   As orthodoxy faded, rationalism gathered strength and, in the eighteenth century, provided a new philosophical perspective that, even in alliance with theology, proved inimical to the task of creating a biblical orthodoxy for Protestantism.[138]

During this decline, theology moved from high orthodoxy through a transitional phase characterized by philosophical eclectecism and indifference to polemical concerns, and ultimately took on, particularly in Germany, a rationalistic form bereft of its scriptural standard.[139]

This transition is particularly evident in the movement of Genevan theology from the strict orthodoxy of Francis Turretin, to the already somewhat rationalizing thought of his orthodox and pietistic nephew and successor Benedict Pictet, to the eclectic and indifferentist theology of the younger Turretin, Jean Alphonse, and his friend and associate Jean Osterwald. Pictet will admit the proofs of God's existence as necessary to theological system,[140] and within a few decades Wolffians like Wyttenbach would argue the necessity of a natural theology grounded in the proofs to any system of revealed theology.[141]

Genuinely orthodox theology in the Reformed and Protestant scholastic tradition was seldom produced after 1720. Nonetheless, as with all such movements, the intellectual model represented by scholastic orthodoxy did not entirely pass away: just as Thomistic theology was written, defensively, after the rise of the Scotist and nominalist critiques and on into the era of the Counter-Reformation, so also was Protestant orthodox theology developed at length by a few remaining thinkers during the Age of Reason. Some, like Johann Friedrich Stapfer and Johann Christoph Beck, attempted to retain the form and the content of orthodoxy by adopting the seemingly helpful and theologically positive philosophy of Christian Wolff while others, like the massively erudite Bernhard de Moor, held to the older orthodoxy still more closely, modeling their theology on the seventeenth-century systems, refusing the advances of the new philosophy, and essentially reproducing the theology of the seventeenth century in great detail without positive recourse to contemporary opinion. The demise of orthodoxy was not so much an obliteration of the form but rather a passing of dominance and a failure to contribute to the ongoing movement and development of theological and philosophical thought.

Part **2**

The Reformed Orthodox Theological Prolegomena

3

The Meaning
of the Terms
Theology and *Religion*

Early orthodox theological systems, written between 1590 and 1620, almost invariably begin with lengthy and detailed discussions of the meaning of the term "theology," of the several kinds of theology, of the possibility of writing true theology, and of the basic presuppositions of that theology. This practice stands in strong contrast with the systematic works of the Reformers and in lesser contrast with the patterns of later Protestant scholastic system. In the era of the Reformation and of early orthodoxy, Calvin, Bullinger, Musculus, Ursinus, Olevianus, Beza, and even Zanchi began their systematic works by simply introducing the first doctrine to be treated—whether knowledge of God, Scripture, or the nature of God. There was no attempt to define the discipline of theology itself. Heppe's *Reformed Dogmatics*, by introducing theology with the topics of natural and revealed knowledge of God, overlooks this development and presents from the outset a somewhat distorted presentation of Reformed system.[1]

The early orthodox flowering is well represented in the systems of Polanus, Scharpius, Walaeus, Alsted, and Gomarus, all of whom elaborate at length on the term *theologia* and its meaning. Scharpius, for example, sets forth in scholastic fashion the basic pattern of his analysis and the subdivisions of his *locus de theologia*. First, he notes, the term must be defined; then the question must be raised and answered as to whether or not such a thing exists—for if there is no theology or if the term does not describe a valid subject for discussion, then the system becomes impossible from the start. Thus the first question following the definition is *An sit?* ("Whether it exists?"); the next question is *Quotuplex?* ("What are its parts?"); and then finally, with a view toward establishing presuppositions and principles, *Quid sit ipsa theologia?"* ("What is this theology?" or "How should theology be considered?").[2] Polanus also raises the question of basic definition and then points toward the division of the subject and a closer definition of *theologia nostra*, our theology.[3]

After 1620 and continuing on to the end of the century, a simpler model was frequently employed. Thus Ames and Maccovius begin, not with the etymological discussion of *theologia* or with the typology of all the kinds of theology found in the systems of Polanus, Scharpius and others, but with theology as known by Christians in this life, "our theology" or *theologia nostra*, and, rather briefly and simply outline a discussion of the topic:

> Theology is considered according to the mode of propounding it (*modus proponendi*), its causes or grounds (*causae sive principia*), its object, and its parts or divisions.[4]

The following discussion observes the more detailed arrangement of the early orthodox by outlining the etymological definition (3.1), the division of theology, generally defined, into true and false theology (3.2), archetypal and ectypal theology, together with the several categories of ectypal theology (ch. 4), before discussing the causes of *theologia nostra* (4.4), the object and genus of theology (ch. 6), its method (ch. 8) and, finally, the *principia* of the discipline (ch. 9).

3.1 The Etymology and Meaning of Theology[5]

For the sake of establishing from the outset an accurate method of exposition, it is necessary to present the meaning and implication of terms. So argues Turretin in the first sentences of his *locus de theologia* with a maxim drawn from "the Philosopher": *verba sunt rerum typoi* ("words are the forms or patterns of things"). Examination of the word *theologia* must precede discussion of the thing.[6] Polanus, similarly, begins his *Syntagma* with the comment that both Aristotle and Clement of Alexandria spoke of right definition as the beginning of knowledge: theological system therefore begins with a discussion of "the word or name theology" (*voce seu nomine Theologia*) before proceeding to the thing or subject matter dealt with. The word *theologia* is of Greek origin, taken over into Latin, and then borrowed or adopted by the fathers of the church from gentile writers. Thus, notes Polanus, Lactantius refers in

his *De ira Dei* to those who know and worship God rightly as *theologi* and
to their knowledge as *theologia*. Early on, moreover, Christians referred
to the apostle John as *Theologus*, "the Theologian," in titles added to
the Apocalypse.[7] Alsted adds to this the fact that church fathers, like
Nazianzus, were called *Theologus* because they wrote about and defended
the doctrine of the Trinity.[8]

The fact that the term *theologia* itself is not a biblical but an
ancient pagan term caused the Protestant scholastics some brief anxiety.
After all, the Reformation was, if nothing else, a profoundly biblical
movement, zealous to avoid anything in religion that could not be
justified from Scripture and careful, particularly in its first several
decades, to formulate its theology upon the text of Scripture and to
avoid the use of classical as well as medieval sources. The classic use
of the term *theologia* by Aristotle and Cicero was not easily assimilated
by Protestant system either on the basis of the ancient inscription to
John as *Theologus* or on the basis of the usage of the fathers of the
church.[9] Some further, preferably biblical, justification was
desirable.[10]

Turretin resolves the problem by making a distinction between the
term *theologia* and its significance:

> The simple terms from which it is composed do occur there, as
> for example, *logos tou theou* and *logia tou theou*, Rom. 3:2; I
> Pet. 4:10; Hebrews 5:12. Thus it is one thing to be in Scrip-
> ture according to sound (*quoad sonum*) and syllables, or
> formally and in the abstract; and another to be in Scripture
> according to meaning (*quoad sensum*) and according to the thing
> signified (*rem significatam*), or materially and in the con-
> crete; "theology" does not appear in Scripture in the former
> way, but in the latter.[11]

Theologia, then, indicates heavenly doctrine (*doctrina coelestis*) and
has, in addition to the scriptural references to *logia tou theou*, words
of God, a series of scriptural synonyms: "wisdom in a mystery" (1 Cor.
2:7), "the form of sound words" (2 Tim. 1:13), "knowledge of truth
according to piety" (Titus 1:1), and "doctrine" (Titus 1:9). Again, the
thing signified by the term is discussed throughout Scripture.[12]

Granting that the term *theologia* can have a legitimate Christian
usage, the Reformed orthodox move on to a more careful etymological
discussion:

> "Theology," derived from the term *theologos* designates prop-
> erly, on the basis of its etymon and its usage by the Greeks,
> not the Word of God (*sermonem Dei*) which is *theou logos*, but
> the word concerning God (*sermonem de Deo*), *peri theou logon*.[13]

The word *theologia*, therefore, has come to mean a word that deals with
God (*sermo qui de Deo agit*) just as *astrologia* means a word concerning

the stars (*sermo de astris*) and not a word of the stars.[14] Scharpius
echoes these arguments and adds that *logos* can be understood internally
as *ratio* or reason subsisting in the mind, or externally as *oratio*,
speech uttered forth. The latter sense is implied in the term *theologia*:
theology is a word about God based upon the utterance or revelation of
God.[15] As is the case with much of the material of this *locus*, these
etymological arguments parallel closely the language of the medieval
scholastics.[16]

Turretin, echoing the remarks of Alsted some sixty years earlier,
argues that this rather rigid separation of *theou logos*, *sermo Dei* from
logos peri tou theou, *sermo de Deo*—word of God from word about God—
results in an inadequate view of theology:

> The term *theologia* used adequately among Christians . . .
> indicates both the word of God and the word about God, which
> two are conjoined, since we cannot speak of God apart from God.
> Thus it may be observed of doctrine that originally (*original-
> iter*) it is from God, objectively (*objective*) deals with God,
> terminatively (*terminative*) looks toward God and leads to God,
> as Thomas Aquinas not at all badly (!) explains, Theology is
> taught by God, teaches of God and leads to God (*Theologia a Deo
> docetur, Deum docet, et ad Deum ducit*). Thus the twofold
> ground of theology (*duplex Theologiae principium*) is embraced
> by this usage: the one, the ground of being (*essendi*), which is
> God; the other the ground of knowing (*cognoscendi*), which is
> his Word.[17]

Although because of the polemical context, Turretin is unwilling to admit
the fact, he has clearly profited from a reading of Aquinas. This
broader etymology, incorporating both the language of "Word of God" and
the language of "word concerning God," provides a firmer basis for the
system and its first principles. Alsted notes, resting on the notion
that *theologia* indicates the divine self-knowledge or Word of God himself, that it is entirely proper both theologically and etymologically to
argue that all who rightly understand "divine things" can be called
"theologians": thus, God, Christ, angels, and Christians—whether the
blessed in heaven or the pilgrims on earth—can justly be called theologians.[18] Specifically, this definition allows the distinction between
an archetypal divine and an ectypal Christic, angelic and human "theology," while also indicating the connection between these theologies. In
addition it points from the etymology of the term directly toward the
statement of the *principia* or grounds of the system, God and his Word.

This type of preliminary definition and discussion also appears in
English systems of the seventeenth century, although the English express
a decided preference for the term "divinity" over the word "theology"—as
is witnessed in the titles of systems by Downham, Ussher, Leigh, and
Watson. This term indicates the knowledge or science concerning "divine"

things, the *scientia rerum divinarum*. "Divinity," writes Leigh, "is the true wisdom of divine things, divinely revealed to us to live well and blessedly, or, for our eternal Salvation. *Logica est ars bene differendi, Rhetorica ars bene loquendi, Theologia ars bene vivendi*." This Divinity is

> such an art as teacheth a man by knowledge of God's will and assistance of his power to live to his glory. The best rules that the Ethicks, Politicks, Oeconomicks have, are fetched out of Divinity. There is no true knowledge of Christ, but that which is practical, since everything is then truly known, when it is known in the manner that it is propounded to be known. But Christ is not propounded to us to be known theoretically but practically.[19]

Even so, Leigh defines theology as *sapientia* rather than as *scientia*: Scripture speaks of knowledge of God as "wisdom" and wisdom (more than science) is a term for certain knowledge (which theology is). Divinity differs, however, from other wisdom and the arts because it is known by divine revelation and has as its end first the glory of God and second the eternal salvation of man.[20]

Since the word *divinity* may be ambiguous, Leigh presents "theology" as a proper synonym but also as a term with a more precise etymology: *theo-logia* indicates a "speech about God." A theologian, therefore, is one who possesses "knowledge of divine things." Thus, the "whole doctrine of Religion is called Theology, that is, a Speech or doctrine concerning God: to signify that without true knowledge of God, there can be no true religion, or right understanding of any thing."[21] We note here a strong continuity with the concerns of Calvin in the first chapter of the *Institutes*: there is an intimate relation between true knowledge of God and true knowledge of self—and the relation is such that true knowledge of God is necessary to all other knowledge.[22] Indeed, we see here in miniature the effects of the work undertaken by the Protestant scholastics throughout the entirety of their theological system. The arguments of the Reformers are not lost but placed in a larger systematic context, in this case, the fundamental soteriological problem of true knowledge of God being set into the context of the basic definition of the discipline.

The definition itself, since it is purely etymological, and since it draws on ancient pagan as well as patristic sources, demands that further attention be directed to the question of the difference between pagan and Christian theology. Most of the orthodox systems proceed to distinguish between pagan and Christian theology and to develop a fairly detailed paradigm identifying the types and forms of both. These paradigms are retained by the high orthodox but, as is the case with many of the sets of basic definitions developed by Protestant scholastics before 1620, the discussion of the paradigm in high orthodox systems is more formalized and much briefer, with greater space and emphasis being given to more recently developed topics—like that of the fundamental *loci* in theology.

3.2 True and False Theology

The term *theology* is used in two ways: it indicates either true or false theology.

False theology (*theologia falsa*) is either of the ancient pagans or of others who err concerning divine things (*de rebus divinis*).

The theology of the ancient pagans was twofold: in part concerning the gods (*de diis*); in part concerning the demons (*de daemonibus*).

The highly refined pagan theology is threefold: mythical, physical and political.

That which treated of the demons was twofold: concerning magic (*magia*) and concerning spiritual interventions (*theurgia*).

Concerning the others who err in divine things, there is the blasphemy of the Jews, the Mohammedans, the pseudo-christians and the heretics.

True theology (*theologia vera*) is either archetypal (*archetypa*) or ectypal (*ectypa*).[23]

The paradigm itself is significant, since it represents the result of early Christian debate with and appropriation of pagan philosophy: the division of pagan religion into the categories of mythical, physical or philosophical, and political or civil comes from the treatise *Divine and Human Antiquities* by the Roman philosopher Marcus Terentius Varro (ca. 47 BC). Varro's paradigm influenced the structure of the first three books of Lactantius' *Divine Institutes* and was ultimately incorporated into a Christian paradigm for all religion by Augustine.[24] Augustine appropriated Varro's schema as a description of false theology and juxtaposed it with the true, Christian theology. Polanus' version of the model simply adds the Mohammedans and the heretics. Dogmatically the model is significant since it sets all non-Christian theology not only under the heading of *theologia falsa*, but also excludes it from participation in and reflection of the divine archetypal theology.

Since the term *theologia* can mean either *sermo Dei ipsius* (a word of God himself, i.e., an oracle or prophecy spoken by God through an instrument) or *sermo de Deo* (a word concerning God; *de divinitate ratio seu sermo*, a concept or word about divinity), the term itself does not indicate the truth or falsehood of what has been said. Polanus notes that, in the latter sense, *theologia* is a word about God just as *cosmologia* is a word about the world. This means that true and false theology must be carefully distinguished at the beginning of theological system. *Theologia falsa, est opinio falsa de Deo, voluntate & operibus eius* ("False theology is a false opinion concerning God, his will and his works").[25] The language is important here: Polanus will not designate false theology as knowledge (*scientia*) or as faith (*fides*)—it is merely opinion. Thus, unlike *scientia*, it does not rest on reason or evidence and unlike faith, it does not rest on authoritative testimony.[26] Pagan theology is "opinionative," writes Junius, "since opinion consists (if such a thing as this does 'consist') purely in our mind and imagination, mere dreams and mockeries in the place of truth."[27] Alsted virtually duplicates this point.[28]

Theologia falsa is a depraved judgment of the soul, falsehood posing as truth, vain and erratic opinion concerning divine powers (*numen*), ignorance of God, fables about divine things. Such is all gentile or pagan theology (*theologia Ethnicorum*). Polanus recognizes a distinction between theology concerned with demons and theology concerned with gods: the former deals with magic (*magia*), the appeasement of evil demons, or with theurgy (the invocation of good demons). More important, however, is the theology concerning the gods, particularly in its "carefully worked-out" (*exquisita*) form. This consists in the *fabulosa* or *theatrica theologia* of the poets and dramatists; the *physica theologia* of the philosophers (a form of natural or rational theology); and the *political seu civilis theologia*, which joined together sacred rites and reverence for government. Although Polanus recognizes that these three forms of *theologia Ethnicorum exquisita* resulted from the efforts of "wise men" and, indeed, rose above the common religion or theology (*theologia vulgaris*) of the day, he will not allow them any perception of religious truth—this despite his occasional positive use of Aristotle—but rather roots all ancient pagan theology in "error of reasoning" and "presumption of wisdom" arising out of a "corrupt nature." Such theology can only contain defective "conclusions and perceptions of God, his nature, works and worship."[29] Virtually the same view is expressed by Junius, while Alsted adds a brief comment on Romans 1:18-23 noting that there is a genuine revelation of the invisible things of God in the created order and therefore the possibility of natural theology—so that the blindness of man and the falsehood of pagan natural theology rest on human, not on divine fault.[30] Of all the writers examined in this study, only Aretius elaborates the patristic argument that the truth in pagan philosophy or natural theology can be understood as an ancient pagan borrowing from the

religion of Israel.[31]   False theology also includes, of course, all contemporary non-Christian religions, which the orthodox typically identify
as "the blasphemies of the Jews, Mohammedanism and "Pseudo-Christianity,"
the latter indicating the heresies of "the Arians, Schwenckfelders,
Anabaptists, and Papists."[32]

What then is true theology (*theologia vera*) and, indeed, what
attests to its possibility and its actual existence?   The standard
definition, introduced into Reformed orthodoxy by Junius, is *sapientia*
rerum divinarum, the wisdom concerning divine things[33] or, at somewhat
greater length,

> the knowledge (*scientia*) or wisdom (*sapientia*) concerning
> divine things, divinely revealed, for the glory of God and the
> salvation of rational creatures.[34]

The same basic definition is used by Polanus who follows Junius closely
throughout this *locus*.[35]   Junius uses the term *sapientia* since
"absolutely all the properties pertaining to intellect, knowledge and the
needs of salvation are most excellently conjoined" in this term.[36]   The
influence of Junius' argument and definition was enormous—particularly
in the Netherlands.

William Perkins' exhaustive treatment of the *ordo salutis*, A *Golden*
Chaine, although technically not a system of theology, contains a concise
definition of Christian or "true" theology in its first chapter:

> The Bodie of Scripture is a doctrine sufficient to live well.
> It comprehendeth many holy sciences, whereof one is principall,
> others are hand-maids or retainers.   The principall science is
> *Theologie*.   *Theologie* is the science of living blessedly
> forever. Blessed life ariseth from the knowledge of God. Ioh.
> 17.3.   *This is life eternal, that they know thee to bee the*
> *only very God, and a Sonne thou hast sent, Christ Jesus.* Isa.
> 53:11.   *By his knowledge shall my righteous servant (viz.*
> *Christ) justifie many.* And therefore it ariseth likewise from
> the knowledge of ourselves, because we know God by looking into
> ourselves.[37]

Perkins' definition of true theology as "the science of living blessedly
forever," drawn from Peter Ramus, is echoed in William Ames' highly
influential *Medulla s. s. theologiae* (*The Marrow of Sacred Divinitie*),
where theology is defined as the "doctrine of living to God."[38]   This
practical emphasis carries over into the works of the continental
scholastics, particularly the Dutch, on whom Perkins' and Ames' influence
was the strongest.   Thus Maccovius: "Theology is a discipline, in part
theoretical, in part practical, teaching the way of living well and
blessedly in eternity."[39] Similarly, van Mastricht:

> This theoretical-practical Christian theology is nothing other
> than the doctrine of living to God through Christ (*doctrina*
> *vivendi Deo per Christum*); or, the doctrine that follows the
> way of piety (*doctrina, quae est secundum pietatem*).[40]

By "theology," therefore, Mastricht does not mean theology generally or abstractly considered (*theologia nude considerata*), but specifically Christian theology: that theology which has been revealed of God principally by the Son who was in the bosom of the Father and which is conveyed in the Scriptures. This excludes a nonscriptural natural theology. In other words, Christian and revealed theology does not utterly exclude natural theology but rather includes it as a greater number includes a lesser. What is excluded is the false natural theology of the "Gentiles." The same argument obtains concerning the use of philosophy and ethics in theology. Only Christian and revealed theology can truly be called theology. "What arises from nature and reason, that is corrupt, half-blind, obscure; it cannot occupy for us the place of a theology that is sufficient for salvation."[41]

Once the definition of the term has been established, the Protestant scholastics recognize that they must also provide a reason for moving from the definition to the thing itself. Definition alone is insufficient; the thing itself, *theologia*, must be shown to exist. Just as Turretin accepted the Aristolelian dictum "words are the forms of things," he and the other Protestant scholastics recognize as correct the Aristolelian assumption that the reality is not the idea or universal known to the mind but the universal in the thing. The establishment of *theologia* as an existent thing, moreover, represents the establishment both of true and of false theology—or more precisely, of the existence of the phenomenon claiming to be *sapientia rerum divinarum* and of the possibility of attaining to a true theology, that is, a genuine wisdom of divine things. The presence of this problematic within the argument leads the Protestant scholastics to state their case in a somewhat circular manner, the prolegomena both laying ground for the system that follows and drawing upon the theological assumptions and conclusions present in that system. Theological prolegomena cannot be entirely *vordogmatisch* or predogmatic: they stand in dialogue with the system and, in fact, are a system in miniature, stated at the level of presupposition.

The orthodox recognize, therefore, that they must provide some ground not only for discussing theology but also for arguing, in the context of their own theological systems, the temporal possibility and actuality of a true theology. Having defined the term, they proceed to discuss the existence of the thing:

> That theology and its object (*Res ipsae*) exist, is taught by the consensus of all mankind: the Object—since God exists and is the *principium* of all that is good in the realm of Nature and since God speaks and acts as God; the Consensus—since all people thus acknowledge this to be so according to the light of nature.[42]

Scharpius similarly argues that all mankind consents to the existence of God outwardly in prayer and worship, taking the name *theologia* for its beliefs and superstitions.   In addition, all men consent inwardly in their consciences that God exists and that there is some knowledge of him.   Scharpius recognizes, however, that these arguments leave him with no grounds for positing *theologia vera*.   He adds, therefore, two further arguments: the church has always testified to the existence of theology and, more importantly, the nature of God as the highest good (*summum bonum*) necessarily leads God to communicate himself to his creatures—the *logos* of God is necessarily *oratio enunciativa*, spoken or enunciated word.[43]

Even more pointedly than Scharpius, Polanus seeks out both testimonies and rational arguments for the existence of *theologia vera*.   The arguments, although neatly syllogistic, are circular in the sense that they rest on belief in the existence of God and in the authority of Scripture—both of these being topics not yet considered, given the order of his system.   In the first place, Scripture contains divine testimony to the existence of theology: Job 12:13 states that "with God is wisdom (*sapientia*) and strength, with him is counsel (*consilium*) and understanding (*intelligentia*)," and similar testimony is found in Romans 11:33 and Deuteronomy 4:6 (i.e., to *sapientia* and *intelligentia* in God and his commands).   In the second place, there is human testimony, both general and special—general testimony in the universal consent of mankind in its philosophical, historical, poetic, and oracular writings; special testimony in the witness of the *Ecclesia Dei*, the church of God.[44]

Polanus' rational arguments draw on points made in Junius' definition and on arguments like those stated by Scharpius.   They are, however, stated more formally and logically:

> 1.   If God exists, it is necessary that theology exist: the antecedent is true, therefore also the consequence.   A related proof: if God is wise (*sapiens*), it is necessary that there be theology: but if God is, he is wise.   Therefore if God exists, it is necessary that theology exist.
> 2.   If God is the source (*principium*) of all that is good in nature, it is necessary that there be theology.   The former is so, therefore also the latter.
> 3.   If God speaks not only of singular things (*res singulares*), but truly of universals pertaining to the right knowledge of himself; then it is necessary that there be theology. That which precedes is true: therefore also that which follows.
> 4.   If God is active, as God, toward all creatures, imprinting on some things obscure vestiges of his majesty, on others a clear image; then it is necessary that there be theology.   The former is so, therefore the latter.[45]

At the very least these "proofs" provide a formal synopsis of the argument for the existence of theology and, as is frequently said of Anselm's so-called ontological argument for the existence of God, they stand as exercises of faith going in search of understanding even if they fall short of being proofs.

Considered as presuppositional statements, the proofs simply declare that God exists, that for God to be God he must be wise, that God is the source of all created good, that God speaks concerning himself in a revelatory manner, and that God in the acts of creation and providence leaves evidence of himself in his handiwork. Such truths are, and must be, the basis for the construction of a body of doctrine concerning God—and, granting these truths, a body of doctrine will be forthcoming. One of these presuppositions—"God speaks not only of singular things, but truly of universals pertaining to the right knowledge of himself"—demands further explanation. This point reflects the barriers to systematic knowing—to wisdom—set in the path of theology by nominalism. If knowledge is merely the perception of particulars, no relationships can exist and no overarching cohesion of ideas can be expressed. For there to be theology, revelation must be a revelation of true concepts, of universals, capable of providing a framework for knowledge. Here, as in the other "proofs," Polanus does not so much prove a point as set aside an objection at a presuppositional level.

The mid-seventeenth-century theologian, Edward Leigh, neatly summarizes these preliminaries. He begins his system by stating that

> In the Preface or Introduction to Divinity, six things are to be considered, 1. That there is Divinity. 2. What Divinity is. 3. How it is to be taught. 4. How it may be learnt. 5. Its opposites. 6. The Excellency of Divine Knowledge.[46]

In the first place, it is clear that there is "divinity" which is simply "a Revelation of God's will made to men" from the "natural light of Conscience, in which . . . many footsteps of heavenly Knowledge and the divine Will are imprinted." The existence of divinity is also clear "from the supernatural light of Grace" and "from the nature of God himself, who being the chiefest good and most Diffusive of himself (*sui diffusium*), must needs communicate the Knowledge of himself to reasonable creatures for their Salvation." It is further manifest by "the end of Creation" which is the glorification of God by his creatures both in this life and in the life to come. And finally the "common experience" of all nations testifying to a sense of God's revelation and will also proves divinity to be possible.[47]

In the high orthodox period, Turretin even more overtly draws on the conclusions of subsequent system: he adds an argument based on the goal or end of creation (*finis creationis*) and another resting on the necessity of salvation (*salutis necessitas*). In the first place, God draws

all creatures to himself that they might know and praise him—theology is
necessary to this end.   In the second place, since man is ordained to a
supernatural end (*ad finem supernaturalem*), there must necessarily be a
supernatural means (*medium supernaturale*) that will lead him toward this
end.   This means can be nothing other than faith, which in turn indicates
knowledge of God, namely, theology.[48] As in Polanus, these arguments or
proofs are not so much logical demonstrations as statements based on
theological presuppositions.   We ought not to suppose that writers so
well trained in the arts of logic and rhetoric failed to recognize this
fact.   Rather, than proofs in the strict sense, these arguments are
intended to show an inner logic of system: they represent a rationalization and formalization of ideas, not philosophical rationalism.

These definitions of true or Christian theology raise in turn a
series of issues that the orthodox deal with as separate topics: the
relation of Scripture to theology, the relation of theology to piety or
religion, and the character of theology as both a theoretical and
practical discipline—whether it is a *scientia* or not.[49]   Another way of
making the same point in a manner that does more justice to the architectonic cohesiveness of the Protestant scholastic systems is to note that
the basic definitions of true and false theology have been constructed in
such a way as to set the presuppositional tone of the whole *locus*,
indeed, of the whole system, and to show the interrelationship between
basic presuppositions and the topics of Christian theology about to be
set forth.   This architectonic cohesion, moreover, particularly in view
of the way it arises out of a collation and exegesis of a whole tradition
(biblical, philosophical, patristic, medieval and Protestant), makes
clear that the development of orthodoxy—of Protestant "right teaching"—
is neither the rise of a theological rationalism nor the creation of
monistic system built around central dogmas, but the realization of an
institutionalizing and catholicizing tendency implicit in the quest for
ecclesiastical establishment.

3.3 Religion and Its Relation to Theology

In one of his more pointed historical excurses into the theological
development of post-Reformation Protestantism, Karl Barth notes the
presence of a separate discussion of "religion" in the theological
prolegomena of several late seventeeth- and early eighteenth-century
orthodox systems. He rightly associates the development of these separate discussions with the rise of pietism, both Reformed and Lutheran,

but incorrectly assumes that the discussion itself is something new to the orthodox of the late seventeenth century and that it represents the intrusion of a generalized conception of "religion" as a human phenomenon into a system which had previously spoken only of "theology" as a revelation of God.[50] In the first place, the orthodox considered theology both objectively as divine gift and subjectively as *habitus mentis* (mental disposition),[51] so that the human, subjective aspect of theology was never excluded from consideration. In the second place, the discussion of religion and of Christianity as true religion, paralleling the orthodox discussion of *theologia falsa* and *theologia vera*, has a long history in Protestantism, reaching back to the Reformers themselves.

Indeed, although Zwingli, Calvin, and Bullinger neither defined nor discussed the term *theologia*, the concept of *religio* was of primary importance to them. The issue at stake here is not the late nineteenth- and early twentieth-century problem of religion as human phenomenon but rather the problem of the right worship of God as raised by the preaching of Reform—or, in other words, the proper establishment of the subjective side of the human expression of relation to God. We encounter, therefore, among the Reformers and the orthodox an interest in the etymology and basic meaning of the word *religio* as piety or, in the typical orthodox definition, the right way of knowing and honoring God (*recta Deum cognoscendi et colendi ratio*).

In practice, we find only a shade of difference between the idea of theology as a wisdom concerning divine things and the idea of religion as the right knowledge and worship of God set forth under the guidance of the *sapientia rerum divinarum*. Thus we see the titles of any number of "instructions" (*institutiones*) in Christian faith and of a large number of confessional documents utilizing the term *religio* rather than either *fides* or *theologia*. In fact, custom tended to dictate that *theologia* be paired with the term *loci communes* and, in the seventeenth century, with *systema*, while *religio* almost invariably was paired with *institutio* and, frequently, in the sixteenth century, with *compendium* and *confessio*. The implication is that the more basic instruction in doctrine is in *religio* while the more detailed and technical instruction is in *theologia*.[52]

The systematic consideration of *religio* was an integral part of the early Reformed systems, appearing as the natural result of inquiry into the doctrines concerning God and his Word. This is the way in which it appears in the writings of Zwingli, Bullinger, Calvin, and Viret. Religion is either true or false, scriptural or idolatrous, the product of revelation or the result of vain imaginings and, although religiosity is viewed as an aspect of all human life—because of the universal *sensus* or *semen divinitatis*—Christianity is viewed not as a human phenomenon but as a product of divine Word. This model is apparent as early as Zwingli's *De vera et falsa religione commentarius* (1525) and it provides the pattern, not only for subsequent discussion of religion in the orthodox systems, but also for the discussion of *theologia vera* and *theologia falsa*. The pagan and the heretical are placed together as false and are viewed as arising from the corruption of human nature, while true religion is the product of grace and revelation and is identified with Christianity.[53]

This systematic approach to religion as the pattern of knowledge and worship directly related to faith and foundational to the elaboration of theology is profoundly evident in the successive editions of Calvin's *Institutes*. In 1536 Calvin identified his work as an "institute" or instruction "of the Christian religion embracing almost the whole sum of piety and whatever it is necessary to know in the doctrine of salvation."[54] What is more, Calvin's expansion of the *Institutes*, in which five chapters on the knowledge of God were added or developed as a kind of prologue, only serves to underscore in those introductory sections the primary emphasis on *religion*, piety and instruction in them.

A pattern similar to that of the *Institutes* is found in Mathieu Virel's *Dialogue de la religion chrestienne* (1582). Virel's work is divided into three books, the first of which deals with the problem of knowledge of God, of man, and of Christ, followed by a chapter on the faith by which Christ's benefits are apprehended. The contents of the volume—essentially the topics of a theological system or an extended catechetical exercise—demonstrate the profound relationship between true theology and right religion in the minds of sixteenth- and seventeenth-century Reformed writers. "Religion," writes Virel, is derived from a word meaning "to bind":

> And it is a spiritual bond, by which men in a certain holy reconciliation are made one with God, and are kept in love and fear, that at length they may be partakers of his heavenly glory, and of the blessed life. Which no religion can do, but that which is Christian, that is to say: that which hath its foundation in Christ.[55]

This can be seen since it is only through faith in Christ that we can be reconciled to God. The proof of this truth we have "out of the word of God, which is most certain, and upon the truth whereof resteth all Christian doctrine."[56]

We have already noted that *religio* tended to be the term used with reference to basic instruction and *theologia* the term used with reference to fully developed theological system. As Protestantism entered the era

of orthodoxy and the emphasis of theological or religious study began to
fall on the full development of system, discussion of *religio* ceased to
be a preliminary concern in theological discussion and, rather than discuss religion, the systems begin to deal with the definition of *theologia*
as the proper prologue to systems of theology.   Nonetheless, *religio*,
defined in terms of the knowledge and worship of God, remained a concern
of theology, a subtopic as it were in theological system.   In the Ramist
models developed by Polanus and Ames, according to which theology was
divided first into doctrines concerning faith and obedience, the former
division began with the definition of *theologia* and the latter division
contained as a part of its preliminary discussions, a definition of
religio.[57]   In other words, the discussion of religion by no means
disappeared from Protestant theology, but merely shifted position under
the influence of a different organizational model.

As the Ramist model declined in popularity and the more teleological, historical and synthetic model in which the topics of Christian life
and obedience were subsumed under discussions of covenant, Law and church
took precedence, the discussion of religion was returned to the prolegomena.   By 1660, as witnessed by the systems of Wendelin and Burmann,
the subject matter of religion is viewed, more or less, as the practically experienced content of theology and theology as the doctrinal
exposition of the subject matter of the Christian religion.   There could
be no genuine theology apart from religion and religion, rightly
conceived, leads to theological exposition.

The larger treatments of *religio* in the high orthodox devote a fair
amount of space to the etymology of the term, much as in the definition
of *theologia*.   Here, however, the etymology is far less clear—due to a
plethora of similar Latin verbs.   Most of the discussions limit the
discussion to three verbs: *relegere*, to gather together, set aside or
re-read; *relinquere*, to relinquish or leave behind; and *religare*, to bind
back or reattach.[58]   Others, like Marckius, add *relegare*, to send away or
put aside; and *reeligere*, to choose again.   The derivation from *relegere*,
indicating specifically a re-reading or reperusal of holy texts, had been
put forth in antiquity by Cicero and was favored by Zwingli and Venema.[59]
The majority of writers, however, follow the Latin fathers (particularly
Lactantius[60] and Augustine[61]) and Calvin[62] in rejecting Cicero's
etymology.   The preferred derivation, seconded by most lexica, is from
religare, to bind back or reattach.[63]

Thus, in the exercise of true religion, man is bound back or
reattached to God.   This etymology can be developed further in terms of
the relationship first broken and then repaired between God and man.

Marckius argues that the derivation from *religare* implies four elements
in religion: 1) God's gracious reconcilation of himself to man; 2) man's
response of true love for God; 3) a practice of moral self-control on
man's part resting on the curative application of salvation (*salutis
cura*); and, 4) an ever fuller submission on man's part to a sincere love
of others.[64] In addition to these basic implications of *religio*, there
is the relationship of *religo*, *religare* to *eligo*, *eligare* ("to choose or
elect"), as Augustine had argued;[65] religion, therefore, rests on the
divine choice of man. Marckius presses the point home by introducing
into his discussion the verb to re-elect (*reeligere*), indicating the
reiteration of God's love (*repetitam Dei dilectionem*) for his fallen
creatures.[66]

In Hebrew, Marckius contends, the idea of "religion" is expressed by
words for the knowledge, worship, love, fear, and invocation of God.
Foremost of all is the usage *via Dei* (cf. Jer. 55:6-9; Ezek. 18:25) which
indicates a form of life devised by God, prescribed by him, perfectly
expressed in him, pleasing to him, and leading toward him. In the Greek
of the New Testament these ideas are expressed by such terms as *eusebeia*
(godliness—1 Tim. 3:16; 2 Peter 1:3), *theosebeia* (piety—1 Tim. 2:10),
eulabeia (reverence—Luke 11:25; Heb. 12:28), *deisidaimonia* (religion—
Acts 17:12; 25:19), *latria* (worship or rites—Rom. 9:4), and *threskeia*
(religion or worship—Acts 26:5; Jas. 1:26-27).[67] Religion may therefore
be defined as *recta ratio Deum cognoscendi & colendi ad hominis pecca-
toris salutem, Deique gloriam*, ("the right way of knowing and honoring
God, for the purpose of the salvation of sinners and the glory of God").
This definition, writes Marckius, draws directly on the sequence implied
in Titus 1:1-2, for true knowledge of God leads to right worship, worship
to salvation, salvation to the glory of God, while the completion or
fullness of God's glory in salvation produces worship and worship yields
knowledge.[68] In Marckius' analysis, the idea of "religion in general,"
with the consequent view of Christianity as a species of religion, is
excluded.

Religious acts can be divided into the categories of those acts
elicited by the very nature of religion and meditation on God and those
commanded mediately by divine ordinance and which have the creature as
their object. This is seen from the two tables of the Law and from
various texts of Scripture (e.g., Titus 2:11, 12; James 1:27; I John
3:21). Or, according to an alternate classification—subjective as
opposed to the foregoing objective description—religious acts can be
viewed as internal, such as love and fear; external, such as building the
temple, sacrifice, or giving of alms; or mixed, such as prayer or hearing

the Word of God. The primary acts of religion, according to Marckius, are elicited and internal—for these are of the very nature of true religion.[69]

Religion, then, can be defined as the *recta Deum cognoscendi et colendi ratio*, "the right pattern of knowing and worshiping God"[70] or *vera religio*, true religion, as *ratio agnoscendi colendique Deum a Deo praescripta ad hominis salutem Deique gloriam* ("the pattern of knowing and worshiping God, prescribed by God for the salvation of man and the glory of God").[71] A somewhat expanded definition of *vera religio* appears in Polanus' *Syntagma*: *vera religio* is *pietas* and consists in acts of worship that are either internal only or both internal and external. Thus, internally *vera religio* consists in "saving faith, true knowledge of God, faithfulness to God, hope in God, love toward God, faithful fear of God, humility before God and patience." When religion is considered in terms of the effect of this inward life on the outward man—*interni simul et externi*, at once internal and external—*vera religio* consists also in "religious and zealous prayer to God for the glory of God" and in "confession of the truth [of the faith] and worship of God in the communion of the faithful."[72]

On the basis of these definitions, we must differ with the view expressed by Barth that the orthodox *locus de religione* harbored the seeds of a "secret catastrophe" that would take place in the eighteenth century. There is not even a seed here of an attempt to place Christianity among the natural phenomena of the world's religions.[73] Burmann's slight modification of the definition in no way shifts emphasis or meaning. Instead of defining "true religion" as "knowledge and worship of God," he defines "religion" as "true knowlege and worship"—the effect of his slight change in language, if any, is to place what Polanus, Wendelin and other scholastics defined as "false religion" entirely outside the category of genuine religion, thus restricting the phenomenon, properly so-called, to Christianity.

The import of these definitions is neatly encapsulated in Walaeus' declaration that "only in the Christian religion are the true and divine marks (*notae*) of religion contained."[74] Walaeus, much to the discomfiture of Barth, argues first that these *notae* are rationally known and then that Christianity alone, in its biblical revelation, satisfies the criteria of true religion.[75] Scripture, therefore, is necessary to true religion. Walaeus enumerates three *notae*: "true knowledge of the true God" (*vera veri Dei notitia*); "a true means of the reconciliation of man with God" (*vera ratio reconciliationis hominis cum Deo*); and "true worship of God" (*verus Dei cultus*). "Nature itself," continues Walaeus,

"teaches that these marks are required in true religion." That Christianity alone contains these marks can be seen by comparison with Judaism
and with Islam: the former represents a partial revelation, the latter
consecrates barbarities and immoralities as religion. Thus the Christian
revelation—both Testaments—is necessary to true religion.[76]

Although Walaeus quite clearly would use reason to prove the super-
iority of Christian revelation and probably fails either to satisfy the
requirements of sceptical reason or to please the heart of piety, he does
not at all broach the question of the partial validity of natural
religion or of the use of natural reason in constructing or deducing a
partially valid religion. We do not have here, then, as Barth argues,
"an unambiguous hint at a general concept of religion which is known by
virture of the voice of conscience or of nature,"[77] nor do we have any
attempt to place Christianity, as a religion, among the religions.
Reason merely recognizes the criteria for discerning "true religion" and
then, by means of these criteria, is forced to admit that only Christianity is "true religion." The other religions do not belong equally to a
category of "general religion"—they are set apart from Christianity as
false. Walaeus' argument, although somewhat rationalistic, remains
within the bounds set by Zwingli and Calvin, and his claim that reason
recognizes certain basic elements in true religion remains within the
bounds of the standard etymology. There is no recourse, even by implication, to a general notion of natural religion on which an idea of
Christian religion can be built.

The phenomenological approach to religion and its tendency to place
Christianity and the other great world religions in the same category
must be traced historically not to those Protestant orthodox who
developed at length the locus de religione at the outset of their
systems,[78] but rather to rationalists like Leibniz and Wolff who not only
evidenced a strong interest in the ethical religions of the Orient but
who also—in direct antithesis to the views of the seventeenth-century
Protestant scholastics—viewed natural theology and natural religion as
the basis upon which valid systems should be built. Only when the
ethical religions of the natural man are recognized as in some manner
valid, indeed, only when the rationalist philosophy comes to view the
legitimate basis for expounding Christian theology as rational religion,
does the problem of religion in general arise for Protestant theology.
This assumption appears earliest among Cartesians like Salomon van Til[79]
and becomes a basic assumption of Wolffian theology.[80] The problem is
intense in the rationalist theologies of the eighteenth century and even

in some of the rational supernaturalist systems,[81] but it clearly does not relate to the Protestant scholastic pattern of definition.

The systematic consideration of "religion" by the orthodox most probably arises from the question of the relationship of religion to theology. Religion, as Wendelin noted, is in a proximate sense the object of theology or the *subiectum de quo* ("the subject concerning which"), inasmuch as all of theology is directed toward the confession of right knowledge of God and the practice of the right worship of God.[82] This point is developed somewhat more clearly by Riissen:

> Theology treats of the knowledge and worship of the true God (*veri Dei cognitionem et cultum*) which is otherwise called Religion. Indeed, Religion is nothing other than the right pattern of knowing the true God (*recta verum Deum cognoscendi ratio*), of which the criteria are: [1] that it teaches about God only through himself, namely through his revelation; [2] that it transmits the true means, recognized as such in all good conscience, by which the sinner is reconciled to God; [3] and finally that it explains, by means of the same revelation, a reasonable worship (*cultum rationalem*), worthy of God.[83]

The statement that religion is the basic subject matter of theology does not, therefore, stand in any tension with the typical orthodox declaration that God and his works are the proper object of theology.[84]. *Theologia* is, as its etymology demonstrates, a word or a teaching; *religio*, also as defined by its etymology, is not a teaching about something but an observance or a practice devoted to something. Both have the same ultimate object, God, but *religio*, even though virtually all the definitions insist that it is knowledge (*cognitio*) as well as worship (*cultus*), does not express itself theoretically so much as practically. In fact, it is the *praxis* of which theology, through right delineation and definition of its object, guides and fosters. This relationship of *theologia* and *religio* is expressed by the orthodox under the discussions of theology as theoretical and practical[85] and in the fundamental articles of theology.[86]

This relationship of religion to theology, together with the parallel distinctions made by the orthodox between *theologia vera* and *theologia falsa*, *religio vera* and *religio falsa*, provides a basis for understanding the relationship between *religio naturalis* and *religio revelata*. Heppe, whose discussion of *religio naturalis* and *religio revelata* was well known to Barth and may have been the initial point of departure for Barth's discussion, mistakenly argues that these two forms of religion "are so related to one another, that the latter is the confirmation of the former (since it absorbs it into itself)."[87] The Protestant scholastics, on the contrary, take such a negative view of natural religion that the only point of continuity between it and revealed religion is the simple, unelaborated confession of the existence of the divine: natural religion, like *theologia falsa*, only serves the argument against atheism by manifesting the universal consent of mankind. Apart from that one point of confirmation by revelation, natural religion stands contradicted and negated by true or revealed religion.[88]

Thus Burmann can say, first, that *religio* so flows from the nature of man and the nature of God that it is the necessary result of "natural reason" and may rightly be termed, in this universal form, *religio naturalis* and second, that this *religio naturalis* is insufficient for salvation since it leads only to idolatry and superstition.[89]   Natural religion knows *that* God exists, but it does not know *what it means* for God to exist and to be the God of sinners.[90]   This paradoxical character of *religio naturalis* makes it capable only of leaving man "without excuse" in his corruption.   Reason teaches the existence of a God who demands worship but, writes Venema,

> in [man's] fallen condition, he cannot deduce without error, even those truths which reason teaches. The fault does not lie in reason's not embracing these truths, but in men's inability, in consequence of the corruption induced by the fall, to use reason as they ought. . . . In the second place, he cannot use his reason aright, because he cannot deduce from it truths for the satisfaction and peace of his own mind.[91]

The disjunction of natural and revealed religion is intensified by the fact that even if man

> could use his reason aright, it would still be insufficient, because it cannot point out to him the way of salvation.   It plainly declares, indeed, that he is a transgressor and that he has forefeited the divine favor,--that God, who is just and holy, cannot, without a full exhibition and vindication of these attributes, re-admit the sinner into his fellowship. But it breathes not a whisper as to the way in which this manifestation may be made, and how, in consistency with these attributes, a reconcilation can be effected between the parties at variance.[92]

Here, then, even in a Reformed system in the eighteenth century, written after rationalism had made distinct inroads into Protestant theology, the orthodox or scholastic model continues to insist that natural reason and natural religion provide no beginning point for salvation and no foundation on which revealed religion can build.   There is no confusion of nature and grace, nature and supernature.   The model for discussion of the problem remains virtually where Calvin and Viret left it--in the concept of a twofold knowledge of God or *duplex cognitio Dei*.[93]   Only in the genuinely rationalist systems is this model set aside--and only in the late eighteenth-century rational supernaturalist systems and their apologetic stance over against rationalism does the problem become an integral part of Reformed or Lutheran systems.   These developments are, in any case, quite distinct from the historical and doctrinal phenomenon designated as Protestant orthodoxy.

4

The Parts or Divisions
of Theology

The theology of the Reformers, even when it attained relatively full systematic expression, as in Melanchthon's *Loci communes*, Calvin's *Institutes*, Bullinger's *Decades*, or Musculus' *Loci communes*, was not a self-conscious intellectual or academic discipline. Whereas all of the writers just mentioned devoted some attention to the issue of the human knowledge of God and to the issue of scriptural revelation, none of them saw fit to discuss the character of theology as an intellectual discipline set in the context of a finite world and accommodated to the forms of human knowing. The same situation obtains in the systematic works of the generation immediately following: Beza, Ursinus, Zanchi, and Olevianus all omit discussion of the discipline. This approach to theology could only be maintained while the Reformation was still in a large sense a protest movement with theological roots and some academic training in medieval models. Once Protestantism had been established as an institutional church with its own confessional orthodoxy and had recognized the need to teach theology in academies and universities, the situation changed and the task of teaching demanded some approach to definition of the discipline, not just in terms of etymologies but also in terms of the problem and the manner of knowing God.

In the decade following 1590 a distinction between *theologia archetypa*, God's knowledge of himself and his works, and *theologia ectypa*, creaturely knowledge of God and works, entered the systematic conceptuality of early Reformed orthodoxy. Althaus correctly points to Franciscus Junius' *De theologia vera* (1594) as the first work to employ this distinction and to make a threefold division in the *theologia ectypa*: the *theologia unionis*, *visionis*, and *viatorum*.   In early orthodox theology, particularly in the works of Junius and Polanus, these categories are all discussed at some length—despite the fact that only the *theologia viatorum* is accessible to man.

This terminology, although it appears somewhat curious to the twentieth-century mind, is in fact the avenue chosen by early Reformed orthodoxy to clarify both the definition of the church's theological task and the nature of the discipline of theology itself.   The terminology echoes traditional distinctions between the pilgrim believer (*viator*) and the blessed (*beati*) in heaven, between the church militant and the church triumphant, and between the light of grace (*lumen gratiae*) given to believers in this life and the light of glory (*lumen gloriae*) given in the life hereafter.   This terminology, in its distinction between a divine archetype and a variety of temporal ectypes, also allows theology to identify both the relationship and the disjunction between God's knowledge of himself and man's knowledge of him.

Althaus argues that these formulations mark the entrance of Thomistic epistemology into the Reformed system.[1]   Two considerations, however, weigh against this argument.   In the first place, Thomist epistemology was present in Reformed thought from the time of Vermigli and Zanchi, not to mention the admiration of a Genevan like Daneau for Aquinas' thought.   Secondly, the distinction beteen God's knowledge of himself and creaturely knowledge of him was such a commonplace in fourteenth- and fifteenth-century scholasticism that its subsequent adaptation by the orthodox does not necessarily point to a Thomistic understanding of the nature of theological epistemology.   The Reformed use of this distinction seems to draw more heavily on the Scotist distinction between *theologia in se* and *theologia nostra* and, like its Scotist predecessor, to hark back to the even more fundamental distinction between *potentia Dei absoluta* and *potentia Dei ordinata*.   Indeed, the presence of what Congar has termed "the constant intervention of disjunctions between the order *in se* and the order of fact" is the hallmark of the Scotist critique of Thomism.[2]

Although Junius was probably the first Protestant theologian to state these distinctions explicitly and positively for use in Reformed dogmatics, the underlying problem addressed by the distinctions belonged the theology of the Reformation from its very beginnings.   One of the elements of late medieval Scotist and nominalist theology that had a profound impact on Luther was its denial of any analogy between God and man and its consequent recognition of the impossibility of formulating a rational metaphysic concerning God. All knowledge of God must rest on authoritative testimony, primarily on that of Scripture. Luther not only denied any recourse of theology to an *analogia entis* between God and man and insisted on the necessity of scriptural revelation, but also argued, in the light of his denial of human merit and his sense of the immediacy of Christ as revealer and savior, against any rational *theologia gloriae* that claimed to describe God as he is in himself and proposed that our earthly theology be a *theologia crucis*, conformed to the pattern of God's revelation in Christ.[3]   Calvin, similarly, allows a glorious revelation of God in creation that ought to be understood by reason—but argues that human beings are so corrupted by sin that apart from salvation in Christ and the saving form of revelation given in Scripture, knowledge of God remains inaccessible to them.[4]   Calvin also distinguishes between the eternal Word and Wisdom of God and the revealing Word given forth in the words of the prophets,[5] the latter being accommodated to human ways of knowing.

After Junius' use of the distinction, it passes into the doctrinal system in the works of such theologians as Polanus, Scharpius, Walaeus, and Heidanus. In these systems a definite limit is set upon human inquiry into the Godhead and a principle of accommodation is utilized to explain the relationship between the true theology known to man and the divine self-knowledge. Thus, the distinction is adapted to an insight present from the very beginning in Reformed theology—that the finite (and sinful) mind of man is incapable of grasping the fullness of divine truth. A similar epistemology characterizes the other Reformed systems of the period, although many—Perkins, Ames, Hommius, Trelcatius, Downham—do not utilize these scholastic terms. The theology of Lutheran orthodoxy, similarly, developed massive and carefully enunciated prolegomena. Beginning with the great *Loci theologici* of Johann Gerhard (1610), the classification of theology provided by Junius carries over into the Lutheran scholastic systems, paralleling the development of the Reformed. We find here, moreover, a substantial agreement concerning the forms of theology and their relationships, the sole exception being the content and extent of the theology of Christ, the so-called *theologia unionis*, where christological concerns raised a major point of debate between the Reformed and the Lutherans.

This means that although the early orthodox discussion of the nature of theology was not highly original either in its terminology or in its content it was, formally, a radical departure from the patterns of sixteenth-century theology and an equally radical return to the scholastic mold of earlier centuries. The change seems to have been accomplished

suddenly, over the space of a decade or so. In the last quarter of the
sixteenth century we see only the beginnings of the use of such distinctions in systematic theological works, while in the first quarter of the
seventeenth century their use seems to be taken for granted. Protestant
school-theology had come of age and the complex, technical vocabulary of
scholasticism had become legitimate in Protestant circles. The work of
adapting the old system to new insights had begun in earnest. Change is
less apparent in the doctrines of the Trinity, the Person of Christ, and
predestination, where the technical vocabulary of essence, nature,
person, subsistence, and cause had been in use throughout the sixteenth
century. In the doctrines of theology and of faith, however, the use of
such terms as *theologia archeypa*, *theologia ectypa*, *habitus*, *actus*, and
so forth marks a new point of departure--as does the technical analysis
of system itself and of the phenomenon of faith that are represented by
these *loci*.

There is one significant difference between the Scotist use of
distinctions between *theologia in se aut divina* and *theologia nostra* and
the Reformed orthodox use of the distinction between *theologia archetypa*
and the types of theology classed under the term *theologia ectypa*.
Scotus develops these distinctions because of new insight into the
epistemological problems involved in writing theology. Although the
soteriological necessity of revelation is not lost to him, his emphasis
falls squarely on the problem of knowledge. The Reformed orthodox
clearly shift ground. The basic epistemological problem remains and the
sense of a drastic limitation of human knowledge concerning God is
everywhere apparent in their prolegomena. But in the work of theologians
like Polanus and Scharpius a new dimension receives emphasis. The
epistemological problem develops both out of the relation of revelation
and reason, theology and philosophy, and out of the soteriological issue:
man *post lapsum* needs revelation not only because of his limited natural
capabilities but because of spiritual blindness caused by sin. The
Scotist epistemological distinctions are now conditioned by Reformed
anthropology.

4.1 Archetypal and Ectypal Theology

The Reformed orthodox generally agree concerning the importance of
distinguishing between archetypal and ectypal theology. Their agreement
is particularly strong in the identification of true human theology as an
ectype or reflection resting on but not commensurate with the divine

self-knowledge.   Disagreements, however, are expressed by the same theologians over the use of the term *archetypal theology*.   Perhaps the clearest and fullest summary of the entire paradigm is found in Polanus' *Syntagma*:

> True theology is either archetypal or ectypal.
>
> Ectypal theology (*theologia ectypa*) is considered either in itself (*in se*) or as it is in rational creatures (*in creaturis rationalibus*).
>
> The ends or goals (*fines*) of the theology communicated to rational creatures are two: the primary and highest is the glorification of God as the highest good (*glorificatio Dei tanquam summi boni*); the secondary and subordinate is the blessedness of rational creatures (*beatitudo creaturarum rationalium*).
>
> The parts of blessedness are two: (1) freedom from all evils and possession of all true goods that rational creatures can possess in God; (2) the vision of God (*visio Dei*), conformity to God, sufficiency in God and a certain knowledge of his eternal felicity.
>
> The vison of God is either obscure or clear.
>
> Ectypal theology considered as it is in rational creatures is either of Christ as he is head of the Church according to his humanity or of the members of Christ's body (*membrorum Christi*).
>
> This latter theology is either of the blessed (*beatorum*) or of earthly pilgrims (*viatorum*).
>
> The theology of the blessed (*theologia beatorum*) is either of angels or of men.
>
> The theology of pilgrims (*theologia viatorum*) has a two-fold pattern: for it is considered either absolutely (*absolute*) or relatively (*secundum quid*).
>
> The theology of pilgrims absolutely so-called and considered according to its nature, is essentially one, eternal and immutable; considered according to its adjuncts it is either old (*vetus*) or new (*nova*).
>
> Theology of pilgrims or our theology (*theologia viatorum seu nostra*) considered relatively or as it exists in individual pilgrims through the activity of efficient causes is partly infused (*infusa*) and partly acquired (*acquisita*).[6]

Quite in contrast to this fairly typical early orthodox interest in developing at length a definition of *theologia archetypa* and of each of the forms of *theologia ectypa*, several of the early orthodox writers—for example, Trelcatius and Gomarus—and most of the high orthodox take the paradigm for granted and, with a sense of impatience, sift through the forms and meanings of theology to set aside quickly those not applicable in order to focus upon our theology, *theologia nostra*.   Thus Turretin:

> The use of the term theology is either equivocal and inappropriate (*abusivus*) when it is applied to the false theology of pagans and heretics; or less than truly appropriate (*minus proprius*) when it is declared of the original and infinite Wisdom, which, apart from us, is known by God in himself according to an ineffable and most perfect mode of knowing; the term, indeed, cannot do justice to the dignity of the thing; or of the theology of Christ (*theologia Christi*) or of the theology of angels (*theologia Angelorum*); or proper (*proprius*),

when it is applied to the theology of sojourning men (*theologia hominum viatorum*), which is distinguished into natural and supernatural theology, as discussed below.[7]

Intellectually and theologically these distinctions and the debate over their use spring directly out of the preceding discussion of the meaning of the term theology and the problem of true and false theology. Etymologically the term *theo-logia* could indicate either the Word of God or words about God—and, if the latter are true, they must rest upon the former.   Thus true *theologia de Deo*, theology concerning God, somehow reflects and is grounded upon the knowledge that God has of himself.   As Alsted comments, true theology, both archetypal and ectypal, is "the indubitable knowledge of divine things."[8]   The basic question to be answered in this segment of the prolegomena concerns the nature of the relationship between the divine archetype and the temporal ectype: is the relationship such that we can ascend by analogy from what is known here to a clear vision of God—the *analogia entis*—or is the relationship such that we cannot conceive for ourselves a perfect theology?[9]   The answer, of course, reflects a series of epistemological, anthropological and soteriological concerns to be developed at length in the subsequent system.   The Reformed orthodox debate echoes the debate over the Scotist distinction between the infinite and perfect *theologia in se* and the various forms of finite theology typical of the fourteenth and fifteenth centuries.   On the one hand, this debate moved toward a clearer statement of the paradigm according to which the various categories of finite theology, classified according to their mode of communication, could be grouped together under the divine archetype, while on the other hand, epistemological concerns somewhat different from those of Scotus brought about modification of the terms and their use.

True theology, both archetypal and ectypal, can be identified as knowledge that stands beyond doubt (*cognitio indubitata*) over against the depraved opinion (*opinio depravata*) of false theology.[10]   The orthodox recognize, then, the necessity of arguing a set of criteria for and a paradigm of true theology, beginning with the divine archetype that must underlie all truth about God and continuing through the several orders of rational creatures capable of knowing God.   Athough theology is diverse or "multiplex" considered according to its modes of communication and the "subjects" or knowers in which it is found, true theology is one according to substance, whether it is found in God himself or in his creatures.[11]   This substantially singular theology, as known infinitely and absolutely by the divine subject, God, is archetypal; as known finitely and relatively by the creaturely subject, ectypal.[12]   There are,

Alsted notes, three causes or grounds for the identification of this *theologia vera*: first, that it arises from the source that is truth itself (*qui ipsissima est veritas*); second, that those who study it receive or achieve truth in their statements; and third, that it is internally harmonious, inasmuch as the mutual agreement and consent of all parts of a given body of ideas with one another's is an index of truth.[13]

Alsted concludes from his discussion of the nature of truth that the truth is one and that there cannot ultimately be more than one truth, that is, no truth can exist in ultimate contradiction with another truth. This conclusion, in turn, points toward the unity of theology and analogically toward the division or distinction of its forms: the divine archetype is theology in the truest sense while all ectypal forms are identifiable as *theologia vera* secondarily because of their "similitude to the archetype." Thus, "theology is and is said to be in intelligent creatures as an image, the archetype of which is in God."[14] "Theology is in God formally and eminently" (*formaliter et eminenter*) as his "essential wisdom." It is not a discursive knowing but a simple intelligence to which all others can be related only by analogy.[15]

The archetype, as Turretin noted,[16] is not in any sense equivalent to our theology: the human mind cannot know the archetype, as such, and the term "theology" cannot be predicated univocally of our theology and of the divine archetype. Nonetheless, as the early orthodox dogmaticians point out, the fact of the divine archetype is crucial to the existence of true yet finite human theology: "Archetypal theology is the divine Wisdom concerning divine things: this we truly adore, but we do not inquire into it."[17] This, adds Junius, is not a definition but rather a description by analogy with things known to us, by the application of our terms to divine things. Wisdom (*sapientia*) is predicated univocally only of God inasmuch as God alone is truly wise—and therefore is predicated equivocally of human beings. Therefore, when predicated of God, wisdom does not indicate a *genus* of wise things of which God is one. The divine *sapientia* is a proper attribute of God: it is divine wisdom in the sense of being identical with the divine essence in its utter simplicity and its freedom from all composition. The *theologia archetypa*, then, is God himself, the identity of self and self-knowledge in the absolutely and essentially wise God.[18]

Polanus thus remarks that the division of theology into the categories of archetypal and ectypal is by analogy. Primarily and principally, *theologia* is *theologia archetypa* and only secondarily and by similitude

is it *theologia ectypa*. This must be the case since all wisdom, goodness, righteousness, power, and other creaturely qualities in rational
creatures are from God in whom they find their archetype--their *imago*.[19]
That there is theology in God appears from the fact that God has wisdom
concerning *rerum divinarum* and from the fact that all perfections "that
are in us, are also in God," but on an exalted level. Thus, "archetypal
theology is the wisdom of divine things that is resident in God, essential to him and uncreated."[20]   This might also be called *theologia
prototypa* or, as the scholastics termed it, *theologia Dei* or "exemplary
theology, to which as to an immutable, primary and primordial idea and
exemplar, all created theology is conformed as a likeness, such divine
theology we adore but do not search into."[21]   This language draws
directly upon that of Junius, with some amplification of definition.

Since, moreover, this "divine knowledge concerning divine things" is
uncreated (*increata*), identical with the form or essence of God (*formalis*), absolute, infinite, utterly simple or incomplex (*simplicissima*), and
utterly simultaneous (*tota simul*), that is, without either temporal or
logical sequence, it must also be incommunicable (*incommunicabilis*), as
indeed are all the divine attributes when defined strictly or univocally.
All that can be naturally communicated to created things of such an
ultimate wisdom are but faint images or vestiges (*imagines aut etiam
vestigia*). There is no analogical path from the divine imprint upon the
created order to a full knowledge of God.[22]   It is therefore God himself
who is the source, origin and efficient cause of what we know in this
life as true theology.[23]   The nature of this archetype and its function
as the source of all that finite creatures know about God poses a final
paradox in the Protestant scholastic discussion of the "attributes" of
archetypal theology: it is both incommunicable (*incommunicabilis*) and
communicative (*communicativa*). The identity of *theologia archetypa* with
the infinite essence of God renders it incapable of communication to
creatures. Nonetheless, God's infinite self-knowledge is transmitted to
things in the created order. In creation, all things receive the imprint
of the divine and the ability of finite creatures to apprehend revelation, to have theology, rests upon the image of God according to which
they have been created.[24]

A somewhat different approach to the problem of *theologia* is evident
in a few of the early orthodox systems. Thus, Trelcatius begins his
introductory remarks by dividing the subject into a discussion of theology and its nature and an analysis of the method he proposes to use
throughout his *institutio*. "Theology" does not indicate the pattern or
knowledge of "God himself" or "that which is in God." God is a "simple

Essence" who "by an indivisible and unchangeable act . . . knows both himself in himself and out of himself all and singular things by himself." What we know of God is his own "revelation or communication" of divine knowledge either "according to the universal nature of all men, or according to special grace and the rule of Scripture in the Church."[25]

In other words, according to Trelcatius, "theology" properly so-called is a word about God known to man. By stating the definition in this way he manifests an early point of disagreement among the framers of the Reformed prolegomena: he refuses to develop the concept of an arche-typal theology and begins with knowledge of God as given in revelation, what Junius, Polanus and Scharpius refer to as *theologia ectypa*. This position can perhaps be viewed as less speculative than that of Junius, Polanus and Scharpius insofar as it refuses to discuss or even to iden-tify a *theologia* that stands beyond human grasp. Although Trelcatius' position never became that of the majority of Reformed orthodox, it was carried forward among the Dutch by Gomarus and Walaeus, both of whom shy away from the identification of a *theologia archetypa* and discuss only revealed theology.[26] It is also echoed, among the later orthodox, by Turretin's reluctance to identify *theologia archetypa* as a "proper" usage of the term *theology*.

This disagreement arises out of the fact that the term *theologia* cannot be applied properly or univocally to both archetype and ectype. Which then is truly theology and who, to reiterate Scotus' Augustinian query, is truly the theologian? Turretin's late orthodox definitions apply the term *theologia* univocally to human theology and view the use of the term as a description of the divine self-knowledge as somewhat less than appropriate (*minus proprius*). Following Junius' argument from the divine attributes, however, some of the early orthodox—like Polanus—argue that the term is used correctly and most properly (*proprissime*) of the divine self-knowledge and only derivatively of our knowledge of God. God, therefore, is properly called "theologian" and is recognized as the first (*primus*), highest (*optimus*) and most perfect (*perfectissimus*) Theologian:

> Theology therefore most properly is that knowledge of divine things which is in the divine mind, so that God alone is called Theologian: and accordingly, God is understood to be the first, highest and most perfect theologian.
> Moreover, this [theology] is a formal wisdom (*sapientia formalis*), absolute or perfect, infinite, utterly simultaneous, incommunicable, and such that only its image or reflection (*imaginem*) can be communicated to rational creatures.
> It is formal: since it is essential (*essentialis*) and the form of God or Deity, which is the purest form (*purissima forma*). . . .

> It is most perfect: since it is not only of all things,
> but is indeed all the knowledge that it is possible for God to
> have concerning all things.[27]

Unlike Turretin's, this position delineates clearly the path of theological knowing as revelational, from God to the creature, rather than as
rational, from the creature to God.   Turretin's view, however, better
reflects the logic of predication in view of the impossibility of a
univocal use of the term *theology* in discussing the relationship between
God's self-knowledge and our knowledge of God—and, of course, neither
Junius nor Turretin intended to imply the possibility of rational ascent
to perfect knowledge of God.

This divergence of opinion arises naturally out of the terminology
itself and the problem of predication.   On the one hand, Scotus' terminology presses a distinction between the infinite, divine and ideal order
(*theologia in se*, or, in Protestant scholastic usage, *theologia archetypa*) and the finite order known to us (*theologia nostra* or *theologia in
subiecto*).   On the other hand, Scotus, the nominalists after him, and
virtually all of the formulators of Protestant theology denied the
Thomist *analogia entis* and declared that no proportion exists between the
finite and the infinite (*finiti et infiniti nulla proportio*).   Late
medieval debate, therefore, adumbrated the quandry of the Reformed
orthodox: Scotus had declared God to be the only true Theologian and
theologia in se to be the only theology properly so-called.

For Ockham, the language of Scotus raised more problems than Scotus
himself had anticipated.   Ockham agreed that God can be known *in se* only
to God himself but then, against Scotus, argued the problematic character
of the identification of God *sub propria ratione Deitatis* as the subject
of theology.[28]   Ockham's nominalism demanded that he view theological
system as a gathered body of discrete subjects each capable of being
known by means of an individual *habitus*.   As one small part of the argument leading to this conclusion, Ockham sought to define more clearly the
limits of *theologia nostra*: he argues a distinction between *theologia
nostra nobis possibili pro statu isto* ("our theology possible for us
proportionate to this present condition") and *theologia possibili per
divinam potentiam in intellectu viatoris* ("theology possible by divine
power in the mind of the pilgrim").[29]   What Ockham has constructed here
is a distinction between the ideal order and the order in fact set into
the context of the human intellect itself: *theologia in se* can now be
identified as an ideal category of *theologia nostra*, normally inaccessible to the human mind but possible under the absolute power of God.

This concept appears to be behind the Reformed orthodox perception of *theologia in se* as the ideal finite case of *theologia nostra*.

The *Annotatiunculae* of John Eck implies another answer to this problem. Eck argues a threefold meaning for *theologia*: knowledge of God in the divine mind (*in mente divina*), in itself (*in se*), and in us (*in nobis*). According to the first of these categories, comments Eck, the maxim of Augustine holds, that "God alone is a theologian, and we are truly his disciples." Much like Scotus' basic definition of *theologia in se*, Eck's definition identifies this category of the knowledge of God as a knowledge proportionate to its object—but now it is defined specifically as knowledge *in intellectu humano*. *Theologia in se*, the pattern to which our theology is subalternate is, according to Eck, the theology of the blessed who know by sight. The theology that human beings have in their pilgrim condition (*secundum statum viae*), the *theologia nostra*, is not proportionate to its object. Rather, it is limited to the knowledge our intellect is capable of accepting through belief.[30] Further redefinition of the term *theologia in se* or theology absolutely considered (*absolute dicta*) occurs among the early Reformed orthodox who use the term in a fashion similar to Eck's usage as a proximate pattern for *theologia nostra*, but identify it not as the theology of the blessed but as the perfect truth of supernatural revelation.[31]

These considerations bring us, finally, to the Reformed orthodox definition of ectypal theology:

> Ectypal theology considered either simply, as they say, or in relation to its various kinds, is the wisdom of divine things given conceptual form by God, on the basis of the archetypal image of himself through the communication of Grace for his own glory. And so, indeed, theology simply so called, is the entire Wisdom concerning divine things capable of being communicated to created things by [any] manner of communication.[32]

Ectypal theology, therefore, includes the theology of union (*theologia unionis*) known by the human mind of Jesus in and through the hypostatic union, the theology of angels (*theologia angelorum*), and the three basic forms of human theology—theology before the fall (*ante lapsum*); after the fall (*post lapsum*) but informed by grace, that is, the theology of pilgrims on earth (*theologia viatorum*); and theology of the blessed in heaven (*theologia beatorum*). The theology of pilgrims can be further divided into natural and supernatural theology. *Theologia ectypa*, in other words, is the category inclusive of all forms and subcategories of finite theology.[33] At this point, too, we can define *sapientia rerum divinarum* in its finite, creaturely application: it is a wisdom consisting both in truths to be known and believed and in things to be done or avoided, belonging, in its perfect form, to the divine image present in rational creatures and conducing to righteousness and blessedness.[34]   All ectypal theology, then, is formed on the basis of the archetype by a communication of grace from Creator to creature.[35]

The distinction between *theologia archetypa* and *theologia ectypa* is further elucidated by the orthodox according to the attributes and modes of each. Archetypal theology, in view of what we have already seen, is uncreated (*increata*), essential, possessed of a definite form (*formalis*), without components or any kind of sequence (*tota simul*), absolute, infinite, and—considered in itself—incommunicable. By way of contrast, ectypal theology is created or produced in creatures by divine communication. Rather than being essential or belonging to the essence of the knower, ectypal theology is habitual (*habitualis*)—in other words, it is a disposition of the mind of the knower and neither the mind itself nor necessarily in the mind. Ectypal theology is also discrete (*discreta*)— that is, composed of distinct parts—finite, and subject to several forms and many variations and, thus, is not absolute, infinite, or formal in the proper sense. All of these attributes point to the fact that ectypal theology is communicable: it is the reflection or image of the incommunicable *sapientia* that is in God and is possible only as a communication from God.[36]

Polanus further states that *theologia ectypa* or *theologia communicata in se* is not simply the knowledge of God that is presently communicated to rational creatures but is that knowledge which "is communicated to [rational creatures] and can be communicated to them by that means which God graciously chooses according to his will, of his inexhaustible fulness, both in this and in the next age." *Theologia communicata in subiecto*, on the other hand, is that knowledge of divine things "communicated according to the mode or capacity for comprehension of those who rightly acknowledge God and who through a profound love in their souls, will live blessedly with him in eternity."[37] Thus the *modus* of theology relates to the ability of each individual to comprehend and perceive knowledge of God as the object of a created intellect. This theology has two ends—the principal and foremost of which is the glorification of God as the highest good (*summum bonum*); the second and subordinate, the beatitude of rational creatures.[38]   There are three possible modes— union, vision and revelation—corresponding with the condition of the finite intellect to which it is communicated. As Alsted comments, ectypal theology "in the subject" is adapted to or modified by the character of the "receiving subject."[39] Thus *unio* is the mode suitable to one in perfect union with God; *visio* to one in the full presence of

God; *revelatio* to one not yet ready for the fullness of the vision of God.[40]

Polanus describes ectypal theology as *sapientia rerum divinarum, a Deo ex archetypo ipsius expressa atque informata per communicationem gratiosam ad gloriam ipsius* ("the wisdom of divine things, expressed and formulated by God from his own archetype by gracious communication, for the sake of his own glory").

> Archetypal theology is the primary idea of theology (*prima idea theologia*), from which ectypal theology is excogitated (*ideatur*), if such a word may be used, and articulated (*exprimitur*): just as the essential truth and goodness in God is the archetype and primary idea of the true and the good, from which all creatures have the idea of the good and the true. Archetypal theology is the *exemplar*: ectypal theology is the *exemplum*, which ought to agree with, correspond with, and resemble the exemplar. Thus ectypal theology is, in rational creatures, a part of the image and likeness of God according to which they were created.[41]

Thus the idea of archetypal and ectypal theology reflects the anthropological doctrine of the *imago Dei* and, by extension, must also reflect the soteriological problem of the fall and the nearly total loss of the *imago*.[42] This pattern of definition became fairly standard: some fifty years later, the English scholastic, Edward Leigh, could declare virtually as a truism that *theologia ectypa* was truly the *theologia de Deo*, the theology concerning God, and was "expressed in us by Divine Revelation after the Pattern or Ideal which is in God," that is, the *theologia archetypa*.[43] The distinction appears as well in the federalist and semi-Cartesian systems of the mid-seventeenth century,[44] and in virtually all of the high orthodox systems at the end of the century.[45]

As we will argue further in the following discussions of the several forms and modes of ectypal theology, this careful and elaborate patterning of definition, though highly dialectical and argumentative in a scholastic sense, cannot be viewed as an inroad of rationalism, nor as a substantive departure from the theology of the Reformation, and certainly not as the development of a form of theology that viewed the theological task as a simple matter or easy encapsulation of divine wisdom in theological system. It is not an inroad of rationalism: the human mind is here radically limited, separated from the infinite divine wisdom, and denied any power of ascent toward the divine apart from divine help. It is not a substantive departure from the theology of the Reformation: there is a formalization of theology but also an attempt to retain in new forms the substance of the Reformation's view of the sovereignty and transcendence of God and of the utterly necessary, gracious character of revelation. It does not view theology as a simple matter: there is recognition of limitation—both of access to the infinitude and perfection of God and of ability of the human mind to grasp divine truths in and of themselves.

4.2 The Causes and Ends of Theology

The question of the causes and ends of theology—the reasons for its existence and the goals toward which it tends—was raised by most of the Protestant orthodox but received a fuller treatment by the Lutherans. The question is significant since it provides a basis for the discussions of the object of theology, of the genus of theology as *scientia* or *sapientia*, and of the character of theology as theoretical or practical. The delineation of first, formal, material, and final causes manifests an essentially Aristotelian perspective and represents one of the ways in which the rise of a scholastic method among Protestants had an effect on the patterns, divisions and definitions within theological system. Nevertheless, we cannot count this development as a sign of radical discontinuity in viewpoint between the orthodox and the Reformers. It represents a difference in degree rather than in kind, insofar as the Reformers themselves thought of problems of cause and effect in Aristotelian terms—as, for example, in Calvin's discussion of predestination. The Reformers simply did not use the model of the fourfold causality as frequently, nor did they apply it to as many issues or problems. For the orthodox, both Reformed and Lutheran, the fourfold causality becomes a model for structuring discussion.[46]

Here, too, the Protestant orthodox were able to draw upon medieval models. Of particular importance to the medieval discussion and of significance to the rise of Reformed orthodoxy because of its availability in printed form in the sixteenth century is the discussion of the causality of theology in the *Summa* of Henry of Ghent. By arguing that theology has as its final cause the goal of human life in the *visio Dei*, Henry was able to provide a basis for answering questions concerning the utility and necessity of theology and concerning the character of theology as theoretical or practical.[47] His identification of the efficient cause or author of theology as God in Christ similarly provides the initial ground for developing answers to a series of crucial questions: the authority of theological knowledge, the identity of valid teachers and hearers of theology, and the proper mode of teaching theology. The proper mode of teaching, in turn, identifies the issue of formal

causality.[48]   The question of material causality enables Henry to move on
to the issue of the proper subject matter of the discipline.[49]

This question of causes and ends of necessity entails the examination of issues and questions belonging both to other sections of the
locus de theologia and to several of the other key loci of the theological system, namely, the doctrines of Scripture, God, grace, and the last
things.   Attention is thereby given to the interrelationship of the loci
and the way in which principles and presuppositions of theology provide a
basis for the system as a whole.   This discussion, moreover, provides the
Protestant scholastics with an opportunity for more diversity of viewpoint than in virtually any other of the topics belonging to the
prolegomena.   Although they agree in identifying God as the first
efficient cause and the glory of God as the ultimate end or final cause
of theology, a variety of views appear in the discussion of intermediate
causality.

The primary model for the discussion of causes of theology comes, as
do the models for many of the topics in the prolegomena, from Junius' De
vera theologia:

> The efficient cause of our theology we argue to be two-
> fold: one principal, the other instrumental.
> The principal and absolute efficient cause of our theology
> is God the Father in the Son by his Spirit inspiring it: so
> that he is the sole author and effecter of this highest and
> most perfect wisdom in his servants.
> The instrumental cause is this wisdom, the logos propho-
> rikos or enunciative word of God: both spiritually and corpo-
> really [i.e., the Word itself, considered essentially, and the
> same Word, considered accidentally in its human instruments,
> the prophets and the apostles].
> The material of theology is divine things: that is to say,
> God and whatever is ordained by God; namely the teachings of
> God that ought to be disseminated concerning his nature, his
> works and his law.
> The form of theology is divine truth, which is considered
> in two ways in theology: either as an entirety viewed as a
> whole, simply, in itself, or as parts considered and duly
> compared one with another.
> The end (finis) of theology is twofold: for the one is the
> highest or remote end and the other nearer (propinquus) and
> secondary or subordinate to it.
> The primary or highest end of theology is the glory of
> God. . . .
> The secondary or subordinate end of our theology is the
> present and future good of the elect. . . .[50]

A second, somewhat different, model is provided by Maccovius:

> The principles of theology (principia theologiae) follow.
> It is either an external (externum) or an internal (internum)
> principle.
> The external principle is twofold, the efficient cause
> (causa efficiens) and the goal or end (finis).

The efficient cause is either concerned with constitution (*constitutionis*) or with acquisition (*acquisitionis*).

The constitutive cause is God himself.

The cause of acquisition is either principal (*principalis*) or less than principal (*minus principalis*).

The principal cause of acquisition is either first (*prima*) or second (*secunda*).

The first is God.

The second is diligent meditation on the divine Word (*meditatio verbi divini*).

The less than principal or instrumental causes (*instrumentales causae*) are, the study of languages, most importantly Hebrew and Greek; of the arts, for example, Grammar, Logic and Rhetoric; and also Philosophy.

The end (*finis*) of theology is twofold: the ultimate end, which is the glory of God . . .; the intermediate, which is the salvation of man.

The internal principle (*principium internum*) is the Word of God (*Verbum Dei*).[51]

(We cite the entire set of partitions, but reserve discussion of those dealing solely with *principia* [the first and the last] for a subsequent section of the study.[52])

Scharpius opens his discussion of the causes of theology by placing the issue of cause into the context of the basic definitions of theology as archetypal and ectypal. Archetypal theology, the infinite and essential truth of God, stands in relation to the finite and communicated truth of revealed theology as *exemplar* to *exemplum* and, therefore, as cause to effect. In addition, the manner or mode of causality, inspiration, indicates that theology is not something innate in men but is rather an action of God, a communication of the divine will effected by the revelatory work of the Spirit in the servants of God. Thus, "the principal efficient cause [of theology] is God the Father, in the Son, by means of the Spirit."[53] The medieval parallel to this argument is worth noting: Robert Kilwardby, for example, argued that man is only the author or efficient cause of teachings that are attainable by rational argumentation—whereas theology cannot be produced by man alone, just as Scripture itself, though written down by men, was produced through the action of the Spirit upon the human authors of the text. God, therefore, is the efficient cause of theology.[54] Similar arguments are found in the theological prolegomena of Henry of Ghent.[55] (Both writers, it should be noted, tend to follow Bonaventure in identifying *sacra doctrina* and *theologia* with *sacra Scriptura*—so that we are also dealing, in these prolegomena, with the beginnings of a formal doctrine of Scripture.[56])

Maccovius similarly identifies God as the *causa efficiens theologiae* but then, in a more detailed argument than that of Scharpius, reinforces, via causality, both the epistemological conception of the necessity of revelation and the soteriological principle of *sola gratia*. God is the efficient cause of theology, not by a direct, unmediated intervention, but through the presentation of his Word to us, through the illumination of our minds and the direction of our wills toward the Word. Thus, argues Maccovius, God is the efficient cause of theology in a constitutive sense, since he is the author of the Word upon which theology effectively rests—the scriptural Word can therefore be called the internal principle of theology. "God is the efficient cause of theology, not in an unspecified way, but through the setting forth of his word. . . . Because he alone is the author of Scripture, which is the one and only internal principle of theology."[57] Gomarus simply identifes God as the source of all theology inasmuch as God is the first truth (*prima veritas*) and highest good (*summum bonum*) and inasmuch as theology has already been recognized, in the order of his theses, as the basis of salvation and human blessedness revealed to us by God.[58]

This declaration that God is the efficient cause of theology, in a constitutive sense, as the author of Scripture, does not satisfy the subjective question of the desire of individuals to engage in the task of meditating upon theological themes or of writing theological treatises. On one level, Scripture itself might be called "theology"—since it fits the definition of *theologia* as *sermone qui de Deo agit*. This was, in fact, a characterization of Scripture and theology found among the medieval scholastics.[59] On another level, however, the work of the orthodox theologian who uses Scripture to construct a theological system differs substantively from the work of the prophets and apostles as they wrote down the *theologia* of the *Verbum Dei internum*. This difference is clearly recognized by the Protestant scholastics in their distinction between *theologia nostra in se*—the perfect, though finite, revealed theology—and *theologia viatorum* considered both *post lapsum* and *in subiecto*. Scripture, then, as a revealed Word concerning God, is ectypal, indeed, *theologia nostra in se*, but it is not involved in sin as we are and the gap between its perfection and our fallenness must be bridged. For this to take place, there must be a cause of acquisition (*causa acquisitionis* or *causa efficiens acquisitionis*) that brings about our acceptance and use of this supernatural truth.

The cause of acquisition, according to Maccovius, can be identified as either a principal or less than principal cause. Since the Reformed allow no synergism in theology but view the acquisition not only of salvation itself but also of saving doctrine as a divine gift, the discussion of the principal cause of acquisition both returns us to God and to Scripture as *principia* and demands that we recognize God himself as the primary cause of acquisition: *causa acquisitionis principalis prima est Deus*.   Thus God, "as he wills, gives us to know the mysteries of his heavenly kingdom by means of his Holy Spirit."[60]   Moreover, since God is the author of theology (*autor theologiae*) questions of curiosity and of doubt are to be rejected in theology and only those questions raised in a docile manner open to instruction (*quaestiones docilitatis*) are to be allowed.   By implication both rationalistic questioning and Cartesian doubt are disavowed as causes of theology.   The secondary cause of acquisition in theology, therefore, must be an attentive meditation on the divine Word (*diligens meditatio verbi divini*), by the grace of the Holy Spirit's illumination, which recognizes that theology is a *supernaturalis disciplina* held apart from private or leisurely speculation and done always with an attitude of reverence.[61]   It is quite clear that the scholastic orthodox never viewed their words as rationalistic, arid and dry, or divorced from piety, as modern scholarship frequently claims.

Granting what has already been said about the causes of theology, the issue of instrumental causality can be considered in two ways—either in terms of the means of revelation by which God makes available to us the knowledge of divine things or in terms of the means by which we interpret his scriptural self-revelation.   Both of these patterns appear in the theology of Reformed orthdoxy.   Junius, Scharpius and the *Synopsis purioris theologiae* follow the first pattern, arguing that the instrumental cause of theology, not by necessity, but by reason of God's mercy upon us in our infirmity, is the ministry of men—that is to say, the ministry of the prophets, apostles and evangelists who were inspired by God the Father, in Christ, by the agency of the Spirit.   This ministry is preserved for us in the word (*sermones*) of the Old and New Testaments.[62]

The pattern of this instrumentality or the way in which the instrumental word is grounded in the eternal *sapientia Dei* is further described by Junius and Scharpius in terms of a series of distinctions concerning word.   These distinctions preserve in yet another form the archetypal/ectypal model of theology.   "The word of man," argues Junius, "is multiplex": there is the innate or indwelling word, called *logos emphytos* by the fathers, which is the intellect itself; then there is the implanted or ratiocinated word, the *sermo inditus* or *logos endiathetos*, which resides in the mind of creatures in accordance with their rational capacity; and, third, there is the *sermo enunciativus* or *logos prophorikos*, the word sent forth or enunciated, which is the outward communication of a word known inwardly to the intellect.   Of these distinctions two can be used analogically of God and all three aid in the discussion of the instrumentality of revealed theology.[63]

The *logos emphytos* or *sermo innatus* belongs to the very nature of its subject and is always actualized in its subject (*semper est actu in subiecto suo*): it cannot be instrumental because it is immanent and intransitive, incapable of being communicated or of passing over into another.[64] Scharpius adds, by way of clarification, that, in the case of God, the *logos emphytos* is the eternal and immutable Word, the Son of God himself.[65] Since the *logos endiathetos* is something that arises in the subject and is not actual in and of itself, it cannot be predicated of God—rather it is the word effected or brought into existence by the Spirit in the human subject. The *logos prophorikos* is a word effected or brought into existence externally or in another: this is, therefore, a suitable term for the word that flows forth from God and which "by its flowing-forth or procession from him produces his effect in those who hear."[66]

This transitive word, the *sermo prophorikos*, differs from human words in several ways. First, it differs insofar as it is sent forth by the Spirit of God and is essentially spiritual, whereas the word of man proceeds through the instrumentality of the human body. Second, the mode of communication of the divine word is spiritual, while that of the human word is corporeal. The divine word is not uttered by a human mouth but comes in the form of dreams, visions and inward inspiration, as well as audible sound.[67] These differences between divine and human utterance bring about some differences in terminology among the Reformed scholastics. Whereas Junius and Scharpius speak of the *sermo* or *logos prophorikos* itself as an instrumental cause and even speak of the Spirit, as divine instrumentality, others, like Polanus and Maccovius, prefer to reserve the language of instrumental or secondary causality for finite human agents or acts. Polanus, therefore, refers to the Word as "the proximate and immediate efficient cause" of theology and views the prophets and apostles as instruments,[68] while Maccovius contents himself with the identification of tools of study as the instrumental causes of theology.[69]

According to this second pattern, the instrumental or less than principal causes of theology are the means of access to and interpretation of the revelation, the traditional "handmaids" or *ancillae* of theology: the study of biblical languages; the arts of grammar, logic and rhetoric; and philosophy.[70] Since the issues of the use of logic and philosophy and of the study of biblical languages are discussed below,[71] we need only note here the emphasis laid upon the proper use of these instruments by the scholastics. The Protestant scholastics maintain the emphasis of the Reformers on the use of the original languages of

Scripture as essential to the theological task—indeed, the seventeenth
century was the golden age of Protestant linguistic scholarship. It was
an era of great orientalists like the Buxtorfs, Lightfoot, Hottinger, and
Walton, and of definitive textual efforts like the London Polyglott
Bible. Nearly all of the dogmaticians had a mastery of the biblical
langugues and many had taught Old or New Testament before attempting to
lecture on theological system. A similar emphasis, harking back to the
medieval "trivium," was laid on the mastery of grammar, logic and
rhetoric prior to further theological (or philosophical) study. Part of
the modern antipathy to scholastic method probably arises from a lack of
education in and appreciation of these latter skills.

These diverse approaches to the instrumental causality of theology
are not mutually exclusive: the former, which identifies the *logos
prophorikos* as instrumental cause, intends to present the instrumentality
by which the scriptural *principium* of theology, itself a form of *theologia ectypa*, is generated; the latter, which identifies linguistic and
other skills as instrumental cause, intends to outline the instrumentality by which the scriptural *principium* becomes the basis of *theologia
nostra*. Both of these views of instrumental causality identify the
materia or *causa materialis* of theology as the "things of God" or "divine
things" revealed in Scripture, and both agree that the *forma* or *causa
formalis* of theology is the truth of God and his revelation, the truth
that is the form or pattern of the *rerum divinarum*.[72]

The *causa materialis theologiae* or material cause of theology is
identical with the subject matter or object of theological discourse.[73]
In short, the *materia* of theology is identical with the efficient cause
of theology and all its effects insofar as it may be known, which is to
say, the material cause of theology is God and all things ordained of
God, according to the manner in which God has chosen to reveal them.[74]
This identification of the material cause is a fairly clear echo of Henry
of Ghent—who not only identified the *materia* of theology as the "subject
of this knowing" but added the crucial qualifier, *inquantum credibile est*
("inasmuch as it is capable of belief"), noting that there is a different
approach to divine things according to natural acquired knowledge,
glorious or visionary knowledge, and mediate knowledge *per fidem*—the
latter being the mode of theological knowing of which we are capable in
this life.[75]

The idea of a formal causality can be argued in two ways for
theology. Gomarus, for example, argues that the *forma* of theology is its
conformity to the theology of God himself (*conformitas ad theologiam
Dei*), whether in the remote sense of adumbrations of divine things known

through the natural order or in the proximate sense of the direct, ectypal reflection of the divine self-knowledge.[76] Here, too, we note the implicit reference to the several modes of communication--natural and either revelatory or visionary--but the form or causa formalis theologiae is ultimately the truth of the divine self-knowledge.[77] The other pattern, as implied in Maccovius' language of a second cause of acquisition and of instrumental causes, identifies the form of theology in a more mediate sense as the pattern given to theology by the proper mode of teaching--and again we note the earlier statement of this perspective in Henry of Ghent's Summa.[78]

The end or goal of theology, in most of the orthodox systems, is defined as twofold: theology has an ultimate or primary end (finis ultimus) in the glory of God (gloria Dei), and an intermediate or secondary end (finis intermedius) in the salvation of man. This secondary goal can also be defined as twofold, just as salvation itself has a twofold implication: either temporal salvation on the "way" to life eternal (salus viae) or eternal salvation, the blessed life in the heavenly homeland (salus Patriae). Thus, the "first fruit," the proximate goal of theology, can also be described in terms reflecting the basic definition of religion: knowledge of the truth, according to piety.[79] Owen describes this eternal, soteriological end of theology as a filling of the blessed with ineffable delight in the eternal praise of God and the Lamb, made possible by "that light of glory in which divine things [are seen] face to face."[80] These goals, of course, correspond with several forms of theology--the ultimate gloria Dei with the theologia archetypa, the finis intermedius or salus viae with theologia viatorum, and the finis intermedius or salus Patriae with the theologia beatorum.[81] Scharpius speaks of the intermediate or secondary goal of theology not as the salvation of man but as salus ecclesiae, the salvation of the church.[82]

Having similarly described the finis or telos of theology as the glory of God, who is the summum bonum, Polanus deals specifically with the highest good. (This discussion is not found in all of the prolegomena but logically is a part of the presuppositional background of theology.) Polanus remarks that in the philosophy of Aristotle the summum bonum and beatitudo are one and the same, but that theology distinguishes between these things. For the summum bonum, according to theology, is God himself inasmuch as he is the primum principium & finis ultimus omnis boni ("the first principle and ultimate end of all good"). This, says Polanus, is confirmed by Scripture (Gen. 15:1; Ps. 16:5;

33:12; 40:5; 73:25; 142:6; 144:15) and can be set forth as the following argument:

> That which is our salvation, glory, strength, shield, and, indeed, all things whatsoever are necessary to our blessedness, that is our highest good.
> God alone is our salvation, glory, strength, shield and all things whatsoever are necessary to our blessedness:
> Therefore God alone is our highest good *summum bonum nostrum*.[83]

Citing Psalm 27:1; 28:7; 62:2, 7; 3:3; 18:2, 3; 1 Corinthians 15:28 and Colossians 3:11, which testify, in the language of the previous syllogism, that God is our salvation, strength, shield, deliverer, glory, refuge, and all in all, Polanus argues that God will "himself alone, without any mediation or means be in eternity the immediate cause and author of all good and all joy for us; and the immediate object in which our joy shall be contemplated."[84]   Again, God is seen to be the *summum bonum*. Even the philosophers must recognize this truth, since "God alone is simply or utterly (*simpliciter*), perfect, absolutely sufficient, and wholly desirable (*summe desiderabilis*), having in himself "the eternal and exemplary forms" of all things.[85]   The blessedness of all rational creatures, then, is the contemplation of and communion with God the Father, Son and Spirit in eternity, consisting in the vision of God (*visio Dei*), conformity to God (*conformitas cum Deo*), sufficiency in God (*sufficientia in Deo*), a freedom from all evils and a possession of all true good.[86]

The highest good, then, is the ultimate end of theology. The concept is distinctly Augustinian, and has substantial precedent in the history of theology; in particular, it received detailed treatment at the hands of the medieval scholastics.[87]   Beyond these historical relationships, there is also the crucial theological relationship of this final causality of theology to the structure of the prolegomena and to the system as a whole. The identification of the end of theology as the vision of God points toward the practical thrust of the Reformed orthodox system. Even in the synthetically organized and nominally speculative system of Polanus, we encounter a sense of theology as soteriological praxis much like that provided by the Ramist definitions of theology as the science of living blessedly forever. The discussion of the *summum bonum* points, therefore, toward the subsequent definition of theology as both theoretical and practical,[88] and this definition, in turn, influences the tone and tendency of the entire system.

At this point, we can note a measure of continuity not only between the Protestant scholastics and the medieval tradition but also between these later Protestant theologians and the theology of the Reformation.

While it is true that, just as we find no genuine prolegomena in the theological systems of the Reformers, we do not find in their writings extended discussions of the causality of theology, it is also the case that the traditional Augustinian perspectives on the goal of Christian theology remained with the Reformers at a presuppositional level. Calvin could write, as a part of his discussion of the relationship of repentance and forgiveness, ". . .the proper object of faith is God's goodness, by which sins are forgiven. . . ."[89]   Calvin also explicitly identifies God as the *summum bonum*.[90]   Thus, a presupposition of traditional theology, noted by the Reformers in the context of soteriological statement, returns to the prolegomena in Protestant orthodoxy.

Finally, we also observe that the language of causality is used by the Reformed scholastics to identify the source, function and purpose of theology without any implication of an overarching predestinarianism. The causal definitions of theology are not linked to any language of necessity nor do they imply any relation between the existence of theology as such and the doctrine of election.   In addition, the discussion of the instrumental causality of theology drawn from Maccovius' *Loci*— despite his supralapsarian view of predestination[91]—in no way indicates a necessity inherent in the instrumentalities by which the first efficient cause brings about the final end of theology.   Thus, again, the theory of predestination as central dogma fails to explain the Reformed system at its presuppositional or principial level.   Similarly, the discussion of the causality of theology in no way represents an incipient rationalism.   In fact, the placement of reason low in the order of causes, at the level of instrumentality, provides the beginning of a solution to the problem of revelation and reason that includes a proper place for both without undermining either the primary function of revelation or the necessity for rational discourse.

4.3 Theology of Union: Christ's Knowledge of God

The problem of the theology of Christ according to his human nature, which enters the theological prolegomena of the Protestant orthodox with Junius' *De vera theologia* (1594), is an essentially christological issue with a long history of its own apart from the development of theological prolegomena.   The church fathers prior to the Council of Chalcedon (AD 451) examined the texts in Scripture where Christ is said to know all things (Matt. 11:27; John 21:17) and those texts where his knowledge is described as limited in some way (Mark 13:32; Luke 2:52), and had either referred the former to Christ's divinity and the latter to his humanity or, on the assumption of a communion of the divine with the human in the hypostatic union and a communication of proper qualities (*communicatio idiomatum*) from the divine to the human nature, endeavored to explain the limitation of knowledge as a hiding of omniscience rather than as an actual lack of knowledge.[92]

The tendency of Western Christology following Augustine was to deny a communication of divine attributes to Christ's human nature and to assume the finitude of his human knowledge. This view raised the further question of the character of Christ's human knowledge which, albeit finite, must nevertheless be higher and more extensive than the knowledge afforded to sinners. Aquinas could argue, on the basis of Jesus' sin-lessness, that Jesus possessed the beatific vision and, on the basis of the hypostatic union, that Jesus' *visio Dei* was virtually infinite.[93] The alternative perspective, resting upon the communication of divine attributes to Christ's humanity, reappeared in the Lutheran Christology of the sixteenth and seventeeth centuries.[94] These two perspectives—the Thomist and the Lutheran—appear as negated views in the Reformed discussion of the *theologia unionis*.

The historical debate, however, only accounts for the forms and patterns of christological argument, not for the presence of the argument in the prolegomena to theological system. To this question we can only offer a tentative answer. The discussion of the *theologia unionis* arises at least in part out of the scholastic drive toward completeness of definition. Christ's knowledge of God, in view of the uniqueness of his person, represents a separate category of theology to be contrasted with the theology of angels and of men either *in via* or *in patria*. As a separate and unique category, it demands discussion as a part of the definition of *theologia* and the isolation of *theologia nostra*. It would also seem, moreover, that the discussion of *theologia unionis* takes on systematic importance in view of the Reformation's tendency, witnessed for example in the epistemology of Calvin's *Institutes*, to define knowledge of God in terms of Christ. The *theologia unionis*, therefore, appears as a basic epistemological category in theology.

> The theology that we call [theology] of union [is] the entire wisdom of divine things communicated to Christ the God-man, that is, as the Word made flesh, according to his humanity.[95]

The idea of a *theologia unionis* does not, therefore, indicate the presence of archetypal theology, known to God alone but somehow delivered in the finite form of Jesus' humanity. Rather, it refers to the knowl-edge of God available to Christ as our Mediator, according to his human

nature.   The Reformed orthodox affirm, of course, that the Word, the
second person of the Trinity, retains the *theologia archetypa* in its
union with the human nature.   There is no kenotic emptying out of divine
essence in the incarnation; the *sapientia Dei* remains an attribute of the
Word.   The issue is that the infinite *sapientia Dei* or *theologia archetypa* cannot be communicated to a finite mind, even to the sinless mind of
Christ Jesus.[96]   Alsted refers to the theology of union as one suitable
to the position and purpose of Christ's person—a *theologia mediatoris* or
theologia oeconomica, that is, a theology of the mediator or a theology
suited to the economy or divine dispensation of salvation.[97]

In defining the efficient cause of theology, Walaeus first notes
that the appointed end of things, the *creaturae rationalis extrema
beatitudo & Dei gloria*, cannot be attained in us unless God himself
communicates with us.   This communication of divine wisdom is accomplished in three forms: by the hypostatic union, by intuitive vision (*per
visionem ut vocant intuitivam*), and by revelation strictly so-called.[98]
The first of these—the theology of union—is that *sapientia* most fully
communicated to the human nature of Christ, the fullness of which both
represents the greatest knowledge of God possible in a creature and that
knowledge necessary to the work of the mediator between God and man.[99]
This communication does not mean—as the ubiquitarians would have it—
that infinite divine wisdom is transformed into a human intellect.
Rather Christ's mind was enlightened extraordinarily by the Holy Spirit
because of the power of union (*ex vi conjunctionis illius cum natura
divina*) with the divine nature.[100]

This limitation of *theologia unionis* as finite knowledge and, therefore, as a form, albeit exalted, of ectypal theology, rests upon two
basic principles: no proportion can be given or made between the finite
and the infinite (*finiti ad infinitum dari proportio non potest*) and
there can be no confusion of natures or transfusion of properties in the
hypostatic union.   Both of these principles can be stated in terms of the
frequently cited Reformed maxim *finitum non capax infiniti* ("the finite
is not capable of the infinite").   We note that the argument is both
philosophical and christological and that the philosophical side of the
argument reflects both epistemological and ontological issues.   On the
philosophical side, Junius' language concerning the absence of analogy or
proportion between the finite and the infinite,[101] like his basic
distinction between *theologia archetypa* and *theologia ectypa*, reflects
late medieval models, specifically the nominalist dictum *finiti et
infiniti nulla proportio* according to which reason cannot move from the
finitude of revelation to the infinite being of God.[102]

The christological problem follows as a result of the philosophical: if the human nature of Jesus, as finite, is incapable in itself of comprehending the infinite knowledge of the *theologia archetypa*, then any equation of the *theologia unionis* with archetypal theology must involve some alteration of the human nature of Jesus. For Jesus to be possessed of an infinite divine wisdom according to his humanity, there would have to be either a communication of divinity to humanity or a transference of divine attributes to Jesus' humanity within the hypostatic union.   But that union takes place without co-mixture or co-mingling, without a confusion of the natures, and thus without either a communication of divinity to humanity or a transference of the divine attributes to the human nature.   Thus Jesus has two natures, two wills, two intellects—a divine and a human—and each has the knowledge that is proper to it. Christ has knowledge or wisdom, then, according to two modes, the divine and the human, the former being essential and incommunicable, the latter being habitual and communicable.[103]

These arguments do not, of course, mean that the Reformed in any way diminish the quality or extent of the knowledge given to Christ.   They view it as the most exalted form of human knowledge of God, higher than either the theology of the blessed in heaven (*theologia beatorum*) or the theology of human beings before the fall (*theologia viatorum ante lapsum*).

> Therefore this theology is the wisdom of divine things communi-
> cated from heaven in the Spirit of God to man, without measure,
> for the sake of the enlightenment of all those who are created
> according to the image of God.[104]

Such a *communicatio sine mensura*, however, cannot be found among all creatures.   Indeed, Junius argues, when the definition passes from consideration of the *theologia unionis in se* to consideration of this theology as it actually exists *in subiecto*, the measureless wisdom of the Spirit appears as an inaccessible source (*fons inaccessus*) and a great abyss (*abyssus magna*) beyond the capacity of angelic and human subjects. Only Christ our Savior can approach such knowledge in his sinless human- ity through the work of the Spirit, for "the Father loves the Son and has given him all things in his hand."[105]

This concept of a *theologia unionis* draws upon the christological concepts of a *communicatio apotelesmatum*, the communication of mediator- ial operations, which bring to completion the work of the two natures, and of the *dona extraordinaria finita*, the extraordinary finite gifts bestowed by the Spirit on Christ's human nature for the sake of his mediatorial work.   In the hypostatic union, Christ is both anointing and anointed (*ungens et unctus*), the divine nature consecrating the human both by uniting with it and by bestowing the gifts of the Spirit. The wisdom of divine things known to Christ, moreover, is a wisdom bestowed in accord with his mediatorial work so that it provides a basis for the ultimate enlightenment or illumination of rational creatures just as Christ's work of salvation provides the foundation of their redemption. The "enlightenment of all those who are created according to the image of God," then, occurs in Christ—so that the *theologia unionis* provides the immediate foundation of our theology, even as the *theologia archetypa* provides the immediate foundation of the theology of union. In other words, the theology of union represents a soteriological or mediatorial principle in the basic epistemology of Reformed system.[106]

Thus, over against the archetypal theology, the *theologia unionis* is to be recognized as ectypal, finite, created, and habitual (*habitualis*), but nonetheless as "truly absolute according to the manner of created nature" (*absolutissima secundum naturae creatae modus*) because of the light of the divine nature united to the human as its *principium* or foundation. In relation to us, therefore, the *theologia unionis* is "as if infinite and close to the infinite" (*quasi infinita & infinitae proxima*). Compared to the measure and limited scope of our wisdom, it appears infinite and can only be called finite in the company of the essential and infinite wisdom of God.[107] Thus Scripture can attribute both growth in wisdom and ignorance to Christ (Mark 13:32; Luke 2:52); and can also say that Christ knows all things (Matt. 11:27; John 21:17)— the former being said in recognition of the finitude of his knowledge, the latter being said in relation to our ignorance.[108]

This view of the *theologia unionis* stands in conflict with the views of the Lutheran orthodox, identified as "ubiquitarians" in the polemical arguments of the Reformed. Indeed, this is a christological debate divorced from its more usual *loci* in Christology proper and in the doctrine of the Lord's Supper. The Lutheran view equated the theology of union with the *theologia archetypa* on the ground that the communication of proper qualities (*communicatio idiomatum*) in the person of Christ implied a communication of the divine majesty, and therefore of the *sapientia Dei*, to the human nature of Christ.[109] Apart from the purely christological polemic, in which both Lutherans and Reformed argued the issue of the *theologia unionis* for the purpose of buttressing their doctrines of the hypostatic union and of the sacramental presence, we can note that the Lutheran concept of *theologia unionis*, insofar as it merges with *theologia archetypa*, has little real function in the prolegomena or in the creation of a theological epistemology, whereas the Reformed view presents a key to the issue of mediation, to the role of Christ as mediator in theological epistemology, and therefore to the way in which Christian theology rests upon Christ as revealer.   In other words, the Reformed concept of a *theologia unionis* bears witness to the perfect accommodation of God to us in Christ that is the basis of redemption and redemptive knowledge.

The debate between the Reformed and Lutherans over the *theologia unionis* remained an issue of importance in theological prolegomena among the Lutherans long after it had ceased to be of interest among the Reformed.   In the late seventeenth century, Calovius and Quenstedt still expended great effort to present christological arguments resting on the *genus maiestaticum* of the *communicatio idiomatum* in order to draw logical errors in the Reformed declaration of the finitude of Christ's human knowledge.[110]   Indeed, the issue appears so settled and is so cursorily treated in the systems of late seventeenth-century Reformed writers like Burmann, Turretin, Heidegger, and Marckius, that the Lutherans were forced to argue with Junius and others of the early orthodox if only for the sake of finding an argument lengthy enough to investigate for errors! The Reformed continue to note the issue as a point of christological dispute in the *locus* on the *communicatio idiomatum*.[111]

Similarly, the Reformed distance themselves from those medieval scholastics who identified the theology of Christ in his human nature with the beatific vision.   Walaeus thus notes the error of the "*Pontificii*" who assume that the *theologia unionis* is an immediate beatific apprehension of the divine by the human nature (*intuitum beatificum humanae naturae in divinam*) as if the human nature of Christ, from the moment of conception, had a direct apprehension or intuition of the wisdom of the divine nature with which it had been united.[112]   This doctrine, notes Walaeus, conflicts with the statement of Luke (2:52) that Jesus grew in wisdom and with the statement of Jesus himself (Mark 13:32) that he was ignorant of the time of the last judgment.

The Roman Catholic attribution of the beatific vision to Christ seems to have remained a greater point of concern among the Reformed than the Lutheran polemic over the *theologia unionis*, though it too tends not to be treated in the prolegomena after the mid-seventeenth century, but to be relegated to the christological *locus* of the system.[113]   Turretin argues at some length about "the nature and extent" of Christ's knowledge, noting that while Christ was performing his work on earth he did not have a glorifed knowledge, nor did he have—as argued previously against the Lutherans—divine omniscience, nor can he be accused of "crass ignorance of many things" as other adversaries claim.[114]   We know from Scripture that Christ lacked knowledge of the time of the last judgment, that he was like us in all things excepting sin, and that he was blessed with profound knowledge of God by the anointing of the Spirit. Christ's knowledge, moreover, was a knowledge suited to his life—and not to an existence beyond passion and death. *Scientia beata*, blessed or beatified knowledge, is therefore excluded, leaving two principal kinds (*species*) of knowledge, *scientia infusa* and *scientia acquisita*.[115]

Although Turretin's argument, like the less elaborate comment of Mastricht, is directed against Roman Catholic doctrine in general, it does manifest a fairly intimate knowledge of the Thomist position in particular. Aquinas had argued that Christ possessed all three species of *scientia*—beatific, infused and acquired—and had pressed the point of the *scientia beata* on the basis of Christ's fullness of divine knowledge and, soteriologically, on the ground that all men potentially have the beatific vision insofar as they are ordained to that end and that all men are ordained to that end in Christ. The sinless soul of Christ must be viewed as having attained that end in this life. Consequently, Christ was at once *viator* and *comprehensor*—*viator* in his passible body, *comprehensor* in his perfection of soul.[116]

"Therefore," argues Turretin, "we confess a twofold knowledge belonging to the human nature of Christ during his earthly life, infused knowledge and acquired or experimental knowledge."[117] The infused knowledge (*scientia infusa*) is a supernatural disposition that knows heavenly things by the light of grace—in the case of Christ, it is given or infused by a special grace of the Spirit that utterly sanctifies his human nature and fills it with the gifts of grace. The acquired knowledge is natural knowledge, gained by the light of reason during earthly life both experientially and by the rational process of drawing conclusions—in the case of Christ, it is untarnished by sin. Finally, Turretin argues against the Roman Catholics that it is also impossible to claim that Christ was at once an earthly pilgrim and a recipient of the beatific vision (*simul viator et comprehensor*). These two conditions are opposed to one another—quite simply, even tautologically, "the *viator* is on the way (*in via*), the *comprehensor* at the goal (*in meta*); the *viator* labors and experiences suffering, the *comprehensor* enjoys the perfect blessedness of the end of his labors."[118] Christ, in his earthly life of suffering and in his death, experienced the existence of the *viator*, not of the *comprehensor*.[119] This argument stands in theological agreement and continuity with the Reformed assumption that the passion of Christ was a suffering of body and soul.[120]

The underlying problem of soteriological epistemology raised here, as in debate with the Lutherans, is concerned with the nature of the knowledge proper to one who is the Mediator for the sake of the execution of his proper work. Christ's knowledge of God as infused by the Holy Spirit and acquired during his life and ministry by the exercise of his intellect must be a true and perfect knowledge of God, higher than that of any sinful man and perfected in and for the sake of the hypostatic union, but—if it is to be true to scriptural passages like Luke 2:52 amd Mark 13:32—it must lack, at least during Christ's earthly life, some of the wisdom of the blessed. In addition, it must conform to the condition or state of Christ so that it reflects first his humiliation and then his exaltation and thereby provides a basis first for the *theologia viatorum* and then for the *theologia beatorum*. The *theologia unionis*, therefore, can be conceived according to two stages, one *in via* and one *in patria*.[121] If this were not so, Christ could not be like us in every way excepting sin and the work of salvation would be jeopardized.

This distinction between the *theologia unionis* and both the *theologia archetypa* and *theologia beatorum* also illustrates the way in which the theological prolegomena both provide foundation for and draw substantively upon the theology set forth in the system proper—without recourse either to rationalistic philosophical principles or so-called central dogmas like predestination. In the first place, the christological emphasis implied in the *theologia unionis* is carried forth soteriologically and eschatologically in the insistence of the Reformed upon mediation in and by Christ as the sole ground of man's union and fellowship with God. If Christ's knowledge of God were the *visio beatifica*, his theology a *theologia beatorum sive visionis*, it would be identical with the theology of the redeemed in heaven and, in effect, the *terminus ad quem* of human theology, nothing more. That being the case, the office of mediator could cease following the final judgment and the humanity of Christ belongs, as it were, to the ranks of the redeemed, without, of course, surrendering the headship and royal power belonging to him through the incarnation. This view, however, the Reformed almost universally reject: they maintain the continuance of Christ's mediation into the eschaton, arguing that our union with Christ as mediator provides the basis for our union with God eternally, insofar as our union with God must always be in Christ.[122] Even so, our vision of God, the *theologia visionis*, must ultimately rest on Christ's relation to God and his knowledge of God for us, the *theologia unionis*. The purpose or goal of this theology of union, then, corresponds with the purpose or goal of

Christ, the anointed one. Just as the purpose of Christ is the redemption and reconstitution of man according to the image of God, so is the
purpose of the *theologia unionis* "the illumination of all those theologians who are created according to the image of God."[123] The theology
of union is the foundation of the theology of all who are in Christ, the
basis for and substance of the vision of God ultimately bestowed upon
believers in their final union with Christ.[124]

   In the second place, we see a similar christological emphasis in the
designation of the object of theology (*obiectum theologiae*)[125] not as God
in se but rather God as he is revealed and covenanted in Christ. This
formulation, in turn, looks from the *theologia unionis* as a mediating
theology between archetypal theology and all other forms of ectypal
theology to the fourfold definition of *verbum Dei*, Word of God, found in
the *locus* on Scripture. There the orthodox recognize that the "essential
Word and wisdom of the Father" is also the Word incarnate and that this
essential Word is the foundation for all forms of the revealed Word,
written or unwritten, external or internal. Here, too, the underlying
thrust is toward the establishment of a christological structure of
mediation. A similar stress on Christ as foundation or mediate principle
appears in the discussion of the fundamental articles of theology.[126]

4.4 Theology as Communicated to Men

   Having defined the one form of ectypal theology present in a
rational creature but not available to human beings generally--the
theologia unionis--we can move into the realm of human cognition and
"theology communicated to men" (*theologia hominibus communicata*). Since
we remain in the category of *theologia vera*, pagan and heretical theologies do not enter the discussion. Strictly considered, such theologies
are the result of the efforts of the human mind, not of divine communica-
tion--their errors, in other words, are not of divine but of human
origin. Nonetheless, *theologia hominibus communicata* is not a simple
category. It must be divided into component parts that correspond with
the several conditions of human beings under grace--before the fall,
after the fall and in the final state of blessedness. In addition, this
theology can be considered either ideally in terms of what it might be
granting its divine object and the divine origin of its cognitive ground,
whether natural or supernatural, or actually in terms of what it is in
the individual knowing subject. We thus can identify the *theologia
beatorum* of the blessed saints in heaven; the *theologia viatorum ante*

lapsum, the theology of earthly pilgrims before the fall; the *theologia viatorum post lapsum* or *theologia nostra*, the theology of pilgrims after the fall or "our theology"--and the latter considered either in itself (*in se*) or in the human subject (*in subiecto*).[127]

Much after the fashion of the medieval doctors beginning with Thomas Aquinas, the Protestant scholastics make an initial division of human theology into two basic categories, based on the words of Paul (1 Cor. 13:12), "For now we see through a glass, darkly; but then face to face: now I know in part; but then shall I know even as also I am known." The distinction is between the knowledge of God accessible to us during our earthly life and that accessible to us in heaven, in the presence of God--or, in the language used by Aquinas in his prologue to the *Sentences*, between our knowledge *in via*, on the way to our heavenly goal, and our knowledge *in patria*, in the heavenly "homeland." The language of pilgrimage and homeland is, of course, rooted in the Augustinian model, drawn from Hebrews 11 (esp. vv. 8-16) and 13:14, of the sojourning people seeking the heavenly commonwealth or "city" of God.[128]

The beginnings of the Protestant use of these categories can easily be seen in Musculus' *Loci Communes*:

> Just as in other things, there is no perfection in man, so is it also in the knowledge of God and godly matters, which is not perfected in any man as long as he lives in this world. . . . But the life to come is grounded upon perfect knowledge, which shall arise in us not by faith, hearing or signs, nor by revelations of the spirit, but by manifest sight, and most assured experience and proof. Then we shall so perfectly know both God and Father, and our Lord Jesus Christ, and the promises of the heavenly life, that there can be nothing more required: which manner of knowledge cannot be conceived by our mind, however faithful it is, as long as we are absent from the Lord in this earthly Pilgrimage.[129]

Even so, there is no perfect felicity in this life which is intended instead by God as an exercise and a discipline for us. Paul, in his first epistle to the Corinthians, tells us of the imperfection of our knowledge that we might not become "haughty and arrogant." We know only in part. Yet that partial and imperfect knowledge is sufficient to us in our present condition: perfection is not present but it is looked for, hoped for.[130] This is none other than the old distinction between *theologia beatorum* and *theologia viatorum*.

The *theologia hominibus communicata* can also be conceived in relation to Christ as the *theologia membrorum Christi*, the theology of the members of Christ. This Polanus defines as "*sapientia rerum divinarum a Christo cum membris suis communicata ad gloriam Dei & membrorum Christi salutem sempiternam*," that is, the wisdom concerning divine things

communicated by Christ to his members for the glory of God and the
eternal salvation of the members of Christ.[131]   This theology is either
the *theologia beatorum* or *theologia viatorum*. The former is also called
theologia clara visionis or, by synecdoche, *theologia visionis*. This
theology of vision, whether of angels or men, is the vision of God and
the perfect knowledge of God communicated in Christ. The latter is that
knowledge of God possible in this world, the knowledge given to earthly
pilgrims, the *viatores*.   Such knowledge of God is properly termed
"supernatural" since it is above (*supra*) and not against (*contra*) nature:
truth does not contradict truth.[132]   It is supernatural by reason of its
mode of manifestation and by reason of its object.[133]

Several of the theses in Gomarus' *Disputationes theologicae* reflect
the logic of Polanus' system on this point: since God himself is the
proper object of revelation, the twofold character of human theology--the
imperfect, partial knowledge of believers *in via* and the perfect knowledge given to those *in patria*--indicates a progress of knowledge toward
the contemplation of God. Thus the *theologia visionis* or *theologia
beatorum* can be described as *theologia teleios*, complete or perfect
theology, that is, a theology that has reached its appointed end, the
visio Dei.[134]

Both forms of human theology relate to the *theologia unionis in
Christo* in a manner analogous to the relationship of the *theologia
unionis* to the *theologia archetypa*. Just as the foundation of Christ's
own knowledge of God is the "prototypical and essential wisdom of God,"

> so also is that theology of union in Christ our Saviour the
> common principle of the remaining theology, whether that of the
> blessed Spirits in heaven, or this possessed on earth by
> wretched men. The archetypal theology is the womb or origin
> (*matrix*) of all others: this ectypal theology in Christ, the
> mother (*mater*) of all the rest: that the source of all (*fons
> omnium*), this as it were the common shelter (*castellum*) or
> means of conception (*conceptaculum*). . . . And so Christ
> sanctifies both of these forms of theology [*theologia beatorum*
> and *theologia viatorum*] in his person: for the practice (*usus*)
> of the lowly theology (*humili theologia*) is in the lowliness of
> the flesh, while that exalted theology is associated with
> (*utitur*) his exaltation, when he is exalted above all names.[135]

The passage is noteworthy both for its christological content and its
metaphors. Not only is Christ's knowledge of God the mediate prototype
for all human knowledge of God, but in addition the forms of human
knowledge of God correspond with the conditions or states of Christ's
person. In other words, the Protestant orthodox definition of theology
in terms of the theology of Christ, of the blessed and of the earthly
pilgrim, serves to emphasize the christocentric character of the saving
knowledge of God, as argued in the concept of the *duplex cognitio Dei*.

Human theology, moreover, on the model of the human pilgrimage toward God, reflects Christ's own pilgrimage of humiliation and exaltation, cross and resurrection.   The christological content of the *theologia viatorum* reminds us of Luther's *theologia crucis*, just as the christological reference of the *theologia beatorum* points to the proper place of the *theologia gloriae*—in heaven and not on earth.   The theology of the blessed, then, belongs to the church triumphant, the theology of pilgrims to the church militant.[136]   These terms—which identify pivotal themes in this *locus* and are of significant import for the system as a whole—are clearly neither rationalistic nor predestinarian as so frequently alleged of the orthodox *principia*.

Junius' metaphors describe the relation of God's archetypal self-knowledge (which is identical with the divine essence) to finite or ectypal theology in terms of motherhood.   This language of motherhood—like the language of *theologia in via* and *theologia in patria*—manifests the rootage of Protestant scholasticism in the medieval and patristic tradition.   This is particularly clear in his traditional use of Proverbs 8:22-32 as a trinitarian and christological passage in which the feminine *chokmah*, *sophia* or *sapientia* is the essential wisdom of God and the second person of the Trinity.

Although considered soteriologically or teleologically the *theologia beatorum* appears as the end result of progress in faith, the Protestant orthodox tend to discuss it first, before the discussion of the *theologia viatorum*.[137]   There are two largely formal reasons for this order of topics.   First, the discussion of *theologia* is arranged in descending order, from the highest and most complete theology to the lowest or least complete theology; second, this descending order concludes the discussion with the *theologia viatorum post lapsum in subiecto*, the pilgrim theology, after the fall, in the individual subject—which is precisely the form of theology that appears in the subsequent *loci* of the system and is, therefore, the point of contact and transition between the definition of theology and the system or body of doctrine as such.

The *theologia beatorum*, then, is a form of the heavenly theology of vision (*theologia visionis in caelis*) "that is communicated to the angels and to the perfect or consecrated spirits of the saints in heaven" and is a "wisdom of divine things" (*divinarum rerum Sapientiam*) suitable to their blessed condition.[138]   The basic definition, comments Junius, indicates that the subject must be presented according to a "threefold argument": with respect to its *modus*, its *subiecti* and its *circumstantia*. Thus the mode is "visionary," the subjects are angels and the spirits of

the righteous, and the circumstances are principally the place (*locus*) of
this theology in heaven.

The visionary mode of communication is a nonphysical or noncorporeal
mode suitable to spirits. Junius defines it as "a permanent and perfect
intellectual light (*lumen intellectuale*), communicated in the form of an
infused habit or disposition, by which light these heavenly creatures see
their creator."   This theology—since it is a permanent and perfect
illumination—might seem identical with the *theologia unionis* on first
consideration, but closer inspection shows it to be distinct and derivative. The theology of Christ is permanent and perfect of itself and in
itself (*a se & in se*) while the visionary theology is perfect only
because of the antecedent theology of Christ upon which it is grounded.
The theology of union rests on the hypostatic union of God and man in
Christ—specifically, on the union of the Logos and its *theologia
archetypa* with the human nature of Christ and the theology known to it.
Even the theology of angels does not arise out of hypostatic union, but
out of a communication of knowledge from God.   The theology of the
blessed, moreover, rests upon the relationship of the righteous to God
made possible by and eternally grounded in Christ. As noted above, it is
a human theology that corresponds with the glorious manifestation of
Christ in his exaltation.[139]

Thus, "the theology of the blessed, this exalted (*excelsa*) theology,
is a wisdom of divine things communicated by the Spirit of God through
the provision of Christ for those who dwell in heaven, according to which
they fully enjoy the eternal, gracious and glorious vision of God to His
glory".[140]   This formulation stands in continuity with the Reformed
teaching of the eternal headship of the incarnate Christ. Although the
doctrine of the *theologia beatorum* is stated primarily in terms of the
"intermediate" state of souls separated from the body (*status medius* or
status animarum a corpore separatarum), it also has an obvious eschato-
logical reference. The definition of *theologia beatorum* points to the
view that the relationship between God and the redeemed must always rest
upon the work of Christ and his continuing mediation, even in eternity.
This point is confirmed by the Reformed discussion of the eternity of the
intercessio Christi and of Christ's *munus regium*.[141]

Although, as we have just indicated, the concept of a *theologia
beatorum* relates to a specific christological and soteriological issue
developed later in the Reformed system, the concept also relates to and,
indeed, arises out of a Reformed reading of the medieval discussion of
theologia beatorum or *theologia in patria* and reflects, in particular,
the question raised by the medieval doctors concerning the way in which

spiritual or noncorporeal beings communicate. Few medieval doctors had hypothesized sonic communication—after all, no spirit, either angelic or human, has vocal chords! The "tongues of angels" noted by the apostle Paul (1 Cor. 13:1) must be the intuitive or immediate communication of minds. Even so, the model for a communication of divine knowledge to a spiritual being must be intellectual rather than sensual, that is, vocal and aural. The doctrine of illumination taught in the Augustinian tradition and emphasized as the ground of mystic contemplation provided the obvious answer in the medieval doctrine of the *visio Dei* or *visio beatifica*. What is significant here, is that this line of argument was not mediated to the Protestant orthodox by the Reformers, who did not discuss the topic, but came from their reading of the medieval scholastic systems.[142]

The category of *theologia hominibus communicata* basic to theological system must, of course, be theology as we know it in this life. This basic category of theology is comprehended by the Protestant scholastics under several distinct names: *theologia revelationis*, theology of revelation; *theologia viatorum*, theology of pilgrims or sojourners; and *theologia nostra*, our theology. All of the terms reflect a reading of the medieval prolegomena, the latter identifiably Scotist. The first of the terms, *theologia revelationis*, refers to the mode or manner (*modus*) of the theology; the latter two to the subjects (*subiecti*) and the circumstances (*circumstantia*) of the theology.

The *theologia revelationis in hac vita*, therefore, can be juxtaposed, according to mode, with the *theologia visionis in caelis*. Whereas the latter rests upon direct illumination and is literally a theology of vision, the former rests not upon vision, since the perfect *visio Dei* cannot be experienced in this life, but on revelation:

> Doubtless the intellectual light of this theology is not lasting, but transient: it is not perfect in an absolute sense (*non perfectum simpliciter*) but can only be called perfect or absolute in a derivative sense (*secundum quid*). Or, if we consider the mode of communication, it is *revelatio*, whereby God is not made manifest, as he is in himself, as the whole object of theology, but as man in his present condition and infirmity is capable of understanding him.[143]

Junius' language here points directly back to the post-Thomist qualification of the concept of *obiectum theologiae*—to Henry of Ghent's *inquantum credibile est*, "inasmuch as it is capable of belief," and to Ockham's *theologia nostra nobis possibili pro statu isto*, "our theology possible for us proportionate to this present condition." In our present infirmity, drawn by the gracious revelation of God's Spirit toward the condition of heavenly blessedness, our theology (*theologia nostra*) is also rightly called *theologia viatorum*, theology of pilgrims.

Junius presents the following definition: "Our theology is the wisdom of divine things, communicated by revelation of nature or of grace through the Holy Spirit for the benefit of those who live on earth."[144] There are, then, two basic modes of communication of revealed theology: nature and grace. The former mode of revelation, nature, represents an internal or immanent ground of communication of divine knowledge (*internum principium communicationis*) insofar as we are part of "nature" and our condition is natural. On the basis of this mode of communication we construct *theologia naturalis*, natural theology. The latter mode of revelation, grace, represents an external ground of communication of divine knowledge (*externum principium communicationis*) insofar as grace comes not from our own nature or effort, but from God. On the basis of this gracious mode of communication we construct a *theologia supernaturalis*, a theology rooted beyond our nature, a supernatural theology. Nonetheless, true natural theology will no more disagree with supernatural theology than nature, as created good by God, will conflict with God's grace.[145]

The orthodox discussion of the mode of communication of theology raises a profound epistemological issue, a corollary of the identification of all finite theology as ectypal. Believers are not given the divine archetype by revelation: they are given an ectypal knowledge of God. This statement in itself, with its assumption of the absence of cognitive proportion between the finite and the infinite, indicates some sort of divine accommodation to human need. The nature of that accommodation, however, underlies and defines the nature of our theology. God does not accommodate his truth to human sin—rather he accommodates his truth to human ways of knowing. Thus, revelation itself, whether supernatural or natural, is suited to the present conditions of human knowing, just as vision is suited to the ultimate conditions of human knowing when we no longer see as "in a mirror darkly." In addition, we recognize that the act of accommodation itself belongs to God: it is God who determines the form of the knowledge that we have of him.

Although we reserve the problem of natural and supernatural theology for subsequent discussion, it is important to note here that natural theology belongs, in the Protestant scholastic schema, to the category not only of *theologia vera* but also of *theologia revelationis* and *theologia nostra*. Since, however, natural theology is not sufficient for salvation and therefore not adequate for the way (*via*) that leads to eternal life, it is not, strictly speaking, the *theologia viatorum* but

only an adjunct of it which is necessarily a *theologia supernaturalis*.[146]
Polanus therefore defines the *theologia viatorum* in tandem with *theologia
beatorum* and in a stricter sense as a form of *theologia membrorum
Christi*, the theology of the members of Christ or of Christ's body.
Whereas Christ is not mentioned in the broader definition of *theologia
nostra*, he necessarily appears in the strictly argued definition of
theologia viatorum:

> The theology of pilgrims is the wisdom of divine things commun-
> icated by Christ through the Holy Spirit to human beings living
> in this earth, by means of gracious inspiration, so that the
> light of the intellect might contemplate God and the things of
> God through its growth; that they might rightly worship God,
> until in heaven they see him clearly and perfectly, to his
> glory. Concerning this, it is written, II Cor. 13:9, 12; Eph.
> 4:11-13; I Peter 1:8.[147]

Polanus concludes,

> The origin [of theology] is divine and supernatural, that is,
> it arises through principles known of themselves by the light
> of a higher science, which is the same as an illumination and
> persuasion through divine revelation in a manner beyond the
> capacity of human reason. This inspired light of heavenly
> power has been poured into our minds.[148]

This view of *theologia viatorum* coincides with what Junius terms
theologia nostra absolute dicta, our theology absolutely so-called: "a
wisdom concerning divine things, inspired by God according to divine
truth, and entrusted to his servants through the enunciative or express
word (*enunciativum sermonem*) in Christ, and also in the Old and New
Testaments . . .,"[149] but it also draws on the Thomistic view of theology
as a subalternate science[150] and accepts a concept of illumination that
probably should be viewed as an inward spiritual gift parallel to the
external light of the Word—and again a Thomistic as opposed to Bonaven-
turan theory of illumination.[151]

In both of these definitions, the human theology indicated is the
highest, truest form of human theology—or, as Junius argues, the essence
of our theology as offered to us by God. *Theologia nostra absolute dicta*
or *in se*, in itself, apart from the several failings, corporate and
individual, of the human knower, is therefore not utterly inadequate to
its subject, the infinite God, the universal ground of all things, their
beginning and end. The mode of communication of this *theologia in se*,
moreover, is and must be divine and an act of grace intended by God to
make the knowledge of his infinite and transcendent being known to us.
Since there is no analogy between the objects of our natural, rational
knowing and God, a divine communication alone is adequate to the divine
subject of theology absolutely so-called.

This sense of the incapacity of the finite for the infinite or of the absence of proportion between the finite and the infinite is clearly present in the language of the Reformers even though they do not use the terms *theologia archetypa* and *theologia ectypa* or *theologia in se* and *theologia nostra*. Thus, Calvin can say, even of the inspired language of Scripture, "It must be recognized that it is somewhat improper" (*improprium quodammodo*) that language used to describe "creatures is applied to the hidden majesty of God."[152] Calvin does not indicate, as one author has argued, that Scripture is "an imperfect and inappropriate instrument at its very best," but rather that the finite vehicle of human language is, in a technical sense, applicable to divine things not *proprie* but *improprie*—as must be the case, given the infinite nature of the subject.[153]

A word of explanation must be inserted here concerning the theological use of the terms subject and object. On the simplest level, the philosophical or theological use of the terms reflects basic grammatical relationships: the subject of a sentence is the idea or thing performing the action, making the affirmation or having the mode of being indicated by the verb; the object is that toward which the action is directed or that which has been predicated of the subject. Thus, in normal theological discourse, God is the *obiectum theologiae*, the object of theology, since he is the One toward whom theological discourse is directed; while the human theologian is the *subiectum theologiae*, since he is the one engaged in the performance of the theological task. Scholastic language, however, tends to use the term *subiectum* with qualifications relating to the direction of an activity or action under discussion. Thus *subiectum quod* or "subject which" tends to indicate passive or noncausal participation in an action, while *subiectum quo*, "subject by which" tends to indicate active or causal participation in an action. That active or causal participation can be further qualified as predicated of the subject (as *subiectum de quo*, the "subject from which," or *subiectum in quo*, the "subject in which"). In this latter usage, God is the *subiectum de quo* of theology, whereas man is the *subiectum in quo* of theology.[154]

This distinction between the subject *de quo* and the subject *in quo* permits the Protestant scholastics to describe the *theologia hominibus communicata*, considered as supernatural or revealed theology, in two ways: in terms of the divine subject by whom the theology is communicated and in terms of the human subject to whom the theology is communicated and in whom the theology is known. As we have already seen, *theologia communicata in se* or *theologia nostra absolute dicta* is perfect and complete even as its author, God, the *subiectum de quo*, is perfect and complete.[155] Theology as it belongs to rational creatures (*ut est in creaturis rationalibus*), or as it is *in subiecto*, is neither perfect nor complete but falls short of perfection and completion both in terms of the mental capacity of the individual subject and in terms of the relationship of the subject to God, grace and salvation. *Theologia hominibus communicata* considered *in subiecto*, therefore, is twofold, according to the two states of earthly mankind: there is a human theology before the fall (*ante lapsum*) and belonging to the state of primal integrity and a human theology after the fall (*post lapsum*) and belonging to the fallen state by the grace of God.[156]

The theology, then, "that God has exhibited perfectly to us by a gracious communication" can only be imperfectly known by us: human theology in the subject is the wisdom of divine things "modified according to the reason that is in human beings" (*modificata pro ratione eorum hominum quibus in est*) and, thus, "mutiliated according to the imperfection of the subject."[157] "Since, in the [human] subject, the nature must always be imperfect, in truth nothing perfect can be comprehended by it."[158] Since, moreover, fallen human nature is not perfected by grace in this life, we cannot expect that Christian theology in the church will ever be perfect. Indeed, Junius concludes, the most that we can say of our theology in this life is that its purity appears in an inchoate form as a result of the work of grace in those who are members of Christ. From these premises, Scharpius argues that man before the fall moved by degrees toward perfect knowledge through better communication of knowledge, use and experience. After the fall, however, debilitated and corrupted by sin, man is incapable of knowing God truly or of living blessedly—human philosophy only serves to frustrate theology. And, in this condition the remaining knowledge of God only serves to leave man without excuse, as Paul testifies in Romans 1:20–21.[159] Thus "this theology, which in the beginning was good in itself, the sinfulness of man renders demonic" (cf. James 3:15).[160]

We have encountered the theme of the *duplex cognitio dei* applied to the definition of theology and related—as ever—to the anthropological problem of revelation and knowledge of God. Prior to the fall man had access to God, according to Scharpius, through "threats and promises, the continuation of sacraments, by grace gathered and perpetuated in the creation."[161] The reference is probably to a sacramental understanding of the two trees of the garden. In any case it represents a knowledge of God sufficient to right conduct—a kind of supernaturally given knowledge of God accessible to the mind and heart unaided by the grace of regeneration. This way is now barred and man must resort to knowledge of God in

Christ, revealed in and defined by the *verbum scriptum*. There alone is
saving knowledge to be found.

Scharpius can therefore conclude concerning supernatural theology
communicated to men, considered as it is in the individual subject after
the fall:

> In the state [of man] after the fall, supernatural theology is
> the wisdom concerning God known in Christ, which is revealed in
> the written word and is thus defined: theology is the wisdom of
> divine things, according to God's truth, inspired by God, and
> entrusted to the servants of God by means of the declared word
> (*per enunciativum sermonem*) in Christ; comprehended in the
> books of the Old and New Testament so as to conduce to the
> glory of God and to the salvation of the Church.[162]

The definition echoes the language of Junius[163] and has parallels in most
of the major early orthodox systems.   The issue addressed by these
definitions is virtually always the problem of true knowledge of God in
the fallen state and the necessity of revelation as centered on and
guaranteed in Christ.

Thus, the distinction between natural and supernatural theology and
its corollary, the necessity of supernatural or revealed theology, leads
Polanus back to the theme of the *theologia viatorum*.   The *theologia
viatorum* can be considered either absolutely or *quatensus est in ipsis
viatoribus* ("as it is in the pilgrims themselves").

> *Theologia viatorum* absolutely so-called and considered accord-
> ing to its own nature, is the wisdom concerning divine things,
> according to divine truth, inspired by God and bestowed upon
> his servants in Christ by his enunciative word, and set forth
> in the Old and New Testaments by the prophets, apostles and
> evangelists, however much of that wisdom was necessary to be
> revealed for the glory of God and the good of elect men.[164]

The term *sermo Dei enunciativus*, Polanus adds, indicates the *logos
prophorikos* by which God explains to us the things concerning himself and
his work: "*Est enim instrumentalis causa sapientiae rerum divinarum in
nobis.*"   In its essence this *theologia viatorum absolute dicta* is one,
eternal and immutable—even as it must be true, holy, and perfect—for it
comes from God.   It is not the same as the two Testaments, but it is
taught in them.[165]

After making the standard distinction between God's archetypal
knowledge of himself and the ectypal theology resting upon it, Owen draws
out the relationship between "our theology" (*nostra theologia*) and this
archetypal "truth" that God has "eternally in his mind":

> . . . upon this [eternal truth] all of our theology depends;
> not, however, immediately, but according to that act of the
> divine will by which [God] is pleased to reveal his truth to
> us: "Indeed, no one has known God: the only begotten Son who is
> in the bosom of the Father has revealed him," John 1:18.   The
> revelation of the mind and will of God: this is the word of

God, the doctrine with which we are concerned and to which all
the thoughts of our minds concerning God, his works, and the
obedience that is owed him ought to be conformed.[166]

After distinguishing between the immanent (*endiathetos*) Word and the Word
sent forth (*prophorikos*) and, under the latter category, between the
unwritten (*agraphon*) and the written (*engraphon*) Word, Owen concludes
that this eternal Word of God, sent forth and put in writing as the
ectypal reflection of the eternal ideal is theology: ". . . the entire
Word of God that is committed to written form, this Scripture is our
theology (*Scriptura ista ita est nostra theologia*).[167]

A further distinction must be made between the truth of Scripture
and the theology that rests upon Scripture:

> *Theologia viatorum* to the extent that it exists in [individual
> subjects], is the wisdom of divine things, communicated to men
> engaged in this life, by God through the Word, modified by the
> reason that is in man, just as wisdom is implanted more in some
> and less in others. . . . This [wisdom] is called, thus, our
> theology in the [human] subject (*theologia nostra in subiecto*):
> obscure theology (*theologia obscura*), with respect to the
> theology of the blessed.[168]

In other words, *theologia viatorum absoluta dicta* and its synonym
theologia nostra in se refer to the body of doctrine, resting upon Christ
as Word and upon the work of Spirit, taught by the prophets and the
apostles—namely, the meaning or substance of Scripture itself in its
perfection—and, when used broadly, to natural theology. *Theologia
viatorum* or *theologia nostra in subiecto* refer to the human attempt to
construct theology resting upon Scripture and, to a more limited extent,
upon natural reason. Scripture, then, is the *principium* of our theology
as such, of the *theologia nostra in subiecto*. Whereas Scripture, as
theologia absolute dicta, is finite but perfect, the human theology based
upon Scripture reflects both the finitude and the imperfection of the
human mind.

In the high orthodox period, the sense of the *theologiae imperfec-
tione* stemming from the orthodox understanding of the ectypal character
of theology and of the *viator* status of the theologian was elaborated at
length by Johann Heinrich Heidegger. Heidegger formally included in his
prolegomena a final discussion of the problematic character of all finite
theology as found in rational creatures. Since we are pilgrims or
wayfarers on the earth, argues Heidegger, our theology must always be
imperfect—*imperfecta semper est*—until it is perfected in the day of the
Lord. Nonetheless, true finite theology, as given to faith by the Spirit
of God through the revelation of the Word, is adequate to its purpose,
the salvation of mankind.[169] This imperfect, wayfaring character of

theology leads Heidegger to argue, against the more typical Reformed pattern, that theology is a totally practical as opposed to a mixed, speculative and practical discipline.[170]

It is also quite clear that the scholastic distinctions between *theologia archetypa* and *theologia ectypa* with strong emphasis laid on the limited and accommodated (though nevertheless true) character of the *theologia viatorum* draw far more heavily upon a Scotist paradigm of the relation of revelation to theology and to human reason than upon a Thomistic model. This judgment is confirmed both in the *locus de Scriptura*, where the necessity of revelation is strongly asserted, and in the *locus de Deo*, where the will is invariably given priority over the justice and goodness of God—even by a reputed Thomist like Zanchi.

Finally, we need to ask what the function of these concepts is in the Reformed system. Why define a *theologia archetypa* which no creature, man or angel can possibly know? Why state the concept of a *theologia unionis* or a *theologia angelorum*—neither of which is attainable by a man in this world or the next? And why mention the *theologia beatorum* which is of no use to us now? What of the *theologia revelata in se*, a perfect if limited truth of God, which cannot correspond to the *theologia in subiecto*, on the one hand because of the natural weaknesses of our minds and on the other because of the loss of our full capacity to relate to God in the fall? What possibly is the use of all these distinctions—if not to humble the theologian and to manifest his system as nothing but dust from the very outset? Theology as it is known to man cannot, in the view of the early orthodox, become a pretentious science. *Theologia revelata in subiecto post lapsum* can hardly be called an overweeningly rationalistic metaphysical system! Looking at the inclusive character and precise definition of the orthodox system from a distance of several centuries, Brunner and others have spoken of the ease with which the orthodox thought they could formulate "correct doctrine"—but closer examination of the orthodox view of the theological task removes this criticism.[171]

The conclusion drawn by both Junius and Polanus is that *theologia nostra* considered in itself is perfect whereas considered in the human subject is imperfect. Thus both Scripture and theological system are our theology, pilgrim theology. We have in our midst the perfect human, ectypal theology, but it cannot be perfectly exposited by us—not because of our finitude, but rather because of our sin and the incompleteness of our sanctification. Our only hope for finding saving knowledge of God lies in the fact that Scripture as transmitted to us in the human form given it by the prophets and the apostles is in fact our theology, *theologia nostra*, and not another theology—and that its perfection is joined to our imperfection according to the christological principle of the *theologia unionis*, that undergirds the entire *theologia hominibus communicata*. The essentially soteriological pattern of the definitions is obvious, as is the way in which the definitions both draw upon and undergird the *sola gratia* and the *sola Scriptura* of the Protestant system of doctrine. Once again, the prolegomena provide the presuppositions for the system and the proper guide to the interpretation of the system. Specifically, they point us toward a theology of grace in Christ and toward Scripture as the *principium cognoscendi* of that theology.

5

Natural and Supernatural Theology

5.1 The Problem of *theologia naturalis*

The Protestant scholastics recognized that the ancient philosophical understanding of God was largely a form of natural theology and that, as such, it represented a limited, nonsaving knowledge of God similar in form and content to the rational metaphysics developed by Christian philosophers. Whereas pagan natural theology, left uncorrected by revelation, could easily be dismissed as a category of *theologia falsa*, the conclusions of Christian, regenerate reason had to be dealt with in the context of theological system—particularly when Christian natural theology corresponded to a portion of the contents of revelation. Similar comments can be made concerning religion. *Religio* arises naturally out of the activity of human reason but, as with natural theology, is immediately subject to the corruption of human nature. Because of this problematic character of natural theology and natural religion, the Reformed orthodox seldom develop a locus of natural theology in either of these topics—never under *theologia falsa* and only infrequently under *religio*.

Theologia naturalis, despite all the problems inherent in its formulation and elaboration, is properly discussed as a form of *theologia vera*, under the category of *theologia viatorum*. This placement of the topic arises from the fact that *theologia naturalis* is neither a theology of union nor a theology of vision, but a theology of revelation. Since the mode of communication of natural theology is revelation, natural theology must be discussed together with supernatural theology. Indeed,

as we have already noted, natural and supernatural theology are viewed as
belonging to the same *genus* of discipline or study.

> The mode of communication of theology is, thus, twofold, by
> nature and by grace: that by way of an internal principle; this
> by way of an external principle, on the basis of which one is
> called natural theology, the other supernatural.[1]

The definition of theology as archetypal and ectypal represents, in part,
a reflection of the Reformed teaching of the creation of man according to
the *imago Dei*.[2]   Natural theology, therefore, as an ectypal form of the
knowledge of God, must be defined in terms of the *imago Dei* and its
almost total loss in the fall.   Just as the *imago* remains, albeit viti-
ated, and in itself is incapable of being the basis for fellowship with
God, so natural theology remains as a *semen religionis* planted in the
soul of man, incapable of being the basis of salvation and serving only
to leave sinful man without excuse.   Even so, natural and supernatural
theology belong to the same knowing subject, the *viator*.   The *viator*,
writes Alsted, is "the elect man trying to reach the heavenly
homeland"—and since we do not deal with the reprobate man and his
theology, we do not deal with a false or reprobate natural theology
opposed to supernatural theology, but with a true natural theology of the
viator, the *electus homo*, subordinated to supernatural theology.[3]

Throughout the previous discussions we have used the terms *natural*
and *supernatural* to describe two types of theology and two kinds of
causality.   Some further definition of terms is necessary as we discuss
natural and revealed or natural and supernatural theology—particularly
in view of the frequent contemporary misinterpretations of and attacks
upon this distinction.   Although a contrast is frequently made, sometimes
even in the scholastic systems themselves, between *theologia naturalis*
and *theologia revelata* (or *theologia revelata sive supernaturalis*), it
should already be clear that the contrast is imprecise insofar as natural
theology is a form of revealed theology.   The precise distinction is
between *revelatio naturalis* and *revelatio supernaturalis* and the forms of
theology resting upon these revelations, *theologia naturalis* and
theologia supernaturalis, the former being conceived according to the
natural powers of acquisition belonging to the mind, the latter according
to a graciously infused power bestowed on the mind by God.[4]   In other
words, natural theology arises out of the order of nature, whereas
supernatural theology, transcending the powers of nature, belongs to the
order of grace.

In addition, even though the terms *natural* and *supernatural* are used
to indicate different orders of causality, those orders are necessarily
interrelated.   Natural and supernatural theology are not utterly distinct

in a causal sense. Alsted points out that the remote causes of both forms of theology are identical, while only the proximate causes are different. Thus in the remote sense, God is the efficient cause and the glory of God the final cause of both natural and supernatural theology.[5] In a proximate sense, however, the efficient cause of natural theology is nature itself and the light of nature, and the final cause is that man be rendered inexcusable in his sin—as contrasted with Scripture and salvation, the proximate efficient and final causes of supernatural theology.[6] Similar comparisons and contrasts, proximate and remote, can be made concerning material and formal causality.[7]

This discussion of natural and supernatural theology occupies a far more prominent position in the Protestant orthodox prolegomena than in their medieval counterparts. What is more, the Protestant discussion draws as much on soteriological as upon epistemological concerns. Whereas Scotus, Aureole, Durandus, and other late medieval theologians saw the critical issue as encapsulated in the denial of a proportion between finite human reason and the truth of God *in se*, the Protestant systems intensify the issue and, indeed, alter its terms by emphasizing the sinfulness as well as the finitude of reason.

Pictet, for example, argues that the existence of God can in fact be known from nature and that this knowledge seems to be partly innate, partly acquired. Man seems to come, through his own mental capacities, to an idea of God and also seems to be naturally able to analyze this concept of God in terms of "the careful observation of created things." Pictet argues that Paul's statement concerning the law in the heart implies an innate knowledge of God while the psalmist's praise of God's handiwork demonstrates a scriptural foundation for the concept of an acquired knowledge of God. "Both these kinds of knowledge" argues Pictet, "are a great proof of God's goodness to man," a benefit to society in general, and provide "an incentive to seek after a clearer revelation" that is "sufficient to leave anyone, who abuses his natural light, without excuse."[8] Special divine revelation is not only to be sought after but is also necessary for salvation for two reasons:

> First, the imperfection of natural knowledge, which was insufficient either for true knowledge or for true worship of God, and which could not, in any way, comfort the human soul against the fear of death, and under the consciousness of sin, because it could not point out the mode of satisfying the divine justice. . . . The second argument is drawn from the great corruption of mankind after the sin of the first parents, their speedy forgetfulness of God and blindness in divine things, their propensity for all kinds of error, and especially to the invention of new and false religions. . . . A revelation beyond the natural was therefore necessary in which God might not only cause to be known, in a clearer manner, his own perfections,

which he had revealed in the first, but also discover new perfections, and reveal "the mystery of godliness."

This supernatural revelation was made through the Word; for, after God had used mute teachers to instruct mankind, he opened his own sacred lips: and after he had, "at sundry times, and in divers manners, spoken unto the fathers by the prophets, in these last days" he has condescended to "speak to us by His Son" (Heb. i.1).[9]

Pictet then concludes by noting that, in view of this distinction, the system he is about to frame is a system of supernatural or revealed knowledge of God.[10]

The question of continuity or discontinuity between the Reformers and the orthodox is raised quite pointedly by these definitions of natural and supernatural theology. According to one line of argument (represented by Althaus and Bizer), the gradual development of the discussion of natural theology and of the positive use of reason represents a turn toward rationalism and, in the view of Althaus in particular, toward a Thomistic model of the relation of reason and revelation.[11] More recently, under the impact of neo-orthodoxy and the Barth-Brunner debate, there has been a tendency among other scholars to argue against any legitimate place for natural theology in Reformed system and to view seventeenth-century discussions of the subject as a deviation from the perspective of the Reformers.[12] As with virtually all of the developments belonging to the rise of orthodoxy, however, the elaboration of a Reformed doctrine of natural theology cannot be represented simply as a manifestation either of continuity or of discontinuity. Calvin and Viret proposed a twofold knowledge of God as Creator and Redeemer, while Musculus addressed the issue of natural and revealed knowledge with a threefold division of the subject.[13] It was the Thomist-trained Vermigli, though, who of all the early Reformed codifiers of doctrine produced the most extended treatment of the problem of natural theology.

The highly influential *locus* on natural theology found in Vermigli's *Loci communes* is drawn from his commentaries on Romans and 1 Samuel. Vermigli's discussion begins with a reflection on Paul's phrase *to gnoston tou theou* (Rom. 1:19), which Vermigli renders as "that which may be known of God." This phrase, according to Vermigli, is restrictive in implication and indicates two categories, at least, of the knowledge of God—things accessible to the natural man and things known only by special revelation, such as justification, forgiveness in Christ and the resurrection of the body. The former category, Paul "reduces . . . to two principal points, namely, the everlasting power and divinity of God." In other words "the workmanship of this world" manifests both the almighty power of God and also the fact that this power is both wise and good in its creative exercise and providential care—and thus is a truly divine power.[14]

There are two opinions concerning the source of this natural knowledge of God. Some, notes Vermigli, would explain it as the result of creation: a certain indication of the Creator and his truth can be perceived in created things. Others believe that God placed in the human mind "certain . . . information, whereby we are driven to conceive excellent and worthy things of the nature of God." On the basis of this natural tendency we learn of God by observing creation. Some claim that pagan philosophers like Aristotle and Plato were in fact instruments or mediators of divine revelation. It is quite true that these thinkers correctly analyzed the order of causes and effects in this world and recognized that such an order cannot go on indefinitely but must come finally to a chief cause which is God. But these evidences of God as cause and protector of all things are equally given in Scripture—as David says, "The heavens set forth the glory of God."[15] Vermigli makes no attempt to restrict the source of natural theology to one or the other of these options. Instead he admits to the fact of natural revelation and the ability of human beings to discern it. Indeed, he indicates a place for the natural knowledge of God in Scripture and, by implication, in Christian theology. All things, says Vermigli, show forth "the eternal power and divinity of God"—but especially human nature which manifests his very likeness and majesty. The soul especially—with its "justice, wisdom, and many other noble qualities," with its sense of right and wrong—testifies to the existence of God, as does the conscience with its inward condemnation of wickedness, love of the good, and presentiment of God's future judgment. There is nothing in the created world so vile that it in some way does not give testimony of God.[16]

This revelation of God in nature renders all inexcusable: no man can explain his wickedness or impiety on the ground of ignorance. All men know of God or can know of him. Vermigli notes that Paul also makes impossible another rationalization—that men lack the strength of will to do the good or to worship rightly. This lack rests on human sinfulness; man's weakness comes by his own fault. Even admitting the universal existence of sin, it is clear that men might still aspire to some good and attempt to avoid evil. But they freely choose to sin—again leaving themselves inexcusable before the Law of God in their hearts and the knowledge of God given in nature.[17]

Vermigli concludes that no matter how clearly God may be *inferred* from nature to be the Creator, it is nevertheless necessary to *know* God as Creator by faith. The article of creation is the first article of the creed. Remove it from the articles of faith and the subsequent related doctrines, including the doctrines of original sin and Christ, will be unable to stand. Faith itself demands that we learn even of creation by revelation.[18] Vermigli thus explicitly sets aside the *analogia entis* of his Thomist teachers:

> The effects by which the philosophers move toward knowledge of God are far inferior to his goodness, strength and power . . . these things are not in him in the same way as we speak of them. For, as in simplicity of nature, so also in goodness, righteousness, and wisdom is [God] other than men. . . .[19]

Beside a natural knowledge of God, therefore, man must have faith revealed "by the Word of God."

> For Christ said, "None can come to me unless the Father draws him." Faith therefore gathers a plentiful knowledge of God out of the Scriptures, as far as salvation requires and as far as our present capacity allows . . . yet we do not reach an understanding of the essence of God.[20]

This perception of the limits of natural theology—clearly not Thomistic in its implications for the use of philosophy and reason in theology or in its denial of analogy between God and creation—carries over into the theology of the Reformed orthodox, including its ambivalence about the value of the purely philosophical doctrine of God as Creator. Daneau and Aretius in the early orthodox period and Riissen at the end of the high orthodox era note that natural theology teaches certain basic truths: that God exists; that he should be worshiped; that man ought to live uprightly; that the soul is immortal; and that virtue is rewarded, vice punished.[21] The doctrine of creation is not included. Instead, *theologia naturalis* is, at its best, defined in terms of the moral or natural law—and these legal truths, the orthodox point out, are not used by natural man to construct a valid ethic. The natural law serves only to leave man without excuse, and its precepts become a valid ethic only through revelation. Heppe rightly notes that the orthodox elaboration of this doctrinal point must be regarded as a defense, in a new context, of the teaching of Calvin and Vermigli concerning the inner sense of the divine shared by all men.[22]

The paradoxical character of natural theology was contested in the seventeenth century by the Arminians and the Socinians. The former argued that the light of nature was in fact a preparation for the light of grace and that the truths of natural theology could provide a basis on which a superstructure of revealed truth might be built; the latter

argued that a "great tradition" of rational or natural truth extended
back to Adam, supplemented by truths of revelation given throughout
history.[23]   Against the distinction between a nonsaving natural
revelation and a saving supernatural revelation, the Socinians argued
that God cannot require of human beings something that he does not
provide: if all God has given to human beings are vague remnants
(*reliquiae*) of the Law, he cannot require of them some higher standard.
To the Arminian position, the Reformed reply that natural theology can be
viewed as a preparation for the "school of grace" but only in the sense
that it renders sinners inexcusable, humbles them and drives them
elsewhere—to grace—for salvation.   There can be no natural,
non-Christian foundation for Christian theology.[24]   The sinfulness of
man both impedes and pollutes natural revelation and places him in need
of a gracious supernatural revelation.   As Maccovius argues, it is
impossible that God could make unjust demands or be the cause of sin, but
it is not at all impossible or improper for God to give his creature,
man, the power to commit sin and become, as it were, a debtor.[25]

The issue for Reformed orthodox theology was not so much the
development of a positive *locus* of natural theology but the defense of a
view of natural theology that taught the existence of such knowledge but
insisted not only on its inefficacy in salvation but also in its
disjunction from the special or supernatural revelation of God.   Here
again we see a point of contact between the prolegomena and the system:
the relation between natural and supernatural theology is soteriologically controlled and reflects precisely the relation between the natural
man in his fallen condition and the regenerate man empowered by grace.
This issue was fully recognized by the Reformed, who viewed the Socinian
and Arminian perspectives on natural theology as controlled by a Pelagian
view of human nature.[26]

5.2 The Distinction Between Natural and Supernatural Theology

> The orthodox indeed uniformly teach that natural theology is
> partly inborn or implanted, such that it is derived from 'the
> book of conscience' by common or basic insights; partly
> acquired, such that it is derived from 'the book of Creatures'
> by the power of reason.[27]

Turretin here cites the two basic sources or patterns of natural
knowledge noted by Vermigli without any technical elaboration. The mind
has both a knowledge that is basic to it (*cognitio insita*) and a
knowledge that is acquired through the powers of reason (*cognitio*

acquisita). The former term demands some explanation. As was strongly implied by Calvin[28] and afterward argued by the Reformed orthodox, the basic knowledge of God, the seed of religion (*semen religionis*) or sense of the divine (*sensus divinitatis; sensus numinis*), is not innate knowledge (*cognitio innata*) in a Platonic sense, nor is it infused knowledge (*cognitio infusa*) so foreign to the mind that without it the mind is blank, a *tabula rasa*.

The Platonic theory, like the Augustinian theory of illumination favored by the more platonizing of the medieval doctors, established a link between the natural man and the realm of divine truth that was not compatible with the Reformed theory of grace and revelation, bound as it was to the epistemological *finitum non capax infiniti*. The theory of a mental *tabula rasa* caused the opposite problem: it so severed the human mind from externals that it raised the possibility of an absolute ignorance of the divine and, therefore, of an excuse for sin (con. Rom. 1:20). Needless to say, this position, too, was repugnant to the Reformed. The Reformed scholastics, therefore, look for a view midway between a theory of *cognitio innata* and a theory of a *tabula rasa*. Such a possibility existed in the concept of *cognitio insita*, defined as an intuitive knowledge or immediate, nonratiocinative apprehension of the divine.[29] Thus Turretin can say that the human mind is not a *tabula rasa* absolutely but only relatively: it does not naturally contain discursive or dianoetic knowledge (*cognitio dianoetica*), that is, acquired knowledge, but it does contain *noesis* or pure intellectual apprehension (*cognitio apprehensiva et noetica*).[30]

Using this concept of *cognitio insita* or *cognitio intuitiva sive apprehensiva*, the Reformed orthodox can argue three basic forms of natural theology, two of them arising immediately and universally in the human mind and one arising as a result of rational examination of the others. First, the universal experience of mankind and the institution of religion in every nation of the world indicate a sense of the divine or of divine power (*sensus numinis*). There is no nation so barbaric, Cicero declared, that it is not persuaded of the existence of God.[31] Second, the human conscience bears witness to a natural law which, Turretin concludes, "necessarily includes a knowledge of God the Lawgiver (*cognitio Dei Legislatoris*)."[32] Knowledge of God, in other words, arises naturally from the contemplation of created things and by inference from the order and government of things.[33] Third, out of these basic apprehensions of the divine, by means of purely rational investigation, pagan philosophers have developed a philosophical natural theology, an acquired natural theology.[34]

In terms of its object and ultimate *source* (God--his power, wisdom and goodness), this knowledge is supernatural, but in terms of the *means of approach* to this knowledge, it is entirely natural.   Scripture expressly testifies, Walaeus notes, that there is nothing spiritual or supernatural in those who are ignorant of Christ: after the fall man is by nature corrupt and devoid of the supernatural.[35]   Against the Socinians and Arminians, who would press this knowledge into the service of salvation, the Reformed note that natural knowledge of God serves only to order society, establish general rules of morality, restrain gross sin, and leave man without excuse in his fallenness.   Any further use of natural theology among pagans would imply salvation by works, apart from grace.[36]   What is more, the natural theology developed by Christians serves not to save souls but to confirm the truths of revelation: in no instance is natural theology salvific.[37]

By way of contrast, a saving knowledge of God is supernatural not only in its object and ultimate source but also in its instrumentality and its acquisition by the mind.   Supernatural theology is mediated by the revealing activity of the *logos prophorikos* and the Spirit, and it is received by a supernaturally given disposition of knowing (*habitus sciendi*) or, more precisely, disposition of believing (*habitus credendi*) distinct from the disposition that receives the natural knowledge of God through perception of the creation.   Although the term was not favored by the orthodox because of its medieval usage in the doctrines of grace and justification, theological knowledge is clearly an "infused" knowledge (*cognitio infusa*) resting, in the receiving mind, on an infused disposition (*habitus infusa*).   In other words, it is not an innate, ingrafted or acquired knowledge, all of which are natural to the human mind.[38] Heidanus notes, however, in a statement reminiscent of pietist attacks on Lutheran orthodoxy, that theological knowledge acquired by study is separable from saving faith: the habit of saving faith must be infused, but the acquisition of theological knowledge is possible even when faith is utterly lost![39]

This disjunction between natural and supernatural theology can be further explained in terms of distinctions in genus, subject/object, efficient cause, material, form, end, and adjuncts.   Polanus argues that only *theologia supernaturalis* is *theologia* properly so-called, since it alone rests upon God's self-revelation in Scripture. *Theologia naturalis*, when it makes a valid claim to truth and is not, therefore, to be classified as *theologia falsa*, is properly a form of philosophy.   It is what the Philosopher calls "theology," which is to say, metaphysics, *prima philosophia*.

> Natural theology is that [knowledge of God] which proceeds from self-evident principles (*principium secundum se notis*) by the natural light of the human intellect according to a human mode of reasoning; and therefore it deals with divine things only as far as the natural light is capable of knowing.[40]

Natural theology belongs, as philosophy, to the genus *scientia*, whereas theology is more properly a form of wisdom (*sapientia*).[41] By way of contrast, Alsted labored, perhaps excessively, to place natural and supernatural theology into the same *genus*. His position is not, however, too far removed from that of Polanus inasmuch as Alsted's definition recognizes the genuine conformity of natural theology to the strict Thomistic view of *scientia* and notes the failure of the definition to fit the case of supernatural theology. Polanus does not address the question of a Christian natural theology; Alsted poses the question and is pressed to define the discipline as a theology rightly so-called.[42] In addition, he cannot equate rational theology with philosophy or metaphysics inasmuch as it is a true knowledge of "divine things" such as is found in the Book of Job and the Psalms: theology, not philosophy of any sort, is presented in the holy books![43]

Natural and supernatural theology differ also with respect to the subject with which they deal, that is, with respect to object. The proper subject or object of theology is divine things (*res divinae*) properly and simply so-called, whereas the subject of natural theology is divine things in part properly but in part improperly so-called, according to human opinion. Natural theology, then, can fall into the difficulty of having its subject dealt with falsely. This problem relates directly to the distinction between the efficient causes of natural and supernatural theology: the efficient cause of the former is nature and the light of nature upon the human intellect, with the light of the intellect itself being the instrument of understanding; the efficient cause of the latter is grace and the light of the Spirit.[44] Thus, natural theology is acquired naturally whereas supernatural theology is acquired in a supernatural way, resting upon the revelation of God.[45]

Furthermore the form and material of natural and supernatural theology differ. The form of supernatural theology is divine truth (*divina veritas*) whereas the form of natural theology, in view of its natural causality, cannot be divine truth. The materials of supernatural theology, moreover, are principles or precepts unknown to nature and graciously revealed (*natura ignota et gratiose revelata*)—such as the

triunity of God and the generation of the Son by the Father.   The
materials of natural theology are principles or precepts ingrafted into
the nature of men (*principia seu praecepta natura hominibus insita*)--such
as the existence of God, the oneness of God and the need to worship God.
Supernatural theology, in addition, contains both Law and gospel, while
natural theology is ignorant of the gospel.[46]   The ends or goals of these
two theologies diverge also, since *theologia naturalis* can not draw man
toward beliefs that do not arise from rational investigation, excite the
emotions to a desire for and love of God, or set aside the dangerous
errors of the world over which Christ has victory.[47]

Supernatural and natural theology differ, finally, as to adjuncts
(*adiuncta*) or attributes.   The former is clear and perfect in itself,
since clarity and perfection are also the attributes of its source and
cause, the Word of God.   The latter, however, is imperfect.   Indeed, the
obscurity and imperfection of *theologia naturalis* obtained in the
original integrity of humanity even prior to the fall--*non finiti ad
infinitum dari proportio potest!*   Thus even antelapsarian natural
theology would have been in need of grace drawing it toward perfection.
After the fall, however, in the corrupt and depraved nature of man, the
principia of natural theology are far more obscure--indeed they are
utterly corrupt and totally disordered (*vitiosissima et conturbatissima*).
Natural theology, therefore, is never, even in itself, capable of
perfection.[48]

5.3 Twofold and Threefold Knowledge of God: The Necessity of Supernatural Theology

Two basic models for understanding the relationship between natural
and supernatural, nonsaving and saving knowledge of God were developed by
second-generation Reformers.   From Calvin, Viret and the editor of
Vermigli's *Loci communes*, Robert Masson, comes a discussion of the
twofold knowledge of God; from Musculus comes a similar model, substantially in agreement with Calvin and Viret, of a threefold knowledge
of God.   Both of these models were retained by the Reformed orthodox and
used as ways of interpreting the problem of natural reason and its
theological perceptions.   Here again we can argue a major point of
continuity with the Reformation in the development of orthodoxy, albeit
not a simple continuity with Calvin's thought or a simple reproduction of
sixteenth-century arguments in the seventeenth century.[49]

Perhaps the clearest and most celebrated statement of the soteriologically reinterpreted discussion of reason and revelation, natural and
revealed theology, is Calvin's distinction concerning the *duplex cognitio
Dei* or twofold knowledge of God.[50]   Calvin identifies the theme of the
entire first book of the *Institutes* as the knowledge of God the
Creator,[51] as distinct from the knowledge of God the Redeemer that he
traces beginning in book two.[52]   This knowledge of God the Creator
belongs *both* to the order of nature and to the general teaching of
Scripture. Pagan philosophy knows something of God as Creator from the
order of nature but, ultimately, because of sin, fails to move from that
knowledge to true religion and idolatrously confuses creature and
Creator.[53] Scriptural revelation, therefore, is necessary for us to have
a true knowledge of God the Creator—and the special revelation of the
gospel promise is necessary for any knowledge of God as Redeemer.

The idea of a twofold knowledge of God appears in a somewhat different form in the writings of Calvin's contemporary, Pierre Viret. Viret
argues that men by nature seek their "highest good" (*summum bonum*) but in
and through themselves are unable to attain it. Man must in fact look to
God as the source of ultimate goodness since no creature is able to
attain that height and since man cannot reach this goodness by his own
devices: "the highest good of man and his true felicity and blessedness,
as well as the means . . . is to know God in Jesus Christ his Son."[54]   It
is insufficient, however, to know merely the fact or truth of Christ
since there are two kinds of knowledge of God, the one faithful, the
other unfaithful. Even the devils believe and tremble! One who believes
unfaithfully fears God not as a good child fears his father but as an
evildoer fears his judge. Only one who believes faithfully in God
through trust in the mercy of Christ can know God as Father.[55]

The contrast between Calvin and Viret is significant, particularly
for the discussion of natural theology. Viret makes a simple bifurcation
between unsaving and saving, unfaithful and faithful, natural and
revealed theology. Those who attempt to reach God through creatures or
through themselves encounter not the highest good but rather a judge of
sin and, indeed, a "cruel tyrant."[56]   Only in Christ is God known as
Father. Viret's language of the knowledge of God as judge and tyrant had
its impact on orthodoxy—but his simple bifurcation was less influential
than Calvin's distinction between knowledge of God as Creator and
knowledge of God as Redeemer, with its implication, spelled out at length
in the argument of book one of the *Institutes*, that knowledge of God as
Creator, albeit a natural knowledge, was available both as a false, pagan
theology and as a true, Christian theology clarified by the

"spectacles" of Scripture.[57] God is manifest as Creator both in the workmanship of the universe and in "the general teaching of Scripture" but as Redeemer only in Christ.[58] In other words, although Calvin speaks of a twofold knowledge of God, he points to three forms taken by that knowledge—a corrupt, partial, and extrabiblical knowledge of God as Creator, a biblical knowledge of God as Creator, and a knowledge of God in Christ as Redeemer.

At the very beginning of his *Loci communes* Musculus deals with the issue of our knowledge of God. He begins by arguing that the "natural and fleshly man" lacks knowledge of "the things of God" and even less "understands or knows God himself." But even the "spiritual man" can lack a "plain and perfect" knowledge of

> those things which concern the Majesty of God, which is so clothed and covered with inaccessible brightness, that the finest part of our mind or understanding can by no means comprehend it. And yet such is our estate as men, that there is nothing which with greater danger we may be ignorant of, than of our God, by whom we were made, and by whose heavenly grace were called to this intent and purpose, that we should know him, obey him, and serve him, unless we will willingly fall into everlasting damnation. So stand we in a profound predicament—with the most mighty and unsearchable Majesty of God on the one side, and the necessity of our salvation on the other side.[59]

Nevertheless, the true knowledge of God is gained only by degrees. The first step, so designated by the initial question of Musculus' system, is the setting aside of impiety and confessing the existence of God. This confession is far from the end of the knowledge of God, but is the necessary beginning, without which "man cannot climb to higher things." The second degree appears as a negative counterbalance to the confession of God's existence: not any God, but the true God must be confessed. "We must know also who is the true God, lest that through the error of Pagans, we happen on any that is not God." As the third, fourth, and fifth degrees, Musculus enunciates the basic articles of biblical faith: we must know God as Creator of heaven and earth, as one in essence and three in person, and as having the particular nature described by the attributes of sufficiency, omnipotence, truth, goodness, lovingkindness, mercy, and justice.[60]

> Sixthly, it belongs also to the true knowledge of God, to know that he is the father of our Lord Jesus Christ, and that he sent him into the world, because of the salvation of man, to be a mediator, redeemer, and saviour, to save all who believe in him, and that he has adopted them to be his sons and heirs of his kingdom. By this knowledge of God we are separated from all nations that are strangers to Christ.[61]

Next, says Musculus, this sixth degree of knowledge must become a matter
of personal faith, to the end that we recognize God as Father "particularly unto each of us, loving, merciful, and the most assured saviour."
Finally, the eighth degree of knowledge is the result of faith manifested
in love, service, and obedience. We must acknowledge God to be the one
true God,

> depending upon him only in clear hope and trust, regarding him
> above all things in heaven and on earth. If a man lack this,
> the saying of the Apostle can be applied to him: they confess
> that they know God, and deny him in their doings.[62]

Knowledge, writes Musculus, depends on two things:

> One is, that the thing which is sought, may be known in deed:
> the other is, that he who would know, be enabled by capacity of
> understanding to know that which he seeks to know.[63]

We can know neither those things that are not nor those things which are
beyond our senses and understanding. Recognizing these restrictions on
all knowledge we can proceed to explain the nature of our knowledge of
God.

To the end that he may be known, "God opens himself to the knowledge
of man" in three ways:

> The first and most general is that which arises from his works.
> The second is more special, declared by his own speech. The
> third is most special of all, which is by his secret
> inspiration.[64]

The first is most general because it is given equally to all people of
all nations. The majesty of God is shown forth in all the world, in
earth and in heaven, so much so "that no man can excuse himself for not
knowing God." Our first knowledge of God and the philosopher's knowledge
of him are founded on "the light and brightness" of his works. Among
other things, the "most constant order," the "endless continuance" of
created things demonstrates the wisdom of the Creator and his "power and
might" in preservation of the world. These good things together with the
"marvellous terror of lightnings and earthquakes, pestilences, gapings of
the ground, strange sights from heaven" and the truth of prophesies which
"plainly pass the limits of man's foreknowledge" the "power of the
godhead to govern all things in the world" is clearly established to the
mind of man.[65]

"The second way that God is known consists in the Word, for God hath
opened himself to our fathers by word and speaking, even from the beginning of the world, until the days of the New Testament."[66] This mode of
revelation is to be considered "special" since it was not given to every
nation but to Israel first and then to the Gentiles by Christ "with the
general gift of salvation to all men."[67]

The third way by inspiration, is by secret revelation of the holy spirit. And this way I call most special, indicating a distinction from the other two, which are indifferent to good and evil, and restricting this way to the   elect, who beside the light of works, and the declaration of words, obtain a most certain knowledge of God, yet rather a feeling and a taste of him, by the lively and effectual inspiration and revelation of the holy spirit of God.[68]

The first two ways of knowing God serve to leave "man's reason . . . utterly void of excuse." The third alone turns "the hearts of men . . . effectually . . . toward the true service of God." Even so, it is the elect of God who by "the inward revelation of the spirit" study the knowledge of God most diligently as it is given in his works and in his Word.[69]

Significantly, both of Musculus' paradigms of the knowledge of God—the eight levels of human knowing and the three modes of divine revelation—retain the distinction between knowledge of God as Creator and Lord and knowledge of God as Redeemer and Father in Christ. In the eightfold model Musculus emphasizes (his sixth degree or level) the necessity of knowing God savingly in Christ—indeed, the whole model hinges on the distinction between true knowledge in the first five degrees and saving knowledge savingly applied in the last three. The three modes of divine revelation, in nature, in Scripture, and redemptively in the Spirit, reflect the implied threefold model in Calvin's *duplex cognitio Dei*.

These models for understanding the knowledge of God carried over into Reformed orthodoxy and, indeed, the specific language of the *duplex cognitio Dei* remained normative. When we speak of a continuity between the Reformers and the orthodox on this point, we define it broadly, as a continuity not with a particular writer like Calvin or Musculus, even though a large portion of their specific language carried over into orthodox theology, but as a continuity of interest in a particular construction of the problem of natural and supernatural theology. In addition, whereas Calvin and his contemporaries were content with the categorical statement of the necessity of saving knowledge in Christ coupled with a recognition of various levels of theological knowledge *extra Christum*, the orthodox saw a need to develop at some length, with attention to their relationships and differences, a whole series of technical distinctions concerning human knowledge of God. Thus Polanus:

> In the first place, knowledge of God (*cognitio Dei*) is twofold (*duplex*): namely of God the creator (*Dei creatoris*) and of God the redeemer (*Dei redemptoris*).
> Knowledge of God the redeemer is knowledge of Christ, which is either bodily or spiritual.

In the second place, knowledge of God is either perfect or imperfect.

In the third place it is either natural or revealed.

Revealed knowledge of God is either spiritual or literal and both of these are either mediate (*mediata*) or immediate (*immediata*).

Further, knowledge of God is either innate (*innata*) or acquired (*acquisita*) or infused (*infusa*).

Moreover, it is either general or special.

Its opposites are a privative ignorance of God and a presumptive knowledge of God (*praesumta notitia Dei*).[70]

The division between natural and revealed or supernatural theology argued under this rubric of *duplex cognitio Dei* places both *theologia naturalis* and *theologia revelata* squarely within the categories of *theologia vera* and, subordinate to that, *theologia ectypa* and *theologia viatorum*. In other words, natural theology as considered by Polanus and the other Protestant scholastics is not necessarily or always a pagan or false theology: it can be a Christian, true theology. What is more, it cannot be severed absolutely from revealed or supernatural theology: it is clearly a form of revelation and its origin and object are supernatural—namely, God. *Theologia naturalis*, in this limited, Christian sense of a *cognitio Dei creatoris*, resting on the natural order but clarified by Scripture itself, is distinct from *theologia super-naturalis* primarily in terms of the mode of revelation and the goal or purpose (*finis*) of theology.[71] The former corresponds with the category of general revelation in Scripture, the latter with special revelation concerning Christ—although, of course, Scripture itself, as the Word of God, is supernaturally given and never in itself natural theology.

This problem of a twofold general revelation or natural theology, together with the typical Reformed emphasis on the necessity of a revelation of God the Redeemer, appears in the model borrowed by Edward Leigh from Zanchi:

There are three Glasses, in which God manifests himself to us:
1. The Glasse of the Creature
2. The Glasse of the Holy Scriptures
3. The Glasse of Jesus Christ: in that Glasse alone God is rightly known and perfectly shines.[72]

Zanchi had made these comments in his *Compendium praecipuorum capitum doctrinae christianae*, a short system written early in his career and based, significantly, on the 1545 edition of Calvin's *Institutes*.[73] In 1545, Calvin had already formulated much of his teaching on the knowledge of God, but he had not yet added the famous language of the *duplex cognitio Dei*. Thus, Zanchi could read the *Institutes* as discussing knowledge of God in creation, Scripture and in Christ—a threefold knowledge. The *speculum creaturarum* is clear by itself (*per se clarum*), the *speculum sacrarum Scripturarum* still clearer (*clarius*), while the third "glass" or mirror, Christ himself, the true image of God is by far the clearest of all (*omnium longe clarissimum*).[74]

Zanchi elaborates at considerable length on the content and the limitations of the *speculum creaturarum*. Inasmuch as God's nature is incomprehensible and hidden from the human mind, only faint marks or signs (*notae*) of the divine majesty can be seen in the creation, but they are clear enough to leave mankind without excuse for its ignorance. As Scripture itself testifies, the created order manifests the majesty of God and, in addition, individual divine virtues, such as the wisdom, power, eternity, goodness, providence, righteousness, mercy, and power of God. From God's righteousness, moreover, the future judgment of sin can be inferred.[75] Such knowledge ought to lead to true religion and to the hope of eternal life. It is not a defect of the mirror, but the defect of our vision that yields up false religion and corrupt knowledge of God and that makes necessary a second mirror for the knowledge of God, the mirror of Scripture.[76]

For the sake of his elect, Zanchi writes, God has provided a remedy to the problem of the sinful distortion of the truths given in the *speculum creaturarum*. Thus the Word of God came to Adam, Noah, and the patriarchs in the form of inward illumination, oracles and visions and then, beginning with Moses, was committed to writing in order to preserve the truth of God from the errors and lies of a sinful world.[77] Scripture, thus, stands as the Word of God, having its own authority prior to the authority of man, prior even to the authority of the church.[78] Following out the implication of Calvin's *Institutes*, which would eventually, in 1559, make a clear division between knowledge of God as Creator and knowledge of God as Redeemer, Zanchi closes his first *locus* with the comment that he will discuss the third "mirror," Christ, at a subsequent point. Since, moreover, Zanchi's subsequent christological discussions do not assume an inward knowledge, given apart from Scripture, the third mirror is to be understood as the scriptural revelation of Christ conjoined with the cleansing effect of redemption in Christ.[79]

Although, therefore, the Protestant scholastics regularly make the distinction between natural and revealed theology, the issue is not quite as simple as the bifurcation would indicate. In the "glass of Holy Scripture," both the "glass of the Creature" and the "glass of Jesus Christ" can be identified. We thus arrive at a model which recognizes two kinds of natural theology (the one pagan and false, the other redeemed and belonging to the category of *theologia vera*) and a supernatural or revealed theology which teaches both of God the Creator--

corresponding at least in part with the *theologia naturalis regenetorum*—and of God the Redeemer. Only the latter category, the theology of God the Redeemer, contributes to man's salvation. The complexity of the model arises from the teaching of the Reformers who were not content to follow the form of the medieval discussion of the knowledge of God and added to the discussion of revelation and reason the problem of the epistemological consequences of sin. Indeed, we find here, despite changes in language, a precise continuity with Calvin's formulation of the *duplex cognitio Dei* and its logical and theological consequences.

Yet another paradigm of some importance, standing in continuity both with the threefold knowledge described by Musculus and Leigh and with the contrast between God as Judge and Redeemer argued by Viret, is found in Charnock's essay on the knowledge of God in Christ. Charnock clearly draws insights from covenant theology into his discussion by distinguishing between the natural, legal and evangelical knowledge of God. The creation provides "a true, though not a full, discovery of God" in which divine attributes like power, wisdom, goodness, immutability, eternity, omniscience, sovereignty, spirituality, sufficiency and majesty can be known. Nonetheless, even before the fall human nature was incapable of knowing "the perfections of God in such a manner as they are discovered in Christ."[80] Since the fall, even this limited natural knowledge has become confused: our reason is utterly insufficient to provide adequate, much less saving knowledge of God.

The legal knowledge of God provides by revelation a knowledge of the moral sovereignty, holiness, and justice (or righteousness) of God. God's holiness appears in his "precepts," his righteousness in his "threatenings"—"nothing of adoption and justifying grace" is represented in the Law. Nevertheless, together with the precepts and threatenings, there was given "a sufficient revelation of God to direct them to Christ, who could only render God visible and intelligible to man."[81] "The evangelical discovery of God by Christ is clearer" than the revelation in creation and in the Law inasmuch as in Christ

> God appears in the sweetness and beauty of his nature, as a
> refreshing light. The creatures tell us that there is a God,
> and Christ tells us who and what that God is.[82]

This evangelical, saving knowledge, however, although clear in itself "as is possible in its own nature" attains for us only "such a clearness as the present state in this world is capable of": it will be "superceded by the light of glory," and even this final knowledge falls short of the fullness of divine knowledge inasmuch as a "created understanding" cannot know an infinite mind as it knows itself.[83]

On the basis of the preceding discussion, a series of distinctions can be made that make sense out of the problem of natural theology and that point to a high degree of continuity between the theology of the Reformers and the thought of their scholastic successors.   Characteristically, these distinctions receive less than adequate treatment at the hands of Barth and scholars like Parker, who tend to follow Barth's presentation of Calvin's views on natural theology.[84]   First, we note a distinction between natural revelation, as placed in the creation by its Creator, and natural theology, as built upon that revelation.   Second, there is the distinction resident in Calvin's thought and the thought of early orthodx writers like Junius and Polanus, between theology *in se* and theology *in subiecto*, between the ideal order and the order in fact.   To this we must also add the distinction between an unregenerate and a regenerate use of natural revelation and the underlying distinction between the *imago Dei* before the fall and its shattered remains in fallen man.   The Barthian readers of Calvin go to great lengths to deny the existence of natural theology, while all that Calvin does is declare such theology useless to salvation.   Calvin, in fact, consistently assumes the existence of false, pagan natural theology that has warped the knowledge of God available in nature into gross idolatry.   Calvin must argue in this way because he assumes the existence of natural revelation which *in se* is a true knowledge of God.   If natural theology were impossible, idolatrous man would not be left without excuse.   The problem is that sin takes the natural revelation of God and fashions, in fact, an idolatrous and sinful theology.   The theology exists and man is to blame because it is sin and sin alone that stands in the way of a valid natural theology.

Parker's interpretation of Calvin's exegesis of Psalm 19:1-9 manifests quite plainly the unwillingness of Barthians to accept the most basic implications of what Calvin says about natural revelation and natural theology—all of which appear to have been quite clear to the Protestant scholastics.   Calvin, as Parker notes, identifies two parts of the psalm: "David celebrates the glory of God as manifested in His works; and in the other exalts and magnifies the knowledge of God which shines *more clearly* in His Word."[85]

Commenting on the first half of the psalm, Calvin extols the revelation of God in nature.   Looking at the second half of the psalm, he argues once again that sinful man is not led to God by natural revelation but is merely left without excuse in his sins.   Only by means of the Word can man come to God, and apart from the Word natural revelation avails nothing, "although it should be to us as a loud and distinct proclamation sounding in our ears."[86]   Brunner was, certainly, incorrect in arguing that Scripture somehow supplements natural revelation—but Barth and Parker are equally incorrect in assuming the "total blindness" of man apart from the Word and in denying natural theology as such. It is clear from the psalm itself and from Calvin's commentary on it that David is not using "the Word" as a key to unlock the otherwise closed doors of natural revelation, but is rather, as one of God's children, looking directly at the book of nature.

Calvin does not deny that there is or can be a genuine natural theology based on natural revelation. Rather his intention is to declare that no natural theology contributes to salvation. This is as true for the regenerate David as it is for the unregenerate Philistine—but David, as one of the redeemed, can recognize the true God in his natural revelation without fashioning an idol. Calvin, therefore, testifies not only to the existence of natural revelation and to the fact of pagan, idolatrous, natural theology, but to the real possibility of a natural theology of the regenerate. Such theology is not saving: it exists as praise rather than as proclamation. Here again, the problem of natural theology reflects the problem of the *imago Dei*: it is not utterly lost, but it provides no basis for man's movement toward God.

Heidegger underscores this contrast between a *theologia naturalis irregenitorum* and a *theologia naturalis regenitorum* in his discussion of the uses of natural theology. Even though it is not salvific, comments Heidegger, the natural knowledge of God (*notitia Dei naturalis*) ought not to be dismissed as useless: it leaves the contentious and obstreperous among the unregenerate without excuse before God (Rom. 1:20) and provides those not yet regenerate but searching in nature for God and salvation with the capability of sensing and discovering the presence of God (Acts 17:27). What is more,

> the regenerate, having been taught the true God and his way of salvation by means of the word of God, may revere all the more the wisdom, power and goodness of God manifest in his works and wonders, and may establish all faith in the one and only God of Israel who alone does such wonders by a return of sorts to the instruction of nature. This use of the works of God is commended magnificently in Psalms 8, 19, 104 and 136.[87]

Mastricht similarly notes a distinction between pagan natural theology, which is a kind of *theologia falsa*, and the natural theology of Christians used as a confirmation of revealed truth.[88]

Du Moulin's foundational treatment of this problem manifests considerable respect for the mind, speaking of it as the greatest faculty of the soul and of knowledge of the truth as the "principal ornament and perfection of the understanding." The greatest height of understanding, moreover, is the knowledge of God. We note here the traditional bipartite view of man as body and soul, the latter being the inclusive term comprising the various spiritual faculties as its organs. Du Moulin's respect for the powers of the mind is tempered, however, from the very outset of his argument by his view of the necessity of revelation: because God is not an object to be perceived but is the fountain of light by which man perceives all things, "God cannot be known . . . unless he infuse our souls with true knowledge of himself."[89]

This necessity of revelation leads Du Moulin to make a distinction between reason and revelation, philosophical concepts and theological doctrines. That man has an inherent knowledge of God is demonstrated both by pagan religion and by his general acceptance of the laws deduced from nature. Philosophers, furthermore, have deduced conceptions of God as Unmoved Mover, as first efficient cause, as Creator and Orderer of the world. Because of this knowledge of God apart from scriptural revelation, Du Moulin sees the need to elaborate upon man's natural ability and define its limits. In the first place, natural knowledge of God is not entirely idolatrous—even though it has been put to wrongful use. Nature conveys some true knowledge of God to man, even if it is insufficient.[90]

Even so, natural theology contains the idea of God as "the most perfect Being, from whom flows and on whom depends all entity and perfection." From this definition follow the attributes of eternity, simplicity, and wisdom. If pagan religions show the sinfulness and idolatry of the wrongful use of this natural knowledge of the divine, philosophy can manifest the more positive ability of the natural man to conceive of God rightly. Philosophy can state the perfections of God, albeit in an imperfect manner. What the natural man lacks is the pure knowledge of God as revealed in his Word.[91] A supernatural revelation is necessary if there is to be any true religion. It alone provides true, saving knowledge, it alone teaches true worship of God.[92] The two components of true religion, knowledge and observance, must rest upon supernatural revelation. The entire discussion of the positive elements of natural theology stands, therefore, within the bounds of the Reformed paradox of the fractured remains of the *imago Dei* and the gift of virtues by common grace. Man's conscience still provides a basic knowledge of the Law, nature still mediates some sense of the divine existence and command, and God still nurtures civic virtues—but none of these gifts is of any soteriological significance.[93]

Turretin can argue, similarly, that salvation, after the fall, depends upon "the revealed Word of the Law and the Gospel." The issue, argues Turretin, is not the existence of natural theology or natural religion: "we may admit, indeed, some sort of natural theology arising from the light of nature, upon which supernatural theology may be built—for example, that God exists, that God is to be worshipped."[94] The issue, rather, is that such natural religion or natural theology cannot provide adequate or proper foundations (*principia adaequata et propria*) for true religion:

> Wherefore Curcellaeus [the Arminian theologian] wrongly distin-
> guishes faith in God from faith in Christ, as if the former is
> absolutely necessary to salvation, the latter only the result
> of divine revelation; for there can be no true and saving faith
> in God, that is not conjoined with faith in Christ, John 14:1.
> For we are unable to believe in God unless it is through
> Christ.[95]

Ultimately, then, natural theology is not a foundation for true knowledge of God, even though it contains some truth. Turretin does not elaborate how this natural theology can be "built" upon—since it is clear that no one can move from natural to supernatural theology apart from the gracious revelation of God in Christ. He may have in mind a pedagogical or legal use of natural theology as described by Charnock and correspond-ing with the Reformed doctrine of the threefold use of the Law, or he may be pointing, much as Pictet would, toward an initial use of the proofs of God's existence in Christian theology, and therefore toward the beginnings of a more rationalistic theology.[96] In either case, however, a sharp line remains between the nonsaving character of natural theology and the salvific character of supernatural theology.

Du Moulin elaborates further upon this problem: reason and the law in nature provide knowledge of God as Creator, as master of life, and as giver of the requirements for right regulation of life. They also give a vague notion of what God is in himself, apart from his relation to external objects. Here Du Moulin clearly allows, albeit in a limited degree, for a metaphysical theory drawn out of nature. Reason and law also give man a sense of terror, an awareness of sinfulness, and a consciousness of just punishment. Yet a definite limit is set upon man's knowledge of God—the corruption of his nature. Indeed, Du Moulin can go so far as to state that without the gospel, all knowledge of God and his works is useless speculation (no matter how correct) and a burden upon the conscience. Only the gospel reveals God as he wills to be toward man—as Father and Redeemer.[97] The problem is not so much the utter unavailability of natural knowledge of God, then, as its inefficacy.

These statements lead Du Moulin to set forth the basic tenets for Christian theological anthropology, including especially the problem of the relation of the fall to the image of God in man. As first created, in God's image, man was characterized by holiness and righteousness. Such was the *imago Dei* in its purity—a spiritual rectitude and a basis

for communion with God.   Then man "revolted from God of his own accord
and by the suggestion of the Devil, whereupon sin came into the world and
by sin death and malediction."   The *imago Dei* was not totally lost, but
disfigured by sin so that there remains in every man some sense of the
divine and a small seed of honesty and justice.   There can now be no
complete and saving knowledge of God through reason or nature, but
because of the remnant of knowledge and because of our perception of the
Law, we are all left without excuse in our sins.   Thus, the entire
anthropological and soteriological structure of Reformed theology must be
brought to bear on the prolegomena, to the end that the initial epistemological statement of the system recognizes the impossibility of saving
knowledge apart from the divine initiative.   Despite the great respect he
manifests for reason and philosophy throughout his treatise, Du Moulin,
like Aretius—and, for that matter, like Calvin—concludes that
revelation supplies man's only hope: the epistemological problem is
surmounted only in Christ, only in the One who reveals God as Father.[98]

Du Moulin and his orthodox brethren, therefore, were unable to
develop a theological epistemology without adumbrating their subsequent
soteriological arguments, the primary point at issue being the theme of
the *duplex cognitio Dei*.   Du Moulin points out that, for the sake of
man's salvation, God sent his only begotten Son into the world to be
united with human flesh.   The Son, who is one God with the Father and the
Holy Spirit, assumed human nature "without diminution of the divinity or
mixture of the natures."   We note here the trinitarian ground motif of
Reformed thought as well as the distinctive christological pattern with
its emphasis on the divine transcendence.   Christ, as the God-man, is the
Mediator who joins and therefore reconciles these otherwise disparate
extremes.   In his human nature, writes Du Moulin, the Son of God performed the work of redemption, fulfilling the laws and making satisfaction for sin.   He is the Author of eternal life to all who believe in
him, for in him we are made sons of God through faith and by the "Spirit
of Adoption."[99]

Du Moulin can therefore write

. . . though God inhabits inaccessible light, he has made
himself visible in some manner in his Son, who is the image of
invisible God and God with us.   Whosoever endeavours to come to
God by any other way shall find him a Judge and not a
Father. . . .[100]

The *duplex cognitio Dei* thus creates a paradox of the union and disunion
of philosophy and theology in the great orthodox systems: on the one
hand, God is the fountain of light by which we perceive all things, while
on the other we cannot truly receive this divine light apart from Christ.

Thus—if as Calvin said—knowledge of God and knowledge of self are intimately related, there can be no truly useful unregenerate knowledge. Philosophy, although it is a crucial adjunct to theology, stands under judgment and even the nominally nonsoteriological *loci* of the system cannot be understood without faith. Again we see that the prolegomena are not an isolated point of departure but in fact depend upon the system they propose to ground.

The impact of the *duplex cognitio Dei* is stronger in some systems than others. In the era of the Reformation Calvin and Viret mark the high point of its influence whereas Musculus and Vermigli develop somewhat different perspectives on the problem and are more open to natural theology. In the era of early orthodxy the situation is similar: the *duplex cognitio Dei* is powerfully enunciated by Du Moulin and Polanus, while its influence is less apparent in the works of Scharpius, Gomarus, Alsted, and Walaeus—although each of the latter sets up barriers to the use of natural theology. Even so, in the high orthodx era, Heidegger and van Mastricht stand out as holding to a clear separation between natural and supernatural theology, while Turretin and Pictet see a vague promise in Christian philosophy. Turretin, moveover, can echo strongly the language of the *duplex cognitio Dei*. At no point is there a clear movement of Reformed theology toward rationalism—rather, we find, in the spectrum of opinion on natural revelation and natural theology, a consistent concern to identify the distinctively soteriological character of Christian doctrine, so that the usefulness of natural theology, even as written by the regenerate, is questioned.

We must object strenuously, therefore, to the all-too-frequent and utterly erroneous claim that orthodox or scholastic Protestant theology generally viewed natural revelation and the natural theology drawn from it as a foundation on which supernatural revelation and a supernatural theology can build. Otto Weber makes this mistake when he declares that orthodoxy fashioned its doctrine of special revelation into "an understanding of the knowledge of God as rational insight into supernatural truths" and thereby came to view special revelation as no more than a completion of our natural knowledge of God and to assume that "Christian knowledge" fits into "the model of rational knowledge."[101]   Rather, supernatural revelation, identified not so much as an unnatural or preternatural way of knowing but as a graciously given way of knowing, provides the context within which all other knowledge must ultimately be understood. The problem is not one of the hegemony of reason over revelation but rather one of the proper use of revelation over against the purely rational or natural.

Alsted's extended *Theologia naturalis* stands, therefore, within the bounds of the Christian community and its theological system. It is an adjunct and not a precondition of that system. Alsted assumes, with Aquinas, that "grace does not destroy nature, but perfects it" and that "grace is not contrary to nature." Nor does he develop an isolated, purely philosophical natural theology: "the foundation (*fundamentum*) of natural theology is threefold, reason, universal experience, and Holy Scripture."[102] In such a system, Alsted can develop proofs of the existence of God, a doctrine of God as Being, a view of the essential attributes of God (but not of the divine affections, like love and mercy), a doctrine of God as Creator and Governor of the world (but not a fully developed *locus* of creation and providence), plus a discussion of angels as spiritual beings, man as microcosm, and physical being in its various properties.[103] Although the discussion is enlightened throughout by biblical references, it remains nonsoteriological in character and observes the strict distinction between natural and supernatural revelation. In addition, the doctrines of natural theology are not proposed as a basis for building a system of supernatural theology. Alsted's work, as the full title shows, is an essay in apologetics designed to refute the "Atheists, Epicureans, and Sophists of the present day."

We are now in a position to comment on H. E. Weber's assumption of a parallel between the relationship of natural to revealed theology and the relationship of Law to gospel.[104] There is, surely, a parallel between the pagan or false natural theology and the preevangelical, elenctical, and pedagogical use of the Law—just as there is a less accurate parallel between the natural theology of the regenerate and the postevangelical, normative use of the Law (the so-called *tertius usus legis*).[105] We find no evidence, however, that the Reformed orthodox recognition of the parallel between natural law and the Decalogue led to a view of pagan natural theology (*theologia falsa*) as a kind of *praeparatio evangelica*: from Musculus to Polanus and Alsted, to Du Moulin, Charnock, Turretin, and Heidegger, this form of natural theology carries with it only the elenctical or condemnatory function of the Law, not the full *usus paedagogicus*. It serves only to leave men without excuse. Even Heidegger who, at the very close of the era of orthodoxy, indicates a pedagogical use of natural law, does so only in the case of the not-as-yet regenerate elect, on the assumption of the operation of grace. We see here an adumbration of the Puritan and pietist soteriological preparationism, not of any kind of philosophical rationalism.

Similarly, we find no evidence that the concept of a natural theology of the regenerate was used by the orthodox as a new basis for

Christian morality.   There is, then, no discussion of Christian natural theology in terms of the *usus normativus legis*.   All of the writers we have examined in this chapter consider the Decalogue as given by supernatural revelation and necessarily so in view of the depth of human sinfulness.[106]   It is typical of the Reformed orthodox that they view the Decalogue as part of the covenant of grace.[107]   The limited function of natural theology, therefore, never serves, in the orthodox systems, as a means of drawing supernatural revelation within the bounds of natural reason.   The opposite is true of the Arminian systems: here we see a distinct effort to bring grace and Christian morality totally within the realm of nature and to create a bridge between Christian theology and philosophical rationalism.[108]   In addition, the high orthodox Lutheran systems, together with the systems of early seventeenth-century pietists like Freylinghausen, do make a cautious equation between natural theology and the pedagogical use of the Law.[109]   Nonetheless, the Lutherans and the pietists, like the Reformed and unlike the Arminians, continue to drive a wedge between the nonsaving and the saving knowledge of God, with the result that the system remains closed to rationalism.   The development, in rationalist systems of the eighteenth century, of a truly foundational natural theology represents a basic alteration of perspective and a loss, not an outgrowth or further refinement, of the orthodox system.

As noted earlier in the discussion of religion,[110] a major change in perspective occurred in the mid-eighteenth century under the impact of Wolffian rationalism.   Reason was viewed as *principium cognoscendi theologiae* and, as a result, natural theology could be viewed as the basic theology upon which a system could be built and to which certain revealed but rationally explicable data could be added.[111]   This identification of reason as a foundation of theology becomes the normative view of eighteenth-century Reformed writers like Venema, Vitringa and Wyttenbach.[112]   Wyttenbach went so far as to argue that not only does revealed theology correct the defect of natural theology and complete its truth but also that natural theology was a necessary prolegomenon to revealed theology.   Inasmuch as revealed theology presupposes but cannot prove the existence of God, natural theology with its theistic arguments is the foundation on which revealed theology rests: the denial of natural theology must lead to the denial of revealed theology.[113]   A similar movement from natural to revealed theology appears in the system of Salomon van Til.[114]   At one level, this development may appear to be a direct descendant of Turretin's brief comment on natural theology as a foundation and Pictet's assertion of the value of the proofs—but at a

more profound level, it marks the rise of a new philosophical perspective
and of a full system of natural theology such as would never have been
countenanced by Turretin or Pictet. There is a certain irony in the rise
of this rationalistic perspective among the Reformed and the Lutherans in
the eighteenth century since it is precisely the structure of theology
argued by the Socinians and the Arminians in the seventeenth century
(albeit on semi-Pelagian rather than purely rationalistic grounds). The
presence of this rationalistic perspective in eighteenth-century theology, therefore, marks the end of genuine Reformed orthodoxy, at least in
those systems that adopt it as the basic perspective for theological
formulation.

The final paradox of the Reformed treatment of natural theology is
that the *theologia naturalis regenitorum*, because it is not saving, can
never become a *locus* of theological system. Although they argue
pointedly that the regenerate can look to natural revelation and discern
the true God, the Reformed orthodox recognize that this discernment so
rests upon the grace of God and the clearer vision of the *opera Dei* made
possible by the general revelation in Scripture that it can never become
the basis even of the doctrine of creation. At very best, the *theologia
naturalis regenitorum* belongs to the church's exercise of praise and to
the ancillary tools utilized by theology in its arguments. It can never
serve as the basis of an argument or the reason for a conclusion. Therefore, natural theology stands at the edge of Christian thought or, to put
the case positively, it exists as a result rather than as a basis for
Christian doctrine. The truths of natural theology are not excluded from
supernatural theology—they are included in the body of revealed doctrine
—not because natural theology is the rational foundation of the system
but because its truths belong to the higher truth—in Maresius' words,
"as a greater number includes a lesser."[115] Natural theology can, in its
discussion of divine essence and attributes, gain some knowledge of *what*
God may be (*quid sit Deus*). It cannot, however, learn *who* God may be
(*quis sit Deus*), that is, the triune, personal God.[116] The system itself
rests entirely upon scriptural revelation for its primary content.[117]

6

The Object and Genus
of Theology

6.1 The Object of Theology

The discussion of the object and genus of theology found in the
Protestant orthodox systems manifests little alteration in substance over
the course of the seventeenth century but considerable development in
detail. The early orthodox were content to state the object, subject or
material cause of theology and to reflect briefly on the traditional
language of theology as knowledge (*scientia*) or wisdom (*sapientia*). The
later systems, especially those written in the second half of the seventeenth century, tend to discuss these issues at greater length and with
broader, freer reference to the medieval materials, as typified by
Turretin's citation of medieval systems for the purpose of providing a
paradigm for debate. The fact of development in detail rather than in
substance may be traced directly to the prior fact that the medieval
materials treat these two issues, object and genus, at such length and
with such exhaustive discussion that the entire Protestant development
from the Reformers to the close of the seventeenth century occurs within
the bounds of this earlier discussion and represents more a positioning
of Protestantism within the paradigm than the creation of a distinctively
Protestant viewpoint.

Once the Protestant scholastics defined with precision the kind of
theology found in their systems—an ectypal theology of earthly pilgrims
considered in the human subject and grounded primarily on revelation—
they found themselves confronted by a series of subordinate questions

that, when answered, would further determine the nature of the discipline. What is the object of theology? What is the *genus* of theology? What is the relationship of theology to philosophy? The order of these questions is important. The relation of theology to another discipline such as philosophy cannot be determined until one understands what kind of discipline theology is—that is, to which *genus* of discipline it belongs. The *genus*, in turn, is determined by the primary object considered by theology. We therefore raise first the question of the *obiectum theologiae*, the object of theology.

> The object of any science is all that is principally treated in it, and to which it refers [as to an authority] all of its conclusions; it can be understood, moreover, either materially (*materialiter*) according to the things considered, or formally (*formaliter*) according to the way in which they are considered (*modus considerandi*).
> Athough theologians speak in differing ways of the *obiectum theologiae*, they more commonly and correctly identify it as God and the things of God (*Deum et Res Divinas*), in such a way that God might be the primary and the things of God the secondary object of theology; as either what is made by God or what is believed and done by men, that is, God considered directly and indirectly (*in recto et obliquo*); or, truly, as God, and things that are of God as his works, and things that are from God as creatures, and things that are directed toward God, as the services of men (*hominis officia*). Thus all things are treated in theology, either because they are of God himself or because they point toward God as first principle and final end (*ut primum principium et ultimum finem*).
> It appears that God is the *obiectum theologiae* both from the word or term itself, *theologia* or *theosebeia*; and from Scripture which recognizes no other principal object; and from the character or conditions of the object that are observed in Scripture: 1. that it is something uncompounded (*incomplexum*); 2. That things are predicated of it denominatively [i.e., not univocally, equivocally or analogically], for example, affections or properties; 3. that whatever is discussed in the subject depends and reflects upon it: God indeed is uncompounded and most simple Being (*ens incomplexum et maxime simplex*); things are predicated of him denominatively, as his attributes; all things depend upon and refer to him and stand in a relation of origination, conservation and dependence to him.[1]

Although Turretin cites no medieval scholastic models, his dependence on them is clear. Richard of Middleton, for example, defined the subject of theological science as discussion of God's attributes and works, the latter consisting of creation, governance, redemption, justification, and glorification.[2] In addition, the basic division of theology into the things concerning God himself and those things that are directed or ordained toward God as to their source or first principle as well as goal or final end is virtually identical to Aquinas' definition of the subject of theology.[3]

These basic definitions of the object of theology exerted a profound influence on the structure of Reformed orthodox theological system. The basic division between doctrines concerning faith and doctrines concerning obedience, observed by Polanus, Ames and Mastricht, is in fact a division between doctrines concerning God and the things of God and doctrines concerning "the things that are directed toward God, as the services of men." The initial division of the doctrines of faith into doctrines concerning God and doctrines concerning the "things of God" appears in virtually all of the Protestant scholastic systems. In other words, the structure of system depends in large part upon the identification of the primary and secondary objects of theology and their treatment in proper order. No central dogmas, such as predestination, control or organize system. Instead, the structure of system arises out of the careful consideration of the *obiectum theologiae*. What is more, the issue of the formal character of the *obiectum theologiae*, the way in which it is to be considered, governs the way in which theological system can be developed following the prolegomena. Here, again, the Reformed orthodox model presses biblical norms, a Christ-centered view of Scripture and an essentially soteriological view of the body of Christian doctrine. In addition, it draws system away from purely metaphysical interests.[4]

Turretin's third article confirms what we have already learned from the etymology of the term *theologia* and adds that God must be the primary or proper object of theology insofar as the God revealed by Scripture is prior to all other things. There can be no object of theology prior to God.

> God is at once the principal and the ultimate object of faith: "Ye believe in God" (John 14:1), said our Lord to his disciples; and says the Apostle Peter, "who by Him," that is, Christ, "do believe in God" (I Pet. 1:21). Believers consider God as the self-existent, uncreated truth, on whom they may rely with the greatest safety; and as the supreme felicity, united to whom by faith, they may become inexpressibly happy. The Creed, accordingly, begins with the words, "I believe in God."[5]

The *obiectum theologiae* and the *obiectum fidei* must, of course, be one and the same. The basic division of theology into faith and obedience identifies the doctrinal section of system as faith, specifically, as the faith which is believed (*fides quae creditur*). Moreover, *fides* is the form of mental assent belonging to theology and believing is the kind of mental disposition (*habitus mentis*) requisite to theology.[6]

Formal identification of the object or subject matter of theology by the Protestant scholastics, like their discussion of archetypal and ectypal theology, looks back to medieval models through the glass of the Reformation.   The Reformers themselves, both first- and second-genera- tion, tend not to discuss this issue, although it is clear that they know and approve of the identification of God as the *obiectum theologiae* or *obiectum fidei*.[7]   In the next generation of writers, we find clearer identification of God as the object of theology and, more importantly, recognition that this identification belongs to the preliminary defini- tion of theology as a discipline:

> The content of all Scripture is the knowledge of God and of ourselves: which is to say, the subject of all theology is God and man, since theology is the knowledge of God: and that consists in two questions, [first] concerning the essence of God and [second] concerning the will of God.[8]

A similar definition occurs in the *schema* or diagram of the *loci* provided by Chemnitz at the end of his prolegomenon.[9]   The bifurcation of topics is typical of Agricolan logic[10] and, moreover, parallels the standard scholastic division of the *obiectum theologiae* into primary and secondary objects—God and the "things of God" or objects of the divine willing.

Beginning with Junius, the Reformed also take up the topic of the object (or subject) of theology as an issue for consideration in the theological prolegomena.   Perhaps because of medieval precedent,[11] the early Reformed orthodox take up this issue as part of the discussion of the causality of theology.   The importance of the topic led, in high orthodox discussion, to a separate chapter on the *obiectum theologiae*, distinct from the consideration of causality.

Junius provides the most extended early orthodox treatment.   The material, subject or object of theology, he writes, is divine things, which is to say, both God himself and whatever God has ordained.[12]   Most simply stated, God alone is the subject or material of theology, inasmuch as all theological discourse must be conducted *sub ratione Dei*, with reference to God as its governing principle.   This means that theology will consider topics that belong to other sciences—angels, also treated by metaphysics; or animals and the elements of things, also treated by physics—but will consider these things not after the manner of meta- physics and physics but with respect to God and in relation to his will. As Alsted comments, explicitly following the fathers and Scholastics, "God is the object of theology in the nominative and the genitive case, that is, God and whatever is of God."[13]   Gomarus, more simply and precisely, notes that the object of theology is defined in terms of revelation:

> The material (*materia*) with respect to which, or the object (*obiectum*) of theology is God openly revealed according to his own goodness, under whom all the things that belong to theology

are considered, not indeed as parts, species or incidental
properties, but as they are either God himself or ordained in
some way by God.[14]

To this basic definition, Walaeus adds a soteriological element:

> The object concerning which theology deals is divine things,
> namely God insofar as he can and ought to be known by us, and
> all things that are from ꞁod, insofar as they depend on God and
> refer both to God and to the salvation of man.[15]

The character of *theologia nostra* as defined in the preceding
sections of the *locus* presses the Protestant scholastics toward a further
qualification of the object of theology and, indeed, toward a clarification of their pattern and method over against certain patterns found
among the medieval scholastics:

> But when God is set forth as the *obiectum theologiae*, he is not
> understood simply or absolutely (*simpliciter*) as God in himself
> (*ut Deus in se*)—indeed, as such he is unfathomable (*akatalep-
> tos*) to us; but as he is revealed and as he has deigned to
> manifest himself to us in the Word. . . . Nor, surely, is he to
> be considered according to deity as such (*sub ratione Deita-
> tis*), as would Thomas Aquinas and many scholastics after him;
> indeed, this way of knowing him cannot be useful (*salutaris*),
> but is deadly to sinners: but he is to be considered as he is
> our God, that is, covenanted in Christ (*ut est Deus noster id
> est foederatus in Christo*), in which manner he has revealed
> himself to us in the Word, not [merely] as something to be be
> known, but indeed as something to be be worshipped, which two
> (knowledge and worship) are comprehended in true Religion, as
> theology teaches.[16]

Turretin's language, contrary to the impression he gives by his
attack on Aquinas, directly reflects the medieval debate over the object
(or subject) of theology. While Aquinas had argued that "all things in
sacred doctrine are treated *sub ratione Dei*," he did not intend to
present theology as an exceedingly metaphysical enterprise, but rather to
indicate simply that theology deals either with God himself (*ipse Deus*)
or with things that are ordered or ordained toward God as to their source
or goal (*habent ordinem ad Deum, ut ad principium et finem*).[17]   It was
clearly Aquinas' intention to provide a more inclusive definition of the
subject of theology than either the traditional Augustinian definition
(adopted by Lombard) of theology as the teaching concerning signs and
things (*doctrina de rebus vel de signis*) or the soteriological definition
of Hugh of St. Victor, the knowledge of the work of reparation or salvation (*opera reparationis*).[18]   Aquinas also rejects the definition of
Grosseteste and Kilwardby of the subject of theology as "the whole
Christ, head and members" (*totum Christum* or *Christus integer, caput et
corpus* or *caput et membra*).[19]

Aquinas' definition is also more inclusive, though certainly not as soteriologically oriented as those presented by his contemporaries. Alexander of Hales defined theology as "the science or knowledge of the divine substance known through Christ in the work of reparation" (*scientia de substantia divina cognoscenda per Christum in opere reparationis*) --a distinct improvement on the Victorine definition but certainly not capable of accounting for all of the topics in Alexander's own *Summa*![20] Bonaventure distinguishes between God, the principle of theology; the *totus Christus*, the subject of theology to which all theology refers; and the broader or more inclusive subject, the universal total of signs and things--attempting to draw together Alexander's improvement on Hugh with the Augustinian definition from Lombard.[21] Aquinas' far more incisive definition was adopted by such thinkers as Henry of Ghent and Duns Scotus.[22] Turretin, apparently, regrets the absence of a strong soteriological thrust in Aquinas and suspects the definition of having a philosophical tendency.

Scotus, in his effort to mark the difference between theology and metaphysics, had noted that the *obiectum theologiae* is God inasmuch as he is God (*Deus inquantum est Deus*) while the object of metaphysics is God inasmuch as he is Being (*Deus inquantum est Ens*).[23] The issue, as Gregory of Rimini states it, is "that God, considered according to deity as such is the subject of theology" (*quod Deus sub ratione deitatis est subiectum theologiae*). Gregory maintains, following the logic of Giles of Rome, that the object of theology cannot be God as such in an absolute sense, but rather God considered in a restricted sense (*non inquantum Deus absolute, sed contracte est subiectum*). This restriction or contraction concerns the capacity of a finite mind to comprehend God: even the *theologia beatorum* does not have as its subject the infinite God absolutely as he is known to himself. The *subiectum* or *obiectum* of *theologia nostra*, concludes Gregory, following Giles, is God inasmuch as the glorifier (*inquantam glorificator*). Giles himself identified the object of theology as *Deus inquantum glorificator et salvator*--a view not at all distant from Turretin's.[24]

In addition, the late medieval scholastic discussion of God as the object of theology *sub ratione deitatis* does not fall under the objections raised by Turretin, but in fact follows much the same logic as Turretin's own discussion of the object of theology broadly considered as the contents of theological system. Peter Aureole thus argues that the consideration of God *ratio deitatis* includes whatever is divine by essence or by participation so that theology takes as its object both God and his creation, governance and salvation of the world, even as it considers Christ according to his divinity and humanity.[25] Rather than assume ignorance on Turretin's part—since, after all, he and his Reformed contemporaries were reading and using late medieval systems—we may suppose an unwillingness to cite these sources while making a rhetorical point against Aquinas and in favor of Protestantism. Turretin presents a modified Thomist definition: God and things directed toward God as their source and goal are the object of theology—yet this object must be understood redemptively, in Christ. The definition is modified, then, in the direction of Alexander and Bonaventure or of Giles of Rome and Gregory of Rimini—a distinctly Augustinian direction.   It is also true that the Reformed prolegomena, as distinct from those of Scotus, Durandus, and Aureole, add to the critique of epistemology a distinctly soteriological dimension by considering the impact of sin and the fall on human reason.[26]   The soteriological note, particularly in terms of its language of the "covenanted" God, not only links Turretin to the Reformers but also to the Cocceians, Burmann and Heidanus.   The latter specifically identifies "the covenanted God" as the object of theology.[27]

A similar set of concerns, drawn out of the medieval debate and, equally, out of the Reformers' concern for the establishment of Christ as the center and focus of all language concerning salvation is reflected in Voetius' discussion of fundamental articles and their relation to the object of theology. Voetius distinguishes between the special, specific object of faith (objectum fidei specialis specifico) which is "Christ or the special application of the promise in Christ" and the general, generic object of faith (objectum fidei generalis generico) which is God or Christ or the Word of God understood simply as the foundation or principium of eternal blessedness. Citing Cajetan, he remarks that the mind understands things in complex or compounded ways—not in incomplex or simple ways—so that it is one thing to ask what must be believed for salvation and another to ask generally the question of the object of theology: the former is a question concerning specific propositions focused on Christ, while the latter is a question concerning simple or incomplex terms.[28]

In his exposition of the obiectum and principium of theology, Burmann similarly notes the central epistemological problems of the necessity and form of mediated knowledge of God.

> . . . hence, the remote object of Theology, or the object to which it tends, is God. . . . Truly, the object from which or formal principle, under which Theology considers this object, and by which we distinguish it from other disciplines, is revelation, or the supernatural light, since that object [i.e. God, the obiectum ad quod] is revealed. On which account this doctrine is called a mystery I Cor. 2:7.

> Indeed, the ground [*principium*] of theology, the connec-
> tion [*complexum*] or basis of knowing, is the Word of God or
> revelation; on which ultimately, all of our conclusions must be
> founded. Hearing is by means of the Word of God: Rom 10:17.
> With thee is the fountain of life. In thy light we see light:
> Psal. 36:9.[29]

Like Rissen, Burmann recognizes the necessity of a relationship between
the Word of God and all mediated knowledge of God and, therefore, points
toward the relationship between Christ as Word and Scripture. The
English scholastic, Leigh, comments that Christ "is called the Word,
because he is so often spoken of and prominent in Scripture, and is in a
manner the whole subject of the Scripture."[30]

We note here a major element of continuity between Protestant
orthodoxy and the theology of the Reformers: despite the considerable
difference in form between the orthodox and the Reformers, the orthodox
system retains the emphasis on revelation in Christ given to Protestant
theology by Luther and Calvin, together with the negative assessment of
the more speculative and metaphysical side of medieval scholasticism.
The definition of the *obiectum theologiae*, like the definition of
theologia nostra, turns away from rationalism and philosophy toward the
view of Christ as the measure or scope (*scopus*) of our knowledge of God.

The debate of the medieval doctors, the Augustinian solution and the
Protestant orthodox view are each reflected in Calvin's discussion of the
obiectum fidei. Although it is often said that Calvin spoke of Christ as
the object of faith, to the point that this interpretation has been
ensconced in the modern subtitle to a section of his *Institutes*, Calvin
in fact comes very close to Turretin's definition:

> When faith is discussed in the schools, they call God simply
> the object of faith, and by fleeting speculations, as we have
> elsewhere stated, lead miserable souls astray rather than
> direct them to a definite goal. For, since "God dwells in
> inaccessible light" (I Tim. 6:16), Christ must become our
> intermediary. . . . Indeed, it is true that faith looks to one
> God. But this must also be added, "to know Jesus Christ whom
> he has sent (John 17:3)."[31]

Or, again, more clearly,

> . . . I subscribe to the common saying that God is the object
> of faith, yet it requires qualification. For Christ is not
> without reason called "the image of the invisible God" (Col.
> 1:15). This title warns us that, unless God confronts us in
> Christ, we cannot come to know that we are saved.[32]

Like Turretin, Calvin ignores the genuine continuity between his
"qualification" of the definition and the theology of "the schools."
There is, as noted above, a certain continuity also between the
Protestant perspective and the Scotist and nominalist theology of the

later Middle Ages with its denial of reason's capacity for the knowledge of God and its insistence on the necessity of revelation. This late medieval theology stands in the background of the Reformation—but the orthodox and the Reformers add to it not only the stress on Christ as the center of revelation but also the sense that not merely human finitude but also human sin stands in the way of a rational or natural knowledge of God. In other words, although the discussion itself and its structure rely on medieval models, the content has been altered along lines dictated by the Reformers and, indeed, the medieval model closest to the Reformed orthodox definition—the Augustinian model of Giles and Gregory —is itself a precursor of the Reformation.

The problem of the *obiectum theologiae* can be further clarified by a discussion of the way in which theology and its perception of God and the *res divinae* as its object compare and contrast with other disciplines and their stated objects. Here again the lines of continuity can most easily be drawn between the Protestant and the medieval scholastics—both in terms of actual medieval models for the Protestant discussion and in terms of the reasons for the discussion itself. The scholastics, medieval and Protestant alike, wrote in the context of the university, where the comparison and contrasting of related disciplines was a fact of daily existence.[33] This contextual issue is made clear in the exhaustive encyclopedic efforts of Protestant scholastics like Keckermann, Alsted and, at the very end of the era of orthodoxy, Buddaeus.

Turretin, for example, recognizes that there is some common ground between theology and the disciplines of metaphysics, physics and ethics— as evidenced by the material objects of these disciplines. Metaphysics deals with God; physics and ethics deal with man, the former with man in a bodily or natural sense, the latter with man in a moral sense. The difference between those disciplines and theology appears not when the object is considered materially (*materialiter*) but when it is considered formally (*formaliter*). Thus theology "treats of God not after the manner of metaphysics inasmuch as he is Being (*Ens*), or as he is capable of being known by means of the natural light (*lumine naturali*), but he becomes known through revelation as Creator and Redeemer; theology deals with creatures not as they are things of nature (*res naturae*) but as they are things of God (*res Dei*)."[34] The system of theology, then, must take care in dealing with nominally metaphysical, physical or ethical topics so that they are given theological form by being viewed under the *duplex cognitio Dei*—God known as Creator and Redeemer—and in terms of a theological or "divine" as opposed to a natural perspective. We note that the *duplex cognitio Dei*, introduced as a formal consideration in theology by Calvin, continues to have an impact on Reformed doctrine in the era of orthodoxy.[35]

Since, moreover, theology takes as its primary object not God considered as Being but God considered in his revelation as Creator and Redeemer, and as its secondary object creatures not as "things of nature but as things of God" and insofar as "they have a disposition and ordination toward God" (*quatenus habitudinem et ordinem habent ad Deum*), the proofs of God's existence are incidental to theology. In other words, the declaration that God is the proper object of theology does not need the proofs for its justification, but can rely on revelation. Turretin writes:

> If theology has its hands full to prove that God exists (*si Theologia probare satagit Deum esse*), this does not arise out of its primary and proper intention, but incidentally, through an external necessity (*ex adventitia necessitate*), truly, for the confutation of profane individuals and Atheists. . . . The axiom "Science does not prove but supposes its subject" is true in human sciences of an inferior status, but theology which is of a higher order follows another method: it reaches out to prove all things that can be proved by its proper means, which is to say, by divine revelation.[36]

In other words, theology does not prove the existence of its primary object but rather justifies what it says concerning both primary and secondary objects on the basis of revelation.

Here too, the Reformed orthodox approach to theology diverges sharply from rationalism. There is no attempt made on the part of the sixteenth- or seventeenth-century orthodox to use the proofs of God's existence to demonstrate the validity of system or as a basis for moving from a rationally established natural theology to a supernatural or revealed theology based on the achievements of reason. This model would appear in the eighteenth century under the impact of Wolffian rationalism but it is quite foreign to the mind of Protestant orthodoxy. Indeed, the orthodox studiously avoid even the Thomist model in which the order of reason parallels the order of revelation. Nor is this point concerning the object of theology and the proofs of God's existence merely a point made tangentially in the prolegomena: it carries through into the *locus de Deo* where the proofs do not belong to the exposition of doctrine properly so-called but rather supply a preliminary denial of atheism as much rhetorical as logical.[37]

By way of conclusion, we note that the Reformed scholastic discussion of the *obiectum theologiae* grows out of medieval scholastic debate and out of the theology of the Reformers, with the result that the Protestant orthodox system, as long as it held to this particular presupposition, would necessarily oppose the incorporation of any of the assumptions of rationalist metaphysics into Christian theology.   In addition, this discussion of God as *obiectum theologiae* functioned to deter the formulation of theological system along the rationalizing lines of the "central dogma" theory as argued by Weber and Bizer. Since God is both cause and object of theology, he must also be identified as the essential foundation (*principium essendi*) of theology.[38]   The way in which God is identified as object, however, in and through Christ the Redeemer as revealed in Scripture, provides the entire system with an epistemological focus and doctrinal pivot quite distinct from the eternal decree, and in accord with the consistent claim of the Reformed that the decree must always be recognized as resting on Christ and known in Christ or through the inward grace of the Spirit.[39]

Furthermore, this view of God as object of theology, inasmuch as it points not only to God as *principium essendi* but to the Christ-centered Scripture as *principium cognoscendi*, points toward a system or body of doctrine that must consider *all* revealed truths and not merely those which can be gathered around or rationalized in the context of a monistic principle. In other words, the doctrine of the triune God and his attributes, together with all of his revealed works *ad intra* and *ad extra*, becomes the controlling factor of theological system—as opposed to any single divine attribute or work whether performed *ad intra* or *ad extra*. We will find, when we investigate the doctrine of the divine attributes and their relation to the divine essence, that this presuppositional corollary of the doctrine of the *obiectum theologiae* carries through into the orthodox system.[40]

6.2 Theology as *scientia* and *sapientia*

The discussion of the *genus* of theology appears in the Protestant scholastic systems both as a continuation of the basic process of definition taking place in the prolegomena and as an evidence and aspect of the self-conscious development of Protestant orthodoxy. In the first place, the problem of *genus* arises once the basic definition of theology has been stated. In the discussion of the *obiectum theologiae*, theology is distinguished even from those other disciplines that are defined, at least in part, as having the same object as theology. Metaphysics and physics are viewed as bodies of certain and evident knowledge acquired by demonstration; ethics is viewed as a body of practical knowledge based upon conclusions drawn from universal principles. Thus, metaphysics and physics are called *scientiae* or sciences, while ethics is a form of *prudentia* or prudence. The question naturally arises for Protestant scholastics as to the relation of theology not only to the specific disciplines of metaphysics, physics and ethics, but also to the kinds (*genera*) of discipline represented by *scientia* and *prudentia*.

In the second place, as noted in the introduction, the establishment of an orthodoxy was but one aspect of the institutional solidification of the Reformation. With institutionalization came the need to teach this orthodox Protestantism in the universities in the context of other intellectual disciplines. In this context, the question was pressed on the Protestant scholastics, just as it had been pressed on the medievals, as to the kind of discipline theology could claim to be and how it might relate, positively or negatively, to other disciplines that claimed the same object. It is worth noting that this question did not arise for the Reformers and that, in their quest for an answer, the Protestant scholastics returned, albeit selectively and critically, to medieval models. Thus in Turretin's fairly elaborate reflections on the object and genus of theology, there is discussion of whether theology is a science, whether it is a form of wisdom (*sapientia*), and whether God is its subject matter—which parallels the issues addressed in the articles in the first question of Aquinas' *Summa*.[41] In this discussion Turretin assumes that theology is nobler or higher than the other disciplines, echoing question 1, article 5 of the *Summa*, and he addresses, as a result of the discussion of *genus*, whether theology is theoretical or practical—the fourth article of Aquinas' first question.

The parallel development of topics does not mean that Turretin and his Reformed scholastic brethren were Thomists in disguise. Turretin distanced himself specifically from Aquinas in the discussion of the *obiectum theologiae* and the definitions given to theology by Junius were indebted more to Scotus than to Aquinas.[42] In the discussion of the *genus theologiae* there is also explicit divergence from a Thomist perspective. The point is, simply, that the paradigm for discussion of the topic arises out of a close reading of medieval models and, in this particular case, the structure of the argument relies, despite frequent disagreement and modification, on the pattern of debate found in the *Summa*.

In the standard paradigm, inherited from Aristotle via the medieval scholastics, there were five distinct *genera* of knowing or intellectual dispositions: understanding or intelligence (*intelligentia*); knowledge or science (*scientia*); wisdom or discernment (*sapientia*); prudence or discretion (*prudentia*); and art or technique (*ars*). Opinion and suspicion (*opinio, suspicio*) are not genuine knowledge and are not classed among the intellectual dispositions. The above terms have, in the scholastic vocabulary, precise meaning. *Intelligentia* indicates a knowledge of principles (*principia*) by spontaneous assent, without demonstration. *Scientia* indicates a knowledge of conclusions derived by demonstration from self-evident first principles. *Sapientia* is an explanation both of principles and conclusions, frequently construed by the scholastics as a knowledge of ultimate purposes. *Prudentia* is a knowledge of practical judgment suited to contingent circumstances. Ars is a knowledge of techniques and skills for bringing about a desired effect or result.[43] We can bring full circle yet another element of the logic of scholastic system if we remember that false or pagan theology, whether mythical, civil or philosophical, was defined as mere opinion which failed to reflect the divine archetype; consequently, this definition formally set false or non-Christian theology outside of the realm of genuine intellectual study.

Where and how does theology relate to this paradigm? Turretin observes that there are three kinds of assent to knowledge: a general, nontechnical sense (*scientia*), faith (*fides*), and opinion (*opinio*). There are also three corresponding dispositions of mind (*habitus mentis*): the disposition of knowing (*habitus sciendi*), the disposition of believing (*habitus credendi*), and the disposition of opining (*habitus opiniandi*).[44] Thus, *scientia* rests upon reason (*ratio*); *fides* upon testimony (*testimonio*); and *opinio* on probability (*probabilitas*). Theology, resting as it does on the assent of faith and consisting in a mental disposition to believe, cannot therefore be precisely equated with any of the other forms of knowing, since all belong to the category of rational *habitus sciendi*. If theology is to be called *intelligentia*, *scientia*, *sapientia*, *prudentia* or *ars*, it must be by analogy only.

The Protestant scholastics, following the medieval doctors, tend to rule out immediately the possibility that *intelligentia*, *prudentia* and *ars* are analogous to theology. *Intelligentia* knows only principles by virtue of their own light; theology knows both principles and conclusions by revelation. *Prudentia* is knowledge concerned only with practice or actions in the civil order; theology is concerned not only with actions or "things to be done" (*agenda*) but also with things to be believed (*credenda*). Moreover, the *agenda* prescribed by theology are spiritual, not civil. Ars is a knowledge directed toward effects or results but, unlike theology, not toward virtuous action.[45] Therefore *scientia* and *sapientia* are the only categories of knowing applicable to theology.

The arguments for classifying theology as *scientia* or *sapientia* are not, of course, original to the Protestant scholastics, but derive from the theological prolegomena of the medieval scholastic systems.[46] According to Aquinas, a distinction needs to be made between primary and subalternate sciences: the former is a science the first principles of which are self-evident; the latter is a science which receives its principles from a higher science. The fact that theology receives its principles by revelation does not prevent it from being a science but rather identifies it as a subalternate science which receives from God by revelation principles that are self-evident in the *scientia Dei*, the science or knowledge of God himself.[47] This Thomistic perspective is evident in several of the early orthodox Reformed systems. The *principia theologiae*, God and his self-revelation, become the basis for legitimate conclusions drawn within theological system and, because of the presence both of principles and of legitimate conclusions, the system can be identified as a subalternate science.[48] Indeed, Alsted can argue that, in this modified Thomistic sense, true or Christian natural theology is genuinely a *scientia*, inasmuch as it has self-evident principles and argues demonstratively while supernatural theology is a subalternate science, inasmuch as its principles are known not by the natural light of the intellect but by revelation and inasmuch as it rests on faith rather than on demonstration. (The qualification of the term *scientia*, however, leads Alsted to prefer "wisdom" or *sapientia* as the genus of theology.[49])

Aquinas, it should be noted, did not think that his identification of theology as *scientia* precluded its identification as *sapientia*. Indeed, he seems unwilling to leave theology in the position of being a secondary or subalternate science without pointing out that theology is in fact the highest form of wisdom. Aquinas answers objections that wisdom, correctly understood, does not borrow its first principles from other sciences but rather uses its principles to prove the truth of the grounds of other sciences. He argues that, first, the derivation of the principles of theology from divine knowledge is not a human borrowing but a derivation, by revelation, from the highest wisdom. Second, Aquinas holds that theological wisdom, as revealed, is distinct from the natural reason used to prove principles, but is nonetheless a criterion by which the truth or falsehood of all other sciences is to be judged. In both cases, theology qualifies as *sapientia*.[50]

If the Thomistic view had been the only antecedent of the Protestant scholastic discussion of the *genus* of theology, there would have been little resistance to the denomination of theology as *scientia* and, in addition, no reason to juxtapose the definition of theology as *scientia* with the alternative view of theology as *sapientia*. The key to the difference between the Reformed orthodox and the Thomistic views is the

critical perspective of Scotus. Scotus had argued that theology, despite
its principles drawn from a higher science and its use of reason to draw
conclusions from those principles, lacked one crucial characteristic of a
scientia: demonstration made on the basis of evidence or evident reasons.
In order for such demonstration to occur, theology must contain "necessary reasons" (*rationes necessariae*) that are evident in themselves (*per
se notis*) either immediately or mediately. However, revealed knowledge
accepted by faith does not belong to the category of self-evident
necessary reason. Theology, in other words, does not rest on natural
light and therefore has no evidence of its object comparable to the
evidence that *scientia* has concerning the contingent order of things.
Therefore theology cannot strictly be called a science.[51]

It is precisely this Scotist critique that we find in the Protestant
scholastic systems:

> [Theology] is not *scientia*, since it does not rest upon
> evidence, but only on testimony; nor does it rest in cognition,
> but directs and ordains it to activity. Nor is it *sapientia*,
> since on account of theology are all aspects of wisdom negated,
> whether the understanding of self-evident principles or the
> knowlege of conclusions.[52]

Among the early orthodox, Scharpius and Alsted had similarly argued that
scientia rests on demonstrative certainty whereas theology rests upon
revelation, and that *sapientia* deals with an understanding of things in
themselves whereas theology deals with an understanding of things *in
Christo* ("in Christ").[53] We note again the antirationalistic tendency of
these arguments and, particularly in Turretin's fairly obvious reference
to 1 Corinthians 1:18ff., the desire to distinguish between theological
wisdom and worldly wisdom. Virtually identical arguments appear in
Walaeus' *Loci communes*.[54]

The fact that theological wisdom is not worldly wisdom or that
theology does not rest on demonstrative certainty in no way implies that
theological knowing is uncertain—only that theology rests upon a certainty specific to theological knowing. Indeed, each order or form of
knowing must have its own kind of certainty. Thus, *prudentia*, a knowledge
of practical and ethical actions, can have only a moral or a probable
certainty (*certitudo moralis* or *certitudo probabilis*), while rational
knowledge, *scientia*, will be characterized by a demonstrative certainty,
what Turretin calls *certitudo mathematica*. Theological certainty or the
certainty of faith (*certitudo fidei*) is a matter neither of moral probability nor of demonstration. Rather theological certainty is an absolute
and infallible certainty that rests upon the truth of God's revelation as

accepted by faith. Thus, Turretin can say that theology rests on testimony, which is to say, upon the certain, authoritative and infallible
testimony of the biblical revelation.[55] Here again, Reformed orthodoxy
distances itself from rationalism, which holds forth the promise of
mathematical or demonstrative certainty.

The twofold end of theology also distinguishes it from *sapientia* and
scientia: the first and highest end is the glory of God, and the subordinate end is the salvation of the church. Theology is, thus, the most
eminent wisdom, having a higher end and, certainly, higher *principia* than
other sciences. The first principles of other sciences are not first
simpliciter but only in their kind. Neither in theology proper nor outside of it are there any higher principles than the first principles of
theology, the foremost of which is God himself; the second, his Word.
Scharpius distinguishes the rule of order, the manner of working, and the
production of effects relating to the Word as *principium theologiae*: God
speaks to us *mediate per verbum* and the *verbum* leads us, likewise mediately, to God through Christ. We cannot know God otherwise than through
the Word.[56]

Owen, whose presentation of the basic questions of the genus and
object of theology manifests a certain degree of impatience with scholastic debate, notes a basic difficulty with all discussion of theology as a
discipline among other disciplines: "The object of theology, since in
some sense it must be God himself, is infinitely more distant from the
objects of all other sciences as those [are] from nothingness itself."[57]
The basis of Christian theology, adds Owen, is shown by the apostle Paul
to be alien to human science and wisdom. His speech and preaching did
not demonstrate human wisdom, but the Spirit and power. Thus, "whether
one considers the origin of theology, or the subject, or the goal, or the
manner of stating and teaching, or indeed the entire nature or practice,
it appears that [theology] can in no way be counted among the human
sciences, either speculative or practical, nor should [theology] be bound
to their rules or methods."[58]

Despite these objections, however, *scientia* and *sapientia* remain the
forms of knowing closest to theology. The contrast between *theologia* and
sapientia arises only when theology, considered as an ultimate explanation of both principles and conclusions, stands over against a worldly
explanation of the same principles and conclusions—and such a contrast
can be maintained only on the basis of a theory of double truth.[59] The
contrast between *theologia* and *scientia*, similarly, rests upon a distinction between the demonstrative certainty of scientific conclusions as
derived from self-evident principles and the certainty of theological

conclusions as derived (logically) from revealed principles. Both of these contrasts are capable of some resolution—and we find the Reformed orthodox using both terms, *sapientia* and *scientia*, with reference to theology as a discipline. Similar, carefully qualified usage prevailed among the Lutheran orthodox.[60]

Among the early orthodox, Trelcatius and Perkins identified theology as *scientia*, without further comment on the meaning of *scientia*. However, both included in their definitions a *posteriori* practical elements not entirely in accord with the basically deductive view of *scientia* as a discipline in which first principles are used as the basis for evident conclusions. Trelcatius thus speaks of the analytical model in theology and of the function of theology as an active or practical discipline;[61] and Perkins almost paradoxically defines theology as "the science of living blessedly forever."[62] The tendency of those who patterned their definitions after Perkins, moreover, was to avoid the issue of theology as *scientia* and to substitute a term not subject to debate, like *doctrina* or *disciplina*: thus Ames,[63] Maccovius,[64] and Mastricht.[65] Walaeus, without further comment, states that theology is a *scientia* or a *sapientia* concerning divine things.[66]

Perkins not only denominated theology a science, he also provided a list of seven secondary sciences which, like the primary science of theology, found their source in "the bodie of Scripture." These are the "attendants" or "handmaids" of theology:

  I. Ethiques, a doctrine of living honestly and civilly.
 II. Oeconomickes, a doctrine of governing a family.
III. Politikes, a doctrine of the right administration of a Common-weale.
 IV. Ecclesiasticall discipline, a doctrine of well-ordering the Church.
  V. The Iewes-Common-weale, inasmuch as it differeth from Church government.
 VI. Prophesie, the doctrine of preaching well.
VII. Academie, the doctrine of governing Schooles well: especially those of the Prophets.[67]

Scripture thus becomes the norm for the humane sciences. It is worth noting that all of the ancillary biblical subjects were developed at length by the orthodox both as separate treatises and as subsidiary themes. Thus we find Keckermann developing treatises on ethics, economics, and politics; Voetius producing a massive treatise on church discipline—including discussions of the commonwealth of Israel as a prototype for church discipline; Heidegger including three *loci* on the Old Testament commonwealth and its laws in his *Corpus theologiae*; and numerous Puritans, incluing Perkins himself, writing treatises on "prophesy," that is, preaching.[68]

A number of writers, particularly those who adopted the Scotist model with its dialectic between *theologia archetypa* and *theologia ectypa*, *theologia in se* and *theologia in subiecto*, use *sapientia* exclusively: thus, Junius,[69] Scharpius,[70] Polanus.[71] Others, recognizing the difficulty of using the terms *scientia* and *sapientia*, argue that no single intellectual faculty or habit of knowing corresponds precisely with theology. Wollebius notes that theology combines the contemplative and active aspects of knowing and is similar, therefore not only to *scientia* and *sapientia* but also to *prudentia*.[72] Burmann notes that theology unites the highest forms of wisdom and prudence.[73] Keckermann alone emphasizes the operative or practical character of theology, defining its genus as *prudentia*: "theology is a religious prudence leading toward salvation."[74] Leigh, rather curiously, speaks of theology primarily as wisdom but also as art or technique.[75] Walaeus argues, echoing Henry of Ghent and other late medieval thinkers, that the object of theology is *res divinae, nempe Deus ipse quatenus a nobis cognosci potest* —divine things, namely God himself insofar as he can be known by us— which is to say, things that pertain to God, that depend upon God and that refer to the salvation of man. Theology, therefore, is rightly called *sapientia* because of its most noble object.[76] Alsted, as noted above, allows a modified use of *scientia* but prefers *sapientia*.[77]

Sapientia, loosely defined, refers to the highest forms of knowledge, to somewhat arcane and difficult concepts, to knowledge resting demonstratively on independent and evident principles, and to the knowledge of those principles. All of these usages of *sapientia*, comments Alsted, can be applied to theology—although its demonstrations have a certainty of faith and rest on supernatural rather than natural principles. Furthermore, the term *sapientia* is typically applied to those disciplines that are more excellent than all others—and theology, in view of its divine subject and of the certainty of its divinely given *principia*, is surely the most excellent of all disciplines.[78]

Among the high orthodox, Turretin in particular felt the need to resolve this issue of *genus* and to select definitively one category of knowing as most analogous to theology. He names no opponent in this *quaestio*, either in the preliminary posing of the question or in the body of his answer—perhaps because the question had been subject to so wide a variety of solutions among the Reformed. Following what can be called the main line of development or, at least, the most logical conclusion to be drawn from the Scotist model present in the intitial divisions of theology, Turretin argues that *sapientia*, wisdom, is most analogous to theology. He solves the problem, tentatively, by setting aside the

Aristolelian paradigm in which *sapientia* was related to *intelligentia* and *scientia* and by using, in its place, what he perceives to have been the ancient Stoic usage: wisdom is "the gathering together (*collectio*) of all habits or dispositions, both speculative and moral."[79]   What is more, Scripture seems to prefer "wisdom" as the designation of the *doctrina fidei*, both in Proverbs and in 1 Corinthians.[80]   In addition, *sapientia* is a proper designation for a knowledge of the most eminent things (*scientia rerum praestantissimarum*)—among which, certainly, are knowledge of God, his works and eternal blessedness.   *Sapientia*, moreover, echoing Aquinas, is an architectonic discipline that directs and judges other forms of knowing.   Even so, theology is a rule for judging all other truths: all not consonant with it must be rejected.[81]

From the outset of the discussion, the orthodox recognized that theology, because it rests on testimony rather than on pure reason, is a disposition of believing (*habitus credendi*) rather than a disposition of knowing (*habitus intellectualis*).   At best, therefore, theology could be called *scientia*, *sapientia*, *intelligentia*, *prudentia* or *ars* only by analogy—since all these are *habitus intellectuales*.   The decision to regard theology as *sapientia*, however, comprising both the self-evident principles known to pure intelligence and the conclusions drawn by science does identify it as an architectonic discipline with a right of judgment over other disciplines.   Theology thus retains its status as "queen of the sciences" and other disciplines function as *ancillae* ("handmaids") that support and serve but never undermine theological conclusions.   The fact that this is said analogically and not univocally not only protects theology as a unique mode of knowing based on revelation but also allows theology to use rational tools in dealing with its *principia* and in drawing its conclusions.   In addition, it opens theology as a discipline to patterns of knowing belonging to *scientia*, *prudentia* and *ars*.

Furthermore, the orthodox hesitancy to equate theology precisely with any human discipline permitted their systems to remain open to forms and patterns of knowing other than those belonging to the five disciplinary categories enumerated by Aristotle.   It is quite correct, as Althaus observed, that the Aristotelian view of *scientia* as a body of demonstratable conclusions would eliminate any kind of historical knowing from the "scientific" disciplines—and it is also correct that medieval scholastic theological "science" was quite ahistorical in its systematic and doctrinal orientation.[82]   (Even those medieval systems in which theology is distinguished from *scientia* are ahistorical in conception.)   The Reformed

orthodox systems, however, tend to recognize the importance of a historical dimension: revelation, covenant and Christology are all rooted in
biblical history and the system itself, in its movement from creation and
fall, by way of covenant, Christology and church, to the end of the age
and the final judgment bears witness to a salvation–historical view of
the body of Christian doctrine.[83] Althaus' critique is, therefore,
blunted: the Aristotelian view of *scientia* is hardly a controlling factor
in an orthodox system that excludes a historical pattern of knowing.

Yet another dimension of the discussion of the genus of pilgrim
theology is noted by Alsted. Because of the encyclopedic nature of his
academic efforts, Alsted produced a separate *methodus* for each species of
theology—natural, catechetical, scholastic, and so forth. His discussion of true theology as including both natural and supernatural theology
together with his methodological division of theology into its several
species demanded that he show how both natural and supernatural theology
belong to the *genus sapientia*. In the first place, natural and supernatural theology, despite their different *principia*, the *liber naturae*
and the *liber scripturae*, have the same subject, God and whatsoever is of
God. The book of nature is simply the self–revelation of God: "God is
the subject of theology, but creatures are made for the manifestation of
this subject."[84] Furthermore, identification of God as the subject of
theology implies that all the actions and works of God belong to this
subject. The identity of subject indicates the identity of the *genus*,
while the distinction of *principia* indicates the presence of mixed
articles or questions within that genus.[85] The argument is not conclu-
sive and Alsted will ultimately confess that natural theology is called
sapientia only by analogy.[86]

Some comment is necessary at this point concerning the importance of
this discussion of *genus* to the orthodox system, particularly in view of
the tendency of much modern theology to ignore this question, the two
notable exceptions being Karl Barth and Wolfhart Pannenberg. It is
inadequate to say that the Protestant scholastics inherited the question
from their medieval models and dealt with it *pro forma* simply because of
its presence in earlier system. There were many issues and arguments set
forth by the medievals that the Protestants chose either to reject or to
ignore. It is also only a partial explanation to note that the scholastic mind strove toward the completion of accurate paradigms and definitions and that theology, like any other discipline, needed to find its
place in the academic curriculum. Both of these explanations are correct
to a certain extent, but what is far more important is the way in which
the use of the inherited paradigm of *intelligentia*, *scientia*, *sapientia*,

prudentia and *ars* was capable of raising and in part resolving questions concerning the relationship of principles to conclusions, the relation of theoretical deduction or synthesis to practical induction or analysis, and the relation of theology as a discipline to other disciplines that claim to guide and direct human life.

In other words, the discussion clarifies the way in which theology has and uses its principles, draws its conclusions, and relates to the conduct of human life. As a subalternate science or derived wisdom, it is *theologia nostra* resting on the *theologia archetypa*, from which it draws its principles or has them bestowed by revelation. It draws conclusions rationally, recognizing that it rests on revelation and not on necessary reasons. And, finally, those conclusions are not merely theoretical as they would be if theology were a science in the strictest sense, but rather, like wisdom, they are eminently practical conclusions which pass judgment on the truth or value of all other ways of knowing and doing and, like prudence, direct human action. This perspective leads directly to the next several topics of the prolegomena: whether theology is theoretical or practical, how philosophy should be used in theology, how theology functions as a discipline, and what the fundamental articles and principles of theology are from which conclusions concerning faith and obedience are to be drawn. From these comments, it should also be clear that this identification of *genus* governs, as it were, the conduct of the entire system.

6.3 Theology: Theoretical or Practical?

One of the debates inherited by the Protestant scholastics from medieval theology concerns the character and purpose of the discipline as theoretical or practical. On this question, moreover, the Reformed scholastics teach no single definitive solution. We have already encountered part of the reason for varied opinion on this point in the basic definitions of theology. Christian theology was frequently explained by the orthodox in terms of its proximate and ultimate purposes—living to God through Christ both now and in eternity—and, in several of the basic definitions, was characterized as "theoretico-practical." Like the medieval doctors, but with a more uniform result, the Protestant orthodox argued the question of whether theology was theoretical or practical or, if a "mixed" discipline, whether more theoretical or more practical. Although explicit discussion of this point has disappeared from modern theological systems, the issue remains as an undercurrent in all discussions of the purpose and, indeed, the reason for theology as a discipline. The answer, of course, like all of the other answers to presuppositional questions raised in the scholastic prolegomena, influences profoundly the subsequent course of theological system.

Like the question itself, the meaning of the terms arose out of the medieval theological tradition—not merely the tradition of scholastic system but also the tradition of piety and mysticism. The adjectives *theoretical* and *practical*, like the nouns from which they derive, *theoria* and *praxis*, *do not* indicate a tendency toward metaphysical rationalization on the one hand and pragmatic enterprise on the other, or a statement of abstract principle on the one hand and of application on the other. To the extent that the scholastic enterprise is interpreted in terms of such a view of *theoria* and *praxis*, it is misinterpreted. The scholastics, both of the Middle Ages and the seventeenth century, understood both words in their basic etymological sense: *theoria* (from the Greek verb *theorein*, "to look at") indicates something seen or beheld; *praxis* (from the Greek verb, *prassein*, "to do") indicates something done or engaged in with an end in view.

Theoria, then, is synonymous with *contemplatio* or *speculatio* and indicates the pure beholding of something. To the scholastic mind, this concept of a pure beholding, with no end in view other than the vision of the thing beheld, must be understood in terms of the *visio Dei* and the ultimate enjoyment of God (*fruitio Dei*) by man. Thus, as Polanus indicated in his basic divisions of the topic of ectypal theology, the ends of theology are the *glorificatio Dei tanquam summi boni* and the *beatitudo creaturarum rationalium*. Insofar as theology embodies this goal in its teachings it is to be defined as *theoria*, *contemplatio* or *speculatio*. Insofar, however, as theology does not embody this end but rather points toward it as a goal, it is *praxis*. Thus, *theoria* may be defined as a teaching (*doctrina*) known in and for itself and *praxis* as a teaching known for the sake of the end toward which it directs the knower.[87]

Unlike some of the issues and paradigms used by the Protestant orthodox, the discussion of theology as theoretical and/or practical has definite roots in earlier Reformed theology, specifically, in the writings of Peter Martyr Vermigli. Vermigli's Thomist training is evident in his argument concerning the balance of theoretical or contemplative elements with the practical side of theology. Significantly, Vermigli does not mention Aquinas—the polemic against Rome was perhaps too intense for him to cite sources—but rather moves toward the problem through a brief discussion of philosophy. The division of philosophy into speculative and practical knowledge relates to our understanding of

Scripture, for "there also we have philosophy, active and contemplative." The things we believe which "are comprehended in the articles of the faith, belong to contemplation." These things are seen to be contemplative or speculative since they are present to knowledge but apart from work. The active aspects of scriptural philosophy are described by the "laws, counsels, and exhortations" of God.[88]

From this we recognize, says Vermigli, that the Scriptures contain a knowledge of God that is both contemplative and active, while the philosophers have simply taken the contemplative path.

> In the holy scriptures the contemplative has the first place: inasmuch as we must first believe, and be justified by faith; afterward follow good works, and that so much the more and more abundantely as we be renewed daily by the Holy Ghost. So does Paul show in his epistles: for first he handles doctrine, afterward he descends to the instruction in manners, and to the order of life.[89]

The Ten Commandments similarly begin with things belonging to "faith or speculative knowledge" and then move on to precepts. The usual human order would be the reverse: men act in order to be justified. Even so the end of philosophy "is to obtain that blessedness or felicity, which may here by human strength be attained." Theological truth, however, comes not by effort but by inspiration of God.

> Even so these things, which a Christian does, he does by the impulsion of the spirit of God. Those things which the philosophers do, according to moral precepts, they do by the guide of human reason. The philosophers are stirred to do those things, because they judge them to be honest and right: but the Christians, because God has so decreed. Those think to profit and make perfect themselves: these, because the majesty of God must be obeyed. Those give credit to themselves: but these give credit to God, and to the works of the law which he has made. Those seek the love of themselves. These are driven by the love of God alone.[90]

From this we may conclude that "speculative knowledge is preferred above the active; since doing is ordained for contemplation, and not contrawise." One may object that contemplation in fact does serve action, since we know God in order to worship him: according to this reasoning "divinity . . . is called actual." Yet divinity contains knowledge which is not actualized, not brought to pass or presently beheld. Indeed the purpose of theology is "that we may know God more and more, until we shall behold him face to face in the kingdom of heaven." The contemplative or speculative aspect of theology is, therefore, foremost in place and importance and the active is derived. This is true both in our present justification and our final glorification.[91]

Vermigli's characterization of theology as both contemplative and active with the active life of obedience springing from the contemplative or speculative ground of faith would prove of central significance for the later Reformed description of theology. Maccovius, Turretin and van Mastricht would speak of theology as a theoretico-practical science and emphasize the grounding of obedience on faith—although they would uniformly reject the intellectualist viewpoint that makes theory of more import than praxis. In addition, this characterization would bear fruit during the early orthodox period, in relation to the Ramist method of organization by division or dichotomy. For Ames, Polanus, and Wollebius the proper division of theology was into the coordinate halves of "faith" and "obedience."

Despite an underlying agreement on the direction of and priorities in theology, Vermigli differs with Calvin in his use of the term *speculation*. Whereas Calvin usually attaches a negative connotation to the term, Vermigli expresses a positive meaning. He calls theology speculative for precisely the same reason that Calvin considers it antispeculative: because it treats of divine revelation, not of human works. The difference arises, most probably, from the Scotist background of Calvin's thought and the Thomistic background of Vermigli's:

> Scotus says that theology is for us a practical science, mainly because revelation is given as a norm for salutary conduct, that we may attain our last end, whereas for St. Thomas theology is primarily a speculative science, though not exclusively, because it deals more with divine things than with human acts. In other words, the main difference between them on this matter is one of emphasis, it is a difference which one would expect in view of St. Thomas's general emphasis on intellect and theoretical contemplation and Scotus's general emphasis on will and love. . . .[92]

Neither Calvin nor Vermigli will tolerate a *posteriori* speculation into the nature of God and his will. However, Vermigli differs from Calvin in that he views a *priori* revealed knowledge of God as "speculative," following the language of Aquinas. Apart from this difference in definition their attitudes share much common ground. Vermigli's language, like Hyperius' distinction between "the metaphysics of Aristotle" and "the metaphysics of Sacred Scripture" makes us pause before we condemn categorically the entrance of "speculation" or "metaphysics" into Reformed theology. Vermigli's Thomism has been filtered through a strong mistrust of unaided reason and a powerful drive to rest the doctrines of salvation on revelation alone. Here, as in Vermigli's earlier statements on the necessity of viewing the doctrine of creation as revealed to faith, we see the other side of his thought which refers to the Scotist and nominalist background—perhaps to his early study of Gregory of Rimini.[93]

Vermigli's understanding of theological speculation or contemplation is not related to an emphasis on metaphysics *per se*. For Vermigli, contemplative theology treats of all those topics given by revelation to faith and, therefore, includes not only those nominally metaphysical topics such as the nature and attributes of God and the Trinity but also the topics belonging to the temporal portion of the *ordo salutis*, such as justification and the atoning death of Christ. In other words the term "contemplative" in Vermigli's system is the exact correlate of the term "faith" in the early orthodox dichotomy, both indicating the exposition of revealed doctrine.

One of the earliest of Reformed thinkers to address the issue of *theoria* and *praxis* in a formal prolegomenon to theological system was Bartholomaus Keckermann. His discussion is of historical and theological importance not only because of its early date (ca. 1592–1601) but also because it *does not* reflect the eventual Reformed orthodox consensus. Like his contemporaries, Perkins and Ames, Keckermann defined Christian theology teleologically in terms of its ultimate goal, the glory of God and the enjoyment of God (*fruitio Dei*). As noted earlier,[94] Keckermann felt justified in arguing, against the tendency of Protestant orthdoxy, that theology was not *sapientia* or *scientia* but religious prudence (*prudentia religiosa*). In accord with this definition, Keckermann denied that theology could be in any way theoretical or contemplative and argued that it was entirely practical—a *praxis* or an "operative discipline" (*operatrix disciplina*). Among the later orthodox, this perspective was held by only a minority, most notably by J. H. Heidegger.[95] Thus, Heidegger can argue in his *Medulla* that theology is totally practical inasmuch as it is directed toward the love and glorification of God and contains nothing other than knowledge of the *praxis* of salvation.[96]

Keckermann's language has strong Scotist overtones: his use of *prudentia* implies a fairly blunt denial of the Thomist view of theology as science or even as wisdom. For Keckermann, as for Scotus, this does not at all imply that God is unknowable but rather that God, to use Scotus' terms, is operable (*operabilis*)—that is, that God is attainable or reachable by a particular kind of action or operation (*operatio*) known to theology. Thus God is known not in a scientific or theoretical sense but in a practical sense as the end or goal of human loving.[97] "Theology," argues Keckermann, "is not a naked knowing (*nuda notitia*) but a faithful apprehension (*fiducia*) such as is rooted in the affections."[98] Thus it is essentially an *operatio* and a *praxis*. Against the Thomist view that theology is both speculative and practical, Keckermann notes that the attempt to make theology a mixed discipline undercuts its unity and, where successful, prevents theology from using a cohesive method. Speculative disciplines argue in a synthetic manner whereas practical disciplines move analytically. Theology must be unified in its subject matter and in its method: it is therefore practical and operative (*operatrix*), a form of *prudentia*.[99]

Beginning in the second decade of the seventeenth century, Protestant scholastics begin to cite in some detail the various opinions of medieval doctors concerning the theoretical or practical character of theology. Whereas earlier use of medieval models, like Junius' appropriation of the Scotist categories of *theologia in se* and *theologia nostra*, had not included citation of medieval theologians by name, the orthodox Protestants of the early seventeenth century both cited theologians by name and frequently identified *loci*—in this case, the prolegomena to commentaries on Lombard's *Sentences*. One of the earliest, if not the first, of the Protestant scholastics to move to this explicit use of the medievals was Johann Gerhard, the great Lutheran scholastic, whose *Loci theologici* appeared in nine volumes between 1610 and 1627.[100] He was followed rather quickly on the Reformed side by Johnann Heinrich Alsted, whose *Methodus sacrosanctae theologiae* was published in 1614.[101] The typology of medieval views on *theoria* and *praxis* rapidly became standardized and is found in virtually identical versions in many of the high orthodox systems.

Turretin, for example, begins his *quaestio*, "An theologia sit theoretica, an practica?," with a section devoted to the "origin of the question." The question, comments Turretin, was debated at length and over a long period by the *scholastics*:

> Some maintained that theology is purely speculative (*simpliciter esse speculativam*), as Henry [of Ghent] in his *Summa*, art. 8, q.3; Durandus in the prolegomena to the *Sentences*, q.6; and Johannes Rada, controversy 3. Others maintained that it is purely practical (*simpliciter practicam*), as Scotus and his followers. Still others argued it to be neither theoretical nor practical, but rather affective or dilective (*affectivam vel dilectivam*), surely more profoundly seated [in the soul] than theoretical or practical disciplines, inasmuch as its goal is love (*finis sit charitas*) and love is not contained within praxis: thus Bonaventure, Albert the Great, and Giles of Rome. Finally, others consider theology to be a mixed discipline, that is, at once speculative and practical (*speculativam . . . et practicam simul*)—whether mostly speculative, as the Thomists argue; or mostly practical, as Thomas of Strasburg.[102]

The question set forth in this paradigm, Turretin continues, is not necessary to an understanding of the true nature of theology (*ad intelligendam veram theologiae naturam*) but to the defense of the church against the Socinians and Remonstrants, who argue that theology is strictly practical, consisting in nothing but obedience to precepts and faith in promises. This perspective removes from religion all fundamental articles—including the Trinity and the incarnation—and, Turretin concludes, ultimately issues in atheism.[103] Whereas the Socinians and Remonstrants would certainly deny that their views led to atheism, they clearly did hope to deny fundamental or necessary articles any role in the determination of normative Christianity.

Following Arminius, Episcopius argues strongly that theology is practical and not speculative. Indeed, on these grounds he attacks the orthodox Reformed use of distinctions between *theologia archetypa* and *theologia ectypa* as vain subtleties without solidity or utility. Theology, he argues, is not based on the example of nature but upon what God in the freedom of his will has conceived as the duties of man. Theology, in general, is nothing other than that teaching which contains a true understanding of God and which, on the basis of this understanding, composes right worship.[104] Theology is a purely practical knowledge which intends only to teach men how to live well and with piety. To say that theology is both speculative and practical is to ignore the fact that "there is nothing in the whole of theology that is not directed toward action."[105]

It is also, therefore, an error to claim that theology is speculative from the point of view of man, but practical from the point of view of God. This claim, argues Episcopius, turns theology into a disquisition on God, his actions and nonactions (or permissions) utterly devoid of human considerations—such as is implied by those who follow the absurdity of a doctrine of absolute predestination.[106] This makes all humanity passive and renders sin nothing but a defective act of God.[107] Episcopius' obvious adversary is Reformed theology. What is significant is that his attack is not simply on the doctrine of predestination but on a wrong perception of theology that turns the discipline away from emphasis on human action toward consideration of doctrines concerning ultimate truths of a transcendent God. If this view of theology were accepted, the Reformed insistence on doctrinal norms would collapse— indeed, the theocentric character of Reformed theology would have to give way to an essentially anthropocentric drive toward *praxis*.

In the context of this debate, it is not at all surprising that Keckermann's definition of theology as *operatrix disciplina* and as pure *praxis* became unpopular—even though in and of itself it implied no departures from the basic doctrines of confessional orthodoxy. The two elements in Keckermann's argument that continued to have an impact on Reformed theology, however, were his perceptions concerning the dominance of the practical and his assumption that the model chosen for theology, theoretical or practical, would have its impact on the method employed in the construction of theological system. Although virtually none of the orthodox attempted to follow Trelcatius by mixing methods within each *locus*, their assumption that theology is both theoretical and practical, contemplative and active, did make impossible the use of either a purely synthetic and *a priori* or a purely analytic and *a posteriori* model in dogmatic system.[108]   In other words, contrary to Turretin's polemical statement, the issue of *theoria* and *praxis* is of importance to an under-standing of the nature of true theology.

Thus, early orthodox thinkers like Polanus and Ames manifest a balance of *theoria* and *praxis* in their basic division of theology into doctrines concerning faith and doctrines concerning obedience. Among the major Dutch theologians of the period, Maccovius' balanced definition was echoed in the theology of Walaeus[109] and Gomarus,[110] while the language of Polanus carries over into the German Reformed theology of Alsted.[111] The Cocceians, Burmann and Heidanus, were viewed with suspicion, there-fore, not only for their views of covenant and their incipient Carte-sianism but also for their tendency to define theology as essentially *praxis*.[112]   Heidanus, whose arguments are considerably more nuanced on this point than Burmann's, argued that theological knowledge, viewed formally and in terms of its method (*ex modo suo*), is speculative—whereas viewed substantively (*materialiter*) and in terms of its object, is practical. God is not contemplated in Scripture as a "purely meta-physical object" but rather as the object of faith, hope and love—not as God *simpliciter* but "as our God" (*ut Deum nostrum*) and "as the covenanted God" (*ut Deum foederatum*).[113]   Heidanus' point concerning the object of theology was, as noted above, drawn into the high orthodox system by Turretin and there linked to the more typical definition of theology as both speculative and practical. Turretin's contemporary, Mastricht, used his theoretical-practical view of theology as a basis for designing the structure of each *locus* in his system—manifesting the practical implica-tion of each article of faith as well as observing the basic division between faith and obedience. There was, moreover, some difference of opinion over the answer to the question both between the Reformed and the Lutherans and among the Reformed themselves.[114]   The truth in Turretin's analysis of the situation is simply that the controversy with the Socin-ians and the Remonstrants most probably helped to determine the final answer—his own, Mastricht's, Riissen's and Maccovius'—to the question. That answer, however, is crucial to the structure and content of theolog-ical system.

Maccovius regarded the issue of the theoretical or practical nature of theology as so important to the construction of system that he let the debate over the issue occupy the opening paragraph of his system:

> A theoretical discipline is something that knows in order that we might know its end (*fine*) only; we know a practical discipline in order that we might act. *Obj.* But God, Christ, &c. cannot be made or acted upon by us. Therefore theology is a purely theoretical discipline. *Resp.* We know God and Christ in order that through this knowledge that we might do something. Thus as I know that God is all-knowing, by this knowledge I also offer him the praise that he knows all my faults, the humble state of my soul and body: from this I am turned to prayers of entreaty and I ask that he overlook the former and graciously support the latter. Thus when I know his omnipotence, I am turned toward him even as my heart is directed toward his statutes: even so this knowlege of omnipotence, wisdom and other attributes of God is theoretical in such a way as to bring about a *praxis* in us. And thus theology consists partly in contemplation (*in contemplatione*) and partly in actio (*in actione*).[115]

This tone-setting paragraph counters both the typical contemporary misunderstanding of Maccovius as an excessively speculative theologian and the equally typical misconception of Reformed orthodoxy as a metaphysically-controlled predestinarian system. Maccovius, who taught at Franecker with the less overtly scholastic Ames, was in fact censured for the perceived excesses of his theological method by the Synod of Dort.[116]   It is an error, however, to conclude from the censure that Maccovius was a purely speculative thinker or, more generally, that the supralapsarian theologians among the Dutch Reformed either forgot the strongly practical dimension of theology taught by Ames or produced systems in which the doctrine of predestination provided an underlying principle governing all other statement. Far more important to Maccovius, as to Perkins, Ames, Walaeus, the authors of the Leiden Synopsis, and to later writers like Mastricht, was the operative or practical implication of all doctrine—including predestination—as it became effective in the mind of the knower.

The character of theology as both theoretical and practical, contemplative and active is determined, therefore, not simply on polemical grounds but primarily on the basis of its subject matter. A purely theoretical discipline is devoted solely to contemplation and has no other goal than cognition; a purely practical discipline is devoted solely to action and has no other goal than the direction of operation (*operatio*) or of *praxis*. It is clear that neither definition applies perfectly to theology:[117] theology contains both *dogmata seu decreta fidei* and *praecepta Christianarum virtutem*—both the required doctrines of faith and the rules of Christian virtue.[118]

The conjunction of the theoretical and the practical can be argued in more detail in terms of the object, subject, ground (*principium*), form, and goal of theology. The object of theology, we have already seen, is God—God as he is known and worshiped, God as the first Truth and highest Good (*ut primum Verum et summum Bonum*). Knowing the highest truth demands contemplation; worshiping and striving toward the highest good demands action. The *subiectum theologiae* or subject *in quo* of theology is man to be perfected (*homo perficiendus*)—both in a knowledge of truth that illumines the intellect and in a love of the good that adorns the will, which is to say, perfected both in faith and in love.[119] In the *principium theologiae*, *theoria* and *praxis* are similarly conjoined: the external principle, the Word, in the Law and the gospel, teaches of things to be done (*facienda*) and things to be believed (*credenda*); the internal principle, the Spirit, is the Spirit both of truth and of sanctification, both of the knowledge and the reverence of the Lord. Even so the *forma* of true religion consists in both the knowledge (*cognitio*) and the worship (*cultus*) of God, and the *finis* of theology and religion is the blessedness of man (*hominis beatitudeo*), consisting in both the vision (*visio*) and the enjoyment (*fruitio*) of God.[120]

This conjunction of theory and praxis in all aspects of theology points to the way in which the orthodox overcome the seeming problem of a mixed discipline with no single proper method, as posed by Keckermann and Trelcatius. Whereas the speculative and the practical are the *differentia* or distinguishing features of inferior disciplines, argues Turretin, in theology, which is a higher and more eminent discipline, it is possible for these characteristics to be conjoined—just as the internal "common sense" (*sensus communis*) that gathers the fruits of experience contains in itself, as in a unity, the *differentia* of the several external senses; or just as rational life (*vita rationalis*) in man contains both "vegetative" and "sensitive" life, that is, the kinds of life found in lower living beings.[121] Turretin's point is simple: the logic of predication recognizes that several species, distinguished from each other by particular characteristics (*differentia*), can belong to a single genus. So is it with theology: the speculative and the practical are *differentia* only at a lower level in the *genus* "discipline," not at the level occupied by theology. This argument for a disciplinary unity encompassing the speculative and practical characteristics of theology reflects the point made previously, in the discussion of archetypal and ectypal theology, that a multiplicity of ways of knowing the substance or object of theology does not indicate a multiplicity of theologies: since there is but one object or substance, true theology is a unity.

Walaeus makes the same point, arguing that theology

> is, however, theoretical in such a way that it consists not in
> vain speculations as engineered by many [medieval!] Scholas-
> tics, but in the true illumination of the mind, which is always
> conjoined with pious affection (cum pio affectu), as the Apos-
> tle says, Titus 1:1, "the teaching (doctrina) that is according
> to piety" (secundum pietatem).[122]

Similarly, his colleague Poliander could note that theory and praxis are
not "opposed differentia" in theology but are closely related conditions
of one discipline that together lead to eternal life.[123]   Although we
have not yet seen an explicit statement concerning a unified method for
theology, there is no logical or theological reason why the definition of
theology as theoretico-practical should preclude unity of method.

Mastricht defines this theologia Christiana theoretico-practica as
that doctrine which inculcates vivendi Deo per Christum. As his text for
this first locus he cites 1 Timothy 6:2-3: "These things teach and
exhort. If someone teaches different doctrine, and consents not to the
wholesome words of our Lord Jesus Christ, and to that doctrine which is
according to piety, he is proud, knowing nothing &c." Mastricht notes
that in the colophon to the Epistle (6:20-21) Paul again urges theologia
vera upon Timothy and bids him flee theologia falsa. The latter is a
doctrine which does not endure, which does not convey sanos sermones
Christi, seu de Christo, and which brings about hatred and strife.[124]
Thus theology is not only doctrina vivendi Deo per Christum but also
doctrina, quae est secundum pietatem.[125] True theology must, therefore,
be expounded according to a method that inculcates doctrine with piety,
theoria cum praxi.

The only issue that remains to be resolved is the balance of theory
and practice. The paradigm employed by the Protestant scholastics noted
two possibilities: a theoretico-practical discipline that is more
theoretical than practical, after the manner of Aquinas' Summa; or a
theoretico-practical discipline that is more practical than theoretical,
following the argument of Thomas of Strasbourg's commentary on the
Sentences. Apart from the exceptions already noted—Keckermann, Burmann
and Heidegger arguing for a purely practical discipine—and apart from
Vermigli's Thomistic emphasis on the theoretical or contemplative side of
the discipline, the Reformed orthodox tend to follow Thomas of Strasbourg, emphasizing the practical:

> That theology is more practical than speculative appears from
> its ultimate goal, which is praxis; granted that not all
> mysteries are regulative of operations or activities, they are
> however impulsive toward operation: indeed nothing [in theol-
> ogy] is theoretical to such a degree and so remote from praxis
> that it does not bring about the admiration and worship of God;

nor is a theory salvific unless it is referred to praxis, John 18;17; I Cor. 13:2; Titus 1:1; I John 2:3, 4; Titus 2:12.[126]

That Thomas of Strasbourg provides the Reformed with a model is significant insofar as Thomas, like the models in our discussion of the object of theology, Giles of Rome and Gregory of Rimini, was a member of the Augustinian order. The Reformed scholastics, when modifying or refusing the patterns both of Thomist or Scotist theology, look to the Augustinian model as an alternative.

It is worth noting that this principial decision to describe the system of theology as theoretical and practical, with emphasis on the practical, coheres with the implications of Reformed soteriology. Just as the various options in the medieval paradigm correlate with theological and philosophical considerations concerning the relationship of intellect and will, so does the Reformed choice of the Augustinian perspective indicate a correlation between the definition of theology itself and a form of soteriological voluntarism. Thomist theology, characterized by a doctrine of the primacy of the intellect was virtually bound to argue the priority of the theoretical or the contemplative. Scotist thought, by way of contrast, with its radical sense of the priority of the will, defined theology as essentially praxis. The Reformed, following the more traditional Augustinian line, balanced intellect and will with an emphasis on the activity of the regenerate will in "living to God" or "living blessedly forever." Calvin, for example, had argued the faithful apprehension of Christ by the "heart" or will to be the chief part of faith.[127] Thus, theology for the Reformed was both theoretical and practical, both intellectual and voluntary, with the emphasis on the practical or voluntary element. Wendelin rather neatly sums up the early orthodox discussion: "True theology is more practical than theoretical, since its goal is the glorification of God and our salvation."[128] Theology and religion are, therefore, the means of obtaining (obtinendi medium) the goal, the glory of God and the salvation of man. This instrumental function of religion and theology underlines their primarily practical character.[129]

6.4 Wisdom and Knowledge as habitus mentis

Few of the Protestant scholastics devote more than a sentence or two to the classification of theology as a disposition of mind or habitus mentis, but that is only because the language was taken for granted and was not a matter for debate. Here again, the underlying materials come from the psychological and epistemological theory of the medieval doctors.[130] It is rather difficult to argue either continuity or discontinuity with the Reformers on this point—they seldom use or dispute the language of *dispositio* or *habitus* in theology nor do they propose an alternative view of how faith resides in the mind. They disparage the language of *habitus gratiae* or disposition of grace, but only because of the semi-Pelagian connotations given it by the teachers of the late Middle Ages.

A strong case can be made, however, for the continuity of the faculty psychology of Christian Aristotelianism during the period of the Reformation and in the theology of the Reformers themselves. Calvin, for example, viewed intellect and will as the faculties or parts of the soul (*partes animae*) and, following the traditional faculty-psychological model, placed the affections below the will as those qualities of soul that desire the things of sense perception and, in turn, influence the will in its choices.[131] The concept of dispositions of intellect and will toward certain objects or kinds of object is an integral part of faculty psychology. In Melanchthon's *Erotemata dialectices*, the single major work from the era of the Reformation in which the faculty psychology is presented, not tangentially as supplying some of the terms for discussion, but in a full positive exposition, the concept of *habitus* receives full definition. "*Habitus*, in Greek *hexis*, is a quality brought about through repeated actions in human beings, according to which people are able rightly and easily to perform those actions which are governed and assisted by a particular disposition or habit."[132] In any case, with the rise of Protestant scholasticism and the need to present a full-scale psychology and epistemology, the language of *habitus* is returned to regular use.

Among the earlier Reformed theologians, the Thomist-trained Vermigli is an exception to the generalization made in the preceding paragraph, though even he did not develop a full-scale psychology. Man's knowledge, he writes, is "either revealed or acquired: theology belongs to the former part, philosophy to the latter." In both cases, wisdom, *sapientia*, is

> a habit (*habitus*) given to the mind of man by God, increased by diligence and exercise, whereby all things may be comprehended in order that a man may reach blessedness. . . . God has implanted a light in our minds and has sown in us the seeds which are the originals of all the sciences.[133]

In other words, the presence of knowledge in the mind is contingent upon the existence in the mind of a disposition for or habit of knowing. A person does not simply know a fact—he must first be *disposed* to know it.

Even among the Protestant scholastics, who adopt without question the entire language of faculty psychology as one of the presuppositions of their discussions of human knowing, we do not find a vast amount of space devoted to the analysis of theology as a *habitus mentis*. The reason for the relative lack of emphasis is quite simple and may, in fact, account for the virtual absence of the theological use of the term in early sixteenth-century Protestant literature. Theology viewed as *habitus* is theology individualized and understood as belonging to the mind of a single human subject, whereas theology viewed as doctrinal system is theology universalized and understood as objective statement made available to all who can read or hear. Thus Wollebius comments: "Christian theology is the teaching concerning God (*doctrina de Deo*) . . . in this place it is considered not as a disposition residing in the intellect (*non ut habitus in intellectu residens*) but as a system of precepts (*sed ut systema praeceptorum*). . . ."[134]

In the scholastic vocabulary, *habitus* indicates any spiritual capacity or disposition of the soul, whether of mind or of will, to be informed by things or beings external to it. These capacities or dispositions, moreover, can be classified both according to origin or cause and according to function or kind. Thus a disposition can be innate or inborn (*habitus insita*), belonging to the nature of the mind or will; acquired (*habitus acquisita*) by an activity of mind or will in relation to something external; or infused (*habitus infusa*) by the activity of some thing or power external to the mind or will. In terms of function or kind, a *habitus* can be a disposition of knowing, strictly so-called (*habitus sciendi*), consisting in the rational activity of mind; a disposition of believing (*habitus credendi*) or a disposition of faith (*habitus fidei*), consisting in the acceptance of received testimony; or a disposition of opining (*habitus opiniandi*), consisting in an opinion concerning something resting neither on rational evidence nor authoritative testimony.[135]

The kind of *habitus*, moreover, is determined by the kind of theology. Natural or philosophical theology is either a *habitus insita* or a *habitus acquisita*; revealed or supernatural theology is a *habitus infusa* in the first instance and, when learned from a system in technical detail, a *notitia acquisita* resting on the infused *habitus supernaturalis*.[136] The implication of these definitions is that natural or rational theology rests upon an innate or inborn capacity of man or, if found in an elaborate, philosophized form that must be learned, on an acquired intellectual capacity. In either case, we are speaking of a rational knowledge, a *habitus sciendi* in the strictest sense. In view of what we have already seen about the limitation of natural theology, we can note here that the disposition of the mind to learn of God through the natural or rational order is, corresponding to the order, a natural or rational disposition subject to the same limitation as the knowledge it receives. Since it belongs to the fallen nature of man, it cannot receive saving knowledge apart from grace. Indeed, the scholastics argue that a separate disposition is needed for a knowledge of revelation.[137]

Revealed or supernatural, which is to say, truly salvific or Christian theology is not a result of fallen nature perceiving truths of God in the world around it—or even of fallen nature *per se* perceiving truths of God contained in revelation. As the Reformers insisted in their doctrine of justification by grace through faith alone, faith itself is a gift of God's grace and neither an innate capacity of man nor a capacity acquired through human effort. The scholastic Protestant classification of theology as a *dispositio supernaturalis*, *habitus supernaturalis* or *habitus fidei* represents an attempt to reckon with this teaching concerning justification in the doctrine of theology itself.[138] As implied in Calvin's theme of the *duplex cognitio Dei* or twofold knowledge of God, there can be no movement from knowledge of God as Creator to knowlege of God as Redeemer apart from Christ and salvation in him. Here too, the theological enterprise, considered as an acquisition of saving knowledge, is impossible unless the disposition of believing (*habitus credendi*) is infused into man by God. Thus, again, the disposition of mind required for a particular order of knowing corresponds with the order of things to be known—a supernaturally given *habitus fidei* or *habitus credendi*, a *habitus theosdotos*, is necessary for the reception of supernatural theology.[139]

The actual language of the Protestant scholastics concerning the *habitus fidei* is clearly influenced in a negative direction by the medieval scholastic view of grace as *habitus infusa* or infused disposition. The Protestant response, consistently present in both the Reformers and the orthodox, had been to deny that grace is a habit infused into the sinner. Grace is a power of God which never becomes a property or predicate of human nature.[140] The psychology of the Middle Ages and of the sixteenth and seventeenth centuries, however, depended on the language of *habitus* as a way of reckoning with the ability of the mind to know or do certain things—and such dispositions are either inborn (*innata*), ingrafted (*insita*), acquired (*acquisita*), or infused (*infusa*). *Habitus innata* and *habitus acquisita* are ruled out immediately by the fall: faith is not something that we have by nature or can gain by effort. Remaining are the terms *habitus insita* and *habitus infusa*: *insita* tended to be used with reference to the result of immediate apprehension while *infusa* carried with it the taint of the medieval doctrine of grace.[141]   Since the former adjective does not apply to the doctrine of faith—insofar as it implies synergism—the latter alone remains applicable.   Rather, however, than speak directly of a *habitus infusa*, the Protestant scholastics tend rather to speak of the divine act of infusing the habit in regeneration or in calling.[142]

The psychology and epistemology of the Protestant scholastics, then, indicates that there can be no saving knowledge in the unsaved—no genuine theology of the unregenerate (*theologia irregenetorum*).   Of course, one could conceivably learn an entire theological system as a set of meaningless distinctions according to the *habitus sciendi*, but none of the materials learned would be effective, none would be capable of use according to the saving intention of theological system.   For Christian theology to be learned as it is intended to be learned, the student or the theologian must be a believer in whose mind there is a disposition of believing, a *habitus credendi*.[143]   Here, it should be noted that the Protestant scholastics reflect the views of the thirteenth-century scholastics—whether Aquinas, Bonaventure or Scotus—and not the views of the nominalists.   The former assumed one *habitus* or disposition for each mode or manner of knowing (i.e., *scientia*, *prudentia*, *ars*, etc.), whereas the latter, based on their views of universals as mere mental abstractions, assumed a distinct *habitus* for each datum of knowledge, which is to say a distinct disposition to know corresponding with each doctrine or even doctrinal point believed.   We note, finally, that this view of theological knowledge as resting upon a divinely infused *habitus fidei* or *habitus credendi* points toward a view of the theologian himself and of theological study as essentially religious.[144]   Theology, understood as a discipline, is a God-given disposition, acquired through study but firmly grounded on an infused disposition of faith.[145]

7

The Use of Philosophy
in Theology

Whereas there is considerable agreement between the Reformed orthodox perspectives on religion and natural theology and the views of the Reformers on those subjects, when it comes to the use of philosophy in theology there is a certain degree of discontinuity. In addition, the Protestant orthodox faced issues similar to those confronted by the medieval scholastics in their work of system building. Luther and Calvin had argued pointedly against the use of philosophical concepts—particularly Aristotelian concepts—in the construction of theology and had consistently ruled out, if not the implicit acceptance of a largely Aristotelian worldview, at least the explicit use of philosophical models. Both Luther and Calvin were reluctant to develop metaphysical discussions of the divine essence and attributes—though neither disputed the truth of the traditional attribution to God of omnipresence, omniscience, eternity, infinity, simplicity, and so forth. This perspective on metaphysical discussion and the related avoidance of the language of essence marks a major difference between the theology of these two Reformers and that of the Protestant orthodox. Much of that difference relates to the problem of the use of philosophy in theology.

The discontinuity, however, is not nearly as pronounced as the views of Luther and Calvin would make it seem.[1] It is quite easy to trace a continuous flow of fundamentally Aristotelian philosophical training from the fifteenth to the seventeenth century. Philipp Melanchthon, the *Praeceptor Germaniae* as he was called, taught courses in Aristotelian logic and rhetoric at Wittenberg throughout the era of the Reformation.

Melanchthon should not be viewed as something of an exception within
Lutheranism: the philosophical faculty of Tübingen numbered among its
members Jacob Schegk (1511-1587), a scholarly Aristotelian who wrote
commentaries on the *Organon*, the *Physics*, and the *Ethics* of Aristotle.
On the Reformed side, the philosophical career of the Marburg professor,
Andreas Hyperius, was as noteworthy as his theological efforts. He not
only wrote the influential *Methodus theologiae* but also the highly
respected *Compendium librorum physicorum Aristotelis*. Examples like this
can be easily adduced to demonstrate the continuity of Aristotelianism
into the sixteenth century.[2]

This recourse to the tradition of Aristotelian philosophy undertaken
both from a humanistic perspective, with its desire to recover the
genuine Aristotle, and from a theologically and philosophically constructive perspective, characterized by a desire to reform and develop the
tradition of Christian Aristotelianism, can and ought to be viewed as an
exercise in "theological self-understanding" growing out of the natural
intellectual development of the Reformation.[3] Lewalter argues that the
clarification of issues in the theological debate between Lutherans and
Calvinists could not ultimately be resolved purely exegetically but
necessarily hinged on the understanding of things (*res*) or of beings
(*entia*), their nature and their conceptualization. Since, moreover, the
debate hinged not merely on the status of ideas but, more profoundly, on
the nature of real things, logic or dialectic by itself was insufficient:
metaphysics was necessary.[4] The purely dialectical approach of Ramus
was, thus, also doomed to failure, while a more traditional Aristotelianism or even a semi-Ramist approach to organization linked to an eclectic
Aristotelianism (as witnessed in the Suarezian metaphysic of J. H.
Alsted) was more likely to succeed in a seventeenth-century Protestant
context.[5]

The medieval dialogue of theology with philosophy also continued on
into the sixteenth century, if not in the writings of Calvin, then quite
obviously in the theology of Vermigli. Vermigli quite pointedly notes
that true philosophy is a "gift of God" according to which rational
creatures discern justice, goodness and other truths implanted in the
mind by God. Philosophy is only to be reproached when it becomes corrupt
"through the inventions of men and the ambitious contentions of philosophers"—such as Stoic fatalism and Epicurean theorization about an "idle
and unoccupied deity."   True philosophy, however, "nourishes and
instructs the soul itself."[6] What is more, philosophy follows a pattern
similar in many ways to theology: it is both an active and practical

discipline and a contemplative or speculative *scientia*, discussing both natural and supernatural causality.[7]

The issue addressed by Protestant orthodoxy, then, was not only intellectually but also historically complex. The Reformation can hardly be said to have ended the intellectual hegemony of modified Christian Aristotelianism. None of the Reformers, not even Luther and Calvin, ceased to view the world as ordered according to the fourfold causality or as fitting into a universe of concentric spheres, each of which was moved by an angelic mover.[8] Nevertheless there had been, beginning with Luther and continuing through the next generation of writers, a tendency to reduce the actual use of philosophical categories in theology and, more importantly, to refrain from lengthy or positive consideration of the great scholastic question of the relationship of revelation to reason. The question returned, rather pointedly, with the success of the Reformation as a churchly movement and with the institutionalization of the Reformation in schools and universities in the late sixteenth century.[9]

7.1 Whether Philosophical Truth Opposes Theological Truth

> The gifts of God do not conflict with one another.
> But philosophy is a gift of God; Exodus 31:3; Psalms 94:10; Sirach 1:1; II Chronicles 1:12; Daniel 2:21, "he gives wisdom to the wise"; Romans 1:19; James 1:17.
> Therefore it does not conflict with a gift of God, which is to say, with theology.
> That which is one and simple cannot be contrary to itself.
> Truth is one and simple, whether conveyed by theology or by philosophy, and is true consistently wherever it is presented (for indeed the distinction of discipline does not multiply truth).
> Therefore truth is not contrary to itself whether presented in theology or in philosophy.[10]

A crucial corollary to the Reformed limitation of natural theology and definition of scriptural revelation as the sole *principium cognoscendi theologiae* is the issue of the relationship of philosophy to theology. For if, as the orthodox Reformed theologians insisted, theology is to be methodically, logically, and therefore rationally argued, it must stand in some positive relation to philosophy or at least be able to utilize the tools of philosophy. The problem of contradiction between philosophy and theology, moreover, was raised with considerable intensity by the reaction of the Reformers against the medieval tradition and by the Protestant doctrine of original sin and near loss of the *imago Dei*.[11] If natural religion and natural theology could produce no true foundation for supernatural theology, but only idolatry and error, how could philosophy, particularly the pagan philosophy of Aristotle, contribute anything to Christian theology?

Debate over this question began in earnest in the thirteenth century following the introduction of the Aristotelian philosophical corpus to the West. Aristotle clearly taught concepts that, although logically acceptable, did not conform to Christian revelation (for example, the uninvolved immutability of the first mover, the eternal existence of matter, and the passing away of the soul with the death of the body). Whereas Aquinas advocated the use of an Aristotelian system corrected by the higher truths of revelation and assumed that even those suprarational truths were never unreasonable, members of the philosophical faculty of Paris, the so-called Latin Averroists, attempted to balance Aristotelian philosophy in its own right over against the Christian revelation by arguing a distinction between philosophical and theological truth—in short, a theory of "double truth" according to which something might be true in philosophy and false in theology, and vice versa.[12]

Yet another element was added to the debate by the Scotist and nominalist contention that rationally deducible concepts and theological system do not necessarily stand in any relation to each other.[13] The issue here is not one of double truth so much as one of a radical diastasis between philosophical, specifically metaphysical, argument and theological argument. It is this perspective that most probably underlies the early Reformation rejection of the use of philosophy in theological formulation.[14] Here, of course, the epistemological problem registered by the Scotists and nominalists is further complicated by the Reformers' strictly Augustinian view of sin and their assumption that sin affects the reasoning process as well as the exercise of the will.[15]

The concept of double truth, which had never entirely disappeared from philosophical discussion, returned to haunt the development of Protestant scholasticism in the debate between the vitriolic Daniel Hoffmann and his colleagues on the philosophical faculty of the University of Helmstedt. This late sixteenth- and early seventeenth-century debate had major repercussions for the creation of a Protestant theological system, whether Lutheran or Reformed. Hoffmann combined the distaste for philosophy and sinful reason inherited by Protestantism from Luther's early polemics with the theory of double truth and produced a theory of "false" philosophical truth set over against "true" theological truth.[16] If such a theory were allowed to stand, the use of reason must be ultimately banned from theology.

The normative Lutheran opinion, as argued against Hoffmann by his colleagues at Helmstedt, was drawn into formal theological prolegomena and stated as a guide to the development of theological system by Johann Gerhard. Thus, in elaboration of the proposition, "What is true theologically cannot be false theologically, for truth is one," Gerhard could argue,

> In themselves considered, there is no contrarity, no contradiction between Philosophy and Theology, because whatever things concerning the deepest mystery of faith Theology propounds from Revelation, these a wiser and sincere Philosophy knows are not to be discussed and estimated according to the principles of Reason lest there be a confusion of what pertains entirely to distinct departments.[17]

Echoing first Luther and then Aquinas, Gerhard can conclude,

> Just as there remains in the regenerate a struggle between the flesh and the spirit, by which they are tempted to sin, so there remains in them a struggle between faith and Reason, in so far as it is not yet fully renewed . . . . The articles of faith are not in and of themselves contrary to Reason, but only above Reason.[18]

The syllogisms cited at the outset of this section from Keckermann represent a Reformed response, contemporary with the Hoffmann debate, to the new challenge of double truth. Keckermann's arguments are duplicated and then expanded at great length by Alsted.[19]

Once a basic answer to the problem of double truth had been formulated—the necessary unity of truth—the debate could be incorporated substantively into theological system. Thus Riissen, at the very end of the scholastic era of Protestantism, poses the question, "Whether Philosophy opposes Theology, i.e., whether the same statement . . . can be true in Philosophy, false in Theology."[20]   The question, argues Riissen, is to be argued in the negative: such opposition arises not out of a double truth but out of an abuse of philosophy, according to which false doctrines based on philosophical or rational excess and error are set over against theological truths.   The impression of an opposition between philosophy and theology is given by those medieval scholastics who set philosophical reason over the testimony of Scripture, by the Socinians who declare that philosophy can be the interpreter of Scripture, and by the "Fanatics, Enthusiasts, Anabaptists, and Weiglians" who by deficient thinking first distort and then reject philosophy.[21]

It is one thing for philosophy to deny a truth, argues Turretin, and quite another for philosophy simply not to teach it: "we do not deny the various theological mysteries not taught in philosophy . . . after all, geometry does not deal with medicine nor physics with jurisprudence . . . granted that philosophy teaches nothing concerning the Trinity and the

Incarnation, it therefore cannot express a negative opinion of these mysteries."[22]   The apostle Paul does not condemn philosophy *per se* but rather the vain and false philosophy of his time that endangers the teachings of the gospel.   It is thus not *vera philosophia* that Paul attacks but the abuse of philosophy at the hand of certain philosophers with inane ideas and pridefully swollen opinion: "he does not, therefore, reject *philosophia in se*, but only the declarations (*dogmata*), of those philosophers who opposed faith in the one true God and in Jesus Christ and the resurrection of the dead."[23]

The proper use of reason and philosophy in theological discourse rests upon recognition of their place and the limits of their competence. Truth, comments Turretin, cannot be set against truth--rather, one truth may transcend another.   Thus truths of sense stand below truths of reason (*infra rationem*), truths of the intellect in immediate relation to truths of reason (*juxta rationem*), and truths of faith above those of reason (*supra rationem*).   Once this pattern is recognized and the hierarchy of truth acknowledged, then rational truth can be used in theological discourse: "grace does not destroy nature but perfects it, nor does supernatural revelation abrogate the natural, but cleanses it."[24]   Thus, on the assumption that faith can belong only to rational creatures, Maresius could comment that "grace is added to reason"--and Wendelin that religion and theology are "necessarily conjoined to reason."[25]   If this balance of faith and reason, grace and nature reflects a Thomistic perspective, it remains true that the separation of philosophical and theological categories noted in the preceding paragraph represents a modification in the direction of Scotism or nominalism.   Here, as in the definition of the *obiectum theologiae* as God revealed in Christ,[26] the diastasis between theology and rational metaphysics and the general Reformed distrust of pure reason stand in the way of an easy alliance between theology and philosophy.

7.2 Philosophy and Reason: Their Competence in Matters of Faith

Although several of the Reformers, most notably Melanchthon and Vermigli, had raised the issue of the use of reason and philosophy, extended discussion of the issue in relation to theological system arose only at the beginning of the seventeenth century with the full flowering of Protestant scholastic system in an academic context.   The debate over double truth and its settlement on the side of the unity of truth can be viewed historically as the point at which discussion became necessary and slight differences in approach to the use of philosophy became a matter of polemical dispute between the Reformed orthodox and their adversaries, both Lutheran and Roman Catholic.   Here, as in the definition and paradigm of theology, the Reformers had provided no models for discussion and the Protestant scholastics were obliged to examine and reinterpret medieval models in the light of their *sola scriptura* principle.

Just as the preliminary divisions or dichotomies of the prolegomena to theological system rule out *theologia falsa* in order to discuss the *theologia vera* of Christianity, so did the debate over the problem of double truth make a distinction between *philosophia falsa* and *philosophia vera* to the exclusion of the former.   Once discussion is limited to true --rightly founded and rightly argued--theology and philosophy, not only does the impossibility of ultimate contradiction become obvious but further definitions, distinctions and relationships must also be discussed.   In the first place, the orthodox note a distinction between philosophical reason and the rational exercise of the mind.   Philosophical reason is a form of discourse consisting in analysis of and argumentation from naturally known principles: it is an intellectual discipline distinct from theology.   The simple exercise of mind or reason, however, is not a discipline--rather, it is the basic work of the understanding that belongs to *all* intellectual disciplines, including theology. Whether or not philosophical conclusions can be used in theology, the exercise of the rational faculty of the soul has its necessary place in theological discourse.[27]

According to Keckermann, metaphysics and logic were to be counted gifts of God made possible by the illumination of the mind by the Holy Spirit.[28]   Such gifts could therefore be used in the service of theological truth.   Keckermann's contemporary, Rudolph Goclenius argued--on the basis of a similar assertion--that the "ideas and terms" provided by logic and philosophy could be used both "properly and analogically" to explicate articles of faith.[29]   After all, *philosophia*, the love of wisdom, ought not to be confused with the *errores philosophorum*.   As Clement of Alexandria wisely noted in his *Stromata*, philosophy properly so-called is not Stoic, Platonic, Epicurean, or Aristotelian--rather, it is whatever these schools of thought have stated correctly.[30]

Even so, philosophy, rightly understood, is simply an instrument aiding in the clear perception of an object.   Historically it served to prepare the gentile world for the Christian faith by confirming and clarifying truths known by the light of nature; individually, it provides a useful preparation of the mind for the reception of theological truth. Philosophy is a lower discipline that prepares the way for a higher.[31]

This potential use of philosophical concepts and categories by theology is facilitated by the similarity of the topics treated by both disciplines and, consequently, by the similarities between philosophical and theological method.   In the realm of philosophy, God, nature and human conduct appear as legitimate topics: metaphysics considers God as Being (Ens) and, in addition, treats of the human soul; physics deals with the natural order; and ethics presents rules of human conduct.   Even so, theology discusses doctrines concerning God, creation, human nature and human conduct.   There are, of course, differences between philosophical and theological treatment of these subjects.   For example, theology considers God as Creator and Redeemer, not as Ens.   Nonetheless, differences in terms and materials do not necessarily point toward disagreement.   In addition, philosophical enquiry, as witnessed by the methods of metaphysics and ethics, is both speculative and practical, both synthetic and analytic, with the result that philosophy and theology are methodologically compatible.[32]

Perhaps the most ambitious attempt during the era of Protestant orthodoxy to manifest the compatibility of philosophy and theology is the system of Nicolas Taurellus.   It serves both as an example of the new striving toward system and intellectual synthesis typical of the late sixteenth and early seventeenth centuries and as a witness to the general unwillingness of Protestant scholasticism to develop in a thoroughly philosophical or metaphysical direction despite its scholastic method and its renewed interest in the relationship of theology to philosophy. Taurellus argued that an adequate metaphysics could arise only in a Christian context and in explicit opposition to secular and pagan authorities, setting forth his position at length in his Philosophiae triumphus, hoc est, metaphysica philosophandi methodus (1573).   He then proceeded, in his Synopsis Aristotelis Metaphysicae ad normam christianae religionis (1596), to rewrite Aristotelian metaphysics by excising or modifying those concepts found to be at odds with revelation.

In order to create a synthesis of theology and philosophy within a Protestant context and without returning to the Thomistic synthesis of the Middle Ages, Taurellus argued that reason itself—not merely the will and the affections—was corrupted by sin.   This argument might have fallen within the bounds of Protestant theological anthropology by allowing philosophy and reason to function for believers—a theologia naturalis regenitorum—but Taurellus made the mistake of arguing a distinction between the substance of our rational faculties, given by God in creation, and the accident or incidental property of corruption, inhering in our faculties after the fall.   Reason needs only to be redeemed by grace and philosophy needs only to be purged of its errors by redeemed reason. After all, Taurellus argued, the faculty of reason is the faculty of the soul through which both theological and philosophical discourse take place: the capability of redeemed reason to develop valid theology ought to be matched by the capability of redeemed reason to develop true and theologically compatible philosophy. Such philosophy would be utterly subordinate to theological truth.[33]

Much of what Taurellus conceived as a synthesis of philosophy and theology depended on the concept of mixed articles of teaching—that is, teachings drawing on two disciplines, such as those concerning the essence and attributes of God, which belong to both theology and metaphysics. One article, however, that Taurellus limited to theology was the teaching concerning the gracious will of God. Theology alone knows of grace and theology alone brings the message of salvation to fallen man. These views might also have been expressed within the context of Protestant theology—but Taurellus added as a corollary to his views on grace and theology that, before the fall, when the work of grace was unnecessary, so too was theology unnecessary. Adam, in his unfallen state, needed only philosophy! We now live under both nature and grace and consequently need both philosophy and theology. Ultimately, in the realms of the blessed, illuminated totally by grace, we will need no philosophy, only the *theologia beatorum*.[34]

Taurellus' reduction of sin to an incidental property, together with his argument that Adam, before the fall and before the need for grace, required only philosophy and not theology for fellowship with God, brought down on his head charges of Pelagianism and, later, Arminianism. The description of sin as an accident had been the view of the Lutheran synergists excluded from orthodox Lutheranism by the Formula of Concord; it was a position equally detested by the Reformed. The assumption that man before the fall was not in need of special grace but could approach God through his rational faculties struck at the heart of Augustinian anthropology, both Lutheran and Reformed.[35]

If Taurellus raised the possibility of philosophico-theological system, the underlying question of the competence of reason in theological matters was raised not by a philosopher within the pale of orthodoxy but by a group of exegetes and theologians already beyond the pale—the Socinians. The earlier Socinians, Lelio and Fausto Socinus, held to the necessity of revelation and argued that Christianity, although its teachings might be higher than those attained by reason, was never unreasonable. As Socinianism developed, however, theologians like Andreas

Wissowatius and Johannes Crellius tended to press the rationality of Christian doctrine to the point that revelation was little more than a divinely sanctioned reiteration of natural theology.[36] The tendency, moreover, of Socinian exegesis and theology was to reject the dogmas of orthodoxy on the ground of their rational unacceptability.

Against the Socinians, the orthodox argue that reason cannot be the principle according to which declarations of the faith are proved (*principium ex quo fidei dogmata probantur*), nor can it be the foundation (*fundamentum*) upon which faith rests since neither the light of nature nor human reason are capable of discovering the things of faith. Turretin provides six reasons for this position: unregenerate reason lies in sinful disregard of the Law and in darkness concerning the gospel; the mysteries of the faith are "above the sphere of reason"; faith is not ultimately grounded on reason but on "the Word that God has spoken in Scripture"; if reason were the *principium fidei*, then all religion would be natural religion, capable of demonstration by the light of reason and numerous statements of Scripture concerning the bondage of reason would be false; reason does not function as a norm of faith since it is either an unregenerate or corrupt reason not only below but also against the faith or it is whole or regenerate reason such as is unavailable to corrupt mankind and such as makes no claim to determine supernatural truths. Reason, illuminated by the Spirit, recognizes that Scripture is the *principium* of faith. The orthodox can, therefore, identify a twofold *principium fidei*: externally and objectively considered, the *principium* is the Word of God; internally and formally the *principium* is the "illumination of the Holy Spirit" or "the supernatural light infused into our minds." The argument here reflects the distinction of theology itself into objective *scientia* and subjective *habitus sciendi*.[37]

Similar arguments against the principial use of reason undergird Maccovius' extensive exposition of the biblical ground for the claim of the subordinate and ancillary status of reason and the suprarational nature of revelation. Maccovius begins with the prophecies of the Messiah in Isaiah, where the prophet declares, "And who has believed what we have been told; and upon whom has the arm of the Lord been revealed?" (53:1). The truth of the Messiah is a stupendous prodigy, argues Maccovius, a miracle. In such matters reason is blind and cannot provide certainty. Even so, Christ himself declares that "flesh and blood have not revealed these things but his heavenly Father" (Matt. 16:17, adapted) and, similarly the apostle Paul declares the gospel to be a scandal to the Jews and folly to the Greeks (1 Cor. 1:23). How can these Socinians, these "acute, rational teachers," fail to recognize the negation of reason by revelation?[38]

Furthermore, argues Maccovius, Scripture indicates that God under no circumstances gives reason the power of judgment in matters of faith (*judicium in rebus fidei*). Instead, we are told to rest our belief upon a hearing of the prophets and a searching of the Scriptures (Luke 16:29; John 5:39). Nowhere does Scripture declare a human standard, whether of the reason or of the will. Indeed, it follows as a necessary conclusion that no extrascriptural norm has been given to us according to which heavenly mysteries can be judged. After all, Maccovius continues, a tailor is not a judge of architecture nor an architect a judge of horses nor a charioteer a judge of metaphysics! Theology, like art, is not to be judged according to general *principia*—such as the critical norm of reason—but according to the special *principia* that belong to it. Thus Christ and the apostles taught the truths of the gospel and advised its careful study without ever having recourse to reason as the basis of judgment or decision concerning the truth of their preaching.[39]

Scripture itself, moreover, provides numerous examples of reason erring in matters of faith. Naaman the Syrian first rejected the counsel of Elijah on the grounds of reason and Nicodemus considered the truth of regeneration to be rationally unacceptable. Thomas doubted the resurrection—again, quite rationally. Indeed, both Christ and the apostle Paul declare that the things of God are hidden from the wise and from those with understanding but are revealed to children, to the foolish and to the weak (Matt. 11:25; 1 Cor. 1:26-27).[40] These arguments all point toward the Protestant hermeneutical principle, *scriptura sui interpres* ("Scripture interprets itself"), and toward a restricted, instrumental function of reason within the bounds of faith.

It was not only Socinian exegesis that caused the orthodox theologians to address the problem of the use of reason as a basic principle. They also faced the philosophical challenge of Descartes and his heirs in the rationalist tradition. This challenge and its implications are nowhere more clear than in the attempt of Heidanus, the semi-Cartesian federalist, to state his acceptance of a rationalistic view of the powers of reason while at the same time distancing himself from the still more rationalistic approach of the Socinians, in particular the notorious Conrad Vorstius and Episcopius. In addition, Heidanus strives to uphold, in continuity with his orthodox brethren, the necessity of revelation for a saving knowledge of God and, therefore, the priority of revelation over reason in theology. Reason does know, innately, the existence of God as the necessary Being. Nonetheless, reason is incapable of serving as a norm of religion after the fall. Reason and experience themselves confirm that true religion "presupposes a foundation other than reason."[41] Heidanus' alliance with Cartesianism is uneasy: Scripture, not reason, must ultimately be the *principium cognoscendi* in theology, while reason has a clearly instrumental role.[42]

Beyond the problem of the principal use of reason, the Reformed also found Cartesianism to be philosophically inadequate and theologically dangerous in its advocacy of the principle of doubt: Descartes began his philosophical pilgrimage toward certainty by doubting everything except his own thinking. To this claim that everything can be doubted, Voetius answers in the negative: some things, like the existence of God and the soul, the providence of God, the immortality and rationality of the soul and the distinction between rational man and the brute beasts cannot be doubted. Nor is it possible to doubt that moral beings such as man ought to do the good and shun evil. These truths, known by both natural and supernatural means, testified to by philosophy and theology alike are beyond doubt.[43] This is not to say that there can be no momentary suspension of judgment for the sake of argument, no academic dispute, or no use of discursive reason for the sake of overcoming doubts: rather doubt may be part of one's method as long as it does not abolish what one genuinely knows, particularly the simple truths implanted in the soul, or as long as it does not lead to the affirmation of falsehood and the denial of truth. Nor, of course, can doubt extend to those things known to theology on the basis of Scripture—inasmuch as Scripture has divine authority and is the "necessary rule of faith and life."[44]

In the mid-eighteenth century, De Moor could sum up the orthodox concern about rationalism with much the same sentiment as encountered in earlier Reformed opponents of Cartesianism. De Moor rejects both the Spinozistic contention that theology deals with piety alone—not with rational truth—and therefore has no dealing with philosophy, and the Cartesian assumptions that faith is not capable of exercising its prerogative over philosophy and that philosophy bears its own independent certainty. Human reason, writes De Moor, has been to a large degree overthrown by the fall—so that any attempt to claim that its certainty stands equal to that of faith is profoundly dangerous.[45] By way of contrast, Vitringa, Venema and Wyttenbach, all contemporaries of De Moor, manifest the new alliance between a genuinely rationalist orthodoxy and the rational supernaturalism of the age.[46]

7.3 The Instrumental Function of Reason

Once it has been recognized that philosophy, like natural theology, has a legitimate though not doctrinally formative or fundamental use in the context of Christian faith, the actual function of reason and philosophy within the system of revealed theology can be outlined. The Reformed orthodox go to some length to emphasize the biblical foundations of their claims concerning the instrumental use of human reason. In the first place, reason can be used to make clear points in divine revelation, as was the case when Christ demanded of his disciples, "Have you understood all that has been said to you? They responded, 'Yea'" (Matt. 13:15). Second, reason must be used in discussion and argument with others, as when the Bereans compared the words of Paul with Scripture (Acts 17:11). Next, reason is necessary in the work of explication, even as Ezra and Nehemiah taught the people reasonably (Neh. 8:9). Fourth, in order to discern falsehood it is necessary "to explore the things that differ" (Phil. 1:10). Finally, reason is useful to vindicate the truth from objections, as Paul himself does in the ninth chapter of Romans.[47]

If the attempt to justify the use of reason biblically appears, at first sight, to be somewhat gratuitous, it nonetheless stands as yet another sign of the genuine opposition between orthodox Protestantism and philosophical rationalism. Whereas philosophical rationalism held reason to be the fundamental principle of valid systematic thinking concerning God and the world, even the last of the high orthodox writers, like Riissen and Mastricht, had reservations concerning the function of reason in theological system. It was indeed important to their essentially biblical system of theology that even the use of reason should have biblical precedent. They press the point, moreover, by making a distinction between reason subjectively and objectively considered: the former is "the rational faculty of soul" according to which man understands and defines intelligible things, whether natural or supernatural, divine or human; the latter is "natural light" (both externally given and internally impressed upon the mind) that is used by the rational faculty in forming concepts and deriving conclusions concerning divine things.[48]

Although fallen reason cannot be the *principium fidei* it is also clear that faith can occur only in rational creatures and that even in Scripture, rational process—both the subjective capacity and the objective light according to which concepts are formed—is integral to the life of faith:

> There is no rule, therefore, apart from scripture. Reason is no such rule, for it is blind, and understandeth not the things of God (I Cor. ii.14, 15). It is liable to error, and is often

deceived; the mysteries of faith are beyond its sphere; the natural man cannot comprehend them. Reason is as it were the eye of the mind, but scripture is the standard, by which it measures the objects proposed. Reason is the instrument which the believer uses in examining the objects of faith by the scripture, as the infallible rule of truth, but it is not itself the rule of these objects of faith.[49]

Reason, therefore, is of great service in describing God's truth; in demonstrating revelation to those who would deny or corrupt it; in illustrating the "mysteries" of religion with examples drawn from history, nature, literature, and philosophy; "in drawing conclusions, and determining the truth of them; in comparing the text with the context, versions with the originals, the decision of ecclesiastical teachers with the scripture; and in distinguishing falsehood from truth, and what is legitimate from what is spurious."[50]

The role of reason in theological discourse cannot, therefore, be "primary and despotic" but rather should be "ministerial and instrumental": like Hagar, reason is a handmaid. Reason does not conclude what can be believed but rather explains and furthers the faith as an instrument employed by the faithful. Thus Paul speaks of religion as rational worship (cultus rationalis)—not originaliter (as if reason were the source and foundation of religion) but subjective et organice insofar as religion is practiced by rational subjects. Similarly Peter speaks of rational and spiritual sacrifice superseding the Levitical code: right religion is cultus rationalis because it is spiritual and internal, not carnal and external.[51] Even so, the rational has an internal, instrumental place in the faith of rational creatures.

The function of reason in theology is not a public and absolute determination of truth in controversy, a iudicium decisionis. Such ultimate authority belongs primarily to God speaking in his Word and secondarily to the pastors of his church. Rather, the proper function of reason is the discernment of truth and falsehood, a judgment of private discretion (iudicium privatae discretionis). This private discretion belongs to the rational subject as a knowing power (potentia cognoscens) that relies upon and operates according to external, objective norms concerning the truth of statements and the truth of connections or relationships between ideas and statements.[52] Human reason has no authority over the incomprehensible—such as the mystery of the Trinity or of the incarnation—but it makes declarations against the patently incompossible —such as transubstantiation and the Lutheran doctrine of ubiquity, which deny objective norms concerning concepts of substance, bodily existence and location.[53]

A further distinction can be made between the truth of statements (*veritas sententiarum*) corresponding with axiomatic rules and the truth of connections or relationships (*veritas connexionum*) corresponding with dianoetic or discursive judgment. The axioms or statements of the faith are provided by divine revelation in Scripture, argues Turretin, while the truth of connections or relationships between these axioms is apprehended by right reason (*recta ratio*). Reason, then, does not introduce into the text of Scripture a meaning that is not present there, but rather serves faith by drawing out legitimate conclusions from the text, by making explicit those truths which are presented implicitly.[54]

The ancillary and confirmatory use of reason follows quite naturally from what we have seen in the discussion of natural theology, particularly of the *theologia naturalis regenitorum*[55] and it is borne out subsequently in the system by the use of reason in the discussion of the divine attributes. Turretin views all of the essential attributes as rationally arguable, but he never introduces the rational argumentation principially: he always introduces his scriptural argumentation first and then, only by way of confirmation, does he use rational argumentation. A similar model is followed by Mastricht.[56] The system, therefore, *never* moves from reason to revelation or from natural to supernatural theology.

The Reformed orthodox recognize, however, that the use of philosophy must be carefully defined so that the potential compatibility of the disciplines does not become the basis for a principial use of human reason in theological matters. Turretin distinguishes between two basic errors concerning the use of reason: the Socinians err *in excessu*, the Lutherans *in defectu*--the former assume that nothing can be believed that is not founded upon reason,[57] while the latter refuse to permit rational judgment between contradictory statements in theology.[58] Reformed orthodoxy attempts to stand between these extremes by affording the proper place to rational judgment in theology. When Turretin attacks the Roman Catholic dogma of transubstantiation as erring, together with Lutheranism, *in defectu*, his uncited medieval models are quite evident.[59]

The instrumental use of reason and, specifically, of rational truths in theological argumentation leads to a distinction between pure articles (*articuli puri*) and mixed articles (*articuli mixti*) in theology. Since theology is a rational discourse and since the truths of theology and of philosophy do not oppose one another, it becomes possible to make statements that include the language and concepts of both disciplines: when theology inquires into the meaning of trinitarian relationships, for example, it asks, in the language of philosophy, whether the persons are really or only rationally distinct from the essence of God.[60] This mixture of language and concepts, in turn, raises the issue of rules for the use of philosophy in theological argument. Thus Alsted argues:

> Since theological questions are of two kinds, simple and mixed, of which the former consist of purely theological terms, the latter of a theological and a philosophical term, no one of sound mind could fail to see that philosophy can be applied to proof only in the latter category, in the former merely to assertion and explanation.[61]

This distinction of *articuli puri* from *articuli mixti* has immediate application in the Reformed orthodox discussion of the doctrine of God. Keckermann, for example, argues that the doctrine of the Trinity can be known only through the revealed Word of God. Philosophy can perhaps illustrate the doctrine of the Trinity by drawing parallels between the threefold unity of the Godhead and the functions of the human intellect or between the divine Trinity and our knowledge of the sun, its light and its heat, but such illustrations neither present nor prove the doctrine. The doctrine of the divine attributes, however, arises both from direct revelation in the Word and from the philosophical use of the *via negationis*, the *via eminentiae* and the *via causationis*—the methods of negation, eminence and causation—by the negation or denial of imperfections in rational creatures, by the exaltation of perfections in rational creatures, and by the delineation of traces of the divine handiwork in the created order.[62]

These general declarations concerning the instrumental or organic use of reason in *articuli mixti* are further qualified in the Reformed scholastic view of the proper construction of syllogistic arguments in which both faith and reason provide elements of the proof. In such syllogisms, reason cannot be the foundation and norm upon which the conclusion rests but only the instrument or means by which a truth latent in the foundation or norm of theology is elicited. In a syllogism, the foundation for all argument is the "middle term," the common ground shared by the major and minor propositions. In theology, "the middle term of the syllogism is not taken from reason, but from scripture."[63] Thus, against the Lutheran doctrine of ubiquity, the Reformed note that reason permits us to say that no genuine body is ubiquitous, while Scripture definitively provides the middle term, that Christ had a "true body." The syllogism is mixed, but the foundation of the logic is scriptural and reason has merely drawn the conclusion intended by Scripture. Even so, the conclusion of such an argument belongs to faith since the subject of the basic proposition is theological: indeed, a rational deduction from a theological proposition must represent a higher truth than a rational deduction from a purely philosophical proposition.[64] In other words, a mixed article can be argued toward a genuinely theological conclusion.[65]

Thus, even when philosophy contributes to a proof in the argumentation of a mixed article, the philosophical element of the argument is not fundamental or constitutive of the truth itself but only serves to elucidate the truth or the relationship between truths. Theology remains the higher truth, but it respects the truths of the rational order. Without noting the similarity between this perspective of Reformed orthodoxy and the revived scholasticism of the Salamanticenes, Keckermann cites the "calumnies" of Melchior Cano against "all evangelical theology." The Spaniard declares that Protestants ignore the rational connections of cause and effect, antecedent and consequent in their views of God and man: such accusations, retorts Keckermann, apply only to the Lutherans![66] At the close of the era of orthodoxy, Pictet could declare,

> In fact, reason and faith, though of a different nature, are not opposed to each other. Hence we maintain that we must not admit anything, even in religious matters, which is contrary to right reason. For although there is much darkness in the human mind, yet no one can deny that there remain some sparks of natural light, and that the mind has in it those principles of undoubted truth, which faith often makes use of for the confirmation of its own doctrines; but what we maintain is, that reason cannot and ought not to bring forth any mysteries, as it were, out of its own storehouse; for this is the prerogative of scripture only. Also, that reason is not to be heard when complaining of its incapacity to comprehend the mysteries of faith: for, being finite, it is no wonder that reason should not comprehend many things that relate to what is infinite; and to reject a mystery because it is incomprehensible to reason, is to offend against reason itself.[67]

The presupposition of this argumentation, despite the pronounced diastasis between divine wisdom in itself and all forms of human knowing including revealed theology,[68] is the essentially Thomistic presupposition that the truths of revelation, though above and beyond reason (supra et praeter rationem), are not unreasonable or contrary to reason (contra rationem). The mysteries of the faith, argues Turretin, are contrary only to corrupt reason—they are simply beyond the natural reach of right reason (ratio recta). No declaration of the faith, however, opposes a reason that is upright and illuminated (ratio recta et illuminata). The reason for this correspondence of revelation with the rational order is that light does not oppose light nor revealed truth natural truth.[69] The consent of reason to the articles of faith in no way implies the dependence of faith on reason, since the relation does not correspond with the relation of cause to effect or of logical foundation to conclusion: faith is prior to reason as a higher to a lower truth, in the context of the essential oneness and self-consistency of truth.[70] What is more, the denial of double truth leads irrevocably to the conclusion that the higher, not unreasonable, truth of faith and revelation illuminates the fallen mind and draws the wreckage of fallen reason toward perfection.[71]

This entire line of argument concerning the proper relation of philosophy to theology, particularly the detailed consideration of the role of reason in the construction of doctrinal conclusions from scriptural materials serves to complete and to illustrate the previous point made by the orthodox in their identification of theology as a science and a wisdom. If reason were not permitted its instrumental role in theology, the discipline could get no further than the exegesis and exposition of Scripture: there could be no systematization and drawing-out of ideas. In this case, theology might be viewed as *intelligentia*, a knowledge of principles—but only in a derivative sense, inasmuch as its principles are not self-evident, but revealed. Just as the initial distinction between archetypal and ectypal theology emphasized the derivative character of our theology, so does the further definition of theology as *scientia* and *sapientia* point toward the use of the principles known by ectypal theology from its archetypal source. The scholastic clarification of the use of reason only serves to underscore the fact that the revealed principles known to the subalternate science or derived wisdom called theology are to be used as a foundation for carefully presented doctrinal conclusions and as indicators of the ultimate divine purpose. The subsequent identification by the Protestant orthodox of Scripture as the *principium cognoscendi* of theology also follows quite naturally from this line of thought.

In summary, Reformed orthodox theology is certainly more open to the use of reason than the theology of either Luther or Calvin. Nevertheless, this openness not only had roots in the Reformation itself, but it also carefully retained the Reformers' sense of the independence of theology from philosophical or metaphysical speculation. The Protestant scholastic use of reason derives *not* from a desire to create a synthesis of theology and philosophy but rather from a clearly perceived and enunciated need to use the tools of reason in the construction of theological system. Not only is rational argument necessary to the elaboration of theological argument, it is also the tool by which conclusions can be drawn in the movement from the text of Scripture to theological formulation. If the Protestant scholastics set aside the antagonism to reason voiced by some of the Reformers, they did so only for the sake of elaborating systematically the theology of their predecessors, in the face of the highly sophisticated Roman Catholic polemic and in view of the need to modify system as they knew it and to draw the tradition of the church into the service of an institutionalized Protestantism.

8
Theology as a Discipline

The natural concomitant of the careful analysis of the meaning of the term *theology* and its relation to the forms of human knowledge of God is an increased awareness of theology proper as an academic discipline. Indeed, these are but two aspects of a single issue. The success of the Reformation led to the establishment and institutionalization of its reforms and of the theology on which those reforms were based. The very success of the theology of the Reformation must be regarded as one of the most important sources of its post–Reformation quest for clarity and self–definition. That definition, in turn, produced a clearer identification of the theological task in its university setting. From the very beginning of Luther's protest, the university and university–trained theologians were at the center of the movement. The process of establishment and institutionalization of the Reformation viewed in terms of the need to train new generations of Protestants in theology led to a reexamination of theology as an academic discipline—and that, in turn, to a clarification of the definitions and presuppositions of that discipline.

As Ong observes in his study of Ramus, the philosophers and theologians of the sixteenth and seventeenth centuries placed considerable stress on the question of method. The *De dialectica inventione libri tres* (1479) of Rudolf Agricola, together with the brief epitome of Agricola's work by Bartholomaus Latomus, were perhaps the most influential works on the logic of organization and argumentation in the first half of the sixteenth century. From the point of view of theology and

theological method, the importance of Agricola's text lay in its methodological use of topics—*topoi* or *loci*—in the organization of knowledge
rather than the typically Aristotelian use of categories of predication.[1]
This methodological model was brought to the service of Protestant
theology as early as 1521 in Melanchthon's *Loci communes*. These "commonplaces" or "universal topics," as elicited from Scripture, became the
model for Protestant dogmatics.

Melanchthon also recognized that topical organization demanded
consideration of a "proper and expeditious way" (*recta et compendaria
via*) of gathering and arranging a subject—in short, a *methodus*.
Melanchthon provides the following definition: "method is a disposition
(*habitus*), namely a science or art making a way or path according to a
definite pattern (*certa ratione*), that is, which invents and opens up a
path as it were through impassible and densely planted places (*loci*),
through the confusion of things (*rerum confusionem*)."[2]   The *loci*, in
short, demand a method.   This method, as we have seen, follows out the
historical order of Scripture while also recognizing the causal priority
of God the Creator and acknowledging the authority of the creeds.[3]

Among second-generation Reformed theologians, one in particular
stands out as carrying the Melanchthonian demand for *methodus theologiae*
toward systematic realization: Andreas Hyperius (1511-64), professor of
theology at Marburg from 1542 on.   His posthumous system, the *Methodi
theologiae, sive praecipuorum Christianae religionis locorum communium*
(1568), not only adopts the *locus* method of exposition but provides some
insight into the issues of order and organization faced by the early
Protestant systematizers.   First, comments Hyperius, the topics viewed as
important by church writers of various ages ought to be weighed and
considered; only the important and necessary articles are to be chosen as
loci.   Once a compend of these *loci* is made, each topic should be
examined in terms of the ages or times of the church: before the fall,
after the fall, prior to the Law, under the Law, under the gospel.[4]   The
scripturae series of Melanchthon are adapted by Hyperius to individual
loci.   All *loci* must be explained: first, in the light of Scripture,
second, in the light of the fathers.[5]

This *locus* method became the standard pattern of theological system
with the publication of the works of Hyperius, Musculus and Vermigli.
Alsted, at the beginning of the seventeenth century, views it as the sole
and proper method for the gathering of theological topics.   He views the
"major parts" or actual species of theology—natural, catechetical,
scholastic, and so on—as primary *loci* and the actual "topics, titles and
subtitles" within these major parts as the secondary and constituent *loci*

of each kind of theological system.[6]   These constituent *loci*, in turn,
are to be the proper subjects of theological declaration and disputation.[7]

Hyperius also notes that the collation of topics yields six major
loci: God, creatures and man, the church, the doctrine of Law and gospel,
signs or sacraments, and the consummation. He has no objection to the
placement of a general *locus* on holy Scripture first, prior to the
doctrine of God, inasmuch as Scripture is the source of all doctrine, but
his preference is to state this ground of theology and to proceed immediately to the first *locus*, the doctrine of God.[8] The doctrine of God--the
divine attributes and the persons of the Trinity--precedes all other
doctrines since they are concerned with the works of God (creation,
providence and administration).[9]   The remaining *loci* proceed in order
from creation, by way of the church and its doctrines, to the final
consummation.   This method, concludes Hyperius, is synthetic (*synthe-
tike*), which is to say, *constitutiva seu compositiva*, moving from general
first principles by way of individual instances or *differentia* of the
principles to the final goal.[10] Hyperius thus establishes the organizational model and the language used to describe its patterns and methods
that would come to characterize scholastic orthodoxy.

Beginning in the second half of the sixteenth century with Hyperius'
Methodus, there is increasing interest in theology as a discipline--and
in the relationship between the discipline of theology as taught in the
academic context and in the life and work of the church.   This language
of method carries over into such early orthodox systems as Trelcatius'
Scholastica et methodica locorum communium institutio and Alsted's
Methodus sacrosanctae theologiae.   In the former title in particular, a
"scholastic instruction" includes both the *loci* or topics and the proper
methodus or "way through" those topics.   Alsted's use of *methodus*
similarly emphasizes the way through or ordering of theology, in this
case, the division of "the whole of theology" into its "members," of the
genus into its species.   Thus Alsted moves through his *Praecognita* or
prolegomena to a separate *methodus* for natural, catechetical, scholastic,
"soteriological" or moral, homiletical and mystical theology.[11]

In addition to this essentially Melanchthonian adaptation of the
idea of method as a way through a body of knowledge, Protestant theology
in the late sixteenth and early seventeenth centuries also had access to
the more strictly logical and philosophical discussion of method typical
of the revived Aristotelianism of the age and developed in its most
compelling form by Jacopo Zabarella (1532--89).   In Zabarella's modified
Aristotelianism, a distinction is made between the *methodus* or "way" of

doctrine and the *ordo* or "order" of doctrine.   Method, for Zabarella, does not order or arrange knowledge so much as make things known. Indeed, method proceeds logically from the known to the unknown, whereas order arranges the elements of a body of knowlege.   The former must have deductive force whereas the latter represents only a clarification of what is already known.[12]

Nonetheless, despite this distinction between the logical rigor of method and the less rigorous patterning of order, Zabarella argued the coherence and coincidence of approach in two cognitive exercises: the *methodus* and the *ordo* of a discipline will follow either the compositive (*compositiva*) or resolvative (*resolutiva*) path.   We have already seen this language in the prolegomena of Zanchi and Hyperius—who had most probably learned the pattern from Renaissance discussions of the logic of Galen.[13]   Zabarella drew on this tradition and used its language to refine his description of method.   The compositive approach moves from cause to effect, from universal to particular, by way of logical demon-stration, and is to be used in theoretical disciplines.   The resolvative approach moves from effect to cause, is less rigorous, and belongs to the practical disciplines.   The compositive method, then, is a *priori* and, when applied syllogistically, locates the effect in the major term while the cause, located in the middle term, forces the conclusion.   The resolvative method is a *posteriori* and proceeds in the opposite manner with the effect as the middle term.[14]

This interest in method is also characteristic of the logic of Petrus Ramus and, by extension, of the theological systems influenced by his *Dialectica*.   Contrary to the contentions of several contemporary scholars, Ramist thought was not a wholesale rebellion against Aristotle, nor was it a radically new departure in logic, nor did it draw theology away from a synthetic and a *priori* model and direct it toward a covenan-tal, salvation-historical and a *posteriori* model of system.[15]   As Jacob Schegk, an Aristotelian contemporary of Ramus, was able to argue, some of Ramus' best ideas were taken directly from Aristotle without citation. Antonius Goveanus, another of Ramus' opponents in debate, could easily show that Ramus' so-called return to Plato and Socrates was hardly more than an elaboration of ideas already found in the handbooks on dialectic by Rudolf Agricola and Philip Melanchthon.[16]   The latter contention is true even of Ramus' famous method of bifurcation: this was one of the trademarks of Agricola's logic.[17]   In addition, whatever genuine objec-tions Ramus did make against the complexities of Aristotelian logic, particularly against the categories of predication, he raised no objec-tions against Aristotelian physics and metaphysics.

The impact of Ramism on the method of late sixteenth-century theology was twofold. We have already noted the impact of Ramus' definition of theology as practical upon the Ramist theological systems of the late sixteenth and early seventeenth centuries. Although any estimate of the importance of Ramus' definition must be tempered by the fact that theology had long been defined as either entirely or partly practical, it remains true that the definition of theology as the doctrine of living blessedly or living to God was appropriated together with the Ramist method of bifurcation and that Ramus tended to influence theology toward an emphasis on *praxis*.[18]   Second, the method of bifurcation was of considerable importance. Again, even if our estimate of Ramus' influence on logic is tempered by a recognition of the practice of bifurcation already resident in the popular Agricolan logic of the late fifteenth and early sixteenth centuries, we must recognize that the practice became of architectonic significance to theology only after it had been put forth by Ramus as the "method of methods."[19]

Finally, the importance of Ramus to the rise of scholastic Protestantism ought to be recognized as essentially methodological rather than theological or philosophical. Moltmann's attempt to associate Ramism with a salvation-historical and a *posteriori* rather than a synthetic, metaphysical or a *priori* approach to theology is simply contrary to fact. A covenant theologian like Olevianus, whose theology avoids metaphysical and a *priori* patterning, argued strongly for Aristotelianism and against Ramism.[20]   Perkins, whose approach is decidedly Ramist, uses the Ramist bifurcations as the organizational pattern of A *Golden Chaine*, one of the most decidedly synthetic, a *priori*, and even metaphysical documents in the history of Reformed theology. Keckermann, a truly a *posteriori* and analytical thinker, avoided Ramism.[21]   What Ramus provided was an impetus toward extreme clarity in the organization of argument, as witnessed by the method of Polanus' *Partitiones*, Alsted's *Methodus* and Ames' *Medulla*, at a time when Protestant theologians were engaged in the primary work of establishing the structure of orthodox dogmatics. In an era characterized by a search for method, for the way through a discipline, Ramism considerably facilitated the establishment of a basic, architecturally cohesive method and, as manifest by Mastricht's late-seventeenth-century system, succeeded in imprinting that clarity on Reformed theology decades after the demise of Ramism as a viable form of logic or dialectic.

A *methodus* or way through theology, as Mastricht argued at the end of the era of orthodoxy, must consider first the nature of God, second, the nature of theology itself, and third, the benefits of the method (i.e., whether it furthers knowledge). Regarding the first of these issues, Mastricht notes that God is not a confused or disorderly God but a God who is declared by Scripture to be decent and orderly (1 Cor. 14:33, 40). This God created rational creatures according to a principle of order and, indeed, in his Scriptures—though arranged perhaps arbitrarily—he manifests a certain logic in the inspiration of his chosen amanuenses. Second, the nature of theology, as noted before, derives from the collation and interpretation of doctrines which are subordinate to and homogeneously dispersed throughout the vast body of Scripture. Third, the method clearly draws together and comprehends the things to be taught, enables them to be retained easily in the memory, and supports its arguments elegantly and well.[22]   Mastricht repudiates both the excessively philosophical method—whether analytic or synthetic—and the nonphilosophical methods of the antitheological Anabaptists and enthusiasts.[23]

The Reformed language of theological *methodus*, then, reflected the main logical and philosophical concerns of the century that extended from the publication of Agricola's logic and the early Renaissance interest in Galen's logical procedures to the renewal of Aristotelianism by Zabarella and his contemporaries. The Reformed writers, following the Agricolan and Melanchthonian pattern, manifest a concern for the overarching logic of the way through the theological topics or *loci* but also, following out the Galenic pattern as found in Hyperius and Zanchi and later developed by Zabarella, demonstrate a profound interest in the actual patterns of argument. Ramus' influence was most powerfully felt at the architectonic level of system. The syllogistic approach, as given impetus by Zabarella's definitions of the compositive and resolvative methods, had more impact on polemical than on positive theology and, with the exception of Wendelin's utterly syllogistic *Systema* (1654), none of the major Reformed systems adopted the syllogism as the sole means of exposition. The definition of theology as both theoretical and practical served also to balance the use of compositive and resolvative approaches in argument— even when the architecture of system tended toward a synthetic or compositive order.

In its method theology accepts reason which, though in itself corrupt, can—illuminated by Word and Spirit—be of use to the theologian in his work. Similarly, theology can reject the excesses of scholasticism without rejecting method itself: artifice and tortuous logic is rejected but method is to be prudently adapted.[24]   Thus the Reformed reject a scholasticism which stands midway between revealed and natural theology and which treats revelation according to the method and arguments of nature, thus setting philosophical demonstration and the thought of Aristotle, Averroes and others equal to, if not above, the Scriptures. Theology must be purified of such error—yet scholastic theology in the sense of revealed theology *quatenus traditur modo scholis familiari* ("to the extent that it is taught in the manner of our schools"), and as Alsted defined it, is useful in polemic against Roman scholasticism, in debate with Gentiles and atheists, and in convincing rational souls of the truth of the revelation.[25] Thus the method of theology begins with Scripture and exegesis, propounds positive doctrine, then settles all controversies and disputed points, and, finally, demonstrates the practical application of doctrine and its usefulness to the individual.[26]

The historical trajectory of theological method from the *loci communes* of Melanchthon, Hyperius and the other early writers of Protestant system to the massive sets of *loci* propounded by the orthodox Protestant theologians of the seventeenth century is marked by a major change in approach: the architectonic *methodus* is maintained, the basic *loci* are set forth, but the approach is, beginning with the generation of Junius, Polanus and Bucanus, a fully scholastic one. This change echoes the change in theological style forged and finalized in the thirteenth century by Aquinas and those who followed his lead. The early Protestant *loci* are primarily exegetical and expository; the later *loci*, beginning with Polanus and his contemporaries, assume the exegesis and then follow a ratiocinative pattern of definition, division and argumentation. Theology has moved definitively from the collation of meditations on *sacra pagina* to the enunciation of a *scientia* of *sacra doctrina*.   In other words, we finally have a genuine systematic or dogmatic theology in Protestant form. Calvin's *Institutes* were by intention an introductory instruction in the reading or study of Scripture; Polanus' *Syntagna* and subsequent Protestant systems are formal scholastic summations of doctrine that weld scriptural and traditional materials into cohesive patterns of argument and, in turn, into an exhaustive and self-contained body of Christian doctrine.

The systematic effect of the *locus* method was to bar the way to the use of overarching motifs in the system and to emphasize the integrity of the topics. The *loci*, as drawn from Scripture and tradition, cannot be easily pressed into the service of a genuinely deductive model. Even when arranged in an *a priori* or synthetic pattern, the *loci* tend to stand independent of one another and to resist any monistic systematizing tendency. Schweizer recognized and noted this methodological issue as creating a problem for the crystallization of the Reformed system—and saw it as pressing the system back toward its confessional foundation for its basic organizational pattern.[27]   It was, after all, Schweizer's intention, as distinct from the intention of the Protestant orthodox, to create a monistic system of doctrine.

The transition from the early *loci communes* to the fully scholastic *loci communes* implies a change in method (in the modern sense of the term) and in underlying intention. As noted before, the literary genre of scholastic system is significantly different from the literary genre of the early Reformation system. The intention of system is now the orderly and logical exposition of all *loci*—and although *methodus* or way through these *loci* draws on earlier paradigms, their exposition is substantially different. This transition, of course, was gradual: the discursive forms of Calvin and Bullinger yield to the *quaestio* of Ursinus and the vast topical treatises of Zanchi. These in turn are modified by an increasingly propositional and logical structure in the era of Ramism. Finally, this is recast into the form of a theoretical-practical, didactic-polemic system that treats each doctrine from all four of these perspectives. We are dealing, in short, with the development of a Protestant scholastic method.

8.1 Scholastic Method

Divinity, Leigh argues, is to be taught and handled methodically, orderly, and logically, according to three basic methods:

> 1.   Succinct and brief, when Divine Truth is summarily explained and confirmed by Reasons, and this Divinity is called Catechetical, Systematical.
> 2.   Prolix and large, when Theological matters are handled particularly and fully by Definitions, Divisions, Arguments, and Answers; and this is called handling of Common-Places, Scholastical and Controversial Divinity. . . .
> 3.   Textual, *which consists in a diligent* Meditation of the Scriptures, the right understanding of which is the end of other instructions.[28]

The student of divinity must be, thus, "of a godly and heavenly mind" and of a "sober . . . studious and diligent . . . honest and good mind." "We must not be too curious in searching out the profound Mysteries of religion, as about the Trinity, predestination; we must be wise to sobriety, and not busy ourselves about perplexed and unprofitable questions, being content to know such things which are revealed to us for our Salvation."[29]

Leigh's statement of theological method serves to clear away two misconceptions concerning the intentions of seventeenth-century theologians. In the first place, the terms *system* and *systematic*, when applied to theology did not, in the seventeenth century, imply anything like the monistic syntheses designated "system" by theologians and philosophers of the nineteenth and twentieth centuries. Instead, *system* here simply indicates the basic body of doctrine in its proper organization, as found in a catechism: a seventeenth-century *systema*, like a *compendium* or a *medulla*, was likely to be a basic survey as distinct from an elaborate system. Second, and more important, the term "scholastic"—contrary to the attempt of several modern authors to define it in terms of an allegiance to Aristotelian philosophy and a use of predestination as a central dogma—indicates neither a philosophical nor a doctrinal position but rather the topical approach of the *loci communes* or "commonplaces" and the method of exposition by definition, division, argument, and answer utilized in the Protestant scholastic theological prolegomena. Burmann, similarly, defined scholastic theology as "nothing other than definitions, arguments, objections, responses and distinctions systematically joined together."[30]

It is also worth noting that, as evidenced by Leigh's description of methods, the term "scholastic" could be used by Protestants in the mid-seventeenth century in a positive, nonpolemical sense which reflected the etymological meaning of the word—a method or teaching "of the schools"—rather than reflecting Protestant distaste for the metaphysical speculations of the medievals. Following the groundbreaking and encyclopaedic efforts of Johann Heinrich Alsted, who entitled his own system *Theologia scholastica didactica, exhibens locos communes theologicos methodo scholastica*, Protestants were in fact able to distinguish between their own scholasticism or school-method and the earlier scholasticism of the medieval doctors. The distinction was made primarily on the assumption of a stronger scriptural and exegetical basis and of a less speculative and more truly ancillary use of philosophy in the Protestant scholastic systems.[31]

Venema's comments on scholastic theology, with their underlying sense of the continuity of Aristotelianism, provide a significant retrospective characterization of the history of theology and its methods:

> The scholastic writers . . . may be regarded as belonging to three different periods. The first begins with Peter Lombard, —a Parisian bishop, who lived in the twelfth century, who regarded the Patristic divines and their writings as a source of theology, and who, after the example of John Damascenus, reduced theology into a new form,—and extends to the days of Thomas Aquinas. The second period begins with Thomas Aquinas, or with Albert the Great, bishop of Ratisbon, in the thirteenth century, and extends to the time of Durandus of St. Portian in the fourteenth. It is characterized by the addition of Aristotle to the sources already mentioned. The third period dates from the days of Durandus to the seventeenth century. Its leading feature, like the preceding, is the rank and authority assigned to Aristotle as a source of theology.

> We cannot but speak with commendation of the order and
> ingenuity of the scholastic method, and of the moderation with
> which it treated all who differed in opinion. . . . And yet
> there were many things in it to be condemned;—especially idle
> and unprofitable speculations, an excessive eagerness for
> disputation, false principles, an ignorance of Scripture and,
> in particular, of the Oriental languages, and a diffuse and
> unpolished style. The systems of Lombard and Aquinas, however,
> deserve to be read.
>   About the time of the Reformation, theology, as a system,
> was presented in a new light, and received many emendations,
> agreeable to reason and the Word of God.[32]

Not only do we encounter no pejorative connotation attached to the term
"scholastic," we also sense the continuity of scholasticism with its
Aristotelian philosophical underpinnings, from the thirteenth through the
seventeenth centuries. The Reformation effects a positive development in
doctrine within the history of scholastic method. Venema seems to
exclude his theology from the category of "scholasticism" only because of
the demise of Aristotelian philosophy.

For the most part, however, the Reformed orthodox are anxious to
distinguish between their own scholasticism and that of the medieval
doctors. Burmann, for example, speaks of the scholastic era coming to a
close with Gabriel Biel's theology at the end of the fifteenth century.[33]
He also provides a careful synopsis of the seventeenth-century Protestant
view of medieval scholasticism:

> To be praised in this *theologica scholastica* are 1. the simple
> and concise kind of language, 2. the accurate and dialectical
> method, 3. the use or support of philosophy and of subjects
> concerned with the natural order (*disciplinarum naturalium*).
> To be rejected, however, are . . . 1. the obnoxious doctrine of
> Papal tyranny, false in many points, 2. the multitude of philo-
> sophical issues, 3. the curiosity over vain questions, 4.
> confusion of issues arising out of an ignorance of ancillary
> languages, 5. obscurity and barbarism.[34]

The scholastic theology of the Reformed both sets aside the errors of
papal teaching—its vain questionings and its failure to use the biblical
languages—and avoids the excessive use of philosophy.[35]

Maccovius presents a similar description of the *modus proponendi
theologiae* together with a somewhat more extensive discussion of the uses
and the appropriate audiences of the two basic approaches, the "succinct"
and the "prolix":

> The model of propounding theology is twofold: one, less-
> cultivated (*rudior*) and less fully-developed (*minusque exquisi-
> tus*), the other most refined and fully-developed (*magis
> exquisitus*).
>   The less fully-developed mode is that which we use with
> reference to children, for the purpose of the knowledge of
> salvation (*ratione salutaris cognitionis*) and of instruction,
> provided that we propound in them, at very least, the principle
> heads (*praecipua capita*) [of doctrine].

The fully developed mode is that which we use with reference to those who, by reason of further progress in heavenly doctrine (*in coelesti doctrina*), the Holy Spirit commonly calls adults, developed ones.[36]

The less fully developed mode of propounding theology, which is, in effect, catechesis, can be reduced to four basic divisions which together comprise the *Elementa fidei Christiana*: the Decalogue, which teaches (1) of the one, eternal, most good (*optimus*), righteous (*iustus*), omnipotent, awesome (*metuendus*), and honored (*colendus*) God; (2) of the Law, its integrity and its use; (3) of the fall and original sin; and (4) of the temporal and eternal misery of sinners; second, the articles of the Apostles' Creed; third, the Lord's Prayer; and fourth, the sacraments. These articles, comments Maccovius, are the foundation of faith and salvation (*fundamentum fidei & salutis*). (We shall return to this foundational or fundamental status of catechesis below in the discussion of fundamental articles in theology and of the impact of the identification of such articles on scholastic system.[37])

The more fully developed mode or method of propounding theology rests upon, indeed, contains the results of the credal or catechetical model but, comments Maccovius, citing Paraeus,

is more devoted to particulars, indeed, with those further topics (*annexa*) and difficulties which commonly arise after the basic issues have been expounded or explained: this method is customarily followed in the schools (*in Academiis*) and observed by all in teaching the Commonplaces of Theology (*Locorum Communium Theologicum*). From this method of propounding theology arises directly the distinction made by theologians concerning the articles of faith (*articulorum fidei*)—that some are universally held (*Catholici*) while others are theological (*Theologici*). . . . Theological science (*scientia theologica*) is sacred doctrine, not entirely directed toward salvation, but which is necessary to theologians for the sake of their profession and for the sake of carrying on and protecting the universal faith (*fidem Catholicam*) in the Church and in the schools.[38]

This statement of method reflects the discussion of fundamental *loci*: the Protestant scholastics recognize that their detailed exposition goes beyond fundamentals—but they also recognize a purpose in their method that relates to the fundamental articles, that of explanation and defense.

The language used by Paraeus also reflects a crucial element of the orthodox theological enterprise: the desire for and emphasis upon catholicity. Protestantism had, from its very beginnings, assumed its identity as the true church—as witnessed by Luther's stance as a *doctor ecclesiae*, a doctor of the church, bound to reform its doctrine, and by Calvin's profoundly catholic claims in his response to Sadoleto.[39] The

Protestant orthodox systems, searching out and defending "right teach-ing," had as their goal the formulation of a universally valid statement of Christian truth. The relationship noted by Paraeus between the funda-mental or catechetical articles to be learned by all and the theological articles of the academic theological science to be learned by the teachers of the church is a relationship grounded in this quest for catholicity. The teacher of doctrine is not given to unbridled specu-lation but rather engages in the most abstruse investigations for the sake of the universal faith of the church, its maintenance and its defense.

Alsted provides a somewhat more complex model but, like Leigh, Maccovius and Paraeus, clearly desires to make distinctions between that which must be taught to all and that which must be elaborated and debated by theologians. Thus, he argues for kinds of theological instruction differing according to the relative place of the human subject in the church: catechetical theology, theology of the confirmand, ecclesiastical theology, and, finally, scholastic theology. Catechetical theology is a preliminary exercise for the novice, while theology for the confirmand is a "more perfect" exercise for those further along the path of religious knowledge. Ecclesiastical theology is a more practical theology that relates to the things of faith, the holy life and the general or popular instruction of the church, while scholastic theology is a more theoreti-cal discipline that differs from ecclesiastical theology not in substance but in mode: it is an essentially disputative form of theology that exists for the defense of the faith.[40]

The Reformed orthodox can thus distinguish two basic types of this *theologia exquisita* or fully developed system of doctrine:

> Theology in this sense is divided by some into didactic and polemical (*didacticam & polemicam*) or, better, into positive and scholastic (*positivam & scholasticam*) theology: of which the former meditates on the analysis and interpretation of Holy Scripture: the latter on the synthesis of commonplaces (*syn-thesi locorum communium*) so that those *loci* that are spread here and there throughout Holy Scripture can be presented in a definite order.[41]

This basic distinction between didactic, "positive" or ecclesiastical theology and the polemical, scholastic or elenctical defense of the didactic theology relates both to the locus-method and to the identifica-tion of theology as a science that draws conclusions from its *principia*. The basic didactic theology of the *compendia* and *medullae* sets forth the basic *loci* and the fundamental or principial statements of doctrine. The scholastic theology of the more elaborate systems develops the principial statements toward their correct conclusions over against the erroneous conclusions of adversaries in debate. As witnessed early on by the practice of Melchior Cano, this is the basic direction of the *locus* method. In the hands of the Protestant writers, however, Scripture is the *principium*, not merely a source of *principia*—and the method as a whole is drawn into the context of the Reformation's *sola Scriptura*. This distinction of methods appears, for example, in Turretin's *Institutio theologiae elencticae*, which is entirely polemical or scholastic; in Pictet's *Theologia christiana*, which is thoroughly didactic and positive, an intentional completion of the system present as polemic in Turretin's *Institutio*; and in Mastricht's *Theoretico-practica theologia*, which attempts to combine the didactic and polemical elements into one system. The same methodological distinctions are apparent among the Lutherans in Baier's *Compendium theologiae positivae* and Quenstedt's *Theologia didactico-polemica*.[42]

None of the preceding statements concerning scholastic, didactic and polemical approaches contained concepts determinative of the overarching structure of theological system and the order and arrangement of its topics. The issues of structure, order and arrangement of system were addressed by the Protestant scholastics according to three primary concerns: the historical implications of the biblical narrative, the methodological implications of the determination of genus, and the purely structural implications of the logic of topical division. None of these concerns, as they were worked out in system, can be viewed as opposing the scholastic, didactic and polemical models. Rather, the structural and organizational concerns operated at the level of system while the strictly methodological models determined the pattern of argument in individual *loci*. In addition, each of the three basic structural concerns were not worked out in all systems: some attended primarily to the historical issue, others primarily to the implications of genus, and still others primarily to the logical division of *loci*.

The historical implications of the biblical narrative for the structure of theological system were recognized by Melanchthon, who spoke of the arrangement of doctrines in *historica series*. This insight into the systematic use of biblical history was adopted not only by Lutheran theologians but also by the Reformed. We see its impact in a limited way on the systems of Calvin and Musculus in the historical movement of doctrine from creation, sin and fall through the Old Testament to redemption in Christ. In Bullinger's theology—the *Compendium christianae religionis* (1556)—the "historical succession" of doctrine takes on a specifically covenantal character.[43] This covenant model, as developed by Ursinus and Olevianus and then transmitted by the Herborn school of

Martinius, Crocius and Alsted, to Cocceius and Burmann, and finally to Witsius and Heidegger, became a central issue in the structuring of system.

Although the debate over covenant theology in the seventeenth cen-tury cannot be discussed at length here, we note that the issue of the debate was not covenant doctrine as such or some basic opposition between "covenant theology" and "scholastic theology." Rather, the issue was Cocceius' notion of a gradual abrogation of the covenant of works and a gradual institution of the covenant of grace and the impact of this notion on the doctrinal value of the Old Testament. What is important to the question of systematic structure and the use of a covenantal *historica series* in Reformed system is the post-Cocceian integration of an expanded covenant exposition into theological system. Whereas Cocceius had produced a pure covenant exposition in his *Summa doctrina de foedere Dei*, Burmann argued the use of "the natural order, the economy of the covenants of God and the administration of human salvation" as a model for the structure of orthodox Reformed system,[44] without the loss of the *loci* of Scripture and God as the beginning point of system. This model, according to which system is not reduced to covenant but covenant occupies a crucial, central and historical position between creation and consummation, was adopted by high orthodox theologians like Heidegger and Mastricht.

The methodological implications of genus seem to have been given their earliest statement by Keckermann, who identified the genus of theology as *prudentia* and classified it as a purely practical disci-pline.[45] This definition led him to the conclusion that the method of theology must be entirely analytical: it cannot proceed speculatively from first cause to final goal but rather analytically—from the final goal assumed by the *praxis*, to underlying conditions that determine the patterns and shape of that *praxis*, to the intermediate or proximate activities and end of the *praxis*.[46] Although Keckermann viewed the analytical systems of Melanchthon and Ursinus as his primary models, his concentration on the purely practical and purely analytical led him away from their historical perspective. The loss of the historical model together with the Arminian and Socinian emphases on theology as practical made Keckermann's views on system virtually untenable in the seventeenth century.

The clarity with which Keckermann perceived the relation of theory, practice and *genus* to method is not evidenced in the words of his contemporary, Trelcatius:

> There is a two-fold method of teaching, the one from Princi-ples, the other to Principles, the one *a Priori* proceeding from

the Cause to the Effect, and from the first and highest to the lowest and last: the other *a Posteriori*, proceeding from the Effect to the Cause, or from the last and lowest to the highest and first: the use of the former is mainly in contemplative sciences, of the latter, in the practical (or active).[47]

Theology, as a science, holds first place in both the contemplative and the active areas of teaching, since it shows both knowledge and right action. Because of this balance, argues Trelcatius, some thinkers have taught theology in an *a priori* manner, others in an *a posteriori* manner. Calvin, Melanchthon, and Ursinus followed the *a posteriori* or analytic pattern while Hyperius, Musculus, Hemmingius, and Zanchi followed the *a priori* (or synthetic) method. Trelcatius comments that his system will draw on both methods, not only "composing the disposition" of the subject analytically, but also "unfolding the invention" synthetically, in order that the full system of theology might be manifest. He will, thus, begin from "first principles" and proceed synthetically, but treat each *locus* analytically.[48]

The assumption on the part of most of the orthodox that theology, as a *sapientia*, combined the theoretical and the practical into a single unified discipline,[49] tended to preclude the use of two distinct and separate methods but did lead, for the reasons indicated by Trelcatius, to a compromise between synthetic and analytic methods. Systems like those of Maccovius, Gomarus, Walaeus, Burmann, Leigh, Turretin, and Heidegger manifest a movement of the system of doctrine as a whole from first principles to ultimate ends—from Scripture and God to the last things—that in a broad and nontechnical sense can be called synthetic and deductive. This very order, however, rests on a teleological perspective as well, so that the goal-oriented *praxis* also has an impact on overarching structure. Beyond this, there is no attempt within individual *loci* to argue in a deductive fashion, but rather the pattern of argument, if not strictly analytic, is generally inductive, moving from Scripture with the use of reason toward doctrinal conclusions.

The final concern contributing to the order of the Reformed scholastic systems is the logic of topical division. This appears most clearly in the Ramist systems and treatises of the early orthodox period: Polanus' *Partitiones* and *Syntagma*, Ames' *Medulla*, Perkins' *A Golden Chaine*, and (to a lesser extent) Maccovius' *Loci communes*. The model is maintained, moreover, in the high orthodox period by Mastricht. Polanus, Ames and Mastricht all assume a basic division of theology into doctrines concerning faith and doctrines concerning obedience. Ramism itself, emphasizing the logical division of a topic into component parts, usually by a progression of bifurcations, did not determine the topics or the divisions chosen, but only the method. Indeed, it was Ramus' contention that a single method, the method of logical bifurcation, served all disciplines.[50] The initial categories of faith and obedience stand upon two precedents—the theological division of Ursinus' catechetical lectures into doctrinal section dealing with redemption and the discussion of Christian life and worship dealing with "thankfulness"; and the standard division of philosophy into metaphysics and ethics. This latter precedent is noted in one of the theses of Ames' *Medulla* added by its posthumous editors.[51] The doctrines of faith, in all of these systems, first consider God, then God's works; next the eternal works of God, then the temporal works; the temporal works of creation, then those of redemption.

The covenant motif and the historical structuring of system between creation and consummation were not pre-empted by any of the other organizational or methodological models: the causally-ordered, theoretical-practical model could easily adapt to a covenant theology. This is clearly the case in Heidegger's *Corpus theologiae* and, somewhat less historically, in Turretin's *Institutio theologiae elencticae*. Similarly the covenant schema could be easily fit into the doctrines of faith in a system like Mastricht's *Theoretico-practica theologia*, where the Ramist model also functioned. What is also clear is that the scholastic method of argument by division and definition with reference to objections from adversaries could be integrated with any or all of these larger structural patterns—as is notably the case in the works of Leigh, Maccovius, Turretin, and Mastricht. Granting, then, the implications of the Reformed orthodox interest in method and their precise conception of the meaning of scholasticism in and for their own theological systems, we must set aside as utterly inapplicable to seventeenth-century Reformed orthodoxy the definition of scholasticism as a predestinarian and metaphysical direction in Protestant thought.

The scholastic method itself exemplifies the problem of continuity and discontinuity between Protestant orthodoxy and both the Reformation and the Middle Ages. The strict logical argument and the use of division and definition, together with the raising of objections and the stating of responses, represents a point of contact and continuity between the Protestant and medieval scholastics. Nevertheless, this continuity is found only in the internal structuring of *loci*; the overarching *methodus*, consisting of the identification and organization of loci, stands over against the medieval scholastic model. The *locus* method was, of course, a development of late medieval logic, but it was also the method chosen early on in the Reformation by Melanchthon as suitable to the construction of a primarily biblical system. The Protestant scholastic method, therefore, stands as part of a development in logic and, particularly, as part of a new interest in method, in the proper patterning of a topic, that began at the close of the fifteenth century and was characteristic of the Reformation.

8.2 The Study of Theology

The distinction between catechetical and scholastic methods in theology made by the Protestant orthodox points directly to their assumption that the study of theology at a fairly detailed level, such as was present in the catechisms and confessions of the Reformed churches and even in the many sermonic expositions of the confessional documents, was not an academic matter. The study of theology was an enterprise intended for all Christians—and the detailed academic study of the subject was to be the practical foundation for sound study on all levels. Mastricht notes that this theological "knowledge of the truth according to piety" (*cognitio veritatis secundum pietatem*) is studied by teachers (*doctores*) and ministers whose office is to understand, teach, interpret, propound, and apply theology. It is also to be studied by magistrates so that they might be acquainted with the Law, as demanded in Scripture (Deut. 17:18–20; Josh. 1:8; Ps. 19:7–14), that they might rightly order the lives of their subjects, guard the church from its adversaries, and govern wisely recognizing the Lordship of Christ. Even so, all Christians should study it so that they might have access to Christian truth, and might advance more and more in it, support their lives by it, and make it known to others.[52]

The work of academic theology, then, as defined by Alsted, is the activity that occupies the student in his study of divine things for the sake of teaching them to others. This study can be further defined in terms of scope, limits and means. Thus, in terms of its scope, theological study seeks the glory of God and the eternal blessedness of the believer and, in a less ultimate sense, the perfection of his intellect, will and speech. In other words, it is an effort of the whole person that relates directly to the conforming of that person to the image of God.[53] In a proximate sense this scope also relates to the ecclesiastical and scholastic forms of theology: the study of theology aims,

broadly, at the general teaching of the church but also, more specifically, at the higher, more systematic discussion of teaching in the
schools.[54]

Alsted further argues that the study of theology must observe
certain limits or bounds. A properly defined period of study, designed
carefully in the light of the demands of the discipline and its scope and
set apart from other times of study, is necessary to proper mastery of
the subject.[55] Similarly, the means of study must relate directly to the
demands, scope and limits of that study. These means, granting the scope
of theology, must be both divine and human, consisting in spiritual
illumination and regulation and in the natural development and care of
mind and body alike.[56] This entire discussion of theological study as
spiritual formation draws directly on the concept of theology as a mental
or spiritual *habitus* or disposition: the disposition is a God-given gift
which, like the grace of redemption after regeneration, demands human
cooperation. In a crucial sense, therefore, the counsels of the orthodox
concerning spiritual discipline in the study of theology grow directly
out of the basic scholastic definition of theology as *sapientia* or
habitus sapientiae.

The orthodox can also cite a series of motives or reasons (*motivae;
rationes*) for the study of this particular discipline. The first of
these, for Mastricht, is the excellence (*praestantia*) of theology, in
view of: (1) its divine origin; (2) the majesty of its arguments insofar
as they rest upon the wisdom of God in Christ and the rule for right
living or the word of life; (3) the use and goal of its arguments in
blessed immortality and the glory of God; (4) its utter certainty resting
on the infallibility of the received testimony concerning Christ (John
3:33); and (5) its purity and sanctity which conduce to the purity and
sanctity of those who possess it. To the excellence of theology can be
added sweetness and delight to the soul arising from study, the necessity
of learning the faith in order to be justified by faith and to receive
the gift of eternal life, and the dangers that may befall those ignorant
of Christian truth—alienation from God and from the covenant of grace,
subjection to the divine wrath and temporal punishments and, finally,
eternal damnation! A further inducement to study arises from the example
of the faithful students of God's Word: the prophets, apostles, and,
indeed, the angels in heaven.[57]

Leigh similarly describes the excellence of theology first, according to its subject matter and, second, according to a list of its
attributes: "it is called 'the wisdom of God,' Prov. 2:10; 3:13; I Cor.
2:6, 7 and 'that wisdom which is from above,' James 3:17." For Leigh,

this divine wisdom of theology has seven characteristics that recommend its careful study: (1) its primary and secondary ends or goals, "the glory of God, that is, the celebration or setting forth of God's infinite excellency" and the blessedness of man; (2) its certainty and truth, transcending all earthly wisdom including the highest philosophy; (3) its cause, the revelation of God; (4) its holiness and the fact that ignorance of it leads to sin and uncleanness; (5) its "delight and sweetness" above all other knowledge; (6) "the excellency of the students of it"—that is, of the saints of the Old and New Testaments, the angels and saints in heaven, and the true church on earth; (7) its enemies: "the Devil and Hereticks oppose it; the Papists would not have the Bible translated, nor the Divine service performed in the mother tongue."[58]

Granting the excellence of the discipline and the other rather pointed incentives to study, considerable attention must be given to preparation for study. Burmann therefore presents his students and readers with a special prolegomenon or preparation (*propaideia et apparatus*) for study. The *propaideia* divides into two parts: first, the attitude of the student and, second, the nontheological intellectual preparation of the student. Primary among the character traits of the theological student is personal piety or spirituality (*pietas*). This piety, essentially a fear of God (*timor Dei*), is, as Scripture teaches, the primary ground (*principium*) of both true knowledge and wisdom (*scientia et sapientia*). The student must apply himself ardently to attaining the goals of man's salvation and God's glory (i.e., the *finis proximus* and *finis ultimus* of theology), and must do so with profound love of the gospel and of Christ, without any desire for personal gain.[59] To this piety must be added the qualities of teachableness (*docilitas*) and zeal (*sedulitas*) or diligence (*diligentia*), manifest, at least in part, through the absence of perverse love, hate, anger, pride, and despair.[60]

Alsted summarizes these issues in a discussion of "the natural gifts required in Theology." Nature provides man with an unformed or inchoate capacity; exercise brings about the highest fulfillment of that capacity. Thus nature embraces all the good qualities and powers of the soul and of the body—the innate readiness of the soul to apprehend and adjudicate, the faithfulness of memory in recording and retaining information, and the quality of eagerness in study; the dignity and sound constitution of body, clarity of voice, and usefulness of members for study. All these gifts are to be maintained and augmented through prayer, temperance and reverent exercise, in the service of theological study.[61] Thus, the gifts of nature are to be developed and sanctified by consistent spiritual discipline—by the cultivation, with the aid of the Spirit, of a holy life of piety before God, justice toward one's neighbors and temperance within one's self. The rule of this life ought to be, therefore, the teaching of Scripture concerning the conduct of a holy life and the examples, in Scripture, of holy living as taught in the lives of the prophets and the apostles. Voetius could similarly and quite summarily argue that theological education could not afford to ignore personal piety—but neither was piety the sole requirement for ministry. Accordingly, Voetius argued even more strongly than Alsted for a coordinated course of study and spiritual discipline, beginning early on in the education of "adolescents." In the course of theology itself, there must be a consistent *praxis pietatis*, a continuing "care and inspection" conducted by private or personal and ecclesiastical mentors, and an ongoing careful examination of students in doctrine, language skills and philosophical tools.[62]

The student of theology, asserts Burmann, must also attend to the sound cultivation of the mind (*bona mentis cultura*) through the study of the liberal arts and sciences and through these studies learn the proper exercise of memory and judgment. Memory is most useful in the study of languages—Latin, Greek and Hebrew—which are also necessary to the study of theology. Burmann notes specifically that barbarity and vulgarity of style are to be overcome. For the study of Latin style he recommends both Cicero and Calvin, commending the latter in particular. As aids to study he notes several contemporary texts on grammar and etymology. The study of Greek points first toward the New Testament, but here too further exercise is necessary for the mastery of style. Burmann recommends the *Ethics*, *Politics and Rhetoric* of Aristotle, the *Enchiridion* of Epictetus, and the writings of Aristophanes and Demosthenes; from the fathers he selects Chrysostom, Nazianzien and Basil the Great; finally, he points the student to ancient and modern lexica—Hesychius and Suidas among the ancients and the "most praised" thesaurus of Stephanus among the moderns.[63]

Burmann also provides advice to the student seeking aids to the study of Hebrew: the grammars of de Dieu, Buxtorf and Alting together with the treatises of à Diest and de Raadt on the proper method of pointing in composition ought to be consulted. Students who have the ability ought also to acquaint themselves with cognate languages: Chaldee, Syriac, Arabic, and the Ethiopic. Burmann recommends further the lexica of Buxtorf, Schindler and Cocceius and, for Arabic, that of Golius. In addition, talmudic study is also useful and the works of Scaliger,

Drusius, Buxtorf, Hottinger, Goodwin, Cappel, and Martinius are to be recommended, among others.[64]

Nor can the student of theology afford to ignore related disciplines such as history, geography, philosophy, mathematics, and medicine. Burmann is particularly concerned to recommend the study of ancient history, the history of the Old and New Testaments, the Reformation, and the Low Countries. In the category of philosophy Burmann notes that Aristotle's works, particularly the *Logic*, have been used with profit by many ages but are, nonetheless, somewhat less than satisfactory. A better philosophy has been provided by René Descartes. This Cartesian philosophy has received expert treatment in la Forge's treatise on the mind, Clauberg's *Logic* and Wittich's *Consensus veritatis revelatae cum Philosophia*.[65] Although Burmann's taste in philosophy was disputed by most of his Reformed contemporaries and Cartesians never gained more than a small following in their circles, the demise of Aristotelianism was recognized by most of the Reformed writers by the end of the seventeenth century. The question they faced was simply the identification of a congenial philosophical perspective; that question, of course, found no easy answer.[66]

Owen, with considerably more caution than Burmann, recommends study of "the arts and sciences," specifically, of grammar, oriental languages, logic, and rhetoric. To these he adds a knowledge of history and the skill, arising from these studies, of the clear communication, without ambiguities, of rational concepts.[67] Owen warns pointedly against the "superficial and disordered knowledge" arising from scholastic vagaries and directs his readers toward the right use of "rational studies" for the construction of theological system (*systema theologica*) and the meditation, day and night, upon the topics of evangelical doctrine (*capita doctrina evangelica*). Even as the ancient fathers, the scholastics and more recent theologians have observed, Owen continues, the student of theology should, above all else, read, know, and retain in his memory both "the things of the faith and the religious life" (*res fidei et negotium religionis*). Although the use of rational concepts is necessary and some philosophy needs to be studied, there is also a great danger in philosophy. As Tertullian, warned, philosophy has spawned heresy—and we know all too well the subtle disputations wrongly brought into theology via Arabian philosophy! True evangelical theology abrogates all such useless philosophy.[68]

In these lists of authors and works to be studied there is an elaboration of the pedagogical heritage of Reformers like Melanchthon and

Hyperius. The former had counseled the reading of the fathers, especially Augustine,[69] and the latter had added to this emphasis on the patristic materials a set of cautious comments on the usefulness of the systematic efforts of John of Damascus and Peter Lombard.[70] Calvin, of course, had cited the fathers with great regularity, while Musculus used the works of the late medieval doctors. In addition, a vast prospectus of materials for the study of theology, replete with citations of Aristotle, Lombard, the fathers and late medieval doctors—all cited under the topics of a theological system—was prepared fairly early in the development of Protestant theology by the Zurich encyclopedist, Conrad Gessner.[71] The influence of his work is difficult to assess, but the tendency Gessner documents is clear: as the Reformation succeeded in establishing churches and the era of confessional orthodoxy dawned, Protestants were drawn more and more to root their theology in tradition.

The study of theology itself demands as detailed a paradigm as does discussion of the preparatory and ancillary disciplines. First and foremost in the study of theology is the reading and study of Scripture upon which all systems and *loci communes* are founded. Burmann here recommends the use of annotated Bibles—Tremellius for the Old Testament, Beza for the New. The movement here from Scripture to system can be made only by close attention to the natural order of things, to the dispensation or economy of the divine covenants and the administration of human salvation. This historical and dogmatic method, argues Burmann, is observed by God himself in Scripture. This is also the method observed in Burmann's own *Synopsis theologiae*. Perhaps out of modesty, Burmann also recommends the use of Cloppenburg's *Syntagma et disputationes*, Owen's *Theologoumena* and Cocceius' two systems (the *Summa doctrina de foedere Dei* and the *Summa theologiae*).[72] Following these recommendations Burmann also provides bibliographical suggestions for the study of the doctrine of Scripture, of each of the dispensations of the covenant, the doctrines of Christ and his work, the sacraments of the New Testament, and the church.[73]

Following his basic counsel Burmann subjoins a series of discussions of theological systems, controversial literature, and older theology (both patristic and medieval).[74] The list is lengthy and cannot be duplicated here. We do note, however, that in the area of systematic or dogmatic theology, Burmann recommends Ames' *Medulla*, Maresius' *Systema*, the *Synopsis purioris theologiae* of the University of Leiden, the disputations of Gomarus and Alting, Ursinus' *Catechetical Lectures*, and Calvin's *Institutes*. Among the Reformers, he comments, after Calvin the most important are Vermigli and Musculus. He also counsels the reading of Luther's sermons, the writings of Chemnitz and Calixtus, the *Loci communes* of Gerhard, and the theologies of Episcopius and Petavius.[75]

Nor does the study of theology stop with dogmatics and polemics: careful attention must be paid to the practical side of theology, to the use and delivery of the doctrines learned. Theology must issue forth in preaching or holy discourse (*oratio sacra*) and other aspects of ministry. To this end, rhetoric and logic must be studied—Quintillian, Cicero, Demosthenes and, adds Burmann, among the more recent writers Ramus and his follower Talon. On the specific task of Christian oration there is Hyperius's *De formandis concionibus* and Keckermann's *Rhetorica ecclesiastica*. For his own readers, Burmann notes briefly the parts of a sermon: introduction, division of the text, grammatical and historical explanation, formal exposition, application and, finally, refutation of error. A distinction needs to be made between incomplex and complex themes, and between dogmatic, moral and historical or exemplary topics.[76] To this discussion Burmann subjoins a lengthy set of suggestions concerning commentators and authors of topical studies of biblical, moral and doctrinal themes.[77] A similar list of commentators appears in Leigh's discussion of the interpretation of Scripture,[78] while Alsted concludes his *Praecognita* with a lengthy discussion of the analysis, study, and interpretation of Scripture.[79]

It is worth noting, by way of conclusion, that the scholastic method of the Reformed orthodox, like their distinctions between theology in itself and theology in the subject, between theological knowledge and the inward intellectual disposition necessary to apprehend that knowledge, and between the faith that is believed and the faith by which we believe, is not only characterized by precision of definition but also by a profound and careful balancing of the objective and the subjective elements as well as the ontological and epistemological aspects of the subject. In the next chapter, the same interest in balance will be evident in the discussion of the *principia* or grounds of theology. Here, we can briefly describe how the balanced approach to study advocated by Burmann was applied to the writing of theological system itself.

The scholastic method was designed specifically for the sake of dealing with both large, architectonic issues and minute, subtopical divisions. The Protestant scholastics manifest, then, a concern for the overarching structure of system and the flow of topics as well as for the careful and orderly division of topics into their component parts. Similarly, balance is also achieved between the exegetical, dogmatic, polemical, and practical emphases of theology. We have already seen how the orthodox balanced the speculative or theoretical with the practical concerns of theology.[80]   The Protestant orthodox also balanced the exegetical, the positive dogmatic and the polemical elements of system—sometimes, as in the case of Scharpius' or Trelcatius' early orthodox systems,[81] developing a polemical rebuttal of opposing views following each positive doctrinal statement, or sometimes, as in the case of Ursinus' catechetical lectures or Riissen's Summa,[82] following the form of the medieval quaestio by posing objections to a thesis and then responding to each of the objections.   Turretin's exclusively disputative or polemical system was consciously paralleled and complemented by his nephew, Benedict Pictet, who wrote an entirely positive system as an expression of Genevan high orthodoxy.[83]

Voetius rather nicely summarizes these concerns in his description of three levels of theological study.   At the first level, students ought to study, as their primary academic effort, according to a threefold pattern of textual or biblical, systematic or dogmatic, and problematic or polemical theology.   The first aspect of study, textual or biblical involves the examination of all the principal books of Scripture and the close exegetical scrutiny of "select loci and themes" in Scripture, specifically the seats (<u>sedes</u>) of doctrines like justification (Rom. 3-4), predestination (Rom. 5), the fall (Gen. 3 and Rom. 5), or the office of ministry (1 Tim. 3).   The second aspect, systematic or dogmatic, ought not simply to sketch out the contents of a synopsis or epitome of doctrine but ought to deal with the whole range of theological topics in depth.   The third, polemical and problematic, should examine all contemporary controversies—such as those between "the orthodox" and the Socinians, Remonstrants, Papists, Anabaptists, Enthusiasts, Libertines, Jews, Epicureans and Atheists.   At the next level, Voetius recommends study of ancillary disciplines like jurisprudence and an emphasis on practical theology; at the third level he recommends history and controversial or disputative theology.[84]

The balance of exegetical with dogmatic, polemical and practical elements of system calls for some further explanation in view of the accusation of "proof-texting" typically leveled against the Protestant orthodox by modern writers.   It is quite true that the orthodox systems cite dicta probantia for every dogmatic statement—and it is also the case that some of these biblical dicta, because of modern critical scholarship, can no longer be used as the seventeenth-century orthodox used them.   Nonetheless, it was never the intention or the practice of the Protestant scholastics to wrench biblical texts out of their context in Scripture or to dispense with careful biblical exegesis in the original languages.   Many seventeenth-century dogmatic theologians began

their teaching careers as professors of Old or New Testament and virtually all of them, whether or not they taught exegesis, were well versed
in the biblical languages. Thus Polanus taught Old Testament exegesis
and was known as a commentator and translator before he was recognized as
a systematic or dogmatic theologian: his system was his final work. In
the era of high orthodoxy, a similar pattern is seen in the work of
Johannes Marckius, whose *Compendium theologiae* was written at the end of
a lifetime of exegetical work.

As we have already noted, the *locus* method itself was designed to
move from biblical and exegetical study of key passages to the collection
of observations and dogmatic conclusions into a body of Christian
doctrine. The *dicta probantia* appear in the orthodox systems, not as
texts torn from their biblical context, but as references to either the
exegetical labors of the theologian himself or, as was more broadly and
generally the case, to a received tradition of biblical interpretation.
It was the intention of the authors of the orthodox systems and compendia
to direct their readers, by the citation of texts, to the exegetical
labors that undergirded theological system. The twentieth century may
not accept all of the results of seventeenth-century exegesis, but it
ought to recognize that the older theology, whatever its faults, did not
fail to appropriate the best exegetical conclusions of its day.

What is more, the detailed form recommended by Burmann for the
preparation and delivery of sermons was followed throughout the orthodox
era. We need to overcome the stereotype of the orthodox sermon,
generated in large part by pietist polemics of the late seventeenth
century--that of a dry, dogmatic declaration inattentive to the spiritual
needs of a congregation. There are dry, dogmatic sermons preached in
every age of the church, some of them by pietists, but the presence of a
few ought not to color our judgment of the many. The basic definition of
theology as both theoretical and practical led to a balance of doctrine
and "use" or application in seventeenth-century sermons.   Indeed,
scholastic attention to form almost invariably assured the presence of
exegetical study, exposition, doctrinal statement, and application in the
Reformed orthodox sermon.[85]

At the close of the era of orthodoxy, this concern for finely
balanced method can be seen in Mastricht's *Theoretico-practica theologia*.
The title itself manifests the concern of the Reformed orthodox that
their theology be valued in and of itself as a statement of doctrine concerning God and his will, but that it also be valued for its results in
the ministry of the church and the education of believers. Mastricht's
system maintains this methodological balance in its use of the old Ramist

division of theology into doctrines of faith and doctrines of obedience.
Both the beliefs of the church and the lives of Christians belong to the
concerns of the theologian, the one being incomplete without the other.
Each *locus* of Mastricht's system, moreover, begins with exegesis, using
the biblical languages, of a text crucial to the doctrinal point at
issue. The exegesis is then followed by dogmatic exposition, a polemical
rebuttal of adversaries and errorists, and then by a practical application. Mastricht adheres consistently to this model throughout his entire
system.[86]

Throughout the orthodox discussions of the study of theology one
senses a singleness of purpose, a sense of the unity of all of the various disciplines and subdisciplines. This unity, moreover, is both objective and subjective. Objectively, all of the subdisciplines tend toward
the single goal of the exposition of Scripture and the collation and
organization of the materials of this revealed "deposit" of faith into a
clearly stated and eminently defensible body of doctrine. Subjectively,
all of the subdisciplines conduce to the training of heart and mind for
the life of faith guided by prayer and meditation and framed by the
personal appropriation of the doctrines both of faith and of obedience.
All of the parts of theological study draw together to attain these two
ends, the objective and subjective, the doctrinal and the spiritual.[87]

Finally, the method here described is balanced in its approach to
traditional and contemporary concerns. The Reformed orthodox adopted a
scholastic method fully conscious of the need to draw that method into
the service of seventeenth-century theology.[88] In addition the works on
philosophy and theology recommended by Burmann and used by the Reformed
orthodox generally in the formulation of their theology bear witness to a
"catholicizing" tendency--a tendency toward theological breadth for the
sake of appropriating for Protestantism great truths of the entire Christian tradition and the best theological insights of the present. Thus,
the fathers, the great medieval scholastics, and the Reformers are to be
read, but the student of theology must also read contemporary works. If,
however, the list of contemporary works is dominated by the Reformed, it
also includes--without indication of polemic--the names of eminent
Lutheran and even Roman Catholic thinkers like Gerhard and Petavius. The
Protestant scholastic was designed to present theology in close dialogue
with the world of thought around it.

9
Fundamental Articles and Basic Principles of Theology

Discussion of the issue of fundamental articles (*articuli fundamentales*) or fundamental theological *loci* (*loci theologici fundamentales*) did not appear as a major issue in the prolegomena of Reformed dogmatics until the era of high orthodoxy in the latter half of the seventeenth century. When it finally appeared, it had both a positive doctrinal source and, more importantly, a polemical point of origin. The positive source was the catechetical basis of many of the Reformed systems of the late sixteenth and seventeenth centuries. We see, for example, a sense of the fundamental or necessary character of the doctrines taught in catechesis in the prolegomenon affixed by Ursinus to his lectures on the *Heidelberg Catechism*. This prolegomenon is of some importance in the development of formal prolegomena to Reformed systems, but in terms of its own intention, it stands primarily as a testimony to the importance of catechesis. This discussion of fundamentals continues to appear, as a result of the catechetical foundation, in later systems built on the model of catechesis—as, for example, Watson's *A Body of Divinity* and Witsius' *Exercitiones sacrae in Symbolum*.

Similarly, when Maccovius discusses theological method, he notes the principal heads of doctrine treated in catechesis (the Decalogue, the Apostles' Creed, the Lord's Prayer, and the sacraments), notes the subtopics of each, and then refers to the whole series as those topics comprising the *fundamentum fidei & salutis*. In other words, there is a series of doctrines the knowledge of which is necessary to salvation. Notably, Maccovius includes the unity and trinity of God, the goodness, justice, and omnipotence of God, the Law, original sin, the two natures and the mediatorial work of Christ, justification, the basic creedal articles, prayer, and Baptism and the Lord's Supper. There is no mention of either predestination or election among these *fundamenta*.[1]

The polemical sources were the views expressed on doctrinal fundamentals by Roman Catholic, Socinian, and Lutheran opponents of the Reformed orthodox. The Roman Catholics—in the canons and the catechism of the Council of Trent and in subsequent polemics by Bellarmine, Cano, Canisius and others—had argued the power of the Roman Church to define the fundamental truths of Christianity. The problem was not only the question of doctrinal norms but also the particular fundamentals defined by Rome over against the Protestant position—such as the doctrines of merit, temporal satisfaction through penance, the sacrifice of the mass, and purgatory. The Socinians raised virtually the opposite issue. Insofar as they defined theology as purely practical and of essentially moral significance, the Socinians could effectively deny the existence of theoretically necessary fundamental doctrines. Socinian polemic, therefore, called into question the theological enterprise of the Protestant orthodox.[2]

Without diminishing the impact of any of these issues on Reformed theology, the ongoing debate with Lutheranism was, certainly, the decisive reason for the development of a major dogmatic discussion of fundamentals in the Reformed system. After the *Book of Concord* (1580) had provided German Lutheranism with a unified confessional statement quite unparalleled in Reformed circles, Lutheran dogmatics rapidly developed into a profoundly confessional theology in which the confessions of the church were viewed as *norma normata*, standardized norms, against which the body of doctrine was to be judged and within which the bounds of right doctrine could be stated with authority. This sense of a set of scripturally defined and standardized confessional norms was translated into a concept of fundamental articles of faith by Nicolaus Hunnius (1585–1643). When Georg Calixt (1586–1656) attempted to use the idea of a limited set of fundamental or constituent articles of faith as a basis for union with the Reformed and, ultimately, the Roman Catholics, his Lutheran brethren successfully argued against his proposals by virtually refusing to acknowledge that any articles of doctrine had less than fundamental status.[3]

In addition to these issues, there was the problem of Cartesian rationalism. In striking a balance between the Socinian denial and the Lutheran proliferation of fundamentals, the Reformed were also forced to deal with the Cartesian notion of certain fundamental principles—

universal doubt, the identification of truth as clear and distinct perception, and the *cogito, ergo sum* of Decartes' system—which, to the orthodox mind, were antithetical to faith. In the polemic with the Cartesians, the Reformed orthodox demonstrate that neither their *articuli fundamentales* nor the *principia theologiae* function as a *priori* principles upon which a whole system of theology can be built deductively.[4]

Finally, the question of fundamental articles, together with the related issue of the grounds or *principia* of theological argument, provide a point of entry into the logic and architecture of Protestant scholastic system. In these two discussions, the Protestant orthodox come closest to discussing the underlying questions of content and structure that must ultimately define the phenomenon of Protestant scholasticism. In other words, it is in consideration of these issues of fundamentals and *principia* that we become capable of addressing the historical questions concerning central dogmas and doctrinal principle put to the Protestant scholastics by nineteenth- and twentieth-century historical scholarship. We have tentatively addressed these questions already in relation to the basic definitions of theology, but here we can see, in terms of specific doctrines and enunciated *principia*, what the Protestant scholastics themselves viewed as the underlying rationale for theological system.

9.1 Necessary Doctrines: Basic Criteria

In their discussion of fundamentals, the Reformed orthodox recognize that there are several distinct kinds of necessity that can be predicated of Christian doctrines and practices and that the identification of valid "fundamental articles" rests upon the prior clarification of the problem of which doctrines and practices are to be defined as necessary and in which way. Witsius begins his discussion of fundamentals, therefore, with a series of distinctions concerning necessary doctrine:

> First we observe that doctrines may be said to be necessary either to Salvation, or to Religion, or to the Church. Thus, a doctrine, without knowledge and faith of which, God does not save adults, is necessary to Salvation; that, without the practice and profession of which no one can be considered conscientious in religious observance, is necessary to Religion; and that, without which none is admitted to the communion of the visible church, is necessary to the Church. There may be articles without which persons ought not to be admitted to the fellowship of the Church, that should not, for that reason, be regarded as absolutely necessary to Religion, or to Salvation.[5]

Similarly, some articles may be necessary to the right practice of religion, but we cannot therefore conclude the damnation of those who refuse to accept such articles.[6] The category of *articuli fundamentales*, therefore, may be restricted to those articles necessary for salvation, namely, those articles necessary to the identification of a person as "Christian" in the most rudimentary sense and which constitute the elements of the faith according to which Christians are justified in the sight of God.

A second distinction relates to the question of theological learning or ability to state explicitly and in detail the meaning of those articles necessary to salvation:

> It is in different measures of clarity, completeness and efficacy that divine revelation, the means of grace, and the communications of the Spirit are enjoyed; and a corresponding diversity takes place in the degrees of knowledge attained by the saints.   In some, it is clear, distinct, steady, and accompanied by a very firm and decided assent; in others, it is more confused, more implicit, subject to occasional wavering, and attended with an assent that is yielded with difficulty. The command of God, indeed, lays an indispensable obligation upon all men, to make every possible effort to attain a most clear, distinct and assured knowledge of divine truth.   It cannot, however, be questioned that the Deity, in his unbounded goodness, receives many into blessedness, whose knowledge even of the principal articles is very indistinct, and such as they are hardly capable of expressing in their own words.   The smallest measure of the requisite knowledge appears to be this, that when an article of faith is explained, the mind so far at least apprehends it, as to recognize and embrace it as true.[7]

There is already the recognition that the Cartesian standard of truth—clear and distinct perception—although certainly desirable in any attempt at exposition of doctrine, is inapplicable to theological knowing at the most fundamental level.   Not only is it impossible for every person to attain the same level of clarity and distinctness of perception, it is also not of the nature of theological truth that it require uniformity and perfection of knowledge either to be perceived as true or to be efficacious.   Precisely to this point, Turretin notes three distinct species of certainty:

> Certainty can be defined as threefold: 1. mathematical; 2. moral; 3. theological.   1. Mathematical or metaphysical certainty is that which is suitable to the first principles of nature both as known in themselves (*per se notis*) and in terms of the conclusions demonstrated on the basis of these principles.   2. Moral certainty, which is perceived with regard to things incapable of being demonstrated . . . but concerning which a prudent person is unable to have doubt.   3. Theological certainty, which is held concerning things that can neither be demonstrated, nor known by nature or through themselves, nor accepted as probabilities on the ground of evidence (*indiciis*) or moral arguments, but that are truly divine and theological things, for example, divine revelation, which therefore support

a certainty not merely moral or conjectural but a truly divine faith.[8]

Since God is neither a natural principle nor a thing that can be known immediately through itself, but rather is known through his self-revelation, theology has its own species of certainty, related to the way of knowing that is specific to theology: faith.

Related to the issue of clarity and fullness of knowledge expressed in the second distinction, is the issue of requirements placed upon faith by historical conditions. Witsius notes a third distinction:

> Times must also be distinguished. It admits of no doubt, that under the bright dispensation of the Gospel, a more extensive and more explicit knowledge is necessary to salvation, than was required under the Old Testament economy; for it is reasonable that both knowledge, and the necessity of knowledge, should increase in proportion to the measure of revelation afforded.[9]

By way of example, a person living under the Old Testament, or even during the life and ministry of Jesus, could be ignorant of doctrine concerning the suffering, death and resurrection of Christ and still be "a true believer and in a state of grace"--but such ignorance is no longer compatible with the conditions of salvation. For confirmation, Witsius looks to Thomas Aquinas: "The articles of faith have increased with the lapse of time, not indeed with respect to the faith itself, but with respect to explicit and express profession."[10]

Whereas the second distinction may be regarded as relaxing possible strictures concerning fullness of definition, this third distinction tends to increase strictures, if not concerning the fullness of the individual knowledge of definitions and details of doctrine, then at least concerning the number of doctrines required for salvation. Taken together, these two distinctions represent the position of Reformed orthodoxy: a definite body of belief with virtually no scholastic definition was required of the laity by the orthodox teachers. Indeed, we have already seen this view expressed in the distinction between the "succinct and brief" catechetical method and the "prolix and large" scholastic method in theology.[11] This perspective is also apparent in the proliferation of catechisms and catechetical lectures in the late sixteenth and seventeenth centuries.

The Reformed scholastics make it clear, therefore, that the designation of certain articles, like the Trinity or the two natures of Christ, as fundamental and necessary for salvation does not constitute a demand that laity become masters of arcane distinctions and difficult concepts --only a confessional level of belief is required. No Christian is required to believe all of the results of scholastic division of a topic and disputation on minutiae. Thus Maccovius distinguishes between those *articuli fidei* that are *catholica* or universal and those that are *theologica* or theological. The catholic or universal are those necessary for faith and salvation—that is, the articles taught in catechesis. The theological articles are those known to and taught by theologians in the course of their work: they are necessary to the work but not to faith. A theologian must know, for example, that the ark was made of cypress or cedar boards and was so many cubits long, for theology explains such things—but this is not necessary to faith. Scripture itself, adds Maccovius, teaches things that are not theological and do not pertain to salvation. A similar point concerning the contents of theological system is made by Voetius.[12]

More precise definition of the category of fundamental articles and its limits occurred in the context of polemical debate with the Socinians, Arminians, Roman Catholics, and Lutherans. The Socinian and Arminian view of *articuli fundamentales*, argues Turretin, errs through defect (*in defectu*) by reducing the category of fundamentals to the point of losing primary doctrines of the faith. The Socinians, on the basis of their definition of theology as entirely practical, set aside the doctrines of the Holy Spirit, the Trinity, the person of Christ, and Christ's satisfaction for sin—claiming that these doctrines were theoretical conclusions reached in schools rather than constituent elements of the Christian religion. The Arminians do not demolish central doctrines but instead, Turretin argues, they reduce the fundamental articles to "faith in the divine promises, obedience to the divine precepts, and the payment of reverence to Scripture."[13]   Turretin here refers not to Arminius himself but to the Arminian or Remonstrant theology of the late seventeenth century, the irenic theology of Curcellaeus and Limborch.

By way of contrast, the "Papists" and Lutherans err on the side of excess (*in excessu*). The Roman Catholics press forward shamelessly as fundamental doctrines worthless "hay and stubble" (*foenum suum et stipulas*)—like the doctrines of the mass and purgatory—while the Lutherans, in reaction to the calls for latitude in fundamentals on the part of syncretists among them, rigidly define as fundamentals both refutations of error and indifferent articles (*adiaphora*). The "orthodox"—Reformed, of course—hold to a middle position between the errors of excess and defect, by neither restricting nor extending the category of fundamentals beyond its proper bounds. Faith, since it includes knowledge as one of its elements, "requires and necessarily includes explicit truths or articles of knowledge and of full assent, and not only of the first principles but of generally essential or eminent articles."[14]

In order to maintain this middle position, Turretin proposes a paradigm for the definition of the *fundamentum* upon which the Christian religion rests. The *fundamentum* can be considered either as simple and personal (*incomplexe et personaliter*) or as complex and natural (*complexe et naturaliter*). The latter division can be defined either loosely (*late*) or strictly (*stricte*). Simply and personally, the term *fundamentum* indicates Christ, the foundation of salvation, the unshakable rock upon which the church is founded.[15] This assumption of a christological underpinning of the whole of doctrine is both the necessary result of the Reformed view of the *theologia unionis* as the mediate principle of all human theology and its corollary, the identification of the *obiectum theologiae* as God revealed in Christ, and the proper prologue to the Reformed scholastic conception of Scripture as the Word of God. Heppe rightly recognized the importance of this distinction between a *fundamentum Scripturae* and the individual doctrines of it, and the conviction that the latter are essentially present in the former, although his truncated presentation of the prolegomena prevented him from manifesting its full significance.[16] In addition, Heppe's treatment also fails to show the precise relation of this conception of Christ as *fundamentum* either to the issue of *articuli fundamentales* or, via this issue, to the structure of the prolegomena or of the system as a whole—at least in part because he severs the topic from the prolegomena.[17]

Ursinus argues "that Christ is taught in the whole Scripture, and that he alone is to be sought there." This, continues Ursinus, is the express teaching of the apostle Paul:

> that the foundation (*fundamentum*) of the doctrine of the church is Christ alone (I Cor. 3:11) and that this foundation (*fundamentum*) is common to the Prophets and the Apostles (Eph. 2:10). The doctrine concerning Christ, therefore, is the sum and scope (*summa et scopus*) of Scripture, and the foundation (*fundamentum*) laid by the Prophets and Apostles, such that those who do not rely upon it are not stones of the temple of God, which is to say, members of the Church.[18]

The point is echoed in the mid-seventeenth century by Leigh who refers to Scripture as "the Revelation of Christ" and distinguishes between Scripture as the "doctrinal foundation" of theology and Christ as "the foundation of foundations" on which Scripture and salvation itself ultimately must rest.[19] Thus, Christ is

> the principal subject of the whole Bible, being the end of the Law and the substance of the Gospel. . . . In this Mystery of Christ, God is revealed in the highest and most glorious way, II Cor. 4:6. There is more wisdome, holiness, power, justice discovered in the Mystery of the Gospel than was known before to men and angels . . .: Christ is the summe of all divine revealed truths.[20]

The connection between Christ as *fundamentum Scripturae* and *obiectum theologiae* (God revealed in Christ) now becomes clear. Christ is the *fundamentum* upon which all fundamental articles rest since he is the preeminent focus of the divine revelation, the sole focus according to which we are able to recognize God as the proper object of theology and on the basis of which theology in all its diverse topics is unified. This view is essentially christocentric in its implications—and it clearly shows that the Protestant orthodox of the sixteenth and seventeenth centuries are not the purveyors of a rationalistic approach to theological system.[21] As important as this model was for Reformed system, it is all the more necessary to distinguish it from the neo-orthodox christocentrism of the twentieth century. The Reformed orthodox make no attempt to use Jesus Christ as the sole index to all points of doctrine. Instead they recognize Christ as the center of God's revelation and as the focus of saving doctrine insofar as the covenant is grounded in Christ and salvation is in him alone. The orthodox point is made clearly by Witsius:

> The doctrine respecting the Lord Jesus, his person and offices, is denominated by Paul a foundation. "Other foundation can no man lay than that is laid, which is Jesus Christ" (I Cor. 3:11). The meaning is, that no man can teach another fundamental doctrine, separate from the doctrine concerning Christ.[22]

In other words, the fundamentals, like the system itself, cluster around and point to Christ while directly supporting faith in Christ, who is the foundation in the simple and personal sense of the term.

In the complex sense, the *fundamentum* refers to the truths that must be believed by all; in short, to the foundation of faith (*fundamentum fidei*). "Complex" here refers to the series of discrete truths belonging to the foundation of faith, in contrast to the simple or uncompounded principial truth that is Christ. This latter sense of *fundamentum*, moreover, is understood either loosely (*late*) or strictly (*stricte*). Loosely, the *fundamentum fidei* or *articuli fundamentales* refers to the "primary rudiments of Christian Religion" taught to catechumens: to the Decalogue, the Apostles' Creed, the Lord's Prayer, the sacraments, and the power of the keys. These texts and topics contain all the doctrines necessary to salvation. Strictly speaking, however, the fundamental articles are precisely those teachings necessary to salvation, the underlying beliefs which cannot be ignored or denied.[23] Thus a distinction can be made, even in the catechetical articles, between truths necessary to salvation and the amplification and elaboration of those truths. For example, it is necessary to know that Christ suffered and died, but a person can be ignorant of the circumstances of his death—namely, that

his suffering took place "under Pontius Pilate" and that he died by
crucifixion between two thieves—and still receive the blessing of salvation.[24]

Scripture, Turretin continues, points to this view of fundamentals.
The apostle Paul (1 Cor. 3:11-13) distinguishes between the true *fundamentum* and those foundations incapable of bringing edification:

> For other foundation can no man lay than that is laid, which is
> Jesus Christ. Now if any man build upon this foundation gold,
> silver, precious stones, wood, hay, stubble . . . the fire
> shall try every man's work of what sort it is.[25]

Turretin reflects both the view of Christ as *fundamentum Scripturae* and
as "foundation of foundations" and the polemic against the "hay and
stubble" presented as fundamentals by the Roman Catholics. Similarly,
Turretin continues, Paul writes that the mature Christian ought to attend
to his calling in Christ and walk according to the divinely given *regula*
(cf. Phil. 3:15-16). Weakness in faith can be permitted (Rom. 14:1) but
teaching that perverts the gospel is anathema (Gal. 1:8). Of course,
nothing can be fundamental that is not given plainly by Scripture since
it is the perfect and sufficient revelation of all things necessary to
salvation.[26]   This basic position excludes the aberrations of the
"Papists and Enthusiasts" who decree fundamentals *extra scripturam*, but
it does not solve the problem of the identification of which scriptural
doctrines are fundamental.

Within these scriptural bounds, further distinctions can be made
with respect to doctrines. The Law itself distinguishes between
necessary moral precepts and ceremonial observation, between what is
absolutely necessary and what is hypothetical and mutable. Thus, some
doctrines are necessary, in a simple or absolute sense, to the essence of
faith (*simpliciter ad ipsum esse fidei*) while others are supportive of
the life of faith and contribute to its *bene esse*. Some doctrines
pertain to the inception of faith (*ad generationem fidei*), others to its
perfection; some are absolutely necessary in and of themselves to all
people, whether immature or mature in faith, others are incidentally or
accidentally important to those mature in faith whose task in life is
preaching or instruction.[27]   Only those doctrines absolutely necessary to
faith and capable of being known by all—even "the simple and illiterate"
—either directly by reading or by an obvious logical consequence of the
text can be defined as fundamentals in the strictest sense.[28]

There is an obvious tension in this argument: fundamental articles
are absolutely necessary to the essence of faith and are given plainly in
Scripture which is the sufficient rule of faith—yet some of the fundamentals are given in such a way that they do not appear on the surface of

the text but must be deduced from it. It would be an error, argues
Witsius, to assume

> that nothing is to be deemed fundamental, which is exhibited in
> any passage in a manner calculated to exercise the industry
> even of the learned. It has pleased God to reveal the same
> truth in the Scriptures "at sundry times and in divers manners"
> (Heb. 1:1). . . . The knowledge of a fundamental article
> consists not in understanding this or the other passage of the
> Bible; but in an acquaintance with the truth, which in one
> passage, perhaps, is more obscurely traced, but is exhibited in
> other places in a clear, nay, in the clearest possible light.
> In fine, we do not concur with the Remonstrants, in requiring
> so high a degree of clearness, as to consider those articles
> alone fundamental, which are acknowledged and maintained
> amongst all Christians as of the most unquestionable authority,
> and which neither are, nor can be controverted. According to
> this rule, hardly anything will remain to distinguish the
> Christian Religion, from the Pagan morality, and the Mahometan
> theology. There is much truth in the remark of Clement of
> Alexandria, "No Scripture, I apprehend, is so favourably
> treated, as to be contradicted by no one."[29]

In the right practice of religion, which consists in obeying the
commandments and hoping in the promises of God, a necessary element is
that special knowledge denominated as faith. Against the Socinians,
Remonstrants and other "Pelagians," the Reformed maintain that the right
observance of religion and true knowledge of its content presupposes
faith in God as the one who works redemption in Christ.[30] This presupposition of faith makes the use of the philosophical principle of "universal doubt" impossible for Christians. Such a principle would place
Christianity on a level with Islam. Similarly, the criterion of *clara &
distincta perceptio* fails to recognize that many of the mysteries of
faith are given by divine revelation and lie forever beyond human understanding—although both in faith and in morals believers ought to seek
clarity and distinctness of statement.[31]

Writing some sixty years after Turretin and Witsius, Johann
Friedrich Stapfer could look back over a tradition of argumentation on
the issue of fundamental articles and draw together a set of concise
definitions. Fundamental articles are "such Truths as are recognized
absolutely necessary to the right knowledge and worship of God and as a
consequence to the attainment of Salvation."[32] This definition, comments
Stapfer, serves as the best criterion for identifying fundamental
articles—indeed, it completes yet another circle of thought in the
prolegomena by returning us doctrinally to the primary definition of
religion as the right way of knowing and worshiping God, *recta ratio Deum
cognoscendi et colendi*. The connection between true theology and right
religion can now be identified at the level of churchly teaching: fundamental articles are "those Truths the profession of which is required for

the encouragement of the church's communion as a society or association [of the faithful in worship]."[33]   Nonfundamental articles are teachings that "do not pertain to the essence and constitution of religion."[34]

Thus, following both the polemic against Rome over the simplicity of truth and the polemic against Cartesians over the principle of doubt and the criteria of truth, the Reformed feel justified in attempting to set forth a series of simple and, in recognition of the mystery of revelation and the hiddenness of divine things (*theologia archetypa*), relatively clear and distinct articles fundamental to the faith.   The polemic has rejected the false criteria of intellectual sophistication and philosophical doubt—but criteria are necessary.   These criteria themselves will reflect the basic stance of Protestantism: neither the general consent of Christians, nor the letter of Scripture, nor the needs of religious practice, nor the ancient articles of the church which deal neither with worship nor with doctrine, nor the determinations of the present church— but only those things necessary to salvation or stated as necessary by Scripture.[35]

9.2 Fundamental Articles and Errors

In view of these biblical distinctions, some conclusions can be drawn concerning various kinds of foundations or fundamentals in theology.   First, there is the underlying foundation, identical with the *obiectum fidei*, the object of faith or, in a formal sense, with the *obiectum theologiae*, the object of theology.[36]   The *obiectum fidei*, viewed in a general or equivalent (*aedequatum*) sense is the *Verbum Dei*, the written Word of God; viewed in a special and proper sense (*speciale et proprium*), it is the doctrine concerning Christ (*doctrina Christi*) together with the principal truths and promises of God (*capitibus et promissionibus Dei*).   In other words, we distinguish between the written Word in its entirety and its saving contents—just as in the doctrine of Scripture a distinction is made between the text of Scripture *quoad verba*, according to its words, and *quoad res*, according to the things or materials represented by the words.[37]   Generally and in terms of the equivalence between the ordained means of revelation and its substance, Scripture is the *fundamentum* and *obiectum fidei*, but it is foundational in such a way that it directs us to Christ and to the promises of God as the special and proper foundation and object of faith.   Fundamental articles of faith, therefore, are drawn directly from Scripture and teach of salvation in Christ.

As Voetius points out, these fundamental articles and corresponding errors can be understood from several points of view. It is one thing to discern an article or error at an objective level, a truth or error as such (*in se*), quite another to faith and error subjectively as they arise out of the disposition (*habitus*) or condition (*status*) of believing or disbelieving, and yet another to grasp the patterns, manner, and degrees of judgment or tolerance, moderation, reception or reconciliation possible in cases of belief and error.[38]   In the first category, some distinction must be made between issues objectively necessary to the being of the church and those necessary to the well-being or salvation of believers, those concerning ritual or polity and those concerning rules or dogmas in the strict sense of the terms, those concerning doctrinal explanations and those concerning beliefs simply necessary in and of themselves, those related to Scripture generally and those concerning the stability of the basic biblical faith.   In the second category, the subjective, errors of ignorance must be distinguished from errors arising from opposition to truth, the internal or mental error from the external error in formal assent and profession.   Here too the condition or state of believers and church must be considered: the condition before the fall is different from the condition after, of the Old Testament from the New and, as the example of doubting Thomas indicates, before the resurrection and after.   Different requirements arise from different states and conditions.[39]

In the third category, distinction is made concerning patterns, manner, and degrees of judgment and tolerance—so that a difference must be recognized between the rules and judgment of particular churches and the general assent of the church universal, visible and invisible. Moderation and some degree of tolerance is required in the first case, while firm judgment is necessary in the latter inasmuch as those who deny universal truths of the church are excluded from heavenly blessedness. Thus it is one thing to tolerate minor corruptions and infirmities with a longsuffering love and quite another to attempt reconciliation with pernicious heresies![40]

Three further distinctions can be made concerning the articles or dogmas of the faith (*dogmata fidei*): they can be defined either as primary and immediate, or as secondary and mediate; as explicit and formal, or implict and virtual; and as positive or negative.[41]   The first of these distinctions refers to the difference between those doctrines which arise immediately from the reading of Scripture (e.g., the doctrines of the Trinity, of Christ as mediator, or of justification) and are primary to the Christian faith and those doctrines which arise by logical derivation as hypotheses or conclusions and which are mediate or secondary to the faith (e.g., the relationship of the two natures in Christ, the *communicatio idiomatum*). This distinction follows the pattern of the Lutheran scholastic differentiation of constituent articles (*articuli constituentes*) from consequent articles (*articuli consequentes*) or, in the language of the "*Lutherani rigidiores*," as Turretin calls them, the "stricter Lutherans" like Calovius and Quenstedt, primary fundamental articles (*articuli fundamentales primarii*) and secondary fundamental articles (*articuli fundamentales secundarii*). The question, of course, is the extent to which secondary or logically derived articles can be considered fundamental.[42]

This question is answered in part by the distinction between the explicit or formal and the implicit or virtual articles. When a doctrine of faith is present in Scripture as an explicit and formal statement it is, of course, necessary. This necessary, foundational character extends, in addition, to those doctrines implied directly by the text and, therefore, virtually present. The implicit or virtually present doctrine, moreover, attains a fundamental or normative status when its formulation becomes an issue of debate between orthodox and heterodox Christians and, in addition, the heterodox formulation leads to an erroneous and soteriologically dangerous understanding of the explicit and formal or primary and immediate doctrines. This argument can be extended to cover doctrines developed as logical conclusions from primary dogmas. Of course, a question arises here concerning the way in which logic, particularly syllogistic logic, can be applied to revealed doctrine and which logical conclusions are in fact essentially biblical and therefore fundamental in a secondary or derived sense.[43]

The third distinction concerning the nature of fundamentals distinguishes between positive and negative articles, and may be regarded as an extension of the previous two categories of doctrine. Positive articles include the doctrines previously noted as primary, consisting principally of affirmative statements of saving truth, such as "Christ is the Son of God" or "the death of Christ was the ransom paid for our sins." Negative articles describe errors both of primary statement and of logical conclusion. Moreover, they specifically consist of falsehoods rejected by orthodox Christians—such as the doctrines of the mass and purgatory. These negative articles identify errors of two sorts, direct or immediate errors and indirect or secondary errors resulting from the application of incorrect logic in doctrinal matters. Blatant heresies fall into the category of direct or immediate error: they subvert primary, immediate fundamentals by overt, explicit contrary statement.   Indirect or secondary error, however, is an indirect subversion of truth.   For example, the popish doctrines of the merit of works and of temporal satisfaction through penance do not immediately subvert the doctrine of Christ's satisfaction, but rather do so indirectly, by way of extension.   So-called negative articles of faith controvert both sorts of error.[44]

This identification of fundamental articles and their distinction both from the *principia* and nonfundamental or consequent articles serves also to identify and distinguish the various kinds of errorist against whom polemic is to be directed.   Those who deny the *principia theologiae* are either classed as infidels or unbelievers.   Those who accept the *principia* but who err in fundamental articles are heretics.   Those who accept both *principia* and *articuli fundamentales* but who separate themselves from the faithful over minor doctrinal issues are schismatics.[45]

The Reformed orthodox generally also note, in connection with the idea of fundamental articles, three kinds of doctrinal error: 1. errors directly *against* a fundamental article (*contra fundamentum*); 2. errors *around* a fundamental or in indirect contradiction to it (*circa fundamentum*); 3. errors *beyond* a fundamental article (*praeter fundamentum*). The first kind of error is a direct attack—such as those launched by the Socinians—against the divinity of Christ or the Trinity.   The second is not a direct negation or an antithesis but rather an indirect or secondary error ultimately subversive of a fundamental—such as a belief in God that refuses to acknowledge his providence.   The third category of error does not address fundamental articles directly or indirectly but rather involves faith in problematic and curious questions (*quaestiones problematicas et curiosas*) that do not arise out of the revealed Word— hay and stubble!—and that, because of their curiosity and vanity, constitute diversions from and impediments to salvation.[46]

This sense of several kinds or levels of error manifests itself in Stapfer's massive *Institutiones theologiae polemicae*.   Stapfer's system, as its subtitle indicates, adopts a scientific arrangement by moving from those adversaries who deny the *principia* of Christianity (the infidels and unbelievers called Atheists, Deists, Epicureans, Pagans and Naturalists), to those who accept either of the principia (Jews, Moslems, Socinians and Latitudinarians or Indifferentists), to those who accept both principia but attack fundamental articles (Papists, Fanatics, Pelagians, Remonstrants and Anabaptists), to those, finally, who agree on fundamentals but who differ on nonfundamental articles (the Greek Orthodox and the Lutherans).   Stapfer feels close enough to the Lutherans to devote a separate chapter to "the consent and dissent of Protestants."[47]

The latter two groups, the Greek Orthodox and the Lutherans, are not viewed as heretics but as schismatics from the Reformed faith.

Stapfer devotes the first two sections of each polemical chapter to the identification of the basic ideas of the heresy and, specifically, to the delineation of its *proton pseudos* or false fundamental, the "primary hypothesis" of the heresy against which he must direct the force of his argument. Thus the false fundamental of the atheist is that there exists "no self-existent substance beyond the world that contains in itself the reason for the existence of this universe."[48] Similarly the false fundamental of the naturalists—Stapfer singles out Matthew Tindal and Anthony Collins—is their assumption that reason alone is sufficient for salvation or ultimate blessedness.[49] Both of these fundamental errors operate to exclude the biblical foundation or *principium* of Christianity: those who hold them are infidels! When he turns to heretics, Stapfer recognizes, again, fundamental errors that mirror, like a "bad eminence," the fundamental articles of the true faith. Thus papists accept revelation and reason but hold as *proton pseudos* the supremacy of the pope which leads to the founding of doctrine on an infallible church rather than on the Lordship of Christ.[50] The Pelagian *proton pseudos*, that fallen man can adequately obey the Law, stands over against the church's insistence on the necessity of grace.[51]

For Stapfer, the Greeks and the Lutherans represent the problem of errors around and beyond fundamentals; neither is to be classed as a heresy. The Greeks deny the doctrine of the procession of the Spirit from the Son as well as the Father, but they do not deny the doctrine of the Trinity. Stapfer here admits the historical problem of the insertion of the *filioque* into the creed, but relies on biblical warrants to justify the doctrine.[52] The Lutherans deny the language of double predestination but nonetheless affirm that salvation occurs by grace alone.[53] Stapfer sees, in the first case, a danger of weakening the doctrine of the Trinity; in the second, a danger of falling into the Arminian error of losing the doctrine of salvation by grace alone.

This paradigm for the identification of fundamental articles and the kinds of error that relate to fundamentals exercised a significant formal influence on the structure of Reformed orthodox system. The way in which issues developed in the prolegomena carry through into the theological system: each doctrinal *locus* of the system was conceived by the orthodox in terms of its relation to fundamental articles. *Loci* are recognized as primary or secondary in their relation to the doctrines of Scripture and each *locus* recognizes and attempts to refute the errors of opponents in terms of their relation to the *locus* itself and to the essentials of the faith. The scholastic method of "definitions, divisions, arguments, and answers" was well suited to the positive and polemical task implied by this paradigm.

As a summation of his argument, and immediately prior to the discussion of the actual fundamental articles, Turretin supplies five criteria for the enumeration of fundamentals. First, they must be catholic or universal (*catholici*) insofar as they are required by the universal or catholic faith as necessary to salvation. Here Turretin explicitly notes the Athanasian Creed, which begins with the words, "Whosoever would be saved must, before all other things, hold to the catholic faith which, except he keep it whole and undefiled, he will perish eternally." Second, a fundamental doctrine must be necessary to salvation in such a way that ignorance of it brings damnation, doubt concerning it brings great danger, and negation of it is impiety and heresy. Third—against the Lutherans in particular—a fundamental article must be such that all the faithful can consent to it without dissent over interpretation, under pain of the anathema of Galatians 1:8 concerning preaching that is contrary to the gospel. "Whence, where there is dissent on fundamentals, no one is able to permit conciliation"—*Unde ubi est dissensus in fundamentalibus, nullus potest dari Syncretismus*. Fourth, *articuli fundamentales* must be such that all theological dogmas (*omnia dogmata theologica*) return to or hark back on them as basic rules of truth—in other words, argues Turretin, the fundamentals are what Paul calls *analogian pisteos*, the analogy of faith. It is by comparison with or measurement against a fundamental that doctrines are known to be true and adequately formulated. Therefore, fifth, fundamental doctrines or articles, properly so-called, must be primary fundamentals or principal truths (*principales veritates*) on which all other fundamentals rest and without which salvation would be subverted.[54]

Having developed a paradigm for the definition of fundamental articles, the orthodox can proceed to the delineation of the actual articles deemed fundamental or necessary to salvation. Here too there is a series of basic categories and criteria.

> First, from the nature and condition of the dogmas themselves; those evidently [are fundamental] that comprehend either the necessary causes or necessary conditions of salvation, whether final or necessary as means, since the negation of causes removes the effect, and negated means cannot lead to a result: thus the grace of God by which we are elected, the merit of Christ by which we are redeemed, and the Spirit by whom we are sanctified are principal causes of salvation, and instrumental faith, John 3:16, 17; true repentance and conversion to God [are] necessary conditions, Heb. 6:2; Matt. 3:2—all these we call fundamental dogmas (*dogmata fundamentalia*).[55]

Witsius similarly argues that "another mark of a fundamental article is, that it be of such a nature, that neither faith in Christ, nor true repentance can exist without it; for as without faith it is impossible to please God, so without holiness, no man shall see the Lord" (Heb. 11:6; 12:14).[56]

From these premises, Witsius can add to the doctrines of grace, faith, repentance and conversion the "articles which respect the existence and veracity of God, and also the gracious rewards which he confers upon his people"—"since it is impossible for anyone to believe in God, unless he knows that he is, and that he is faithful in all his sayings; and since it is impossible also for any one to love and serve him, unless he believe that he is the rewarder of those that seek him."[57] Similarly, since faith is not implicit, but presupposes knowledge, "the knowledge of Christ is necessary to salvation (John 17:3; 20:31)"—and this knowledge, in turn, rests (together with the honor that must be paid to Christ according to John 5:23) on the doctrine of Christ's equality of dignity and identity of substance with the Father. Against the Socinians, therefore, the orthodox maintain as a fundamental, necessary to faith, the doctrine of the divinity of Christ.[58]

Second, a whole series of articles are known to be fundamental by the express declaration of Scripture (ex ipsius Scripturae declaratione). Among these doctrines are the doctrine of God as One and Three (de Deo Uno et Trino), as positively attested by John 17:3 and negatively by 1 John 2:23; the doctrine of sin (Eph. 2:1; 1 John 1:10); the doctrine of Christ's person, natures and work; the doctrines of the gospel of Christ, faith, and justification apart from works; the doctrines of sanctification and true worship of God; and finally, the doctrines of the resurrection and of life eternal.[59] Virtually all of the orthodox systems cite a wide variety of texts—dicta probantia—which are intended for use, not crassly as proof texts for citation without exegesis, but as points of reference to the long-established results of the church's exegetical tradition. The dicta probantia or proving texts serve not to circumvent study of the text but to indicate received interpretation leading from exegesis to doctrine.

Third, "the character of fundamental articles can be sought from the Apostles' Creed, in which the Fathers drew together from the writings of the Apostles a summary of fundamental doctrines."[60] In other words, the Creed provides an index to fundamental doctrine but does not survey the fundamental doctrines exhaustively—particularly since it deals only with theoretical articles of the faith and not with the equally fundamental

practical articles concerning worship.   Moreover, not even all theoretical fundamentals are explicitly stated in the Creed.   We read nothing of
the grace of God, the satisfaction of Christ, and the providence and
conservation of God, though these doctrines may be viewed as present
implicitly in the Creed by way of logical consequence and analogy (per
consequentiam et analogiam).   Finally, the Creed witnesses to the truth
of Scripture not so much according to the actual language of the text
(quoad verba) but rather according to the meaning (quoad sensum).   Thus
it may be said, with Hilary, that fundamentalia non sunt in verbis, sed
in sententia ("the fundamentals are not in the words but in the meaning")
and that heretics are identified not by rejection of the Creed per se but
by rejection of its doctrinal implications, as is witnessed in the cases
of the anti-Trinitarians, both Sabellian and Arian and by the papists who
distort the doctrines of Christ's death, the church and the remission of
sins.[61]

A fourth criterion can be added from Witsius: "if any article is
stated as necessary to be known, which cannot be understood, unless some
other article shall have been previously understood and believed; that
other article must also rank among those which are necessary."[62]   We
know, for example, by the express declaration of Scripture that salvation
by grace alone in Christ is a necessary or fundamental doctrine.   But the
doctrine of salvation by grace alone cannot be understood "unless we know
that sin has plunged us into so deep an abyss of misery, that our deliv-
erance surpassed our own power, and even the united exertions of all
creatures."[63]   Therefore, the doctrine of universal sinfulness is also a
fundamental article of faith.

The Reformed scholastics refuse to move beyond the basic enunciation
of categories and criteria to an explicit list of fundamental or necessary articles.   To attempt such a list, says Turretin, would be "rash and
useless":[64] rash, because Scripture itself nowhere precisely defines such
a category of doctrines; useless, since there appears to be no limit to
the ways in which heretics—whether papist, Socinian or Anabaptist—
manage to err in fundamental issues.   This absence of an explicit and
restrictive list, moreover, impugnes neither the perfection of Scripture
nor the value of the church's confessions as norms of doctrine, since
Scripture remains sufficient in its revelation of doctrines necessary to
salvation and the ancient creeds provide satisfactory criteria for the
determination of fundamentals.[65]

The unwillingness of even the most scholastic of the later Reformed
orthodox—for example, Turretin and Heidegger—to counter the Lutheran
expansion of the category of fundamentals to points of contemporary

doctrinal dispute with a list of counterfundamentals defined from the Reformed point of view explains in large measure the absence of a pietistic critique of system among the Reformed. Whereas the attempt by Calovius and Quensted to include virtually the whole of theological system in the category of fundamental doctrines brought down upon Lutheran orthodoxy the pietist charge of substituting dogmatic accuracy for Christian faith and of losing sight of piety amid a tangle of rigid doctrinal requirements; the Reformed avoided the charge almost entirely by limiting the category of fundamental doctrines. In the early eighteenth century, during the transitional period between high orthodoxy and the Age of Reason, a more tolerant and latitudinarian view, expressing a concern parallel to that of the pietists, was voiced by theologians like Jean Alphonse Turretin: only the basic creedal articles strictly necessary to Christian faith could be identified as fundamental. Other points of contention, such as those separating the Reformed and the Lutherans, could be set aside. Although a stricter orthodoxy continued to be represented by writers like Stapfer and De Moor, the younger Turretin's views were more characteristic of the age and its increasingly rationalistic approach to theological issues.[66]

In a positive sense, it is clear that the Reformed discussion of *articuli fundamentales* also maintained a precise and careful distinction between the status and function of Scripture, catechism or confession, and theological system in the church, while demonstrating the theoretical and practical interrelation of these three forms of *doctrina*. What is more, this series of distinctions and relationships points toward the issue of doctrinal or theological *principia*, toward the doctrine of Scripture as *principium cognoscendi*, and toward the development of theological system both on the basis of that *principium* and in both formal and material relation to catechetical and confessional models.

9.3 The *principia theologiae*

The identification of theological *principia* is the final and most truly foundational discussion presented within the prolegomena of theological system. Here the orthodox theologians penetrate still deeper into the substance of theology, deeper even than the identification of fundamental articles of the faith. Here they address the *sine qua non*, the necessary and irreducible ground of theology, apart from which not even the fundamental articles of the faith could be set forth and no articles of theology, fundamental or derivative, could be correctly stated.

Long before the development of theological prolegomena in the Middle Ages, the Greek word *archē*, indicating a beginning, source, or first principle, had been definitively identified with the Latin word, *principium*. It was the term selected by Rufinus in his translation of Origen's *On First Principles*, the *Peri Archōn* or *De Principiis*. It was also the term used by Jerome to translate *archē* in John 1:1. Once this fact of the history of the term and its translation has been recognized, the roots of the search for a *principium* can be extended back into the intellectual history of the Western world to Aristotle's declaration that all *archai* or first principles are the ground or "first point from which a thing either is or comes to be or is known . . . of these some are immanent in the thing and others are outside."[67]

The historical and philosophical roots of the Reformed language of *principia* were made clear from the very outset of the discussion in the early orthodox period. Sibrandus Lubbertus argues at the beginning of his treatise on the principles of Christian dogmatics that "all arts and all disciplines and sciences have identifiable *principia* from which solid arguments and precepts are deduced." Just as arithmetic, geometry and physics have first principles, so does theology: there must be a "true, immediate, utterly necessary prior and knowable" principle that is the "cause of all doctrines in the Christian religion."[68] From Aristotle and Iauellus, Lubbertus draws the argument that the *principia* of any given discipline must be identified as a *principium essendi* or principle of being and a *principium cognoscendi* or principle of knowing: the former is necessary for the existence of the discipline, the latter for knowledge of it.[69] If the doctrines of Christianity are to be true, certain, necessary, and divine, so must be the *principia* on which they rest: human authority is, therefore, ruled out at the level of *principia*.[70]

As noted earlier in another context, the orthodox Protestant prolegomena are dogmatic, not predogmatic declarations. Neither here, in the identification of *principia*, nor anywhere in the prolegomena have we stood outside the bounds of theology and, on nontheological grounds, identified the basis of right argumentation. The first principles, the sources and foundations of theological argument, have been assumed and implied from the outset in the definition of theology and in the contrast between archetypal and ectypal theology. The archetype and the *archē* must be identical. In addition, the identification of God and his self-revelation as the *principia* or grounds of theology merely serves as a preliminary statement of the doctrines of God and of Scripture that stand at the beginning of the system and, in fact, like the entirety of the prolegomena, as a reflection upon the contents of the theological system as a whole in terms of the underlying rationale for its existence.

The form of this primary statment, moreover, is clearly determined not only by the original contrast between archetypal and ectypal theology but also by the systematic commitment to the connection between divine archetype and human ectype that must characterize any legitimate system of theology. This desire to make clear the connection between the divine and human knowledge of the divine was resident in the consistent effort of the orthodox to argue the relationship between all forms of ectypal theology and the divine archetype in terms of the *logos prophorikos* or Word sent forth. Here the discussion focuses on the divine archetype as the ultimate and essential foundation of theology and on Scripture as the divinely and therefore authoritatively and infallibly given cognitive foundation of theology. Acknowledgment of these two foundations or *principia* in turn legitimizes the movement toward system.

In addition, by way of closing yet another circle of argument in the orthodox prolegomena, this final discussion of *principia* must be viewed as the culmination of a process of reasoning begun in the distinction between archetypal and ectypal theology and crystallized around the identification of the genus of theology. Just as the identification of theology as a subalternate science that derives its principles from a higher science places the imprint of the archetypal/ectypal model upon the discipline of "our theology," so does the identification of *principia* arise from the claim that theology is a kind of *scientia* and return to the language of archetype and ectype. In other words, the archetype is the higher science that supplies the principles used as the basis of conclusions in the ectypal, subalternate science. Granting the relation between archetype and ectype, the archetypal divine self-knowledge is one of the principles of ectypal theological knowing, that is, the *principium essendi*. The means by which the archetype definitively reveals itself, Scripture, must be the *principium cognoscendi* required by the subalternate science for its existence as a discipline. These definitions, in turn, demand a hermeneutic that will draw conclusions from the scriptural principle.

This point is clearly made by Chandieu in his proposal for a legitimate scholastic method for Protestant use. For Chandieu, the use of scholastic form is legitimized by the identification of the correct *principia*: Scripture, not reason, must supply all of the *principia* or *axiomata* used in theology. In addition, since these axioms arise out of revelation they cannot be demonstrated nor do they rest on human knowing (*scientia humana*). Theological *principia* rest upon the wisdom of God.[71]

The affirmation of Scripture as *principium cognoscendi* thus follows from the basic definitions and divisions of theology presented by the orthodox at the beginning of their prolegomena. All true theology reflects the divine archetype and that archetype cannot be known in and of itself but only through a gracious self-revelation. Reason, therefore, cannot be the cognitive foundation of theology inasmuch as it cannot know God in and of himself and inasmuch as it is not a divine self-revelation but only an instrument for understanding revelation. Since, moreover, the archetype infinitely transcends nature and since the ultimate end of theology is of grace and not of nature, the natural order and its revelation cannot be the cognitive foundation of Christian theology. What remains is the divine self-revelation in and through the Word as recorded in the biblical witness. Thus, the Word of God written is the *principium cognoscendi theologiae*.

When, therefore, the Protestant orthodox introduce a separate discussion of *principia theologiae* or foundations of theology into their prolegomena, they tend to place it at the end of the prolegomena as an introduction to or preparation for the next two *loci*: Scripture, the *principium cognoscendi theologiae*; and God, the *principium essendi theologiae*. These *principia* or foundations of theology are argued by the Protestant scholastics according to two basic patterns. The majority simply point to the logic of the situation: theology has been shown to exist and anything that exists and is also capable of analysis must have two foundations or grounds—an essential foundation that guarantees its existence and a cognitive foundation that makes knowledge of it possible. Thus theology which both is and is known must have an essential foundation (*principium essendi*) and a cognitive foundation (*principium cognoscendi*). The other pattern of derivation is causal and arrives, by somewhat different logic, at the same result.

The first of these patterns, descriptive of the logic of knowing something, is neatly and closely argued by Hoornbeeck:

> In theology, the foundation (*principium*) is twofold: of being and of knowing (*Essendi et Cognoscendi*), namely, that by which it is and that by which it is known; the former establishes or presents the knowable object (lit., the knowable thing and the object: *scibile et obiectum*); the latter brings forth knowledge and gives form to the subject: the former is God, the latter is the word of God himself, as is manifestly expressed and indicated in holy Scripture.[72]

Virtually identical is the statement of Edward Leigh:

> Two things are to be considered in Divinity: First, the Rule of it, the Scripture or Word of God. Secondly, the Matter or

parts of it concerning God and man. *Principium essendi* in Divinity is God the first Essence; *Principium cognoscendi*, the Scripture, by which we know God, and all things concerning him.[73]

Leigh notes that, like many divines of his day, he will begin with the Scriptures. That there may be a revelation of God is apparent not only to Christians but also to pagans—and it is eminently reasonable. Moreover, Christians should be well satisfied that they have such a revelation in view of the supernatural character of the truths of the gospel. These truths are a matter of God's "grace and favour," they exceed the powers of natural reason and "illumination and elevation of the faculties of the soul was necessary for the right reception of them."[74]

> There are three general Characters whereby we may know any Word to be the Word of God, and a Religion to be the true Religion; 1. That which doth most set forth the glory of God. 2. That which doth direct us to a rule which is a perfect rule of holinesse toward God, and righteousnesse to men. 3. That which shews us a way suitable to God's glory and men's necessity, to reconcile us to God. The word of God sets forth God's glory in all the perfections, and is a compleat rule. . .[75]

A somewhat more developed statement of this logical pattern is found in Trelcatius' *Scholastica methodus ss. theologiae*. After his statement of definitions, Trelcatius moves on to his system proper and in an initial chapter deals with the "first principles" of theology. All sciences, he argues, have proper principles above which the mind cannot ascend—since these principles are indemonstrable. Divinity alone begins with the absolute, first principles of things which depend on no other matters; whereas the basic principles of the other sciences are only first relative to the science for which they provide the foundation, the basic principles of theology are prior to any other "principle of Being" or "principle of knowing."[76]

> For there are two Principles, the one of the thing, the other of knowledge, the former out of which other things are produced, the latter on which the knowledge of other things depends.[77]

In theology this division may be explained as

> God and the Word: God is the Principle of being, the first cause of Divinity, from which springs both the end of Divinity and the means to this end: the Word is the Principle of knowing, by which the end of Divinity and the means unto it may be known.[78]

Both these principles are first in their spheres, since nothing exists prior to God and nothing was known or spoken prior to his Word. (Of course, in the case of true or Christian natural theology, Scripture cannot be the *principium cognoscendi*. Alsted, who developed one of the more massive treatises on natural theology in the era of early orthodoxy, counts nature as the *principium* of natural theology, Scripture as the *principium* of supernatural theology.[79]) This identification of Scripture as *principium cognoscendi* also indicates the Protestant orthodox acceptance of a dynamic view of the biblical Word much like that of the Reformers: whereas God is the remote or first efficient cause and therefore *principium essendi theologiae*, the living Word of God is "proximate and immediate efficient cause" and therefore the *principium cognoscendi* of theology.[80]

This language of *principium cognoscendi* and *principium essendi*, like most of the structures we have already examined, has clear medieval precedent though here, as before, the Protestant scholastics clearly make modifications in the language and implication of scholasticism in view of the teachings of the Reformers.   In the fourteenth century, in the face of the critique of the definition of theology as *scientia subalterna*, it became quite common to define theology as a *habitus* or disposition of knowing conclusions drawn from the *principia theologica*, the articles of faith and the Holy Scriptures.[81]   The Protestant scholastics, of course, identify Scripture alone as *principium* and subordinate all churchly articles of faith to it—but their reason for identifying a *principium cognoscendi* is identical.   In the absence of *principia per se nota*, theology must identify the principles upon which it is founded and attest their certainty.   Even so, among the late medieval scholastics, Marsilius of Inghien identifies God as *principium theologiae*, the self-revealed ground of the existence of theology.[82]   This language can be viewed, moreover, as a simple extension of the fairly standard medieval identification of the Trinity as the *principium essentialis* of all created things.[83]   The Protestant scholastic use of the terms *principium essendi theologiae* and *principium cognoscendi theologiae* represents, nonetheless, a significant development in theological system.   The medieval doctors had used similar language but had never stated the two *principia* as a basic division of topics at the beginning of system leading to a fully developed *locus de Scriptura sacra* prior to the *locus de Deo*.   The doctrine of Scripture stated so pointedly as *principium theologiae* is, thus, both a descendant of the medieval system and a specifically Protestant development resting upon the *sola Scriptura* of the Reformers.

The medieval scholastic identification of theology, objectively considered, with the divine revelation in Scripture, coupled with the notion of theology as a subalternate science—a science consisting in first principles known from a higher science and in the conclusions drawn from those principles—led several of the teachers of the fourteenth century, notably Gregory of Rimini and Pierre d'Ailly, to develop a language of *principia* similar to that of the Protestant scholastics.   Gregory had argued that all theological disputes were to be adjudged by *dicta* resting on Scripture, inasmuch as the *principia* of theology are the truths resident in the canon of Scripture and all other theological truths fall into the category of conclusions "following by necessity" from the biblical *principia*.[84]   D'Ailly assumes the same relationship between *principia theologiae* and the conclusions properly belonging to theology (*conclusiones proprie theologicae*) and argues that the *principia* of theology are "the verities of the holy canon" of Scripture.[85]

There are crucial elements of continuity and discontinuity to be noted in this developing language of *principia theologiae*.   On the one hand, neither Gregory of Rimini nor Pierre d'Ailly give us precisely the formulation of the Protestant scholastics: Scripture for them, provides the divine truths that are the *principia theologiae*.   In other words, there are many *principia* from which conclusions may be drawn.   We may associate this sense of multiple *principia* with the nominalist denial of universals and *genus*.   The Protestant development of the idea, however, finds in Scripture itself, as the source of divine truths, a single *principium* of theology.   We may associate this sense of a single *principium* both with the Protestant tendency, noted in Vermigli, Zanchi, Polanus, Keckermann, Alsted and others, away from a nominalist philosophical stance and with the Reformation emphasis on *sola Scriptura*.   On the other hand, on the side of continuity, we must recognize that both the Reformation and orthodox Protestantism stand in a direct line of doctrinal development from the great scholastic systems of the thirteenth and fourteenth centuries insofar as medieval doctors presented a clear doctrine of Scripture as the ultimate cognitive ground of theology.[86]   We must also recognize that the Protestant orthodox appropriation and modification of scholastic language of *principia* points toward the doctrinal continuity, despite formal discontinuity, of the orthodox with the Reformers.

As Congar has pointed out, the typically medieval language of the sufficiency of scriptural revelation for salvation, even when coupled with comments like those of Scotus concerning the necessity of revelation, ought not to be understood over against the comments of the same theologians concerning the necessity of the *magisterium*, the teaching office of the church.[85]   In a limited sense, the protests of Wycliffe and Hus, which did pose the sufficiency of Scripture against the authority of the church, provide adumbrations of the Protestant view of Scripture as *principium cognoscendi*.   Of greater importance to the development of the idea of Scripture as *principium cognoscendi*, however, is the early Reformation declaration and subsequent confession of *sola Scriptura*. The majority of sixteenth-century Reformed confessions, like the First and Second Helvetic, the Gallican and the Belgic, juxtapose the doctrines of Scripture and God as the contents of the first several chapters or articles. The Protestant scholastic declaration of *principia*, therefore, is distinctly Protestant and, if structurally and methodologically different from the theology of the Reformers, is based directly on the theology of the Reformation.

It is also probable that the Protestant scholastic view of Scripture as the *principium cognoscendi* rather than as a body of *principia* functioned as an unstated but important factor in the decision, noted in a previous chapter, to identify the *genus* of theology as *sapientia* or wisdom rather than as *scientia* or knowledge in a strict sense. Since Scripture is not to be viewed precisely as a body of *principia* drawn from a higher science, theology does not fit perfectly into the definition of a subalternate science. Of course, the hermeneutic of drawing legitimate conclusions in theology from the explicit statements of Scripture remained as part of the legacy of theological method mediated from the medieval scholastics by the more systematically oriented Reformers and their adoption of the locus method to the Protestant orthodox. Nonetheless, the definition of Scripture as a unified *principium*, together with the definition of theology as a kind of wisdom not based on evidence of reason, prevented the Protestant orthodox from adopting the very view of Scripture they are frequently accused of holding—Scripture as a set of conveniently-numbered divine propositions. The divine archetype is simple, nondiscursive, and nonpropositional: the propositional nature of language belongs to the accommodation of truth to our ectypal patterns of knowing. Exegetical study of the entire *principium* rather than a collation of propositions would necessarily undergird the formulation of Christian doctrine.

In terms of the larger question of continuities and discontinuities in the history of doctrine, the medieval language of *principia theologiae* and of the sufficiency—indeed, the authority and infallibility—of the biblical revelation stands as an important terminological precedent for the Protestant scholastic discussion of *principia* and of the doctrine of Scripture.[88] We can identify, then, a continuity of scholastic language —but a discontinuity of implication inasmuch as the *sola Scriptura* has set aside the authority of the church over the meaning of the text. Even so, we note a discontinuity of language between the Reformers and the

Protestant scholastics—but a clear continuity of theological implication despite the formalization of statement.

When the question of *principia* is considered causally, we again raise the question of an essential or external foundation since theology obviously is not self-caused. In addition to this external ground, all disciplines also have their own inward or internal basis, a *principium* belonging to the discipline itself. Maccovius, accordingly, speaks not of a *principium essendi* and *principium cognoscendi*, but of a *principium externum* that operates as an efficient cause and a *principium internum* that stands as the material substratum of the discipline as provided by the operation of the efficient cause.[89] In this approach to the *principia* we encounter yet another reflection of the medieval prolegomena and, in addition, the probable dogmatic source of the language of principles or foundations of theology. Whereas the medieval scholastics devoted little space to the explicit discussion of *principia*, they were profoundly concerned to delineate the causal grounds of theology—God being the efficient cause and scriptural revelation the material cause of theology.[90]

The designation of Scripture as *principium internum* demands some explanation, particularly since it stands in contrast with the frequent Reformed designation of Scripture as *principium cognoscendi* and, even more pointedly, with Mastricht's view of Scripture as *principium cognoscendi* received inwardly by faith at the inception of spiritual life.[91] The difference arises not only because of Maccovius' causal consideration of *principia*, which places God external to the theological enterprise and the Word internal to it, but also and perhaps primarily because of his careful definition of Scripture as one form of Word and his equally careful recognition of the way in which that Word must be known inwardly if it is to be the *principium* of our theology. According to its essence, the Word is "that celestial doctrine which the holy books contain" and, as such, precedes both logically and chronologically all written forms. The Word is, therefore, *Verbum internum* when it comes to the prophets and apostles. The written form of the Word is, therefore, an incidental property or accident.[92] The Word, of course, is *principium theologiae* according to its essence—and, thus, in this sense, *principium internum*. Maccovius' definition simply regards the written Word as external to the individual believer and identifies the Word as received by faith as *principium internum*. Moreover, faith receives inwardly not the accidents but the essence of the *doctrina caelestis*.

Polanus, rather more directly, argues that Scripture is *principium cognoscendi* insofar as it is the place where the immediate cause of our theology is given:

> The immediate and proximate efficient cause of our theology is the Word of God, which, consequently is the foundation (*principium*) of our theology. The first principle, indeed, into which all theological doctrines are resolved is, "Thus said the Lord" or "God said" (*Dominus Dixit, seu Deus Dixit*). This foundation is one or whole and necessarily so, both because all the Prophets and Apostles call us back to this alone, as is witnessed by all of Scripture; and because God cannot be understood except through himself (*non potest Deus nisi per Deum intelligi*).[93]

In other words, Scripture must be the *principium theologiae* in a causal sense since the infinite and transcendent God and his self-knowledge must remain inaccessible to us apart from the Word of revelation—again, an echo of the archetypal/ectypal model of theology and of the epistemological dictum *finitum non capax infiniti*. Theology, considered as finite but true, cannot have a human cause or a humanly constructed foundation.

The art of living to God does not belong to the natural potential of man but is truly a *facultas acquisita*, the rule of which is prescribed by God and set forth in his Word, the sacred Scriptures.[94] Thus Scripture is the norm for Christian living and theology: it is called the *theologiae principium*. Mastricht's text for his second *locus* is 2 Timothy 3: 16, 17—"All Scripture is inspired by God, and is useful for doctrine, for refutation, for correction, for instruction in righteousness, that a man of God might be perfect, to all good works perfectly instructed."[95] From all this it follows that *sacram Scripturam, perfectam esse Deo vivendi regulam*, a conclusion that is corroborated internally by a multitude of texts in Scripture.[96]

This causality of the Word, moreover, points us directly back to God as the *principium essendi*, since Scripture, as the cognitive foundation of theology, is the result of the *logos prophorikos*, the word sent forth, the instrumental cause of theology.[97] The *logos prophorikos* points back to its source, the *logos emphytos* or immanent Word, which is the mind of God himself, the divine Logos. This is not merely an ultimate cognitive foundation but also, of course, the essential foundation, in Maccovius' language, the *principium externum* and *causa efficiens* of theology or, in the usual language of orthodoxy, the *principium essendi*.

As a final point in the discussion of *principia*, we raise the issue of the internal reception of the Word, the *principium cognoscendi*. Following the instrumental language of Junius, according to which the Word sent forth to the minds of the prophets and apostles (*logos prophorikos*) could also be viewed as the basis for a word concerning God implanted both in the minds of the authors of Scripture and in the minds of their hearers (*logos endiathetos*), Maccovius and Alsted had spoken of the inwardly known Word of God as the *principium internum* of theology.[98] This approach to the problem found confirmation in the already established doctrine of the *testimonium internum Spiritus Sancti*: an inward Word of the Spirit, opening the minds of fallen creatures to the truth of God, must accompany the externally preached Word of God. Riissen, therefore, can speak of *verbum internum* as one of the necessary forms of Word in the communication of the promises of the gospel.[99]

These definitions, however, provide only a limited identification of the internal principle of theology. They do show how the Word, considered as *principium cognoscendi externum*, is brought into the human mind and established as the cognitive ground of our theology, *theologia nostra*. But the definitions fail to come full circle. The human mind, before the internal testimony of the Spirit, could not receive the Word. Something, indeed, has been changed within the soul that now makes it receptive to the gospel. The full development of this discussion belongs, of course, to soteriology, but the identification of the subjective ground of reception does belong to the principial and preliminary sections of theological system. The orthodox, indeed, had always asserted that theology, as a form of knowing, whether *scientia* or *sapientia*, could belong only to rational creatures: salvation itself is offered to rational creatures and to them alone[100] and they were in agreement that reason was necessary to theological discourse.[101] The use of reason was defined, however, as instrumental and ancillary, and the Cartesian notion of a principial function of reason was rejected by all but a few of the Reformed orthodox.[102]

In the seventeenth century, under the impact of rationalism and particularly in the wake of the seemingly constructive and theologically congenial rationalism of Leibniz and Wolff, a considerable number of the late scholastic systems elevate reason from an ancillary to a principial status. Thus, Venema:

> There are included in the preliminary points (*prolegomena*) the sources and principles from which our doctrines are drawn. For, if the science of theology be certain, so must its principles, which are, as it were, the springs from which it proceeds. Now these principles are two, the one innate, the other revealed,--reason and revelation.[103]

This affirmation of reason as *principium cognoscendi internum* constitutes a major departure from the perspective of the Reformers and the Protestant scholastics of the seventeenth century and, when conjoined with the rationalist definition of truth as *clara et distincta perceptio*, clear and distinct perception, it had the tendency to obscure not only the role of faith in theology but the underlying epistemological vision of Reformed theology that the human mind, unless aided by grace and presented with supernatural revelation, is incapable of knowing the deepest truths of God.

The extreme result of this line of thought can be seen in the theological systems written in the eighteenth century under the direct tutelage of Wolffian rationalism. Baumgarten's *Theses dogmaticae*, Vitringa's *Doctrinae christianae religionis*, and Endemann's *Institutiones theologicae dogmaticae* present the standard theological prolegomena, with Baumgarten even noting the distinction between archetypal and ectypal theology and arguing that theology, in the strictest sense, is revealed theology drawn from Scripture. Yet, neither Baumgarten nor Endemann see fit to present a doctrine of Scripture at the formal beginning of system. Baumgarten presents his doctrine of Scripture in the second part of his system, following the *ordo salutis* and preceding discussion of Law and gospel and of the sacraments. He also acknowledges throughout his system the status of Scripture as *principium cognoscendi*—but he omits preliminary presentation of the problem of revelation and reason, supernatural and natural theology. Baumgarten strongly implies that reason and natural theology provide a solid point of departure, albeit nonsaving, for revelation and supernatural theology.[104] Vitringa identifies both reason and revelation as *principia theologiae* and proceeds to deal first with reason, viewing it as the cognitive foundation on which revelation must build.[105] Endemann relegates Scripture to the final *locus* where it merely serves to confirm the results of reason. Reason, in Endemann's theology, has finally become the sole *principium cognoscendi*.

A similar and perhaps still more pointed principial use of reason can be seen in the *Institutiones theologiae polemicae* of Johann Stapfer. Although we must allow a more crucial role of reason in polemical theology, inasmuch as the orthodox defined the instrumental and organic role of reason in polemics in terms of the use of reason to refute rational errors in the views of one's opponents, it is also clear that Stapfer has moved farther into the realm of the purely rational than the principles of a high orthodox system like Turretin's *Institutio theologiae elencticae* would allow. The contrast is instructive: whereas Turretin's *Institutio* looks structurally like a positive system, Stapfer's does not. Turretin begins with a standard theological prolegomenon and doctrine of Scripture, defensively stated; Stapfer begins with a chapter on the method of polemics, a second chapter discusses cautions to be observed in polemical argument, and then moves to his "demonstration of theological truths," beginning with the proof of God's existence.[106]   Whereas the proofs are not essential to Turretin's polemic, Stapfer's argument is clearly founded upon the rational demonstrability of God.   In addition, Stapfer not only identifies "Reason and Revelation" as the "twofold *principium*" of his system, he also assumes, in his arguments for the existence of God, the validity of the Wolffian "principle of sufficient reason."[107]

Stapfer argues at length that revelation is necessary in view of the fall.   For all that reason and the "religion of nature" provide a basis for moral actions in the doctrines of the essence and attributes of God, of God as Creator and preserver,[108] they do not provide a truth sufficient to the salvation of sinners.[109]   Stapfer can only argue this point rationally after he has, by reason alone, defended the doctrine of the divine essence and attributes, of creation, providence and the immortality of the soul, of the dependence of man upon God, of the potential of man in the natural state, and even of the plight of man in his sinful condition.[110]   Rational argument dominates the system.

The first hints at this principial use of reason, found in the writings of several Reformed theologians of Cartesian inclination at the end of the seventeenth century—notably Wittich and Braun—elicited an angry response from the last generation of high orthodox theologians. These writers, particularly the Dutch Reformed, raised the question of a resident principle, in man, upon which theology might rest, or, in the language of scholasticism, of a *habitus* of the soul upon which theology might be internally grounded.   The earlier development of the prolegomena, particularly the discussions of the object and genus of theology and of the role of reason and philosophy in theological system, had already provided the orthodox with grounds for an answer.   All that remained was for an antirationalist or anti-Cartesian, like Mastricht, to formulate it in relation to the issue of *principia*.

In brief, Protestant scholastic theology had defined the divine object of theology as given truly and fully in revelation alone, and had recognized that the *genus* of theology was not precisely *scientia*, *sapientia*, *intelligentia*, *prudentia* or *ars*, because theology rests not on rational evidence but on testimony, that is, on the witness of revelation.   As part of this discussion of *genus*, then, came the recognition that the mental disposition or *habitus* by which theological knowledge is received cannot be a *habitus sciendi*, a disposition of knowing, but a *habitus credendi*, a disposition of believing or a *habitus fidei*, a disposition of faith.   Once theological truths are received by the *habitus credendi*, then reason can use those truths as a basis for drawing conclusions—but reason itself is never an ultimate ground of theological argument. With this theological basis fully in view, Mastricht answers the principal question by placing a *locus de fide salvifica*—a doctrine of saving faith—immediately between his doctrine of Scripture and his doctrine of God as a statement concerning the way in which revelation, external to the mind as objectively given Word, becomes effective inwardly. It is *fides*, not *ratio*, that provides the point of entry into the doctrine of God.[111]

With the conclusion of the discussion of the *principia theologiae*, we come not only to the end of the orthodox prolegomona but to the point at which we can survey the principles and presuppositions of Reformed orthodox system and make some judgments concerning the character of Protestant scholasticism. Of course, we are not in a position to make claims concerning the organization of all orthodox systems (although some general remarks are surely in order), nor are we in a position to assess the contents of individual *loci* in the system. Instead, we can assess the way in which the prolegomena point toward the system and define its method, its contents and the relationships between its *loci*. We are entitled to assume that the prolegomena are genuine and that what they indicate to be the chief concerns of system are indeed the basic issues, principles and structures of the system in all of its *loci*.

As argued in the introduction and illustrated by the discussions of natural theology, of the use of reason and philosophy, and of the *principium cognoscendi theologiae*, the Reformed orthodox system was hardly rationalistic, nor was it metaphysically inclined. In addition, the scholastic view of the object of theology—God as revealed, the primary object; and all the works of God, the secondary object—together with the *locus* method of exposition by topic, the scholastic approach to the division and definition of topics, and the discussion of Scripture as *principium cognoscendi*, points toward a concern for elaborating each and every topic of Christian theology on its own terms. Apart from the doctrines of Scripture and God, the orthodox system allows no *principia* or monistic organizing principles.

Beyond these largely negative conclusions that define the phenomenon of Protestant scholasticism over against several erroneous but, unfortunately, frequently reiterated characterizations, we can also provide a positive description of the Protestant scholastic system, both in terms of its development and in terms of its final form. In its method the Protestant scholastic system depended upon the traditional scholastic pattern of the establishment of topics by careful division of the subject, the definition of topics through disputation with adversaries—the *quaestio*--and, finally, the elaboration of conclusions through the use of logical and rhetorical tools. This concentration on the parts of the whole, together with the organization of system by *loci* militated against the establishment of synthetic unity and aided the development of a system characterized by exhaustive, comprehensive treatment of all topics and by analytic rigor.

For overarching organization of system the Reformed orthodox relied on teleological and historical issues. Typically, they move from the statement of *principia*, through creation, fall and redemption, to the last things with an emphasis on the covenant as the historical or econom- ical form of the divine work of salvation. Apart from this patterning, however, we find virtually no interest in deducing one doctrine from another but, instead, a desire to place exegetically established doc- trinal *loci* at their proper points along the historical-teleological line of the system. In each *locus* moreover, we can expect the methodological and epistemological definitions of *theologia nostra*, its limits, its genus, its object, the extent of its use of philosophy and reason, to establish the boundaries of argument, just as the *principia*, Scripture and God, limit and define what can be known and said about each aspect of the divine work.

These stylistic, methodological and architectonic interests of the Protestant orthodox did, of course, mark a major alteration of attitude and approach from the systematic essays of the first and second genera- tion Reformers. Theology is now seldom discursive, and the catechetical models of the sixteenth century have been superceded by the more synthe- tic or a *priori* model of scholastic system. The style is propositional and the argumentation is rigorous. Where Calvin and his contemporaries had been content with the more rhetorical enthymeme, the orthodox state all of their premises precisely and in full syllogistic form. If the systems are not rationalist in their presuppositions, they are rational in form and in argument.

Beyond this, it is also fairly clear from the prolegomena that the Reformed orthodox system is primarily a soteriological system, rather than a speculative, philosophical or metaphysical one. We recognize this: (1) from the definition of our theology as a theology *in via*, searching out its salvation between fall and eschaton; (2) from the limits placed on natural theology; (3) from the redefinition of a natural theology of the regenerate as belonging to Christian praise rather than to "fundamental theology," as it were; (4) from the emphasis on the object of theology as God revealed and covenanted in Christ; and (5) from the stress upon the character of theology as theoretical-practical with the emphasis upon *praxis*. A system with presuppositions such as these would only with great difficulty enter the realm of speculative rationalism and, then, only to its ultimate destruction. The tendency of these presuppositions, spelled out in the system as a whole, was toward the establishment of a system scholastic in form and method but essentially in continuity with the teachings of the Reformers.

In his study of "Dogma in Protestant Scholasticism," R. S. Franks argued cogently that "in systematizing and working out the practical doctrines of the Reformation, the seventeenth-century Scholasticism . . . preserved faithfully the central affirmations of the reformers . . . ."[112] Franks argues continuity with the theology of the Reformation on the issues of grace, faith, justification, and church and legitimate development from the Reformers' pronouncement of *sola Scriptura* to the orthodox theologians' doctrine of Scripture. His perspective on the Protestant scholastic use of philosophy is also worthy of note:

> The philosophical element in the new Scholasticism, viz. the doctrines of God and the world, was practically taken over bodily from mediaevalism, and in reality presents no new growth when compared with its predecessor. The bold speculative outlook of the Middle Ages is lost. There is no longer the same independent interest in the philosophical problems of epistemology and metaphysics in their religious application. We have instead merely a statement of what may be called in modern phrase "the approved results" of the earlier scholastic investigations. . . .[113]

Our examination of the Reformed orthodox prolegomena has substantiated Franks' perspective and, in addition, permits some refinement of his generalization concerning the Protestant use of medieval scholastic philosophy. While it is quite correct that the Protestant orthodox borrow from the medieval scholastics and manifest little or no "independent interest in the philosophical problems of epistemology and metaphysics" in their relation to theology, it is also quite clear that the borrowing was hardly uncritical. The Protestant scholastics were not "boldly speculative" in these areas because they had learned well at the hands of the Reformers—their borrowings reflect a wariness of excessive rationalism and excessive speculation. Indeed, the several places where we have noted a strong kinship between the Protestant scholastic and medieval scholastic systems, the Protestants seem to be treading a carefully marked path of Augustinianism and modified Thomism.

In brief, we found some genuine kinship with Henry of Ghent on the issue of causes of theology, with Giles of Rome and Gregory of Rimini together with Henry of Ghent on the object of theology, with Thomas of Strasbourg on the speculative/practical balance of theology, and with Duns Scotus on the overarching issue of the relationship of God's self-knowledge (archetypal theology) to our theology. Henry of Ghent and Giles of Rome represent a cautiously modified Thomism inasmuch as they attempt to synthesize the tradition of Augustinian theology with Aristotelian philosophy but attend closely to the dangers of such a synthesis. Giles, together with Gregory of Rimini and Thomas of Strasbourg, represents the Augustinianism of the Order of Saint Augustine, a branch of which would produce Staupitz and Luther and, later on, Peter Martyr Vermigli and Jerome Zanchi. Scotus' perspective on theology, moreover, represents an Augustinian vision of divine transcendence in union with a critical perspective on the limits of human reason over against the more optimistic synthesis proposed by Thomas Aquinas. In each case, the Reformed scholastics seek out a position more critical of the powers of human reason and more traditionally Augustinian than that of Aquinas, without, however, moving over into a fully nominalistic perspective. The scholasticism they chose, in other words, as the approved results of earlier investigations was the scholasticism most attuned to the theology of the Reformers.

In effect, the process of development that we have just traced in the prolegomena represents the attempt of succeeding generations of Protestants to come to terms with the establishment of the great sixteenth-century protest as a church in its own right and with the need of that new ecclesiatical establishment to be orthodox and, indeed, "catholic" in the broadest sense of the term. The establishment of orthodoxy or "right teaching" through scholastic method and the establishment of ties to the tradition through recourse to patristic and medieval sources manifest a successful process of institutionalization and catholicization. To fault the Protestant scholastics for producing an all-encompassing dogmatic system of right teaching and thereby "domesticating" the dynamic theology of the Reformation is, in fact, to fault Protestantism for its success in surviving as a church. Protestant orthodox theology is different from the theology of the Reformation—more so in form than in substance—but it is this very difference that marks its historical and doctrinal importance in the life of the Protestant churches.

Abbreviations

art. article

Baier–Walther *Compendium theologiae positivae*, adjectis notis amplioribus . . . denuo edendum curavit, C. F. G. Walther, 3 vols. in 4. St. Louis: Concordia, 1879.

cap. caput (chapter)

CO *Ioannis Calvini opera quae supersunt omnia.* Edited by G. Baum, E. Cunitz, and E. Reuss. 31 vols. Brunswick: Schwetschke, 1863–1900.

DLGT Richard A. Muller. *Dictionary of Latin and Greek Theological Terms, Drawn Principally from Protestant Scholastic Theology.* Grand Rapids: Baker Book House, 1985.

DTEL Heinrich Schmid. *Doctrinal Theology of the Evangelical Lutheran Church.* Trans. Charles E. Hay and Henry Jacobs. Minneapolis: Augsburg, n.d.

Glaubenslehre Schweizer, Alexander. *Die Glaubenslehre der Evangelisch–Reformirten Kirche dargestellt und aus den Quellen belegt.* 2 vols. Zurich: Orell, Füssli and Comp., 1844–47.

obj. objection

par. paragraph

PL *Patrologia cursus completus. Series Latina.* Ed. J.-P. Migne. 221 vols. Paris, 1844–55.

prol. prologue/prolegomenon

q. question

RD Heinrich Heppe. *Reformed Dogmatics set out and illustrated from the sources*, Foreword by Karl Barth; revised and edited by Ernst Bizer; trs. by G. T. Thomson. Grand Rapids: Baker Book House, 1978.

RE *Realencyclopaedie fuer protestantische Theologie und Kirche.* Edited by A. Hauck. 3rd ed. 24 vols. Leipzig: J. C. Hinrich, 1896–1913.

Sent. *Sententiarum*, i.e., a commentary on the *Sentences* of Lombard.

Notes

Chapter 1. The Study of Protestant Scholasticism

1. See François Wendel, *Calvin: The Origins and Development of His Religious Thought*, trans. Philip Mairet (New York: Harper & Row, 1963), pp. 144–49.

2. See below, 8.1, and *The Lutheran Cyclopedia*, s.v. "Scholasticism in the Lutheran Church," for one of the clearest and most precise definitions of the phenomenon of Protestant scholasticism. Also see *The New Catholic Encyclopedia*, s.v. "Scholastic Method" and "Scholasticism," and the excellent description of Protestant scholasticism in Robert Preus, *The Inspiration of Scripture: A Study of the Seventeenth Century Lutheran Dogmaticians* (London: Oliver and Boyd, 1955), pp. xv–xvi.

3. Cf. Brian Armstrong, *Calvinism and the Amyraut Heresy: Protestant Scholasticism and Humanism in Seventeenth Century France* (Madison: University of Wisconsin Press, 1969), p. 32; with John S. Bray, *Theodore Beza's Doctrine of Predestination* (Nieuwkoop: De Graaf, 1975), pp. 12–14; and below, 8.2.

4. Otto Ritschl, *Dogmengeschichte des Protestantismus*, 4 vols. (Leipzig and Göttingen, 1908–27).

5. Hans Emil Weber, *Reformation, Orthodoxie und Rationalismus*, 2 vols. (Gütersloh, 1937–51).

6. E.g., I. A. Dorner, *History of Protestant Theology*, trans. George Robson and Sophia Taylor, 2 vols. (Edinburgh, 1871); and Wilhelm Gass, *Geschichte der protestantischen Dogmatik*, 4 vols. (Berlin, 1854).

7. E.g., Basil Hall, "Calvin Against the Calvinists," in *John Calvin*, ed. G. E. Duffield (Appleford: Sutton Courtney Press, 1966), pp. 18–37; R. T. Kendall, *Calvin and English Calvinism to 1647* (Oxford: Oxford University Press, 1979); Holmes Rolston, III, *John Calvin versus the Westminster Confession* (Richmond: John Knox, 1972).

8. Gerhard Ebeling, *The Study of Theology*, trans. Duane Priebe (Philadelphia: Fortress, 1978), p. 134.

9. Ibid., p. 134.

10. Ibid., p. 134.

11. Ibid., pp. 134–35.

12. J. S. Whale, *The Protestant Tradition* (Cambridge: Cambridge University Press, 1962), p. 121.

13. See Paul Oskar Kristeller, *Renaissance Thought: The Classic, Scholastic, and Humanist Strains* (New York: Harper & Row, 1961), pp. 24–47; John Dillenberger, *Protestant Thought and Natural Science: A Historical Interpretation* (Nashville: Abingdon, 1960), pp. 51–54; and Charles B. Schmitt,

Aristotle and the Renaissance (Cambridge, Mass.: Harvard University Press, 1983), pp. 10-33.

14. The division of orthodoxy into early, high, and late periods draws upon the excellent brief analysis of Reformed theology in Otto Weber, *Grundlagen der Dogmatik* (Neukirchen, 1955) I: 140-48; cf. the translation, *Foundations of Dogmatics* (Grand Rapids: Eerdmans, 1981-82) I: 120-27. Weber's survey of the era of orthodoxy is one of the more accurate and balanced accounts presently available.

15. This so-called "pragmatic" reason for the rise of orthodoxy was argued by several seventeenth- and eighteenth-century writers and, more recently, in a modified form by Ernst Troeltsch who viewed pedagogical rather than polemical needs as the basis of the development of orthodoxy. See the discussion in Robert P. Scharlemann, *Thomas Aquinas and John Gerhard* (New Haven: Yale, 1964), pp. 14-16, and the somewhat more detailed presentation of the history of scholarship, on which Scharlemann is obviously dependent, in Ernst Lewalter, *Spanish-jesuitisch und deutsch-lutherische Metaphysik des 17. Jahrhunderts* (Hamburg, 1935; repr. Darmstadt, 1968), pp. 8-19.

16. See Richard A. Muller, "*Vera Philosophia cum sacra Theologia nusquam pugnat*: Keckermann on Philosophy, Theology, and the Problem of Double Truth," in *Sixteenth Century Journal* XV/3 (1984): 341-65.

17. See below, 8.1.

18. Alexander Schweizer, *Die protestantischen Centraldogmen in ihrer Entwicklung innerhalb der reformierten Kirche*, 2 vols. (Zurich, 1854-56); Wilhelm Gass, *Geschichte der protestantischen Dogmatik; Ernst Troeltsch, Vernunft und Offenbarung bei Gerhard und Melanchthon* (Göttingen, 1891); and cf. Scharlemann, *Aquinas and Gerhard*, pp. 15-16; Lewalter, *Metaphysik*, pp. 11-14.

19. See below, 2.4.

20. Robert Bellarmine, *De controversiis christianae fidei adversus hujus temporis haereticos* (Rome, 1581-93).

21. Muller, "*Vera Philosophia*," pp. 363-64.

22. Cf. Peter Petersen, *Geschichte der aristotelischen Philosophie im protestantischen Deutschland* (Leipzig, 1921; repr. Stuttgart, 1964), p. 208, with Ernst Lewalter, *Metaphysik*, pp. 35-38.

23. Scharlemann, *Aquinas and Gerhard*, p. 18.

24. See Charles Singer, *A Short History of Scientific Ideas to 1900* (London: Oxford University Press, 1959), pp. 218-97. Singer traces the loss of the Aristotelian-Ptolemaic worldview and shows how the new scientific worldview could not coalesce before Newton. On the problem of orthodoxy and rationalism, see below, 2.5.

25. Cf. E. M. W. Tillyard, *The Elizabethan World Picture* (New York: Vintage, 1942), pp. 24-25, 66-67; and Arthur O. Lovejoy, *The Great Chain of Being* (Cambridge, Mass.: Harvard University Press, 1936), pp. 183-207.

26. See Dillenberger, *Protestant Thought*, pp. 39–41, 52–54; Schmitt, *Aristotle and the Renaissance*, pp. 28–33, 103–9; Petersen, *Geschichte der aristotelischen Philosophie*; and Charles Schmitt, *John Case and Aristotelianism in Renaissance England* (Montreal: McGill–Queen's University Press, 1983); and Armstrong, *Calvinism and the Amyrant Heresy*, pp. 127–28.

27. Schmitt, *John Case*, pp. 9–10.

28. See in particular Episcopius, *Institutiones theologicae*, in *Opera* (Amsterdam, 1650), vol. 1; and Richard A. Muller, "The Federal Motif in Remonstrant Theology from Arminius to Limborch," in *Nederlands Archief voor Kerkgeschiedenis* 62/1(1982): 102–22.

29. See Alexander Schweizer, *Die Glaubenslehre der evangelisch-reformirten Kirche dargestellt und aus den Quellen belegt* (Zurich, 1844–47) I: 89, 130–31.

30. See Richard A. Muller, "The Debate over the Vowel Points and the Crisis in Orthodox Hermeneutics," in *Journal of Medieval and Renaissance Studies* 10/1 (1980): 53–72.

31. See John Gurr, *The Principle of Sufficient Reason in Some Scholastic Systems, 1750–1900* (Milwaukee, Wis.: Marquette, 1959), pp. 51–90.

Chapter 2.   The Development of Theological Prolegomena

1. Otto Weber, *Grundlagen der Dogmatik*, (Neukirchen, 1955) I: 10; *Foundations*, I: 4–5.

2. Hugh of St. Victor, *Eruditionis didascalicae libri vii*, in *PL* 176, cols. 739–838; also, *The Didascalion of Hugh St. Victor*, trans. Jerome Taylor (New York: Columbia University Press, 1961).

3. Hugh of St. Victor, *Summa sententiarum septem tractatibus distinita*, in *PL* 176, cols. 43–45.

4. Hugh of St. Victor, *De sacramentis christianae fidei*, in *PL* 176, cols. 183–86.

5. Ibid., col. 185.

6. Ibid., col. 183.

7. Cf. Yves M.-J. Congar, *A History of Theology*, trans. Hunter Guthrie (Garden City: Doubleday, 1968), pp. 79–80; with Johannes Beumer, *Die theologische Methode: Handbuch der Dogmengeschichte* (Freiburg: Herder, 1972), I/6: 72–73; and note the discussions of theology as *scientia* in Alexander of Hales, *Summa theologica* (Quaracchi, 1924–58), intro., q.i; Thomas Aquinas, I *Sent.*, prol., art. 1,q.2, in *Opera Omnia* (Parma, 1852–73), vol. 6; Albertus Magnus, *Summa*, prol., q.1 in *Opera* (Paris, 1890–99), vol. 1; and, on this development, see Ulrich Koepf, *Die Anfänge der theologischen Wissenschaftstheorie im 13. Jahrhundert* (Tübingen: J. C. B.

Mohr, 1974), pp. 125–54; also note the important essay on "Theology as Science in the History of Theology" that appears as chapter four of Wolfhart Pannenberg, *Theology and the Philosophy of Science*, trans. F. McDonagh (Philadelphia: Westminster, 1976), pp. 229–96.

8. See Peter Lombard, *Sententiae in IV libris distinctae*, editio tertia, 2 vols. (Grottaferrata: Collegii S. Bonaventurae ad Claras Aquas, 1971–81). On the sources, composition and subsequent editing of the *Sententiae*, see ibid., I: 117*–29*, 143*–44*; Lombard's contribution to theological prolegomena is in *Sent.*, I, dist. 1, cap. 1–2.

9. Aristotle, *Nichomachean Ethics*, VI.3–8:1139b–1142a, in *The Basic Works of Aristotle*, edited by Richard McKeon (New York: Random House, 1941), pp. 1024–1130; see further below, 5.1.

10. William of Auxerre, *Summa aurea* (Paris, 1500), fol. 131d, 254c; cited in Congar, *A History*, pp. 89–90.

11. Robert Kilwardby, *De natura theologiae*, ed. Friedrich Stegmüller (Aschendorff, 1935), cap. 2, 3, 4, 5.

12. See Alexander of Hales, *Summa theologica*, intro., q.i, cap. 1–2; q.ii, memb. 3, cap. 3; Bonaventure, I *Sent.*, prol., q.1, in *Opera* (Quaracchi, 1882–1902), cf. Pannenberg, *Theology and the Philosophy of Science*, pp. 8–11.

13. Alexander of Hales, *Summa theologica*, intro., q.i, cap. 4, art. 2.

14. Cf. Congar, *A History*, pp. 120–21.

15. M. D. Chenu, "*La théologie comme science au XIIIe siecle*," in *Archives d'Histoire Doctrinale et Littéraire du Moyen Age* 2(1927): 53–56.

16. Ibid., pp. 62–65.

17. Thomas Aquinas, *Summa theologiae*, 5 vols. (Madrid, 1962–65) I^a, q.1, art. 2–8; and cf. Pannenberg, *Theology and the Philosophy of Science*, pp. 229–230.

18. Augustine, *De doctrina christiana*, I. ii–iii; II. vii. 9–11, in *PL* 34.19–20, 39–40.

19. See Henry of Ghent, *Summae quaestionum* (Paris, 1520), art VIII, q.iii., on the goal of theology viewed as praxis.

20. Gordon Leff, *Medieval Thought: St. Augustine to Ockham* (Baltimore: Penguin, 1958), p. 241.

21. Cf. Gerard of Boulogne, *Summa*, q.3,a.3; q.4,a.1.; with Paul de Vooght, *Les Sources de la doctrine Chrétienne d'après les theologiens du xive siecle et du début du xve siecle* (Paris, 1954), pp. 33–52 [Gerard's *Summa* is found in de Vooght, pp. 265–483].

22. Congar, *A History*, p. 130.

23. The dictum, "Deus solus theologus est, nos vero sumus discipuli eius" is cited by the medieval teachers as a maxim drawn from Augustine's *De doctrina christiana*. I have not found the maxim verbatim in Augustine (cf. Walter Moore's annotation in his edition of Johann Eck, *In primum librum sententiarum annotatiunculae* [Leiden, 1976], p. 16), but there are several passages in Book IV that point in this direction: true wisdom does not belong to us but descends from the Father of Lights (IV.v.7); God assists us in discourse about him and gives us an eloquence beyond our powers (IV.xviii.37; xxix.62). These passages coincide with the language of Henry of Ghent who cites *De doctrina christiana*, IV, as indicating that "God alone is the teacher of sacred scripture" and that no one can learn the truth of blessed living unless made "teachable" by God (*Summae quaestionum*, art. XI., q.1).

24. Durandus de Saint Pourçain, *In Petri Lombardi sententias . . . libri IV* (Venice, 1571), prol., q.1.

25. Peter Aureole, *Scriptum super primum sententiarum*, ed. Eligius Buytaert (St. Bonaventure, New York, 1952), I, proem., 1, q.A, 2–3.

26. Cf. Congar, *A History*, pp. 154–65.

27. See below, chapter 8, and August Lang, *Die Loci theologici des Melchior Cano und die Methode des dogmatischen Beweises. Ein Beitrag zur theologischen Methodologie und ihrer Geschichte* (Munich, 1925).

28. Cf. Heiko Oberman, *Masters of the Reformation: The Emergence of a New Intellectual Climate in Europe*, trans. Dennis Martin (Cambridge: Cambridge University Press, 1981), pp. 64–110.

29. Cf. Yves M. J. Congar, *Tradition and Traditions: An Historical and Theological Essay* (New York: Macmillan, 1967), pp. 116–17, 138–39, with Heiko Oberman (ed.), *Forerunners of the Reformation* (New York, 1966), pp. 53–65.

30. Cited in Roland Bainton, *Here I Stand: A Life of Martin Luther* (Nashville: Abingdon, 1950), p. 185.

31. Cf. the interpretation of "right reason" in Martin Brecht, *Martin Luther: His Road to Reformation, 1483–1521*, trans. James L. Schaaf (Philadelphia: Fortress, 1985), p. 460.

32. Paul Althaus, *The Theology of Martin Luther*, trans. Robert C. Schultz (Philadelphia: Fortress, 1966), p. 3.

33. Cf. Oberman, *Forerunners*, pp. 53–65; with Althaus, *Theology*, p. 3.

34. Cf. Reinhold Seeberg, *Textbook of the History of Doctrines*, trans. Charles Hay (Grand Rapids: Baker Book House, 1977), II, pp. 191–94; Otto Scheel, *Martin Luther: Vom Katholizismus zur Reformation*, (Tübingen, 1921), II; 173. For a somewhat more moderate view of Biel, see Heiko Oberman, *The Harvest of Medieval Theology: Gabriel Biel and Late Medieval Nominalism*, revised edition (Grand Rapids: Eerdmans, 1967), pp. 68–89. Oberman does concur in the strict separation of natural and revealed knowledge. On Trutvetter, see E. G. Schwiebert, *Luther and His Times: The Reformation from a New Perspective* (St. Louis: Concordia, 1950), pp.

168–69, 173; and Oberman, *Masters*, p. 250. Also see Congar, *A History*, pp. 135–36; and see the extended discussion of the background of Luther's early theology in Alister E. McGrath, *Luther's Theology of the Cross: Martin Luther's Theological Breakthrough* (Oxford: Blackwell, 1985), pp. 27–92.

35. Cf. Congar, *A History*, pp. 155–56; with T. M. Pégues, "Théologie Thomiste d'apres Capréolus: De la voie rationelle que nous conduite a Dieu," in *Revue Thomiste* 8 (1900): 288–309. Also see L. Charlier, *Essai sur le probleme théologique* (Paris, 1938), pp. 15–25; and cf. the excellent analysis of early twentieth-century debate on the "nature and method of theology" according to the medieval scholastics in Auricchio, *The Future of Theology* (Staten Island, New York: Alba House, 1970) pp. 121–90.

36. Cf. Walter von Loewenich, *Luther's Theology of the Cross*, trans. Herbert Bouman (Minneapolis: Augsburg Press, 1976), pp. 70–77; Regin Prenter, *Luther's Theology of the Cross* (Philadelphia: Muhlenberg Press, 1971), pp. 13–14.

37. Paul Vignaux, *Luther, Commentateur des Sentences* (Paris, 1935), pp. 24–30.

38. Althaus, *Theology of Martin Luther*, p. 21.

39. See below, 6.1.

40. Philipp Melanchthon, *Loci communes* (1533) in *Opera quae supersunt omnia*, vol. 21 (Brunswick: Schwetschke, 1854), col. 253–54. The definitive study of Melanchthon's concept of historical or scriptural *series* is Peter Fraenkel, *Testimonia Patrum: The Function of Patristic Argument in the Theology of Philip Melanchthon* (Geneva, 1961), pp. 52–109.

41. Philipp Melanchthon, *Loci praecipui theologici* (1559), in *Opera*, col. 603.

42. See below, chapter 8.

43. Philipp Melanchthon, *Brevis discendae theologiae ratio*, in *Opera*, vol. 2, cols. 455–62.

44. Ibid., cols. 456–57.

45. Philipp Melanchthon, *Loci praecipui theologici* (1559) in *Opera*, vol. 21, col. 607–08.

46. Ibid., col. 607–8; cf. *Loci communes* (1541), in ibid, col. 349.

47. Cf. the *Loci theologici Germanice* in *Opera*, vol. 22, col. 66; with *Loci communes* (1541) in *Opera*, vol. 21, col. 349.

48. See below, 6.2.

49. See below, 1.3 and 3.1.

50. Martin Bucer, *Summarischer Vergriff der Christlichen Lehre und Religion* (Strasbourg, 1541), articles 1-4; cf. the critical text in Martin Butzer, *Deutsche Schriften*, vol. 17 (Gütersloh: Gerd Mohn, 1981), pp. 122-24. The earlier document, *Das ym selbs niemant sonder andereen leben soll . . .* is found in *Deutsche Schriften*, vol. 1 (Gütersloh: Gerd Mohn, 1960), pp. 44-67.

51. Cf. the comments in George R. Crooks and John F. Hurst, *Theological Encyclopedia and Methodology on Basis of Hagenbach*, rev. ed. (New York: Hunt E. Eaton, 1894), p. 123. I have not been able to obtain a copy of this document.

52. See Benjamin B. Warfield, "On the Literary History of Calvin's Institutes," in *Calvin and Calvinism* (New York: Oxford University Press, 1931), pp. 373-428; and Jean-Daniel Benoit, "The History and Development of the *Instituto:* How Calvin Worked," in *John Calvin*, ed. G. E. Duffield (Appleford: Sutton Courtney Press, 1966), pp. 102-17.

53. See below, 5.2 and 5.3.

54. Vermigli's *Loci communes* (London, 1576; 1583) are a posthumous compilation, gathered from Vermigli's exegetical, doctrinal and philosophical works by Robert Masson and arranged by him after the pattern of Calvin's *Institutes*. Although there must always be some question concerning the applicability of Calvin's outline to Vermigli's thought, there can be no doubt of the impact of the *Loci* on the rise of orthodoxy.

55. See below, 5.1 and 5.2.

56. John Patrick Donnelly, "Calvinist Thomism," in *Viator* 7(1976): 441-45.

57. Cf. Muller, "*Vera Philosophia*," pp. 343-44.

58. Musculus, *Loci communes sacrae theologiae* (Basel, 1573), cap. 1, lxi; and see below, 5.3.

59. See below, chapter 8.

60. Andreas Hyperius, *Methodi theologiae* (Basel, 1568), pp. 2-6.

61. Robert Preus, *The Theology of Post-Reformation Lutheranism* (St. Louis: Concordia, 1970-72), I: 82-88. Preus surveys Hyperius' work at length, viewing him as essentially Lutheran. Perhaps more correctly Hyperius should be viewed as a Melanchthonian mediating figure whose views on the Lord's Supper would ultimately be received with more enthusiasm by the Reformed than the Lutherans.

62. The first printing of this work bears the title, *De recte formando theologiae studio* (Basel, 1556); the later editions, titled as above, appeared in 1559, 1572, and 1582.

63. Cf. Andreas Hyperius, *De theologo, sive de ratione studii theologici, libri iiii* (Basel, 1559), pp. 455-507.

64. See below, 8.1 and 9.3.

65. Jean Barnaud, *Pierre Viret, sa vie et son oeuvre* (Saint–Amans, 1911; repr. Niewkoop, 1973), p. 694.

66. *Briefs et divers sommaires et catechismes de la doctrine chrestienne* . . . (published under a similiar title in 1561).

67. *Exposition de la doctrine de la foy chrestienne, touchant la vraye cognoissance & le vray service de Dieu: & la Trinité des personnes en l'unité de l'essence divine: & la manifestation d'iceluy en la creation tant du grand que petit mode, & en sa providence en toutes creatures, & principalement en la nature humaine: & la naissance & accroissement & estat ordinaire de la vraye que de la fausse Eglise* (Geneva, 1564).

68. See below, 5.1.

69. Zacharias Ursinus, *Explicationes catecheseos*, in *Opera theologica*, edited by Quirinius Reuter, 3 vols. (Heidelberg, 1612), I, col. 51.

70. Jerome Zanchi, *Operum theologicorum*, 8 vols. (Geneva, 1617), VIII, col. 319. Zanchi discusses, at length, the problem of the knowledge of God in his *Compendium praecipuorum capitum doctrinae christianae*: cf. *Opera*, VIII, cols. 621–639, and below, 5:3.

71. Ibid., col. 319.

72. Benedict Aretius, *Examen theologicum, brevi et perspicua methodo conscriptum* (1557; Lausanne, 1579); *SS. theologiae problemata, seu loci communes, et miscellaneae quaestiones* (1573; Geneva, 1589).

73. Benedict Aretius, *Theologiae problemata*, I–II.

74. Antoine Chandieu, *De verbo Dei scripto* . . . . *Praefatio de vera methodo theologice simul et scholastice disputandi*, in *Opera theologica* (Geneva, 1593), pp. 7–9; and cf. Ritschl, *Dogmengeschichte*, I: 183–85. Note that a similar interest in a properly biblical use of scholastic method is evident in Reformed theology throughout the seventeenth century: cf. Benedict Pictet, *Theologia christiana* (Geneva, 1686), praef. and below, 8.1.

75. Cf. Francis Junius' early (before 1590) *Theses theologiae* with his later theses and with his *De vera theologia*, thesis 5 (1594), in *Opuscula*, ed. Abraham Kuyper (Amsterdam, 1882), pp. 289–90, 104–5, 41.

76. See below, particularly chapters 2 and 6.

77. Cf. Arminius, *Opera theologica* (Frankfurt, 1635), pp. 22–58 (the orations *De obiecto theologiae; De authore & fine theologiae;* and *De certitudine sacrosanctae theologiae*) and pp. 269–72 (disputations *De ipsa theologia; De methodo qua theologia informanda est; De beatitudine, fine theologiae; De religione;* and *De norma religionis verbo Dei*).

78. See below, 5.1 and 5.2.

79. See below, 7.2 and 7.3.

80. See below, 2.5 and 7.3

81. Cf. Franz Burmann, *Synopsis theologiae et speciatim occonomia foederum Dei* (Geneva, 1678); with Abraham Heidanus, *Corpus theologiae christianae* (Leiden, 1686), I: 8, 11.

82. Maresius, *Collegium theologicum sive systema breve universae theologiae* (Groningen, 1659), I.xv–xxiii; cf. Voetius, *De ratione humana in rebus fidei*, in *Selectae disputationes theologicae*, 5 vols. (Utrecht, 1648–69), I, pp. 1–12.

83. Richard A. Muller, *Christ and the Decree: Christology and Predestination in Reformed Theology from Calvin to Perkins* (Durham, N.C.: Labyrinth Press, 1986), pp. 1–2, 176–80, 226 n.1.

84. Hermann Bauke, *Die Probleme der Theologie Calvins* (Leipzig, 1922), pp. 22, 30–31.

85. Cf. Bizer, *Frühorthodoxie und Rationalismus* (Zurich, 1963), pp. 6–9; Basil Hall, "Calvin against the Calvinists," pp. 18–37; and Walter Kickel, *Vernunft und Offenbarung bei Theodor Beza* (Neukirchen, 1967), pp. 128–29.

86. Cf. Muller, *Christ and the Decree*, pp. 79–84.

87. Cf. Richard A. Muller, "Perkins' A *Golden Chaine*: Predestinarian System or Schematized *Ordo Salutis?*" in *Sixteenth Century Journal*, IX/1 (1978), pp. 69–81.

88. Cf. Muller, *Christ and the Decree*, pp. 86–87, 162, 168.

89. See below, 9.3.

90. See below, chapter 8.

91. Thomas Aquinas, *Summa theologiae*, Iᵃ, q.23, art. 1; cf. introduction to the *quaestio* where the subject of the first article is given alternatively as "*utrum Deo conveniat praedestinatio.*" Alexander of Hales placed predestination in the doctrine of God under the topic "*De scientia Dei relate ad salvanda,*" that is, under the *scientia Dei* (*Summa theologica*, V, Sec. ii, q.4). In neither case is a predestinarian metaphysic indicated.

92. Cf. Zanchi, *De natura Dei*, lib. V. cap. 2 in *Opera theologicarum* (Geneva, 1617), II; with Maccovius, *Loci communes theologici* (Amsterdam, 1658), xxv.

93. Muller, *Christ and the Decree*, pp. 149–54, 156–59.

94. Ibid., pp. 178–81.

95. Cf. Althaus, *Die Prinzipien, der deutschen reformierten Dogmatik in Zeitalter der aristotelischen Scholastik* (Leipzig: Deichert, 1914), pp. 126–78, where Althaus argues the issue of natural and revealed theology under the rubrics of covenant and Law/gospel; also pp. 191–97, where he attempts to relate the doctrine of the decrees to the problem of knowledge of God.

96. *RD*, pp. 1–11.

97. Schweizer, *Glaubenslehre*, I: 138–39, 144–45, 188–90.

98. Ibid., p. 45; Schweizer also uses the more famous Schleiermacherian term, "schlechthinige Abhängigkeitsgefühl," feeling of utter dependence (p. 72); and cf. pp. 64, 79–80.

99. Cf. Schweizer, *Glaubenslehre*, I: 101 on the deduction of the system from the doctrine of God; and ibid., pp. 40–52, 135–49, on the implications of absolute dependence.

100. Armand Saintes, *A Critical History of Rationalism in Germany from Its Origin to the Present Time* (London: Simpkin, Marshall and C., 1849), pp. 12, 17.

101. Ibid., pp. 27–28.

102. Ibid., pp. 43–47.

103. Ibid., pp. 51–52, 54.

104. Ibid., pp. 64–68.

105. Ibid., pp. 92–96.

106. J. M. Robertson, *A History of Freethought, Ancient and Modern to the Period of the French Revolution*, 4th rev. ed. (1936; repr. London: Dawsons, 1969), I: 498, 503, 509; cf. W. E. H. Lecky, *History of the Rise and Influence of the Spirit of Rationalism in Europe*. (New York: Appleton, 1884), I: 79, 371.

107. Robertson, *History of Freethought*, I: 507.

108. John Fletcher Hurst, *History of Rationalism* (New York: Eaton & Mains, 1901), pp. 334–36.

109. Hans Emil Weber, *Reformation, Orthodoxie und Rationalismus* (Darmstadt: Wissenschaftliche Buchgesellschaft, 1966), I/2, pp. 268–69.

110. Ibid., pp. 270–71.

111. Ibid., pp. 274–77.

112. Ibid., pp. 278–79.

113. Ibid., p. 283.

114. Ibid., pp. 287, 288.

115. Ernst Bizer, *Frühorthodoxie und Rationalismus* (Zurich: EVZ-Verlag, 1963).

116. Ernst Bizer, "Die reformierte Orthodoxie und der Cartesianismus," in *Zeitschrift für Theologie und Kirche*, 55 (1958): 306-72.

117. Bizer, *Frühorthodoxie*, pp. 6-15 (on Beza), pp. 16-32 (on Ursinus), pp. 32-50 (on Daneau). We note the improbability of arguing development through such diverse topics; cf. Muller, *Christ and the Decree*, pp. 6-7.

118. Contra Bizer, *Frühorthodoxie*, p. 9.

119. Dillenberger, *Protestant Thought*, pp. 65-66.

120. See below, 7.2-7.3.

121. See below, 9.3 and note the descriptions of the assumptions of eighteenth-century rationalist dogmatics in Saintes' *Critical History* (pp. 64-86) and Hurst's *History* (pp. 126-39, 199-207).

122. Bernhard de Moor, *Commentarius perpetuus in Joh. Marckii compendium . . .*, 6 vols. (Leiden, 1761-71); Johann Alexander Doederlein, *Institutio theologi christiani in capitibus religionis theoreticis*, 2 pts. (Nuremberg, 1787); Samuel Friedrich Morus, *Commentarius exegetico-historicus, in suam theologiae christianae epitomen*, 2 vols. (Halle, 1797-98).

123. Bizer, *Frühorthodoxie*, p. 6.

124. Cf. Friedrich August Tholuck, *Vorgeschichte des Rationalismus*, 4 vols. (Berlin, 1853-62)

125. See below, 6.2, and cf. 7.2.

126. See Richard A. Muller, "Scholasticism Protestant and Catholic: Francis Turretin on the Object and Principles of Theology," in *Church History* 55/2 (June, 1986): 193-205.

127. See below, 7.3.

128. Cf. Ernst Lewalter, *Spanisch-jesuitische und deutsch-lutherische Metaphysik des 17. Jahrhunderts* (Hamburg, 1935) for a discussion of the influx of traditional Aristotelian metaphysics into the Protestant university.

129. See below, I.4; 5.1; 6.3; 6.1; 6.2; and 7.3.

130. Frank Thilly, *A History of Philosophy* (New York: Henry Holt, 1941), pp. 221-22.

131. Cf. below, 7.2.

132. Cf. Gass, *Geschichte*, II: 243–44, 303–4.

133. Bizer, "Cartesianismus," pp. 371–72.

134. Ibid., p. 367.

135. See below, chapter 8.

136. Cf. Michael Heyd, "From a Rationalist Theology to a Cartesian Volun-tarism: David Derodon and Jean-Robert Chouet," in *Journal of the History of Ideas*, 40 (1979): 527–42.

137. Cf. Dorner, *History*, II: 252–63; with Bengt Hägglund, *History of Theology*, trans. Gene Lund (St. Louis: Concordia, 1968), pp. 335–39; and Dillenberger, *Protestant Thought*, pp. 163–67, 173–78.

138. See Dillenberger, *Protestant Thought*, pp. 167–73, 178–90.

139. Cf. Hägglund, *History*, pp. 343–51; with Dillenberger, *Protestant Thought*, pp. 173–78, and Weber, *Foundations*, I: 129.

140. Pictet, *Theol. chr.*, I.i.1.

141. Wyttenbach, *Tentamen theologiae dogmaticae*, 3 vols. (Frankfurt, 1748–49), prol. 7–9; and see further, below, 5.3.

Chapter 3. The Meanings of the Terms *Theology* and *Religion*

1. Cf. *RD*, pp. 1–11.

2. Scharpius, *Cursus theologicus* (Geneva, 1620), col. 1.

3. Cf. Polanus, *Syntagma theologiae christianae* (Geneva, 1617), I.i–ii.

4. Maccovius, *Loci communes theologici* (Amsterdam, 1658), I.

5. Cf. the summary in *DLGT*, s.v. "theologia"; with the discussion in Robert Preus, *The Theology of Post-Reformation Lutheranism* (St. Louis: Concordia, 1970–72), I: pp. 110–14.

6. Turretin, *Institutio theologiae elencticae* (Edinburgh, 1847), I.i.1; cf. Alsted, *Praecognita*, in *Methodus sacrosanctae theologiae* (Hanover, 1614), I.i.

7. Polanus, *Syntagma*, I.i; cf. John Owen, *Theologoumena*, I.i.4, in *Works* (Edinburgh, 1847), vol. 17; and Poliander et al., *Synopsis purioris theologiae*, ed. Herman Bavinck (Leiden, 1881), I.ii.

8. Alsted, *Praecognita*, I.i.

9. Scharpius, *Cursus theologicus*, col. 1.

10. Owen, *Theologoumena*, I.i.1–2; Alsted, *Praecognita*, I.i.

11. Turretin, *Inst. theol.* I.i.2.

12. Ibid., I.i.5; cf. Heidanus, *Corpus theologiae*, I (p. 1).

13. Franciscus Gomarus, *Disputationes*, I.i, in *Opera theologia* (Amsterdam, 1644).

14. Walaeus, *Loci communes*, I, in *Opera omnia* (Leiden, 1643), p. 114; similarly, Heidanus, *Corpus theologiae*, I: 1.

15. Scharpius, *Cursus theologicus*, col. 1.

16. Cf. Johannes Altenstaig, *Lexicon theologicum* (Köln, 1619), s.v. "*theologia*."

17. Turretin, *Inst. theol.* I.i.7.

18. Alsted, *Praecognita*, I.ii.

19. Edward Leigh, A *System or Body of Divinity* (London, 1664), p. 2.

20. Ibid., p. 3.

21. Ibid., I.i.

22. John Calvin, *Institutio christianae religionis*, I.i.2–3, in *CO*, vol. 2.

23. Polanus, *Syntagma*, Synopsis Libri I; cf. Wollebius, *Compendium theologiae*, ed. Ernst Bizer (Neukirchen, 1935), praecognita, I.i.

24. Augustine, *De civitate Dei*, VI.v–viii; VII.xxxiii; VIII.1, in *PL*, 41, cols. 180–187, 221–22, 223–25.

25. Polanus, *Syntagma*, I.i.

26. See below, chapter 6.

27. Junius, *De vera theologia*, i.

28. Alsted, *Praecognita*, I.iii.

29. Polanus, *Syntagma*, I.i.

30. Junius, *De vera theologia*, i.

31. Aretius, *Theologiae problemata*, I: 4, citing Justin Martyr, *Second Apology*; Tertullian, *Apology*, c. 44; and Eusebius, *Praeparatio evangelica*, ix.3.

32. Alsted, *Praecognita*, I.iii.; cf. Poliander et al., *Synopsis purioris*, I.xxvi.

33. Junius, *De vera theologia*, i.

34. Walaeus, *Loci communes*, I: 114; cf. Poliander et al., *Synopsis purioris*, I.ix.

35. Polanus, *Syntagma*, I.ii.

36. Junius, *De vera theologia*, ii.

37. William Perkins, A *Golden Chaine*, p. 11, col. 1, in *Works* (Cambridge, 1612–19), vol. I.

38. Cf. Peter Ramus, *Commentariorum de religione christiana* (Frankfurt, 1576), I.i; with William Ames, *Medulla ss. theologiae* (London, 1630), I.i.1.

39. Maccovius, *Loci communes*, I.

40. Mastricht, *Theoretica-practica theologia* (Utrecht, 1724), I.i.xxxvi.

41. Ibid., I.i.16.

42. Junius, *De vera theologia*, i.

43. Schapius, *Cursus theologicus*, cols. 1–2.

44. Polanus, *Syntagma*, I.ii.

45. Ibid., I.ii.

46. Leigh, A *System*, I.i.

47. Ibid.

48. Turretin, *Inst. theol.* I.ii.1.

49. See below, 3.3; 6.2; 6.3.

50. Karl Barth, *Church Dogmatics*, ed. G. W. Bromiley and T. F. Torrance, 4 vols. (Edinburgh: T. & T. Clark, 1936–1969), I/2, pp. 284–91.

51. See below, 6.4.

52. See below, 8.2, on the distinctions between catechetical, ecclesial and scholastic theology.

53. Ulrich Zwingli, *De vera et falsa religione commentarius*, in *Sämtliche Werke*, ed. Emil Egli, Georg Finsler and Walther Köhler, vol. III (Leipzig, 1914), pp. 639-40, 643; cf. Ursinus, *Explicationes catecheseos*, cols. 47-48.

54. Cf. John Calvin, *Institution of the Christian Religion* trans. Ford Lewis Battles (1536; rev. ed. Grand Rapids: Eerdmans, 1986).

55. Mathieu Virel, *A Learned and Excellent Treatise Containing all the Principall Grounds of Christian Religion* (London, 1594), I.i.

56. Ibid.

57. Cf. Polanus, *Syntagma*, IX; Ames, *Medulla*, II.iv; on Ramus and Ramism, see further, below, chapter 7.

58. Cf. Polanus, *Syntagma*, IX.i; Herman Venema, *Institutes of Theology* (Edinburgh, 1850), ii.

59. Zwingli, *Commentarius*, pp. 639-40; Venema, *Institutes*, ii.

60. Lactantius, *Divinae institutiones*, IV. 28, in *PL*, 6, cols. 535-38.

61. Augustine, *De civitate Dei*, X.3, in *PL*, 41, cols. 280-81.

62. Calvin, *Inst.* I.xii.1.

63. Cf. Johannes Marckius, *Compendium theologiae christianae* (Groningen, 1686), III.i.

64. Cf. Ibid., III.i.

65. Augustine, *De civ. Dei*, x.3, *PL*, 41, cols. 280-81.

66. Marckius, *Compendium*, III.i.

67. Ibid., III.iv.

68. Ibid., III.ii.

69. Ibid., III.v.

70. Burmann, *Synopsis theol.* I.ii.4; cf. Maresius, *Collegium theol.*, I.vii.

71. Wendelin, *Christianae theologiae systema maius* (Cassel, 1656), I.i.

72. Polanus, *Syntagma*, Synopsis libri IX.

73. Barth, *CD* I/2, p. 287.

74. Walaeus, *Loci communes*, II: 125.

75. Cf. Barth, *CD*, I/2, p. 285.

76. Walaeus, *Loci communes*, II: 125; cf. Burmann, *Synopsis theol.* I.ii. 18–19.

77. Barth, *CD* I/2, p. 285.

78. Cf. Burmann, *Synopsis theol.*, I.ii; Marckius, *Compendium*, III.

79. Salomon van Til, *Theologiae utriusque compendium* (Leiden, 1719), II.ii.

80. Cf. Wyttenbach, *Tentamen theol.*, prol., 7–8; Johann Reinbeck, *Betrachtungen ueber die in der Augspurischen Confession*, 4 parts (Berlin, 1731–41), I.vii–xxx.

81. Cf. Campegius Vitringa, *Doctrinae christianae religionis* (Arnheim, 1761–86), i.28; Doederlein, *Inst. theol. chr.*, prol. I.i–iii; Knapp, *Lectures on Christian Theology* (New York, 1859), intro., 1, 3, 4.

82. Wendelin, *Christianae theol.*, I.i.

83. Leonhard Riissen, *Summa theologiae didactico–elencticae* (Frankfurt and Leipzig, 1731), I.iii.

84. Further, below, 6.1.

85. Below, 6.3.

86. Below, 9.2.

87. Heppe, *RD*, p. 7.

88. Cf. Burmann, *Synopsis theol.*, I.ii,12–13; Venema, *Institutes*, ii, pp. 23, 27–28; Heidegger, *Corpus theologiae christianae* (Zurich, 1700), I.33.

89. Burmann, *Synopsis theol.*, I.ii.7–8, 12.

90. Cf. Cocceius, *Summa theologiae*, I.xvii (*RD*, p. 4); and Heidegger, *Corpus theol.*, I.xiii.

91. Venema, *Institutes*, ii, p. 27.

92. Ibid., p. 28.

93. See further, below, 5.3.

Chapter 4. The Parts or Divisions of Theology

1. Althaus, *Die Prinzipien*, pp. 230–31.

2. Congar, *A History*, p. 130.

3. Cf. Paul Althaus, *Theology of Martin Luther*, pp. 25–34; and von Loewenich, Luther's Theology of the Cross, pp. 44–49, 75–77, 106–7.

4. Calvin, *Inst.* I.ii.1; II.vi.1.

5. Ibid., I.xiii.7.

6. Polanus, *Syntagma*, Synopsis Libri I.

7. Turretin, *Inst. theol.*, I.i.9.

8. Alsted, *Praecognita*, I.iv.

9. The homiletical implications of this view of the imperfection and limitation of human knowledge of God are clearly outlined in Stephen Charnock, *A Discourse of the Knowledge of God in Christ*, in *The Complete Works of Stephen Charnock* (Edinburgh: Nichol, 1864–66), vol. 4, pp. 127–28, and in his *A Discourse of the Knowledge of God*, in *Works*, vol. 4, pp. 38–41.

10. Alsted, *Praecognita*, I.iv.

11. Maresius, *Collegium theol.*, I.iii; cf. Poliander *et al.*, *Synopsis purioris*, I.iii.

12. Poliander *et al.*, *Synopsis purioris*, I.iii–iv.

13. Alsted, *Praecognita*, I.iv.

14. Ibid.

15. Ibid.

16. Turretin, *Inst. theol.*, I.i.9.

17. Junius, *De vera theologia*, iv; cited verbatim in Alsted, *Praecognita*, I.iv.

18. Ibid.; cf. Scharpius, *Cursus theologicus*, col. 2.

19. Polanus, *Syntagma*, I.iii.

20. Ibid.

21. Ibid.

22. Cf. Junius, *De vera theologia*, iv; Alsted, *Praecognita*, I.iv.

23. Junius, *De vera theologia*, v; cf. Owen, *Theologoumena*, I.iii.2.

24. Alsted, *Praecognita*, I.iv. The discussion in this and the two preceding paragraphs reflects the problems of the classification and predication of divine attributes and once again establishes the intimate relationship of the prolegomena to the theological system as a whole. Further discussion of these two problems is planned for *Post-Reformation Reformed Dogmatics*, volume 3.

25. Lucas Trelcatius, *Scholastica et methodica locorum communium institutio* (London, 1604), Lib. I, pp. 1-2.

26. Gomarus, *Disputationes*, I.xv-xvii; Walaeus, *Loci communes*, I.

27. Polanus, *Syntagma*, I.iii.

28. Ockham, I *Sent.*, prol., q.ix, in *Opera* (St. Bonaventure, New York: The Franciscan Institute, 1967), vol. I.

29. Ibid., p. 268.

30. John Eck, *In primum librum sententiarum annotatiunculae*, edited by Walter Moore (Leiden: Brill, 1976), prol., p. 16.

31. See below, 4.4.

32. Junius, *De vera theologia*, v.

33. E.g., Scharpius, *Cursus theologicus*, col. 2; Polanus, *Syntagma*, I.iii; Turretin, *Inst. theol.*, I.ii.6.

34. Junius, *De vera theologia*, v.

35. Ibid.

36. Junius, *De vera theologia*, v.

37. Polanus, *Syntagma*, I.iv.

38. Ibid.

39. Alsted, *Praecognita*, I.v.

40. Cf. Junius, *De vera theologia*, v; Leigh, *A System*, I.i; Henry of Ghent, *Summa*, art. XIX, q.ii, arg. 1, resp.

41. Polanus, *Syntagma*, I.iv; cf. the virtually identical argument in Alsted, *Praecognita*, I.v.

42. See below, 5.1.

43. Leigh, A *System*, I.i.

44. Cf. Burmann, *Synopsis theol.*, I.36–37; Heidanus, *Corpus theol.*, I: 1–2.

45. E.g., Turretin, *Inst. theol.*, I.ii.6; Heidegger, *Corpus theol.*, I.v; Riissen, *Summa theologiae didactico–elencticae* (Frankfurt, 1731), I.i; Mastricht, *Theoretico–practica theol.*, I.15.

46. For the Lutheran view, cf. Johann Wilhelm Baier, *Compendium theologiae positivae*, edited by C. F. G. Walther, 3 vols., (St. Louis: Concordia, 1879) I: pp. 36–44.

47. Henry of Ghent, *Summa*, art. VIII.

48. Ibid., art. X–XIV.

49. Ibid., art. XIX.

50. Junius, *De vera theologia*, theses 28, 29, 30, 24, 25, 31, 32, 33, respectively.

51. Maccovius, *Loci communes*, I–II (pp. 3–5, 10).

52. Below, 9.3.

53. Scharpius, *Cursus theologicus*, col. 6; cf. Junius, *De vera theologia*, thesis 29; and Alsted, *Praecognita*, I.v.

54. Robert Kilwardby, *De natura theologiae*, 3.

55. Henry of Ghent, *Summa*, art. IX, q.1–2.

56. Cf. Bonaventure, *Breviloquium*, I.ii, in *Opera*, vol. 5.

57. Maccovius, *Loci communes*, I (p. 3); similarly, Poliander et al., *Synopsis purioris*, I.xiii.

58. Gomarus, *Disputationes*, I.xviii–xix.

59. Cf. Bonaventure, *Breviloquium*, prol., 1.

60. Maccovius, *Loci communes*, I (p. 3).

61. Ibid.

62. Junius, *De vera theologia*, xv; Scharpius, *Cursus theologicus*, col. 6; Poliander et al., *Synopsis purioris theologiae*, I.xiv.

63. Junius, *De vera theologia*, xv; Scharpius, *Cursus theologicus*, cols. 6–7.

64. Junius, *De vera theologia*, xv.

65. Scharpius, *Cursus theologicus*, col. 7.

66. Junius, *De vera theologia*, xv; so also Poliander et al., *Synopsis purioris*, I.xv.

67. Cf. Scharpius, *Cursus theologicus*, 7.

68. Polanus, *Syntagma*, I.xiv.

69. Maccovius, *Loci communes*, I.

70. Cf. Maccovius, *Loci communes*, I (p. 4).

71. See 6.2; 6.3; 8.2.

72. Cf. Junius, *De vera theologia*, xiii–xiv; Maccovius, *Loci communes*, I; Polanus, *Syntagma*, I.x.

73. See further, below, 6.1.

74. Gomarus, *Disputationes*, I.xx; cf. Alsted, *Praecognita*, I.v.

75. Henry of Ghent, *Summa*, art XIX, q.ii, arg. 1, resp.

76. Gomarus, *Disputationes*, I.xxi.

77. Alsted, *Praecognita*, I.v.

78. Henry of Ghent, *Summa*, art. XIV, q.1.

79. Poliander et al., *Synopsis purioris*, I.xviii, xxi.

80. Owen, *Theologoumena*, I.iii.6; cf. Charnock, A *Discourse of the Knowledge of God*, in *Works*, Vol. 4, pp. 82–84.

81. Cf. Maccovius, *Loci communes*, I (p. 5); Polanus, *Syntagma*, I.iv, xiv; Alsted, *Praecognita*, I.v.

82. Scharpius, *Cursus theologicus*, col. 7.

83. Polanus, *Syntagma*, I.v.

84. Ibid.

85. Ibid.

86. Polanus, *Syntagma*, I.vi; cf. Alsted, *Praecognita*, I.x.

87. Cf. Henry of Ghent, *Summa*, art. VIII, q.1, resp.

88. See below, 6.3.

89. Calvin, *Inst.* III.iii.19; cf. III.ii.1 and below, 6.1, on the object of theology.

90. Calvin, *Inst.* III.xxv.10.

91. Cf. Maccovius, *Loci communes*, XXV (pp. 209–10).

92. E.g., Hilary of Poitiers, *De trinitate*, IX. 58–75 in *PL*, 10 cols. 327–43.

93. Thomas Aquinas, *Summa theologiae*, I, q.113, a.4, ad 1.

94. Cf. *DTEL*, pp. 16–17.

95. Junius, *De vera theologia*, vi.

96. Cf. Ursinus, *Tractationes theologicae* (Neustadt, 1589), p. 314; Junius, *De vera theologia*, vi; Polanus, *Syntagma*, I.vii; Walaeus, *Loci communes*, I; Alsted, *Praecognita*, I.vi.

97. Alsted, *Praecognita*, I. vi.

98. Walaeus, *Loci communes*, p. 114, col. 2; cf. Junius, *De vera theologia*, v.

99. Walaeus, *Loci communes*, p. 115, col. 1; cf. Polanus, *Syntagma*, I.vii.

100. Walaeus, *Loci communes*, p. 115, col. 1.

101. Junius, *De vera theologia*, vi.

102. See Heiko Oberman, "Some Notes on the Theology of Nominalism," in *Harvard Theological Review* (1960): 57–60.

103. Cf. Junius, *De vera theologia*, vi; Polanus, *Syntagma*, I.vii; Walaeus, *Loci communes*, I; Alsted, *Praecognita*, I. vi.

104. Junius, *De vera theologia*, vi; cf. de Moor, *Commentarius*, I.viii, pp. 30–31.

105. John 3:35, cited by Junius, in *De vera theologia*, vi.

106. Cf. Junius, *De vera theologia*, vi; Polanus, *Syntagma*, I.vii.

107. Junius, *De vera theologia*, vi; cf. Polanus, *Syntagma*, I.vii; and Poliander et al., *Synopsis purioris*, I.v.

108. Cf. Turretin, *Inst. theol.*, XIII.xiii.4, 7.

109. Cf. *DLGT*, s.v. "*communicatio idiomatum.*"

110. Cf. Baier–Walther, I.p.4, and *DTEL*, pp. 16–17, with Preus, *The Theology of Post–Reformation Lutheranism*, I: 167–73.

111. E.g., Turretin, *Inst. theol.*, XIII.viii.19; Mastricht, *Theoretico-practica theologia*, V.x.31.

112. Walaeus, *Loci communes*, I (p. 115a).

113. E.g., Turretin, *Inst. theol.*, XIII.xiii; Mastricht, *Theoretico-practica theologica*, V.x.31.

114. Turretin, *Inst. theol.*, XIII.xiii.2.

115. Ibid., XIII.xiii.1, 3.

116. Cf. Aquinas, *Summa theologiae*, I, q.113, a.4, ad 1; III, q.8, a.4, ad 2; III, q.9, a.2–4.

117. Turretin, *Inst. theol.*, XIII.xiii.1.

118. Ibid., XIII.xiii.12.

119. Cf. Mastricht, *Theoretico-practica theologia*, V.x.31.

120. Cf. Voetius, Wollebius and Keckermann in *RD*, pp. 464–65.

121. Cf. Turretin, *Inst. theol.*, XIII.xiii.12–14.

122. See Richard A. Muller, "Christ in the Eschaton: Calvin and Moltmann on the Duration of the *Munus Regium*," in *The Harvard Theological Review*, 74/1 (1981): 51–59.

123. Alsted, *Praecognita*, I.vi.

124. Cf. Muller, "Christ in the Eschaton," pp. 57–59.

125. See below, section 6.1.

126. See below, 9.1.

127. Cf. Alsted, *Praecognita*, I.xvi, xviii.

128. Cf. *DLGT*, s.v. "*viator.*"

129. Musculus, *Loci communes sacrae theologiae* (Basel, 1573; trans. London, 1578), lxi.

130. Ibid.

131. Polanus, *Syntagma*, I.viii.

132. Gomarus, *Disputationes*, I.xliii.

133. Ibid., I.xliii.

134. Ibid., I.xlv–xlix.

135. Junius, *De vera theologia*, vii.

136. Alsted, *Praecognita*, I.vii.

137. Cf. Junius, *De vera theologia*, vii–viii; Polanus, *Syntagma*, I.viii–ix.

138. Junius, *De vera theologia*, vii; Alsted, *Praecognita*, I.vii.

139. Ibid.; de Moor, *Compendium*, I.ix, p. 34.

140. Junius, *De vera theologia*, vii.

141. See Muller, "Christ in the Eschaton," pp. 51–59.

142. Cf. Aquinas, *Summa*, Iª, q.58, art, 4; q.107; Scotus, *Opus Oxoniense* II, dist. 9 in *Opera omnia*, edited by Luke Wadding (Paris: Vives, 1891–95), vol. 8; Gabriel Biel, *Collectorium circa quattuor libros sententiarum* (Tübingen, 1501), II, dist. 9, art. 2, dubia ii–iii; Alsted, *Praecognita*, I.vii.

143. Junius, *De vera theologia*, viii.

144. Ibid.

145. Ibid., ix; cf. Alsted, *Praecognita*, I.viii.

146. Ibid., I.viii.

147. Polanus, *Syntagma*, I.ix.

148. Ibid., I.xiv.

149. Junius, *De vera theologia*, xii; cf. Alsted, *Praecognita*, I.viii, xvi.

150. See below, 6.2.

151. Cf. Gilson, *The Philosophy of St. Bonaventure*, trans. Dom Illtyd Trethowan and Frank J. Sheed (Paterson: St. Anthony Guild, 1965), pp. 349–64; with Aquinas, *Summa*, II/2ae, q.172, art. 2, resp.

152. John Calvin, Commentary on Hebrews 1:3 in *CO* 55, col. 12.

153. See Ronald S. Wallace, *Calvin's Doctrine of the Word and Sacrament* (Grand Rapids: Eerdmans, 1957), p. 113.

154. See Junius, *De vera theologia*, xii.

155. Cf. Scharpius, *Cursus theologicus*, col. 3; Polanus, *Syntagma*, I.iv.

156. Cf. Polanus, *Syntagma*, I.iv.

157. Junius, *De vera theologia*, xvii.

158. Ibid.

159. Scharpius, *Cursus theologicus*, col. 3.

160. Ibid., col. 3.

161. Ibid., col. 3.

162. Ibid., col. 4.

163. Cf. Junius, *De vera theologia*, xvii.

164. Polanus, *Syntagma*, I.xii.

165. Ibid.

166. Owen, *Theologoumena*, I.iii.2.

167. Ibid., I.iii.3.

168. Polanus, *Syntagma*, I.xiii.

169. Heidegger, *Corpus theol.*, I.67–69; cf. de Moor, *Commentarius*, I.x (p. 36).

170. Heidegger, *Corpus theol.*, I.70; see further, below, 6.3.

171. Emil Brunner, *The Christian Doctrine of God; Dogmatics: vol. 1*, trans. Olive Wyon (Philadelphia: Westminster, 1950), p. 28; cf. the similar comments in Armstrong, *Calvinism and the Amyraut Heresy*, p. 194; and Bray, *Theodore Beza's Doctrine of Predestination*, p. 14.

Chapter 5. Natural and Supernatural Theology

1. Junius, *De vera theologia*, thesis xiv; cf. Maresius, *Collegium theol.*, I.iv–v, on *theologia viatorum* as both natural and revealed or supernatural; also Poliander et al., *Synopsis purioris*, I.vi–vii.

2. Alsted, *Praecognita*, I.xiii.

3. See above, 4.1.

4. Cf. Riissen, *Summa*, I.iv–vii; Heidegger, *Corpus theol.*, I.vii, ix, xii–xiv; Turretin, *Inst. theol.*, I.ii,7; Junius, *De vera theologia*, ix–xi; with *DLGT*, s.v. "revelatio generalis/revelatio specialis."

5. Alsted, *Praecognita*, I.x.

6. Ibid., I.xiv.

7. Ibid., I.xii.

8. Pictet, *Theol. chr.*, I.ii.2,4.

9. Ibid., I.iii.2–3.

10. Ibid.

11. Cf. Althaus, *Die Prinzipien*, pp. 73–95; and Bizer, *Frühorthodoxie*, pp. 32–50.

12. Karl Barth and Emil Brunner, *Natural Theology*, comprising *Nature and Grace*, by Emil Brunner, and the reply, *No*, by Karl Barth, trans. Peter Fraenkel [London: G. Bles, 1946]; Karl Barth, *The Knowledge of God and the Service of God According to the Teaching of the Reformation* [The Gifford Lectures, 1937–38], trans. J. L. M. Haire and Ian Henderson [London: Hodder and Stoughton, 1938]; Edward A. Dowey, *The Knowledge of God in Calvin's Theology* [New York: Columbia University Press, 1952]; T. H. L. Parker, *The Doctrine of the Knowledge of God: A Study in Calvin's Theology*, rev. ed. [Grand Rapids: Eerdmans, 1959].

13. See below, 6.3.

14. Peter Martyr Vermigli, *Loci communes* (London, 1583), I.ii.1.

15. Ibid., I.ii.3.

16. Ibid., I.ii.5.

17. Ibid., I.ii.8.

18. Ibid., I.ii.12.

19. Ibid., I.iv.14.

20. Ibid., I.iv.15.

21. Lambert Daneau, *Christianae isagoges ad Christianorum theologorum locos communes libri II* (Geneva, 1588), in *RD*, p. 3; Aretius, *Theologiae problemata*, I: 1–2; and Riissen, *Summa*, I.vii.

22. Cf. Heidegger, *Corpus theol.*, I.10–11; Turretin, *Inst. theol.*, I.iii.5; iv.8–9; Leigh, A *System*, I.i; Junius, *De vera theologia*, x.

23. Cf. Turretin, *Inst. theol.*, I.iii.4; iv.1; citing Socinus, *Praelectiones theolgicae*, ii.

24. Alsted, *Theologia naturalis*, I.i, in *Methodus* as book III.

25. Maccovius, *Loci communes*, i, p. 5.

26. Cf. Walaeus, *Loci communes*, I (p. 116).

27. Turretin, *Inst. theol.*, I.iii.4 [virtually identically given in Riissen, *Summa*, I.iv]; cf. Pictet, *Theol. chr.*, I.ii.2.

28. John Calvin, *Inst.*, I.iii.1–3; v. 1–2.

29. Cf. *DLGT*, s.v. "cognitio" and "cognitio intuitiva."

30. Turretin, *Inst. theol.*, I.iii.11; cf. de Moor, *Commentarius*, I.xii (p. 41).

31. Cited by Riissen, *Summa*, I.iv; and used by Calvin, *Inst.*, I.iii.1.

32. Turretin, *Inst. theol.*, I.iii.5; cf. Pictet, *Theol. chr.*, I.ii.3.

33. Walaeus, *Loci communes*, I (pp. 115–16).

34. Cf. ibid.; with Owen, *Theologoumena*, I.vii.13; and de Moor, *Commentarius*, X.xii (p. 42). De Moor (p. 47) cites Calvin, *Inst.* I.v, in support of his point.

35. Walaeus, *Loci communes*, I (p. 116).

36. Cf. ibid., with Turretin, *Inst. theol.*, I.iv.; and with Owen, *Theologoumena*, I.iv. 8–10.

37. Mastricht, *Theoretico-practica theologia*, I.i.18–19; note that even Heidanus, whose theology was open to Cartesian influences, agrees on this point (*Corpus theologiae*, I: 2, 13–14; and see below, 7.2.

38. Turretin, *Inst. theol.*, I.vi.4; and see further, below, 5.3, on theology as *habitus*.

39. Heidanus, *Corpus theologiae*, I: 3.

40. Polanus, *Syntagma*, I.x.

41. Ibid., and see below, 6.2.

42. Alsted, *Praecognita*, I.xiii; and see below, 6.2, on the problem of *genus*.

43. Ibid., I.xiv.

44. Ibid., I.xiv.

45. Polanus, *Syntagma*, I.x; cf. Owen, *Theologoumena*, I.vii.28.

46. Polanus, *Syntagma*, I.x; cf. Junius, *De vera theologia*, x; Walaeus, *Loci communes*, I (pp. 118–119).

47. Polanus, *Syntagma*, I.x.

48. Cf. Junius, *De vera theologia*, x; Polanus, *Syntagma*, I.x; Alsted, *Praecognita*, I.xvii.

49. See Richard A. Muller, "*Duplex cognitio Dei* in the Theology of Early Reformed Orthodoxy," in *The Sixteenth Century Journal*, X/2 (1979): 51–61.

50. Calvin, *Inst.*, I.ii.1; vi.1, 2; xiii.9, 11, 23–24; II.vi.1.

51. Ibid., I.ii.1.

52. Cf. ibid., II.vi.1.

53. Cf. ibid., I.iii–v.

54. Pierre Viret, *Exposition familière sur le Symbole des Apostres* (Geneva, 1560), p. 13.

55. Ibid., p. 15.

56. Ibid., p. 15.

57. Calvin, *Inst.*, I.vi.2.

58. Ibid., I.ii.1.

59. Musculus, *Loci communes*, i.

60. Ibid., lxi.

61. Ibid.

62. Ibid.

63. Ibid.

64. Ibid., i.

65. Ibid.

66. Ibid., i.

67. Ibid.

68. Ibid., i.

69. Ibid.

70. Polanus, *Syntagma*, *Synopsis Libri* IX.

71. See above, 4.2; 5.2.

72. Edward Leigh, A *System*, I.ii, citing Zanchi; and note the identical paradigm in Aretius, *Theologiae problemata*, I (p. 3).

73. Zanchi, *Opera*, VIII, col. 617–18.

74. Ibid., col. 627. The chronology of Calvin's and Zanchi's work may indicate that Zanchi influenced Calvin toward the formulation of the concept of *duplex cognitio Dei*.

75. Ibid., cols. 628–29.

76. Ibid., cols. 630–31.

77. Ibid., cols. 631–32.

78. Ibid., col. 633.

79. Ibid., col. 638; cf. col. 710ff., i.e., *locus* 7, *De fide* and *locus* 8, *De Symbols Apostolico*, where Zanchi speaks at length of faith and of knowledge of God in Christ. See especially col. 712 where Zanchi quotes Calvin's definition of faith (from *Inst.* III.ii.7).

80. Charnock, A *Discourse of the Knowledge of God in Christ*, in *Works*, vol. 4, pp. 115–18; cf. Cocceius, *Summa theologiae*, I.xvii (cited in *RD*, pp. 4–5).

81. Ibid., pp. 123–24.

82. Ibid., p. 125.

83. Ibid., pp. 127–28.

84. Cf. T. H. L. Parker, *Knowledge of God*, pp. 34–36.

85. *CO*, 31, col. 194, my italics; cf. Parker, *Knowledge of God*, pp. 34–36.

86. *CO*, 31, col. 199.

87. Heidegger, *Corpus theol.*, I.12.

88. Mastricht, *Theoretico-practica theologia*, I.i.18.

89. Pierre Du Moulin, A *Treatise of the Knowledge of God* (London, 1634), p. 2.

90. Ibid., pp. 3-9.

91. Ibid., pp. 25-26; cf. pp. 4-9.

92. Polanus, *Syntagma*, I.xi.

93. Cf. the citations from Heidegger, Witsius, Keckermann, and the *Leiden Synopsis* in *RD*, pp. 291-92, 364-65.

94. Turretin, *Inst. theol.*, I.iv.3.

95. Ibid., I.iv.20.

96. Cf. ibid. with *DLGT*, s.v. "usus legis"; and Charnock, A *Discourse of the Knowledge of God in Christ*, pp. 123-24; cf. Pictet, *Theol. chr.*, I.i.1.

97. Du Moulin, A *Treatise*, pp. 24-25, 36.

98. Ibid., pp. 55-58; cf. the similar christological argument in Aretius, *Theologiae problematae*, I: 4; and Calvin, *Inst.*, I.ii.1; vi.1.

99. Du Moulin, A *Treatise*, pp. 56-57.

100. Idid., p. 57.

101. Weber, *Foundations*, I: 217.

102. Alsted, *Theologia naturalis*, I.i.

103. Ibid., II, ad fin; cf. de Moor, *Commentarius*, I.xviii (p. 60), on the contents and limits of natural theology; also Pictet, *Theol. chr.*, I.ii.6.

104. Hans Emil Weber, *Reformation, Orthodoxie und Rationalismus*, I/2: 274-77.

105. Cf. *DLGT*, s.v. "usus legis."

106. Cf. Turretin, *Inst. theol.*, XI.i.22-23; with the opposition of the Decalogue in the Westminster *Shorter* (*ad fin.*, following q. 107) and *Larger* catechisms (qq. 91-97); and note, e.g., Junius, *Theses theologicae*, XXIII.3; Wollebius, *Compendium*, XIII.i., propositions 7 and 8.

107. E.g., Turretin, *Inst. theol.*, XII.v.23; Hermann Witsius, *De oecono-mia foederum Dei cum hominibus libri quattuor* (Utrecht, 1694), IV.iv.

108. Muller, "The Federal Motif," pp. 115, 118–19, 121–22.

109. Cf. the citations of Calovius and Reusch in Baier–Walther, I: 9; with Johannes Freylinghausen, *Fundamenta theologiae christianae* (Magde-burg, 1734), I.i.1; and note the still more positive view of natural theology and natural religion in the late eighteenth–century pietist, Knapp, *Christian Theology*, Intro., I.ii.4–5.

110. Above, 1.4.

111. Cf. Sigmund Jacob Baumgarten, *Theses dogmaticae* (Halle, 1767), prol.; and Samuel Endemann, *Institutiones theologiae dogmaticae* (Hanover, 1777–78), prol.; with the pointed statement from Johann Christoph Beck's *Fundamenta theologiae naturalis et revelata* cited in *Glaubenslehre*, I: 187.

112. Cf. Venema, *Institutes*, proleg. and ch. 1 (pp. 8, 10–11); Vitringa, *Doct. chr.* I.16–17; Wyttenbach, *Tentamen theol.*, prol., 4–5.

113. Wyttenbach, *Tentamen theol.*, prol., 7–9; a similar point is implied by Pictet, *Theol. chr.*, I.i.1.

114. Van Til, *Theol. comp.* cf. I.i.4 with II.i; and on the validity of rational theology see I.iv.1, 3, 6.

115. Cited in *Glaubenslehre*, I: 187.

116. De Moor, *Commentarius*, I.xviii (pp. 60–61).

117. See below, 7.2 and 7.3, on the use of philosophy and reason in theo-logical system; and cf. Heidegger, *Corpus theol.*, I.12.

Chapter 6. The Object and Genus of Theology

1. Turretin, *Inst. theol.*, I.v.1–3.

2. Richard of Middleton, *In IV libros sententiarum* (Venice, 1507), prol., q.1.

3. Thomas Aquinas, *Summa theologiae*, I^a, q.1, art. 7; and see further, below, this chapter.

4. Cf. Muller, *Christ and the Decree*, pp. 169–71; and below, this chapter.

5. Hermann Witsius, *Exercitationes sacrae in symbolum* Amsterdam, 1697 *Sacred Dissertations on . . . the Apostles' Creed*, trans. D. Fraser, 2 vols. (Edinburgh, 1823), IV.i.

6. See below, 6.2; 6.4.

7. Cf. John Calvin, *Inst.*, II.vi.4; III.ii.1.

8. Martin Chemnitz, *Loci theologici* (Wittenberg, 1653), p. 12, col. 2.

9. Ibid., p. 13.

10. Cf. below, chapter 9.

11. E.g., Henry of Ghent, *Summa*, art. XIX, q.2; and Bonaventure, I *Sent.*, prol., q.1–4, deal with the *materia*, the *causa formalis*, *causa finalis* and *causa efficiens*, respectively.

12. Cf. Junius, *De vera theologia*, thesis 24.

13. Ibid., xiii; cf. Alsted, *Praecognita*, I.ix.

14. Gomarus, *Disputationes*, I.xx.

15. Walaeus, *Loci communes*, p. 114; cf. Poliander *et al.*, *Synopsis purioris*, I.xii.

16. Turretin, *Inst. theol.*, I.v.4; cf. Aquinas, I *Sent.*, prol, art. 4 and *Summa theologiae*, I^a, art. 7.

17. Aquinas, *Summa theologiae*, I^a, q.1, art. 7, corpus. Note that Aquinas *does not* use the phrase *sub ratione Deitatis* but rather *sub ratione Dei*.

18. Cf. ibid.; with Peter Lombard, I *Sent.*, dist.1, cap.1; and Hugh of St. Victor, *De sacramentis christianae fidei*, c.2, in *PL* 176, p. 183; also see Congar, *A History*, pp. 124–25.

19. Robert Grosseteste, *Hexaemeron*, ed. Richard Dales and Servus Gieben (London: Oxford University Press, 1982), I.i–ii.1; Robert Kilwardby, *De natura theologiae*, ed. Stegmüller (Aschendorff, 1935), pp. 16–17; and also see E. Mersch, "L'objet de la théologie et le 'Christus totus'" in *Recherches de science réligieuse*, 26(1936): 126–57; and Per Erik Persson, *Sacra Doctrina: Reason and Revelation in Aquinas*, trans. Ross Mackenzie (Philadelphia, 1970), pp. 242–44. Mersch (pp. 139–40) cites a fragment of Grosseteste including the same view of the object of theology as expressed in the *Hexaemeron* and notes (p. 145) that this definition reappears in the theology of Ulrich of Strasbourg (d. 1277), a pupil of Albert the Great.

20. Alexander of Hales, *Summa theologica*, I, intro., q.1, cap. 3, art 1, resp.

21. Bonaventure, I *Sent.*, proem., q.1; cf. *Breviloquium*, prol., cap. 4; cf. also Mersch, *Sacra Doctrina*, 142–43.

22. Henry of Ghent, *Summa*, art xix, q.2; Scotus, *Op. Oxon.*, prol. 3, q.2.

23. Scotus, *Op. Oxon.*, prol. 3,q.2.

24. Gregory of Rimini, *Lectura super primum et secundum sententiarum*, ed. Damasus Trapp and Venicio Marcolino (Berlin: de Gruyter, 1979–81), prol., q.4, art. 2; cf. Giles of Rome, *Primum sententiarum* (Venice, 1521), prol. 1,q.3; similarly, John of Paris, *Commentarium in libros sententiarum*, ed. J.-P. Muller (Rome, 1961), prol. 1, "[theologia] de Deo principalius agat ut est reparator . . ."; and Marsilius of Inghein, *Quaestiones Marsilii super quattuor libros sententiarum* (Strasbourg, 1501), prom., q.3, art. 4: "eius subiectum esse deum: inquantum est finis vitam viatoris..."; also cf. the spectrum of medieval definition summarized in Congar, *A History*, pp. 124–25 with the discussion in Ulrich Koepf, *Die Anfänge der theologischen Wissenschaftslehre*, pp. 82–87.

25. Peter Aureole, *Scriptum* I, proem., sec. 5, art. 4b.

26. Cf. Pannenberg, *Theology and the Philosophy of Science*, p. 235; but also note Lawrence F. Murphy, "Gabriel Biel and Ignorance as an Effect of Original Sin in the Prologue to the *Canonis missae expositio*," in *Archiv für Reformationsgeschichte*, 74(1983): 5–23 and 75(1984): 32–57.

27. Heidanus, *Corpus theologiae*, I: 7.

28. Voetius, *De articulis et erroribus fundamentalibus*, in *Sel. Disp*, II, p. 515.

29. Burmann, *Synopsis theol.*, I.ii.52–54.

30. Leigh, *A Treatise*, II.16.

31. Calvin, *Inst.*, III.ii.1.

32. Ibid., II.vi.4.

33. Cf. W.4. Zuylen, *Bartholomaus Keckermann: Sein Leben und Wirken*, (Leipzig: Noske, 1934) pp. 20–21.

34. Turretin, *Inst. theol.*, I.v.5; cf. the similar presentation by Scotus in P. Parthenius Minges, *Ioannis Duns Scoti Doctrina Philosophica et Theologica* (Quaracchi, 1930), I, pp. 510–11, 520–21.

35. Cf. Muller, "*Duplex cognitio Dei*," pp. 59–61.

36. Turretin, *Inst. theol.*, I.v.6.

37. Cf. Polanus, *Syntagma*, II.iv.

38. See below, 9.3.

39. Cf. Muller, *Christ and the Decree*, pp. 78, 110, 157, 221 n.168.

40. Cf. *DLGT*, s.v. "attributa Dei"; "opera Dei essentialia"; and "simplicitas." I plan to discuss this issue at length in a continuation of

the present study, *Post-Reformation Reformed Dogmatics*, III. *The Triune God.*

41. Aquinas, *Summa theologiae*, Iª, q.1, art. 2, 6 and 7.

42. Contra Althaus, *Die Prinzipien*, p. 232.

43. Cf. Aristotle, *Nicomachean Ethics*, VI.3–8:1139b–1142a; with Altenstaig, *Lexicon theologicum*, s.v. Ars; *Intelligentia*; *Prudentia*; *Sapientia*; *Scientia*; and note also Durandus, *Sent.*, prol., q.1, par.2.

44. Cf. Turretin, *Inst. theol.* I.vi.2; Alexander of Hales, *Summa Theologica*, intro., q.i, cap. 1, obj. 3; also note Gregory of Rimini, I *Sent.*, prol. q.1, art. 2: the *habitus* requisite to theology is described here as a *habitus creditivus*, the conclusion being drawn that it is not possible for an infidel to be a theologian. (The character of theology as *habitus* will be discussed further below, 6.4).

45. Cf. Scharpius, *Cursus theologicus*, col. 4; Wollebius, *Compendium*, praecognita, I.ii; Turretin, *Inst. theol.*, I.vi.5; Maresius, *Collegium theol.*, I.x.

46. Cf. Alexander of Hales, *Summa theologica*, intro., q.i, cap. 1–2. Alexander defines theology as *scientia* but frequently has recourse to the term *sapientia* and takes considerable pains to show that theology is not like the other sciences.

47. Cf. Aquinas, *Summa theologiae*, I,q.1,a.2.

48. E.g., Trelcatius, *Scholastica et methodica locorum communium institutio* (London, 1604), I: 6. On the originality and significance of Aquinas' position for medieval scholastic theology, see M.-D. Chenu, "La théologie comme science au XIIIe siecle," p. 33.

49. Alsted, *Praecognita*, I.ix.

50. Aquinas, *Summa theologiae*, I,q.1,a.6.

51. Scotus, *Op. Oxon.*, prol., q.3, art. 2 and 4.

52. Turretin, *Inst. theol.*, I.vi.5.

53. Scharpius, *Cursus theologicus*, col. 5; Alsted, *Praecognita*, I.ix.

54. Walaeus, *Loci communes* I (p. 114).

55. Turretin, *Inst. theol.*, II.iv.22; cf. I.vi.5; and also see Richard A. Muller, "Scholasticism, Protestant and Catholic," pp. 197, 201; and note the similar view of certainty expressed by Alsted, *Praecognita*, I.ix.

56. Scharpius, *Cursus theologicus*, col. 7–8.

57. Owen, *Theologoumena*, I.ii.1.

58. Ibid., I.ii.2.

59. See below, 7.1.

60. Cf. Baier-Walther, I: 32-35.

61. Trelcatius, *Schol. meth.*, I: 6.

62. Perkins, *Works*, I: 11.

63. Ames, *Medulla*, I.

64. Maccovius, *Loci communes*, I.

65. Mastricht, *Theoretico-practica theologia*, I.i.xxxvi.

66. Walaeus, *Loci communes*, I (p. 114); similarly, Poliander in the *Synopsis purioris*, I.x-xi.

67. Perkins, *A Golden Chaine*, p. 1.

68. Cf. Keckermann, *Operum omnium quae extant* (Geneva, 1614), vol. II; Voetius, *Tractati selecti de politica ecclesiastica*, 2 vols. (Amsterdam, 1885-86); Heidegger, *Corpus theol.*, XII-XIV; and Perkins, *A treatise concerning the only true manner and method of preaching*, in *Works*, vol. II.

69. Junius, *De vera theologia*, ii.

70. Scharpius, *Cursus theologicus*, col. 5.

71. Polanus, *Syntagma*, I.iv.vi.

72. Wollebius, *Compendium*, proleg. i.2.

73. Burmann, *Synopsis theol.*, I.ii.50.

74. Keckermann, *Systema sacrosanctae theologiae*, in *Operum omnium*, vol. II, ad fin, separate pagination, I.i.

75. Leigh, *A System*, I.i, p. 2.

76. Walaeus, *Loci communes*, I (p. 114).

77. Alsted, *Praecognita*, I.ix.

78. Ibid.

79. Turretin, *Inst. theol.*, I.vi.7, citing Stobaeus.

80. Ibid.

81. Ibid.; cf. Alsted, *Praecognita*, I.ix.

82. Althaus, *Die Prinzipien*, pp. 241-43.

83. As noted above (2.2), the theme of scriptural and historical series derives from Melanchthon.   For the methodological impact of this historical emphasis, see below, chapter 8.

84. Alsted, *Praecognita*, I.ix.

85. Ibid., and see below, 7.3, for a discussion of mixed articles.

86. Ibid., I.xv.

87. Cf. Turretin, *Inst. theol.*, I.vii.3-4; Mastricht, *Theoretico-practica theologia*, I.i.20; Maccovius, *Loci communes*, I; and note Pannenberg, *Theology and the Philosophy of Science*, pp. 234-35.

88. Vermigli, *Loci communes*, II.iii.9.

89. Ibid., I.ii.13.

90. Ibid., I.ii.13.

91. Ibid.

92. Frederick Copleston, *A History of Philosophy*, 9 vols. (Garden City, New York: Doubleday, 1985), II: 496.

93. Vermigli, *Loci communes*, II.iii.9.

94. Above, 6.2.

95. Cf. *Corpus theologiae*, I.70.   Puritan theology also tended toward emphasis on theology as practical or "directive" knowledge.   See, e.g. Charnock, *A Discourse of the Knowledge of God*, pp. 50-51.   In view of this Protestant orthodox tendency to balance theory and praxis in definitions of theology, we must reject as a major misinterpretation Barth's argument that the orthodox chose a Scotist definition of theology as a *scientia practica* and tended to emphasize religiosity rather than objectivity in their view of theology: see *CD*, I/1, pp. 85, 191-92.

96. Cited in *Glaubenslehre*, I: 145.

97. Cf. Scotus, *Op. Oxon.*, prol. q.iv, n.42.

98. Keckermann, *Systema*, I.i.

99. Ibid.

100. Cf. Johann Gerhard, *Loci theologici*, edited by E. Preuss (Berlin, 1863-75), I, proem. 11-12.

101. Alsted, *Praecognita*, I.v, ix.

102. Turretin, *Inst. theol.*, I.vii.1.

103. Ibid. I.vii.2.

104. Episcopius, *Institutiones theologicae* I.ii. Cf. Arminius' oration, *De obiecto theologiae*, in *Opera*, p. 26, col. 1. Arminius argues that *theologia in via* is purely practical whereas the heavenly theology of the blessed, *theologia visionis*, is theoretical or contemplative; also note *Disputationes privatae*, I.v–vi, in *Opera*, p. 269.

105. Ibid.

106. Episcopius, *Institutiones*, I.ii.

107. Ibid.

108. See further below, ch. 8, on theology as a discipline; and 9.3, on theological *principia*.

109. Walaeus, *Loci communes*, I.i; cf. Maccovius, *Loci communes*, I, cited below, n.58.

110. Gomarus, *Disputationes*, I.x.

111. Alsted, *Praecognita*, I.ix (esp. p. 63).

112. Cf. Burmann, *Synopsis theol.* I.ii.51.

113. Heidanus, *Corpus theologiae*, I: 7.

114. Cf. Baier–Walther, I: 6–7, where theology is defined as *scientia practica*.

115. Maccovius, *Loci communes*, I.

116. Cf. S. D. van Veen, s.v. "Maccovius, Johannes' in *RE*, vol. 12, pp. 36–38.

117. Turretin, *Inst. theol.* I.vii.3–4.

118. Walaeus, *Loci communes*, I:114.

119. Turretin, *Inst. theol.* I.vii.6.

120. Ibid.

121. Ibid., I.vii.8.

122. Walaeus, *Loci communes*, I: 114.

123. Poliander, *Synopsis purioris*, I.xxiii.

124. Mastricht, *Theoretico-practica theologia*, I.i.2.

125. Ibid.

126. Turretin, *Inst. theol.*, I.vii.25.

127. Cf. the definitions of theology from Perkins, Ames and Maccovius, cited above, 1.3; with Calvin, *Inst.*, III.iii.33.

128. Cited in *Glaubenslehre*, I: 145.

129. Ibid.

130. Cf., e.g., Durandus, *Sent.*, prol. q.1, par. 6-8.

131. See Calvin, *Inst.*, II.i.9; ii.2,12.

132. Melancthon, *Opera*, 13, col. 535; and cf. the discussion of *habitus* in Johannes Wallmann, *Der Theologiebegriff bei Johann Gerhard und Georg Calixt* (Tübingen: Mohr, 1961), pp. 65-71.

133. Vermigli, *Loci communes*, II.iii.5.

134. Wollebius, *Compendium*, praecognita, I.ii; cf. Owen, *Theologoumena*, I.iii.1.

135. Cf. Bucanus, *Institutiones theologicae* (Geneva, 1602), XXIX.2; Turretin, *Inst. theol.*, I.vi.2; also, Altenstaig, *Lexicon theologicum*, s.v. "habitus".

136. Alsted, *Praecognita*, I.ix.

137. Cf. Turretin, *Inst. theol.*, I.vi.2-3; with Charnock, A *Discourse of the Knowledge of God*, pp. 26, 60.

138. Cf. Maccovius, *Loci communes*, lxx, pp. 629-30.

139. Maresius, *Collegium theol.*, I.xi. Cf. Biel, *Sent.*, prol., q.Vii, nota 2; and the Lutheran view in Baier-Walther, I: 70-71; and Wallmann, *Der Theologiebegriff*, pp. 71-75; with Turretin, *Inst. theol*; I.vi.4; and Junius, *De vera theologia*, v.

140. Cf. Maccovius, *Loci communes*, xxii, pp. 166-67; with Turretin, *Inst. theol.*, III.xx.7-9.

141. See above, 3.3.

142. Cf. Maccovius, *Loci communes*, lxxi, p. 690; Turretin, *Inst. theol.*, XV.viii.1.

143. Cf. *DLGT*, s.v. *"theologia irregenitorum"* and *"fides . . . (1) fides historica;"* with Alsted, *Praecognita*, I.ix.

144. See below, 8.2.

145. Maresius, *Collegium theol.*, I.xi.

Chapter 7. The Use of Philosophy in Theology

1. Cf. the more extended discussion in Richard A. Muller, *"Vera Philosophia cum sacra Theologia nusquam pugnat*: Keckermann on Philosophy, Theology and the Problem of Double Truth," in *Sixteenth Century Journal*, XV/3 (1984): 343–65.

2. Cf. Schmitt, *Aristotle and the Renaissance*, pp. 34–64.

3. Lewalter, *Metaphysik*, pp. 31–33, 41.

4. Ibid., pp. 35–37.

5. Alsted, *Methodus metaphysicae* (Herborn, 1620).

6. Vermigli, *Loci communes*, II.iii.7–8.

7. Ibid., II.iii.6.

8. Cf. Calvin's comment on Ephesians 1:5–8 and Ezekiel 1:1–24; 10:8–16 in *CO*, vol. 51, col. 148–15; vol. 40, col. 21–54, 213–220; touching on causality and angelic movers, respectively.

9. Cf. Muller, *"Vera Philosophia*, pp. 341–65.

10. Keckermann, *Operum omnium*, I, cols. 69–70; cf. Alsted, *Praecognita*, II.x.

11. Cf. Muller, *"Vera Philosophia,"* pp. 341–45.

12. See F. van Steenberghen, *Thomas Aquinas and Radical Aristotelianism* (Washington, D.C.; CUA Press, 1980), pp. 75–110; and Etienne Gilson, *Reason and Revelation in the Middle Ages* (New York: Scribner, 1938), pp. 37–85. For further bibliography see Muller, *"Vera Philosophia,"* p. 345, n.13.

13. Cf. Leff, *Medieval Thought*, pp. 264, 280–81.

14. Cf. Oberman, *Harvest*, pp. 32–42.

15. Cf. Calvin, *Inst.*, I.iv.1–2; II.ii.12.

16. See surveys of the Hoffmann controversy in Dorner, *History of Protestant Theology*, II: 110–13; and Bernhard Pünjer, *History of the Christian*

Philosophy of Religion, trans. W. Hastie (Edinburgh: T. & T. Clark, 1887), pp. 178–90; see also *RE*, s.v. "Hoffmann, Daniel."

17. Gerhard, *Loci theologici*, in *DTEL*, p. 33.

18. Ibid., pp. 34–35.

19. Alsted, *Praecognita*, II.x.

20. Riissen, *Summa*, I.vii.

21. Ibid.

22. Turretin, *Inst. theol.*, I.xiii.7.

23. Ibid., I.xiii.9; cf. Maccovius, *Loci communes*, i, pp. 9–10; and de Moor, *Commentarius*, I.xxi (pp. 71–72).

24. Turretin, *Inst. theol.*, I.xiii.3; cf. Maresius, *Collegium theol.*, I.xv; and note the parallel with medieval theology, e.g., Thomas Aquinas, *Summa*, I, art.1, q.8, ad 2; and Henry of Ghent, *Summa*, art.X, q.3.

25. Both cited in *Glaubenslehre*, I: 188–89.

26. Above, 6.1.

27. Cf. Keckermann, *Praecognitorum*, in *Opera*, col. 35; Voetius, *De ratione humana*, 2; Turretin, *Inst. theol.*, I.viii.8–9; and note, e.g., Henry of Ghent, *Summa*, art.XVI, q.7, ad 1 et ad 2, on the relation of faith to understanding as a rational faculty of mind.

28. Keckermann, *Praecognitorum*, col. 69.

29. Rudolph Goclenius, *Dialectica Rami*, as cited by Puenjer, *History*, pp. 171–72.

30. Cited by Turretin, *Inst. theol.*, I.xiii.6.

31. Riissen, *Summa*, I.vii; cf. Alsted, *Praecognita*, II.xi.

32. Cf. Keckermann, *Praecognita*, col. 68; Turretin, *Inst. theol.*, I.v.5; xiii.7; with de Moor, *Commentarius*, I.xxi: 71–72.

33. Cf. Puenjer, *History*, p. 116.

34. Ibid.

35. Cf. F. A. Bente, *Historical Introductions to the Book of Concord* (St. Louis: Concordia, 1921, 1965), pp. 144–52.

36. Cf. Puenjer, *History*, pp. 199–200; Earl Morse Wilbur, A *History of Unitarianism* (Boston: Beacon, 1945), I: 571–72.

37. Turretin, *Inst. theol.*, I.viii.5; cf. Voetius, *De ratione humana*, 2–3.

38. Maccovius, *Loci communes*, i, p. 6.

39. Ibid., i, pp. 6–7.

40. Ibid., i, p. 7.

41. Heidanus, *Corpus theologiae*, I (pp. 8, 11, 14).

42. Ibid., I (p. 18); II (p. 53).

43. Voetius, *Appendix de dubitatione philosophica*, in Sel.Disp., III, pp. 847–48.

44. Ibid., pp. 849, 853–55.

45. De Moor, *Commentarius*, I.xxi; and cf. Voetius, *De ratione humana*, 3.

46. Cf. below, 9.3.

47. Riissen, *Summa*, I.xi; note the similarity between this argument and the basically Augustinian view of the relation of faith and understanding found in Alexander of Hales, *Summa theologica*, intro., q.ii, cap. 4.

48. Turretin, *Inst. theol.*, I.viii.1.

49. Pictet, *Theol. chr.*, I.xi; cf. Chandieu, *De vera methodo*, p. 10.

50. Ibid.

51. Turretin, *Inst. theol.*, I.viii.8, citing Romans 12:1 and 1 Peter 2:5.

52. Cf. Turretin, *Inst. theol.*, I.ix.2; Riissen, *Summa*, I.xi.

53. Cf. Turretin, *Inst. theol.*, I.ix.9.

54. Ibid., I.viii.11–12; cf. Maresius, *Collegium theol.*, I.xvii.

55. Above, 5.3.

56. Cf. Turretin, *Inst. theol.*, III.iii.5–6; ix.9–12; x.3–6; with Mastricht, *Theoretico-practica theologia*, II.vi.1–4; vii.1–4, etc.

57. Turretin, *Inst. theol.*, I.viii.2–3.

58. Ibid., viii.2; x.1–16; see below, 6.3.

59. E.g., Henry of Ghent, *Summa*, art. X, q.2, *ad obj.*, argues that reason cannot prove the authority of Scripture but can properly accept Scripture, as the norm for reason and for all human wisdom.

60. Keckermann, *Praecognitorum*, col. 37.

61. Alsted, *Theologia scholastica*, p. 7 (cited in *RD*, p. 11); *Praecognita*, I.ix.

62. Keckermann, *Praecognitorum*, col. 32.

63. Turretin, *Inst. theol.*, I.vii.14; cf. Keckermann, *Praecognitorum*, col. 38.

64. Turretin, *Inst. theol.*, I.viii.15–16; Riissen, *Summa*, I.xi, controversia 1; Maresius, *Collegium theol.*, I.xviii.

65. Alsted, *Praecognita*, I.ix.

66. Keckermann, *Praecognitorum*, col. 38; citing Cano, *Loci theologici*, IX.3.

67. Pictet, *Theol. chr*, I.xi.

68. See above, 4.1; 4.4.

69. Turretin, *Inst. theol.*, I.viii.18–19.

70. Cf. Riissen, *Summa*, I.xi, controversia 1.

71. Heidegger, *Medulla theologiae*; cited in *Glaubenslehre*, I: 188.

Chapter 8.   Theology as a Discipline

1. Walter Ong, *Ramus, Method, and the Decay of Dialogue* (Cambridge, Mass.: Harvard University Press, 1958), pp. 104–5.   Also see Neal W. Gilbert, *Renaissance Concepts of Method* (New York: Columbia, 1960), pp. 119–28.   On Ramus and the impact of Ramism on Reformed theology, see further, below, this chapter, section 2.

2. Philipp Melancthon, *Erotemata dialectices*, in *Opera*, 13, col. 573.

3. *Loci communes* (1533), in *Opera*, vol. 21, col. 253, 254; and *Loci communes* (1545) in ibid., col. 603; and cf. above, 2.2.

4. Andreas Hyperius, *Methodi theologiae* (Basel, 1568), pp. 8–9.

5. Ibid., p. 10.

6. Alsted, *Praecognita*, II.cxxx.

7. Ibid., II.cxxxii, cxxxiii.

8. Hyperius, *Methodi theol.*, p. 12.

9. Ibid., pp. 12–13.

10. Ibid., p. 15; cf. *De theologo*, pp. 455–507 on the detailed division of the six basic *loci*.

11. Alsted, *Praecognita*, II.cxxix.

12. Gilbert, *Renaissance Method*, p. 171.

13. E.g., Jeremias Triverius, *In texnhn* [i.e., *technē*] *Galeni clarissimi commentarii* (Lyons, 1547); and cf. the discussion in Gilbert, *Renaissance Method*, pp. 105–7.

14. Gilbert, *Renaissance Method*, pp. 171–72.

15. Cf. Ong, *Ramus*, pp. 142–48, 207–12; Puenjer, *History*, p. 119; Muller, *Christ and the Decree*, pp. 140–47.

16. Cf. Ong, *Ramus*, pp. 214–20, 258–59.

17. Ibid., pp. 146, 199–200.

18. Cf. above, 3.1; 3.2; 6.3.

19. Ong, *Ramus*, pp. 225–69.

20. Cf. Lyle Bierma, "The Covenant Theology of Caspar Olevian" (Ph.D. Dissertation, Duke University, 1980), pp. 229–38; with Jürgen Moltmann, "Zur Bedeutung des Petrus Ramus für Philosophie und Theologie im Calvinismus," in *Zeitschrift für Kirchengeschichte*, 68(1956–57); 295–318; and Muller, *Christ and the Decree*, ch. 6, n.1.

21. William Perkins, *A Golden Chaine*, pp. 11–16; and note Richard A Muller, "Perkins' *A Golden Chaine*: Predestinarian *System or Schematized Ordo Salutis*," in *The Sixteenth Century Journal*, IX/1 (1978): pp. 69–81. Keckermann's *Praecognitorum logicorum* are oriented toward Zabarella and Suarez and away from Ramus. Cf. Gilbert, *Renaissance Method*, pp. 214–20; with Peter Peterson, *Geschichte der Aristotelischen Philosophie*, pp. 127–43, especially p. 138 on Keckermann's critique of Ramism.

22. Mastricht, *Theoretico-practica theologia*, I,i,4.

23. Ibid., I.i.6.

24. Ibid., I.i.6.

25. Ibid, I.i.25.

26. Ibid., I.i.5.

27. Schweizer, *Glaubenslehre*, I: 192.

28. Leigh, A *System*, I.i.

29. Ibid.

30. Burmann, *Synopsis theol.* I.ii.44.

31. Cf. Mastricht, *Theoretico-practica theologia*, I.25, citing Alsted specifically as the basis for the distinction; with Burmann, *Synopsis theol.*, I.42, 46–47.

32. Venema, *Institutes*, prolegomenon (pp. 7–8).

33. Burmann, *Synopsis theol.*, I.ii.46.

34. Ibid., I.ii.47; cf. the similar objections, at length, in Voetius, *De theologia scholastica*, in *Selectarum disputationum theologicarum* (Utrecht, 1648–69), I: 12–29.

35. Mastricht, *Theoretico-practica theologia*, I.25; cf. Owen, *Theologoumena*, VI.viii.11; Alsted, *Praecognita*, I.xviii; Pictet, *Theol. chr.*, praef.

36. Maccovius, *Loci communes*, I.

37. See below, chapter 9.

38. Maccovius, *Loci communes*, I (p. 2).

39. Cf. Calvin's letter to Sadoleto in *CO*, vol. 5, cols. 385–416 with its reflection (col. 392) on the famous Vincentian Canon.

40. Alsted, *Praecognita*, I.xviii.

41. Burmann, *Synopsis theol.*, I.ii.42; cf., in the eighteenth century, the similar view of method in van Til, *Theol. comp.*, II.i.

42. Cf. Baier-Walther, I: 43; *DTEL*, p. 19; and Preus, *The Theology of Post-Reformation Lutheranism*, I: 34–35; and note Lang, *Die Loci theologici des Melchior Cano*, pp. 90, 209–10; also, on Cano and Protestant orthodoxy, see Pannenberg, *Theology and the Philosophy of Science*, pp. 244–45.

43. Cf. Heinrich Bullinger, *Compendium christianae religionis* (Zurich, 1556), II.vii–viii.

44. Cf. Burmann *De studio theologico*, I.4; with *Synopsis theol.*, I.i.7–16; and with Schweizer's discussion of method and architectonic issues in *Glaubenslehre*, I: 89, 130–31; note also the discussion of high orthodoxy below, 1.3.

45. Above, 6.3.

46. Keckermann, *Systema*, I.i.

47. Trelcatius, *Schol. meth.*, I (p. 6).

48. Ibid., pp. 7–8.

49. See above, 6.3.

50. Cf. Gilbert, *Renaissance Method*, pp. 128–44; Ong, *Ramus*, pp. 225–69; and cf. Donald K. McKim, "The Function of Ramism in Perkins' Theology," in *The Sixteenth Century Journal*, 16/4 (1985): 503–17.

51. Ames, *Medulla* [1648], I.ii.6.

52. Mastricht, *Theoretico-practica theologia*, I.28.

53. Alsted, *Praecognita*, II.i.

54. Ibid.

55. Ibid., II.ii.

56. Ibid., II.iii,v.

57. Mastricht, *Theoretico-practica theologia*, I.i.29.

58. Leigh, A *System*, I.i.

59. Burmann, *De studio theologico*, I.3, in *Synopsis theol.*, ad fin.

60. Ibid., 4–5; cf. Heidanus, *Corpus theologiae*, I (pp. 4–6).

61. Alsted, *Praecognita*, II.v.

62. Ibid., II.iv; cf. Voetius, *Exercitia*, pp. 4–31.

63. Burmann, *De studio theologico*, I.6–8.

64. Ibid., I.9–10, cf. Alsted, *Praecognita*, II.iii,iv.

65. Burmann, *De studio theologico*, I.17.

66. Cf. above, 2.4.

67. Owen, *Theologoumena*, VI.ix.11–12.

68. Ibid., VI.ix.13–15; cf. viii.2,9.

69. Cf. Melancthon, *Brevis discendae theologiae ratio*, Opera, 2, col. 459.

70. Hyperius, *Methodi theol.*, pp. 5–6.

71. Conrad Gessner, *Pandectarum universalium . . . liber ultimus de theologia* (Zurich, 1549).

72. Burmann, *De studio theologico*, II.1–4; cf. Voetius, *Exercitia*, p. 37 for a slightly different list: Voetius recommends Drusius' Old Testament, the New Testaments of Beza and Piscator, the *loci* or *medullae* of Ames, Gomarus, and Maccovius, and the longer systems of Polanus, Alsted, and Wendelin.

73. *De studio theologico*, II.5–12.

74. Ibid., II.13–27.

75. Ibid., II.13, 15.

76. Ibid., III.1–14.

77. Ibid., III.24–38.

78. Leigh, A *System*, I.iii–iv.

79. Alsted, *Praecognita*, II.xii–cxxviii; discussion of this material lies beyond the scope of the present volume inasmuch as it belongs to the doctrine of Scripture.

80. See above, 6.3.

81. Cf. Scharpius, *Cursus theologicus*; and Trelcatius, *Schol. meth.*, noting the polemical section at the end of each chapter.

82. Cf., e.g., Ursinus, *Explicationes catecheseos*, in *Opera theologica* (Heidelberg, 1612), I, cols. 163–65; with Riissen, *Summa*, III.ix., controversia (against the Anthropomorphites).

83. Pictet, *Theol. chr.*, praef.

84. Voetius, *Exercitia*, v–viii (esp. pp. 31–36, 45–47, 59–61). The greater part of Voetius *Exercitia* is a vast, six-hundred page isagoge on all theological disciplines that provides an analytical bibliography for theological study so vast that it charts a course far beyond the basic pattern of academic theological study.

85. Burmann, *De studio theologico*, III.4–9; and note the similar method, with emphasis on piety and application, in Johannes Hoornbeeck, *Tractatus de ratione concionandi* (Leiden, 1645) and David Knibbe, *Manuductio ad oratoriam sacram* (Leiden, 1679). The early orthodox homiletical pattern is well illustrated in Andreas Hyperius, *De formandis concionibus sacris* (Basel, 1552), translated as *The Practis of Preaching* (London, 1577). See further, Edwin C. Dargan, A *History of Preaching* (Grand Rapids:

Baker, 1954), II: 76–81, 137–49, 168–85; and for examples of a Puritan and Reformed style, strongly orthodox in its doctrinal content, cf. any of the sermons of Thomas Manton in *The Complete Works of Thomas Manton*, 22 vols. (London: J. Nisbet, 1870–75), but note particularly the sermon on Mark 10:27 in vol. 17, pp. 82–95, where Manton emphasizes the scholastic distinction between *potentia ordinata* and *potentia absoluta* but draws it out at length with reference to the text; also see Owen's sermons in *The Works of John Owen*, ed. William Goold (London, 1850–53), vol. 8.

86. Cf. Mastricht, *Theoretico–practica theologia*, pp. 1–5, 51–65, 65–75, etc.; with Richard A. Muller, "Giving Direction to Theology: The Scholastic Dimension," in *Journal of the Evangelical Theology Society*, 28/2 (June, 1985): 184–86.

87. Cf. Edward Farley, *Theologia: The Fragmentation and Unity of Theological Education*, (Philadelphia: Fortress, 1983) pp. 51–53.

88. Cf. Lewalter, *Metaphysik*, pp. 31–33, where a similar contemporizing effort is noted in the Protestant use of Aristotelian metaphysics.

Chapter 9. Fundamental Articles and Basic Principles of Theology

1. Maccovius, *Loci communes*, I (pp. 1–2); cf. Polanus, *Syntagma*, I.ii.

2. Turretin, *Inst. theol.*, I.xiv.1.

3. Cf. Dorner, *History*, II: 185–203.

4. Turretin, *Inst. theol.*, II.iv.22; cf. Mastricht, *Theoretico–practica theologia*, I.ii.34.

5. Witsius, *Exercitationes*, II.ii; cf. the identical point in Voetius, *De articulis et erroribus fundamentalibus*, in *Sel. Disp.*, II, p. 513.

6. Witsius, *Exercitationes*, II.ii.

7. Ibid., II.iii.

8. Turretin, *Inst. theol.*, II.iv.22.

9. Witsius, *Exercitationes*, II.4.

10. Cf. Thomas Aquinas, *Summa theologiae*, II^{iiae}, q.1, a.7.

11. Above, 8.1.

12. Maccovius, *Loci communes*, I (p. 2); cf. Voetius, *De articulis et erroribus fundamentalibus*, in *Sel. Disp.* II, pp. 513–14.

13. Turretin, *Inst. theol.* I.xiv.1.

14. Voetius, *De articulis et erroribus fundamentalibus*, in *Sel. Disp.*, II, p. 516; Turretin, *Inst. theol.*, I.xiv.1, 2, 8; cf. Riissen, *Summa*, I.xii; Marckius, *Compendium*, III.xii.

15. Turretin, *Inst. theol.*, I.xiv.4; cf. Heidegger, *Corpus theol.*, I.49.

16. *RD*, p. 42.

17. Cf. ibid., pp. 42–46.

18. Ursinus, *Loci theologici*, in *Opera*, I, col. 427–28.

19. Leigh, A *System*, I.ix.

20. Ibid., I.i.

21. Cf. Heidegger, *Corpus theol.*, I.56.   This perspective carries over into the Protestant orthodox discussion of Christ and of Scripture as "Word of God."   See Richard A. Muller, "Christ—the Revelation or the Revealer? Brunner and Reformed Orthodoxy on the Doctrine of the Word of God," in *Journal of the Evangelical Theological Society*, 26/3 (Sept. 1983): 309–19.

22. Witsius, *Exercitationes*, II.x.

23. Turretin, *Inst. theol.*, I.xiv.4.

24. Ibid., I.xiv.5.

25. Ibid., I.xiv.6.

26. Witsius, *Exercitationes*, II.v.

27. Turretin, *Inst. theol.*, I.xiv.7.

28. Witsius, *Exercitationes*, II.vi.

29. Ibid., II.vi.

30. Marckius, *Compendium*, III.vi.

31. Turretin, *Inst. theol.*, I.xiv.20.

32. Johann   Friedrich   Stapfer,   *Institutiones   theologicae   polemicae* (Zurich, 1756–57), IV.1802.

33. Ibid., IV.1803.

34. Ibid., IV.1805.

35. Marckius, *Compendium*, III.xii.

36. See above, 6.1.

37. Cf. Turretin, *Inst. theol.*, I.xiv.8; with ibid., II.xiii.14; Voetius, *De articulis et erroribus fundamentalibus*, in *Sel. Disp.*, II, pp. 514–15.

38. Voetius, *De articulis et erroribus fundamentalibus*, in *Sel. Disp.*, II, pp. 517.

39. Ibid., pp. 517–24.

40. Ibid., pp. 525–26.

41. Marckius, *Compendium*, III.ix.

42. Cf. Turretin, *Inst. theol.*, I.xiv.8 with Baier–Walter, I: 49–68.

43. Witsius, *Exercitationes*, II.vi,xi.

44. Cf. Turretin, *Inst. theol.*, I.xiv.8, 10; with Riissen, *Summa*, I.xii–xiii.

45. Stapfer, *Inst. theol.*, I.36–38.

46. Riissen, *Summa*, I.xiii; cf. Turretin, *Inst. theol.*, I.xiv.9.

47. Stapfer, *Inst. theol.*, Tom. V., cap. xx.

48. Ibid., II.vi.8.

49. Ibid., II.x.6.

50. Ibid., IV.xiv.6.

51. Ibid., IV.xvi.6.

52. Ibid., V.xix.38–45.

53. Ibid., V.xx.80–82.

54. Turretin, *Inst. theol.*, I.xiv.19; cf. Voetius, *De articulis et erroribus fundamentalibus*, in *Sel. Disp.*, II, pp. 531–32.

55. Ibid., I.xiv.20.

56. Witsius, *Exercitationes*, II.vii.

57. Ibid.

58. Ibid.

59. Cf. Riissen, *Summa*, I.xiv; Marckius, *Compendium*, III.xiii; Turretin, *Inst. theol.*, I.xiv.21; Voetius, *De articulis et erroribus fundamentalibus*, in *Sel. Disp.*, II, pp. 533–34.

60. Turretin, *Inst. theol.*, I.xiv.22.

61. Ibid.

62. Witsius, *Exercitationes*, II.xi.

63. Ibid.

64. Turretin, *Inst. theol.*, I.xiv.25.

65. Ibid., I.xiv.26; cf. Witsius, *Exercitationes*, II.xv–xvii.

66. Cf. J. A. Turretin, *Brevis & pacifica de articulis fundamentalibus disquisitio* (Geneva, 1719).

67. Aristotle, *Metaphysics*, V.1. (1013a, 18–20), in *The Basic Works of Aristotle*, ed. R. McKeon (New York: Random House, 1941), p. 752.

68. Sibrandus Lubbertus, *De principiis christianorum dogmatum libri VIII* (Franecker, 1591), I.i (pp. 1–2).

69. Ibid., pp. 2–4.

70. Ibid., pp. 5–6.

71. Chandieu, *De vera methodo*, pp. 9–10.

72. Hoornbeeck, *Antisocinianismus*, I.i.1, in *Summa controversiarum* (Utrecht, 1653).

73. Leigh, A *System*, I.ii, (p. 6); cf. Wollebius, *Compendium*, praecognita, I.iii.

74. Ibid., p. 6, [margin].

75. Ibid., p. 6.

76. Trelcatius, *Schol. meth.*, I.i

77. Ibid.

78. Ibid.

79. Alsted, *Praecognita*, I.ix; cf. idem., *Theologia Naturalis*, I.i, where Alsted notes that *natura* here indicates "reason, universal experience, and the Book of Nature (*Liber Naturae*)." Similarly, Maresius, *Collegium theol.*, I.xxiii, identifies reason as the *principium* of natural theology, Scripture as the *principium* of revealed theology.

80. Cf. Alsted, *Praecognita*, I.xvi.

81. Cf. Peter Aureole, *Scriptum* I, proem. sect. 1, q.A.3; and Pierre D'Ailly, *Quaestiones super libros sententiarum* (Strasbourg, 1490) prol., q.1, art. 2.

82. Marsilius of Inghien, *Quaestiones Marsilii super quattuor libros sententiarum* (Strasbourg, 1501), I, proem., q. 2, art. 3.

83. Cf. Altenstaig, *Lexicon theologicum*, s.v. "*Principium Theologicae*".

84. Gregory of Rimini, *Sent.*, I, prol., q.1, art.2; cf. the citations and argument in De Vooght, *Les Sources*, pp. 105-6; also note Henry of Ghent, *Summa*, art. X; John Hus, *Super IV Sententiarum*, edited by Wenzel Flaj-shans and Marie Kominkova (Osnabrück, 1966), I, dist. 1, q. 4; II, inceptio, q. 1, art. 6-9; Scotus, *Op. Oxon.*, prol., q. 2.

85. D'Ailly, *In Sent.*, I,q.1, art 3; see also the discussion in De Vooght, *Les Sources*, pp. 235-36.

86. Cf. De Vooght, *Les Sources*, pp. 254-56; I hope to develop this whole issue of the continuities and discontinuities in the doctrine of Scripture at length in a subsequent volume.

87. Congar, *Tradition and Traditions*, pp. 116-18, 138-39; cf., on Scotus, Minges, I: 534-41.

88. E.g., Henry of Ghent, *Summa*, art VIII; and Scotus, *Op. Oxon.*, prol, q.2, n.14; IV, dist. 3, q.4, n.14; dist. 14, q.3, n.5.

89. Cf. Maccovius, *Loci communes*, I, cited above, 4.2.

90. Cf. Kilwardby, *De natura theologiae*, 2, 4; and Henry of Ghent, *Summa*, art. XIX; and above, 4.2.

91. Mastricht, *Theoretico-practica theologia*, I.ii.1 and II.i.1.

92. Maccovius, *Loci communes*, II: 10-11.

93. Polanus, *Syntagma*, I.xiv.

94. Mastricht, *Theoretico-practica theologia*, I.ii.1.

95. Ibid., I.ii.1.

96. Ibid., I.ii.3.

97. See above, 4.2.

98. Maccovius, *Loci communes*, I; Alsted, *Praecognita*, I.xvi.

99. Riissen, *Summa*, I.ii.1.

100. Cf. Burmann, *Synopsis theol.*, I.ii.6.

101. See above, 7.2; 7.3.

102. Cf. Ernst Bizer, "Die reformierte Orthodoxie und der Cartesian-ismus," pp. 371-72.

103. Venema, *Institutes*, prolegomena, p. 8.

104. Baumgarten, *Theses dogmaticae*, I.i.1-10 (prolegomena); II.x. (scripture). Baumgarten, who presented his theses first in 1736 as a development and supplement to Freylinghausen's *Fundamenta theologiae christianae*, argues the preliminary, nonsaving character of natural theology but does not argue the revealed source of system as pointedly as Freylinghausen (cf. *Fundamenta*, I.i.). In addition, Baumgarten's exposition is a formal prolegomenon, where one would expect a more cautious approach to natural theology, mixed articles, etc.--while Freyling-hausen's comments occur in a brief introductory description of the knowledge of God that echoes the language of the *duplex cognitio Dei*. The tendency of Lutheran orthodoxy to postpone discussion of the scrip-tural *principium* until the *locus* of Word and Sacrament--i.e., until ecclesiology--conjoins in Baumgarten's *Theses* with the tendency of rationalism to ignore Scripture as *principium*. The more orthodox alter-native is seen in Baumgarten's contemporaries Rambach and Weismann: cf. Johann Jakob Rambach, *Dogmatische theologie oder Christliche Glaubens-lehre* (Frankfurt and Leipzig, 1744), I.iii; and Christian Eberhard Weismann, *Institutiones theologiae exegetico-dogmaticae* (Tübingen, 1739), locus III, where Scripture appears as *principium* even though it will be treated again, later, in a different manner, under the topic of Word and Sacrament as means of grace.

105. Vitringa, *Doct. chr.*, I.16.

106. Cf. Turretin, *Inst. theol.*, I and II; with Stapfer, *Inst. theol.*, I, II, III.i., sections 270-96.

107. Stapfer, *Inst. theol.*, I, sections 6 and 30; III.i., sections 274, 283, 289, 291, 293, 294, 296.

108. Ibid., III.xii., section 956.

109. Ibid., III.xii., sections 960-63.

110. Ibid., III.i.-xi.

111. Cf. Mastricht, *Theoretico-practica theologia*, II.i.

112. R. S. Franks, "Dogma in Protestant Scholasticism," in *Dogma in History and Thought* (London: Nisbet, 1929), p. 117.

113. Ibid., p. 115.